MW00335724

KEYS TO
SELF-REALIZATION
A Self-Counseling Manuel

KEYS TO SELF-REALIZATION

A Self-Counseling Manual

Marilyn Jean Enners

1469 Morstein Road
West Chester, Pennsylvania 19380 USA

AUTHOR'S DEDICATION

With gratitude and love, I dedicate this work to Emilia Rosine Schelling, a.k.a. "Mimi." Your strength, faith and love have sustained my restless spirit, for you have taught me the True Meaning of "Generosity of Spirit." Thank you Mimi for consenting to be the "channel" through which I entered the earth plane.

To Yeasuf and "Papa," your gentle guidance and patient teachings fed a hungry heart, and lifted this child toward the Light, for you have taught me that a true "Master" serves unselfishly and unconditionally. Thank you for the blessings you have given to me.

To Diana Marie Rothman, M.D., and John Henke, M.D., two superior physicians whose empathetic support has made the physical body meet the demands of my spiritual essence. And to so many others who have been, and still are, unconditional and unfailing in their support and belief in my work. Your love has made my path so much more joyful.

Before the light in *all* of you, I stand both humble and proud. You have made me realize that I am, indeed, entitled to miracles!

AUTHOR'S ACKNOWLEDGEMENTS

I would like to take this opportunity to gratefully acknowledge the invaluable contributions of John Tyksinski, a sensitive, artistically creative mind who has added so much beauty to this book with his unique designs and down-to-earth advice.

And to Douglas Congdon-Martin, whose gentle "suggestions" helped me to achieve a long-cherished goal. I really do appreciate all that you "put-up" with while working with me. You helped make this book a joyful experience.

I would also like to mention my heart-felt gratitude to Peter Schiffer for his enthusiastic acceptance of my work. You are a very special man, Peter, and your "miracles" are just around the corner.

Copyright © by Marily Jean Enners
Library of Congress Number: 89-50408
ISBN: 0-914918-91-5
Manufactured in the United States of America

All rights reserved. No part of this work may be reproduced or used in any form or by any means – graphic, electronic, or mechanical, including photocopying, mimeographing, recording, taping or information storage and retrieval systems – without written permission from the copyright holder.

Published by Whitford Press,
A Division of
Schiffer Publishing, Ltd.
1469 Morstein Road
West Chester, Pennsylvania 19380
Please write for a free catalog,
This book may be purchased from the publisher.
Please include $2.00 postage.

CONTENTS

INTRODUCTION

In our search for Enlightenment and Knowledge, there are many different Spiritual "Tools" or "Keys" available to us to unlock the Gate of our Subconscious Mind, that part of us which serves as a "Channel" to our Higher Self. This Gate represents the pathway of knowledge to behavior patterns we have established both in this lifetime and in previous incarnations. These "Keys" merely unlock the Gate or remove barriers so that you can discover who you are, what gifts you are blessed with, where you are going, what potentials are present. But the most important element of all is that these "Keys" can help to reveal what Challenges and Lessons you have subconsciously chosen to face in order to experience and grow in Awareness.

These "Keys" have many different names, such as Numerology, Color Symbolism, Astrology, Dream Analysis, Meditation, Psychometry, Palmistry, Prayer, Tarot, and many others. The "Tools" or "Keys" that you use in the process of removing limitations or barriers to your Higher Self are, of themselves, unimportant. What is important is for you to unlock the Gateway of your Subconscious. Once this Gate is unlocked, the "Real" work begins with your very first Lesson or Challenge on the Path of Enlightenment: the Lesson of Discernment, of learning to recognize what is Illusion and what is Truth, on the physical Earth Plane as well as the multi-leveled Astral Plane you touch during your Dream State or in Meditation.

Numerology, Color Symbolism, Astrology, Crystals, Mandala Designs, Minerals, Dream and Meditation Symbols, and Tarot, as "Keys" or "Tools", can help you to understand yourself, the world you have created on the Earth Plane, and the people around you. All of us, whether we are consciously aware of it or not, are deeply involved in the same struggle for Spiritual Growth and Enlightenment. The Earth Plane or Physical-Material Plane is our "school-room" our "Laboratory" for learning and experimentation, and sometimes the Earth Plane is even a joyful playground. Using the Astrology, Numerology, Dream/Meditation Analysis, Color Symbolism, Mandalas, or Tarot as Guides will reveal potentials, "energies" or "vibrations" which are, of themselves, neutral in expression, but can be transformed into negative or positive forces by your will, your Free Will.

Free Will means the ability to make your own choices, your own decisions. It is a gift from the Creator, a gift that makes us co-creators with the most powerful force in the Universe. By utilizing our Free Will we can change the direction of our lives at any time we choose to do so simply by choosing to see the situation facing us in a different light. But it also means we are responsible for the choices and decisions we make, no one else. This is the Law of Karma, the Law of Cause and Effect. Free Will does not mean that we can establish the curriculum here in the "Earth School", but it does mean we can elect what we want to take or experience at any given time.

Many times we will blame others or fate or unkind circumstances for the pattern our lives take. This mistaken idea forces you to feel like a victim. WE ARE NOT VICTIMS OF THIS EARTH PLANE UNLESS WE ALLOW OUR-SELVES TO BE SO. WE are the creators of our Reality, no one else. Nothing happens to us by chance, nor are there just random coincidences in your life. All that you are, all that you have been, and all that you will be, is of extreme importance to the Spiritual Evolution of this planet. You, as an individual with Free Will, are extremely unique, one of a kind. There is no one else like you, anywhere or anytime. Therefore, you have a special place and a special purpose in the Tapestry of Creation. Subconsciously, and during your Dream State, you are in constant communion with the Higher and Lower Astral Realms, but once back in the physical body with its inherent limitations, you will not consciously remember what was revealed to you, just vague bits and pieces unless the Gateway or Channel to the Subconscious has been opened. The Higher Self will never interfere with your choices, or prevent you from exercising your will, that is not its purpose. Your Inner Teacher or Higher Self does not demand to be heard and will not come to you on a conscious level without being invited to do so by you. That is the law of the Universe.

On a deeper, more spiritual level, the Higher Self is also referred to as the Holy Spirit. That part of ourselves which is in a state of perfection and in perfect communion with the Creator. It is this part of ourselves which we are seeking to rejoin on a conscious level. It is our Ego which places the barriers to this union as a means for perpetuating that feeling of isolation and separateness by using Illusions and Deceptions on the Earth Plane and the lower astral planes. When there are barriers to Truth, then it is easy to fall prey to the illusion we are victims, and when we attack or strike out at others because we fear being attacked ourselves, we strengthen the hold of Illusions fostered by our Ego. The purpose of this book, which is presented to you in three parts, is to provide you with some of the "Keys" needed to unlock your psyche from the stranglehold of Illusions. Self-Realization dispels the darkness the Ego would trap you in. There are many "Keys", and many "Paths" available to you which will assist you in achieving the goal of Self-Realization. I have chosen, in this book, to give you a few of those "Keys" or "Tools" to work with. Part One of this book is titled: "Symbolic Keys to Self-Realization. In this section the following chapters appear.

The First Chapter of this book is entitled: "Number Symbolism. This chapter will introduce you to the components of a Numerology Profile and show you how to discover your personal numerical vibrations. Definitions of the esoteric meanings of Numbers are also included in this chapter along with the astrologi-cal and planetary affiliations. In building a solid foundation for metaphysical knowledge it is important to see the inner-connectedness between Numerol-ogy, Astrology, Color, Dream Symbolism and the Tarot.

The Second Chapter of this book is entitled: "Symbolism of the Alphabet". This chapter deals with the special individual meanings behind each letter of the alphabet. When constructing a Numerology Profile, one of the major compo-nents concerns the name you were given at birth. Each letter of your name, and especially the first vowel of your name, exerts a subtle but powerful influence over your personality. Understanding the energies inherent to your nature, as revealed by your name, allows you to utilize the energy in a progressive positive manner.

The Third Chapter of this book is entitled: "Chakra Symbolism". In this chapter, the focus is on defining the meanings of the seven Chakras or "Power Centers" of the human body. Understanding what the chakras are is very important for it is through the chakras that we absorb and utilize energy. If you know how to open your chakras up, you will be able to use their power to cleanse yourself of negative influences or energies. Each of the 7 Chakra's of the body vibrate to color, to sound, to the subtle pulsations of the planets. Therefore, learning what affects the Chakra Centers is a vital "key" to a balanced mind and spirit, and greatly influences your ability to gain awareness.

The Fourth Chapter of this book is entitled: "Color Symbolism". This chapter deals with the hidden meanings behind Color and how different shades or hues affect you on a subconscious level. Color is very spiritual in its definition and is often seen in prophetic dreams, in meditation, and in other "messages" from the subconscious. The colors we are attracted to, that we wear, that we surround ourselves with in our homes and offices reveal many hidden facets about ourselves. Knowing the meaning of Color will also assist you in understanding the people around you and what emotional state they are in. It can be an invaluable "tool" when used properly. When interpreting Dreams, Mandalas, or Meditation experiences, the colors we see or remember have a great deal of importance in understanding the message being relayed to you.

Color Symbolism is very important when mastering the "Keys" pertaining to the Tarot. Both color and the symbols used on the Tarot have a great deal of metaphysical meaning and mystical wisdom that cannot be ignored. Astrological Signs vibrate to certain colors as well as to certain Minerals, Gems, and Crystals. The colors in your "aura" reveal intimate details about your state of health and how you cope with stressful situations, with problems, what the environment around you is, and how you see yourself.

The Fifth Chapter of this book is entitled: "Dream and Meditation Symbolism". In this chapter, the symbols which appear during the dream-state and while meditation are explored in depth. Learning the esoteric and metaphysical meanings of objects can release you from cultural, racial, or religious prejudice and allow you to see the object as it really is. The attainment of Pure Truth and Agape, without the distraction of Illusions, is what Self-Realization is all about. With this goal in mind, you are encouraged to keep a "dream journal" or meditation journal in which to record the symbols you see. Dreams are one of the ways the Universe seeks to touch our minds and offer us the guidance we ask for.

The Sixth Chapter of this book is entitled: "Astrological Symbolism". In this chapter, the esoteric and metaphysical meanings of the twelve Zodiac Sign are explored in depth, allowing you to uncover the hidden influences behind the astrological signs which affect you on a personal level. As with Color, each Astrological Sign vibrates to certain Crystals, Minerals and Gems, which leads us to the information contained in the next chapter.

The Seventh Chapter of this book is entitled: "Geological Symbolism. This chapter is concerned with the metaphysical and historical meanings behind

Crystals, Minerals, and Gems. The chemical components found in minerals, gems, or crystals affect the physical body, which in turn affects the emotional and mental bodies demonstrating the inter-connectedness between us and the mineral kingdom. This information is one of the "Keys" which can assist you in the goal toward Self-Realization. The more knowledge one has, or the more "Keys" one has, the easier it is to open the Gateway to your subconscious and keep it open.

Part Two of this book is concerned with the practical application of the symbolic "keys" in Part I. The Eighth Chapter of this book is titled: "Meditations. In this chapter different meditation exercises are presented for you to experiment with. I have a couple of excellent meditation exercises that work beautifully in opening up the Chakra Centers so that the channel to your creative Subconscious Mind and your Higher Self is established. Suggestions in personal preparation for meditating is also offered in this chapter in the event meditating is unfamiliar territory to you .

The Ninth Chapter in this book is titled: "Practical Exercises. This chapter is focused on personal experimentation with different techniques in order to gain enlightening experiences. I have included a Yoga Breathing exercise in this chapter which has a cleansing affect on the mental and emotional mind. It is also beneficial for asthma sufferers or for people who have respiratory problems. I know this from personal experience since I have had chronic bronchial asthma since I was a child, and when I am having breathing difficulties the Yoga Breathing exercise I have described in chapter 9 gives me great relief.

The Tenth Chapter in this book is entitled: "Mandala Designs". In this chapter I have included a variety of different Mandalas for you to color and experiment with. When creating your mandala, color is the vital tool used to interpret the hidden meaning your subconscious is relaying to you. What colors you choose when coloring these designs reveal your emotional state at that time. It also shows a great deal about you as a person and how you cope with stressful situations, with problems, what the environment around you is, and how you see yourself.

Part Three of this book is titled: "The Tarot and Self-Realization. In chapter 11, an introduction to the Tarot is presented along with instructions on how to prepare yourself for using Tarot Cards, for the proper frame of mind is essential when seeking enlightenment. The Tarot is not meant to be used lightly or as a game. It is a "Tool" to be used with a constructive purpose in mind, and not as a means of entertainment. I have also included several different types of Lay-Out Spreads for you to try and experiment with. These spreads will help you to get started, but I urge you, under the guidance of your Inner Teacher, to develop, design and experiment with your own Lay-Out Spreads. You may discover that a layout of your own design will bring the spiritual and intuitional knowledge you are seeking.

The following chapters deal with the Spiritual and Symbolic aspects of the Tarot, beginning with the 22 Major Arcana followed by the four Minor Arcana Suits. As examples and as references, I use two different decks, the Rider-Waite Tarot Deck and the Mary Hanson-Roberts Tarot Deck because of their extensive use of Color and Symbolism. The symbols used in the Tarot Cards do, for the most part, have their origins in mystical esoteric literature, including the Bible. It combines the religions of Judaism, Christianity, Hinduism, Buddhism, Taoist, Zen, Moslem, as well as other belief systems. Each Tarot Card conveys a Spiritual Lesson or Challenge for the individual working with the Tarot to use as a tool for You will find that each of the Tarot Cards described and defined in this book has a great deal of knowledge and wisdom to offer to you. How you use this information, how you interact or "interface" with the energy vibrations around you is part of the Spiritual Challenge or Lesson you have consciously or unconsciously attracted to you. The important thing to remember is that the Tarot merely shows potentials in your life, what you do with these potentials and energy patterns is a matter of Free Will.

Seek the white wind and let it lift you to your rightful place in the Universe. You are about to embark on a wonderful and exciting journey, a journey that will bring you home to your True Self, your True Reality. Always remember...

"Yesterday's sorrows are behind you
melted into the mists of time.
Tomorrow's promise is yet to materialize
though it grows in substance and form.
Today is your gift from the Universe
yours alone to shape and mold.
Give yourself permission to accept your golden opportunities."

Part I:
SYMBOLIC KEYS
TO SELF-REALIZATION

CHAPTER ONE

THE SYMBOLISM OF NUMBERS

To begin forming your Foundation of Knowledge, the first step is to understand the esoteric and metaphysical meaning of Numbers. Each number has its own special vibration, a positive and negative side which emits an energy that can be utilized. Numbers symbolize universal principles and laws which reveal, in part, the cycle of evolution for all life. This evolution is not only of the physical plane, but also gives a great deal of insight into the Spiritual Evolution of all beings. Manifestation on the Earth Plane is the result of the Evolutionary Steps symbolized by numbers.

The following information will deal not only with the ancient metaphysical wisdom symbolized by numbers, but also with the way numbers relate to us now. Pythagoras, the father of modern mathematics and an avid practitioner of the science of Numerology, discovered the effect of numbers on the Universal Pattern of life.

This ancient Greek Scientist saw how intricately numbers were intertwined with human destiny, a destiny which he, and others, believed was and is mathematically calculable.

Numerology, according to Webster's Dictionary, is a system of occultism involving divination by numbers. The word "Occult" means mystical-esoteric studies; that which is hidden, secret, mysterious, beyond normal human understanding. Numerology comprises all of these elements and more. It is a fascinating way to gain insights into your "true" nature and the Karmic Path you have chosen to walk in this life. Numerology also reveals what influences you are under in this present incarnation and what you are here to accomplish or what goals you have chosen for yourself. Numerology, Astrology, Dream Analysis, and Tarot, are all interconnected, and to study one of these "Keys" automatically leads you to study the others.

What are the esoteric meanings of numbers? What is a Numerology Profile? What are the components which comprise this type of Profile? How do I calculate the numbers that vibrate to me? In order to answer these questions, I have included instructions on how to determine which number represents your Life Lesson Number, your Path of Destiny Number, your Soul Number, your Outer Personality Number, and your Karmic Challenges. There is also a brief description of what each of these number categories mean.

Knowing how these number categories pertain to you personally, and then seeing, in a Tarot Spread, the number pattern that emerges from the Cards themselves will give you an even deeper insight into the Self-Counseling session you are participating in. The purpose of this chapter is to present you with the first of the many "keys" needed to unlock the gateway which leads you up the path toward Self-Realization.

THE LIFE LESSON NUMBER

Also called the "Birth-Path Number", this number symbolizes the lessons you have chosen to experience and learn in this lifetime. The Life Lesson Number has a powerful influence over your choice of "vocation" or what course you choose to direct your energies toward. This number is a permanent one and cannot be changed or modified in anyway because it is calculated from your birth date, (month, day, and year). This number reveals potential career opportunities plus the karmic lesson you came into this incarnation to master and then use in a positive creative manner. The Life Lesson Number represents the Cosmic Gift you were given at birth in order to accomplish your personal destiny. Here is an example of how to calculate your Life Lesson Number.

Birth date: 12/24/1953

    (1+2=3) (2+4=6) (1+9+5+3=18)

add the month, (3), to the day, (6), and to the year (18):

    3+6+18=27   2+7=9

Nine is the Life Lesson Number for this birth date. This was calculated by reducing the sum to a single digit. If the sum had been a *Master* number, such as 11, 22, 33, 44, 55, 66, etc., the sum would *not* be reduced to a single digit. Here is another example:

Birth date: 11/4/1926

    (1+9+2+6=18) 11+4+18=33

The Life Lesson Number for this birth date is a Master number 33 and is not reduced to a single digit. I didn't reduce the month when adding because it is a Master number.

In order for you to understand how to calculate your Path of Destiny Number, Soul Number and Outer Personality Number, you need to understand the relationship between each letter of the Alphabet and the number it corresponds to. The following diagram shows how the Alphabet breaks down in relation to numbers. Using this diagram, you can break down any name or word into its numerical value.

THE ALPHABET AND THE NUMBERS

1	2	3	4	5	6	7	8	9
A	B	C	D	E	F	G	H	I
J	K	L	M	N	O	P	Q	R
S	T	U	V	W	X	Y	Z	

THE PATH OF DESTINY NUMBER

This number is derived from the total numerical value of all the letters in the entire name as was given at birth. This number should be reduced to a single digit unless it is a Master Number. The Path of Destiny number shows what you must do in this lifetime or incarnation. It also reveals what you came here to manifest, what choices you made before entering your physical body. It is the Key to your abilities as well as serving as a source of Inspiration. The Path of Destiny represents your aim in life, it shows both the spiritual and material path you are walking in this lifetime and what is necessary for you to accomplish in order to advance your Soul's Level on the Evolutionary Spiral.

However, it is important to point out that this number expression is influenced by the Soul Number, which is the numerical value of the Vowels in the full name given at birth, and by the Outer Personality Number, which is the numerical value of the consonants in the full name given at birth. These two numbers have a modifying effect on the Path of Destiny Number and should be taken into consideration. All though you may modify your full name somewhat by name changes, marriage, nicknames, etc., the birth name influence is always the power behind the changes you make and this influence will persist in its desire for expression throughout your life. Here is an example of how to calculate your Path of Destiny Number:

$$1\ 97\quad 51\quad 5\quad 5 = 33$$
FULL NAME   Marilyn Jean Enners
$$4\ 93\ 5\quad 1\ 5\quad 55\ 91 = 47\quad 4+7 = 11$$

$$11+33 = 44$$

Because the Vowels in my name are a Master Number 33, I have not reduced it to a single digit. When you add 4+7 together it becomes a Master Number 11. Since both numbers are Master Numbers, I added them together to determine the total numerical value of my full given name at birth. 44 is a Master Number as well, therefore, this number is not reduced to a single digit either. This gives me the Master Number 44 as my Path of Destiny Number. Here's another example:

$$19\quad 9\ 15\quad 1\ 5 = 31\quad 3+1 = 4$$
FULL NAME   David Michael Drake
$$4\ 4\ 4\quad 4\ 38\quad 3\quad 49\ 2 = 45\quad 4+5 = 9$$

$$4+9 = 13\text{: } 1+3 = 4$$

The total numerical value of this name is 4. The Vowels in this name add up to 31. When you add 3+1 it equals the number 4. The Consonants in this name come to 45. Adding 4+5 equals 9. To get the total numerical value of the Vowels and the Consonants add 4+9 which equals 13. Since 13 is not a Master Number, it is added together to equal the number 4. Therefore the Soul number, (vowels), of this name is a 4. The Outer Personality Number, (consonants), of this name is a 9. But the Path of Destiny Number, (total), is a 4.

THE SOUL NUMBER

This number is calculated from the total numerical value of the vowels found in the full given name at birth. It is important for me to stress that you must use the entire name as it was given to you at birth. Just a first name and last name is not enough. If you have two middle names, they must be included in the calculations. Occasionally, however, babies are only given two names at birth, in that event the only thing you can do is use just the two names. But that is the only exception to the rule.

The Soul Number reveals your true nature, that fragile essence which many people seek to protect from a "hostile" world. This number represents your inner core, who you really are beneath the "mask" you show to others. Because the Soul Number reveals the deeply intimate aspects of your personality, very few people are aware of what you are really like deep down. The Soul Number also indicates what personality traits you have developed in previous lifetimes.

The Soul Number is what you, your Subconscious Self, desire-even need-to express in someway. This desire or urge can be so powerful in its intensity that it may overwhelm any other numerical vibrations which affect you. This number is very important to understand because it reveals the pattern of spiritual growth and enlightenment you have attained over many lifetimes. The energies of the Soul Number is a powerful force which has great influence over your actions and choices in the present lifetime.

THE OUTER PERSONALITY NUMBER

This number is calculated by adding together the numerical values of the consonants in the full given name. The Outer Personality Number reveals how you appear to other people; however, it does not necessarily indicate your true nature. This number also shows how people expect you to act because of the "image" you project in order to safeguard your vulnerabilities. The Outer Personality Number represents the Conscious Self and how you want to impress or appear to others. This number can also reveal what you secretly dream or fantasize about.

The word "Personality" is an off shoot of another word "Persona", which means "Mask" and therefore represents the "mask" we present to others. A pleasant personality is really essential to achieve the goals you set for yourself. It is important to understand this because it is through the vibration of your Outer Personality Number that the other Vibrational Urges, the Soul Number, The Life Lesson Number, and the Path of Destiny Number are expressed. Our Outer Personality also serves as a shield, granting us the illusion of safety or protection.

KARMIC CHALLENGES

By using the date of birth, we can determine what special karmic lesson is very important for you in this incarnation. It is a number that subtly influences your life in unseen ways, therefore I think it is important to know what that number is. Here is an example of how to calculate your Karmic Challenge.

(3) (6)   (9)

BIRTH DATE: 12/24/1953

This needs to be reduced to 3 separate single digits, which I have demonstrated. Even if one or more of the numbers are Master Numbers, they must be reduced to a single digit. Then you set these 3 numbers up as follows:

3 6 9
3 3
0
6

First, I subtracted the 3 from the 6 and came up with 3. Next I subtracted the 6 from the 9 and came up with 3 again. Third step was to subtract 3 from 3 which gave me 0. It is this Third Step which results in your Karmic Challenge. For me it is a 0. The Four Step reveals the Sub-Karmic Challenge which is calculated by subtracting the 3 from the 9 which gives me a 6. This sub-karmic challenge does not have the influence of the Main Karmic Challenge, but it still affects me in very subtle ways.

If the first number had been a 7 rather than a 3, I would still have subtracted 7 from 6 and arrived at the number 1. The method is simple, you subtract the smaller number from the larger number. It doesn't matter which one comes first. For example:

$1 + 9 + 5 + 7 = 22$ (22 must be reduced to a single digit: 4)

BIRTH DATE: 9/8/1957

9 8 4
1 4
3
5

Since I can't subtract 9 from 8, I subtracted 8 from 9 to derive the number 1. I can't subtract 8 from 4, but I can subtract 4 from 8 to derive the number 4. Third step is the subtraction of 1 from 4 which results in 3, the Karmic Challenge. 9 can't be subtracted from 4, so I reverse the order and subtract the 4 from 9 to derive the number 5, which is the Sub-Karmic Challenge. This is a fairly simply formula, but it can seem complicated when written out like this.

VOWEL INDICATORS

It was taught in the ancient temples of Lemuria, Atlantis, Egypt, and Greece, that "vowels" are sacred elements in the alphabet. The priests and priestesses believed that the first vowel in an individual's first name was the "energy" that drew the spiritual essence or "soul" into the physical body. The first vowel in a name indicates important "Karmic Merits" an individual is gifted with in their present incarnation, (karmic merit means "earned" reward).

Metaphysical scholars and Numerical Adepts have found through careful research that the first vowel does have a profound influence on us. It sets the "tone" for our inner personality. If the first vowel in a name is repeated anywhere else in our name, the vibrational influence is greatly increased. However, if that same vowel is found more than 3 times in a name it can cause an imbalance or set up special spiritual challenges for us to face.

MISSING LINKS OR KARMIC INDICATORS

When you are calculating the numbers in your name and birth date, there usually are one or two numbers which do not appear. These missing numbers or "links" are called "karmic indicators" and reveal certain qualities you need to concentrate on in your present lifetime. This is due to the actions and choices you made in previous lifetimes. For example: If you are lacking the number "2" in your name, it symbolizes a need to develop qualities of cooperation and mediation, qualities you did not develop or utilize properly in a previous lifetime. The missing number could also indicate that in a previous lifetime you over used the qualities of the number 2 and became a "wishy-washy" sort of individual, never able to make up your mind or you were unable to withstand any type of pressure.

Therefore, "missing links" or "karmic indicators" serve as challenges or lessons we are in need of experiencing or "re-experiencing" in order to achieve growth and awareness as spiritual beings. Even more importantly, karmic indicators symbolize Sub-conscious behavior patterns established in the past which can surface and manifest in our actions when we are under stress, often without us even being consciously aware of it.

THE BASIC MEANING OF NUMBERS

The symbolism of numbers has been studied and utilized as a source of wisdom for many millennia. Some metaphysical scholars believe they can trace the art of number symbolism back to the civilization of the Tridents. Understanding the esoteric and metaphysical meanings of Numbers can serve to guide or inspire you when faced with choices and opportunities in your life.

Numbers have an "inner-connectedness" with Astrology and the planets of our solar system. Each Zodiac sign vibrates to a specific number expression as do each of the planets or "heavenly bodies" used in astrological interpretations. In this section, along with the basic meaning behind the numbers themselves, the astrological and planetary ties will also be defined so you will be able to develop a deeper awareness of the continuity or "fluidity" of the Universe.

NUMBER 0
This number has the potential of all numbers. It can be all, or nothing. In the ancient temples, the number 0 symbolized the never-ending link which exists between humankind and all other life-forms, a link that was experienced both in joy and sorrow. The number 0 represents the feminine aspect of the Creator, the "Goddess Energy" which is pure, unformed and unlimited. This number represents the Hand of the Mother preparing the way, releasing undreamed of potentials and possibilities. The Hand of the Mother Goddess offers opportunities for Transmutation and Transformation. The number 0 incorporates both the Alpha and Omega energies, and yet it is more, for it has no beginning and no end, it is eternal and Infinite. The shape of zero, (0), is oval, symbolic of an egg or the womb, which represents the seed of creation, and the seeds of change.

NUMBER 1
This number represents the inventor, the pioneer, it is a leader or creator on the physical plane. Number 1 is an individualist, an originator. This number contains the aspects of creation and self. In the ancient temples, the number 1 taught the priests and priestesses the importance of becoming a Channel for the Eternal, Spiritual Forces which control, sustain, and nurture life in the Universe.

Number 1 represents the Male Energy Force or Principle. In the Oriental philosophies, this energy is referred to as the "Yang" energy. It is raw energy, pulsating and in a state of kinetic motion. The number 1 seeks to establish its identity in the Universe, to utilize the gifts the Creator has bestowed upon it. Number 1 has a fierce need or desire to manifest on the physical plane because it has the power to choose how its energies will be directed. It has the choice of being a constructive, powerful, creative force, or choosing to be a negative, destructive whirlwind raging through life, contributing nothing but the ashes of ruins.

Number 1 is, by its very nature, positive and mental in its expression. Its element is Fire. One is the I AM of creation, signifying unity with all. It represents the true Self-Consciousness, Self-Awareness of Being, but it can degenerate all of its potential into the pettiness of Ego. The Spiritual Lesson inherent in number 1 is Unity with the Creator and through this Unity, experience a "one-ness" with all of creation. The Keyword for number One is: beginning.

Astrological and Planetary affinities: The Number One vibrates to the Zodiac sign of Aries and to the planet Mars.

NUMBER 2
This number represents the peacemaker, the diplomat, it is changeable and adaptable. Number 2 is balance, union with another, a pair. It has the aspects of

rhythm and harmony, of peaceful cooperation with others different from itself. In the ancient temples, the number 2 taught the priests and priestesses the importance of attuning their hearts and minds with the wisdom of the ages, of creating a union between themselves and their Spiritual Guides or Teachers.

Number 2 symbolizes the Female Energy Force or principle. It is a receptive energy that is termed the "Yin" energy in Oriental philosophy. Number 2 is gestation, a time of germination when things begin to take shape and form. Two seeks to assimilate diverse experiences, to find a common thread that runs between different creations. Two collects and synthesizes details. It has the awareness of opposites and can give unconditional acceptance of those differences. Two has the great power to act as a bridge between opposites, to give understanding and nurturing. Negatively, number 2 can be indecisive, juggling opposites and increasing the separateness, rather than acting as a stabilizing and unifying bridge between two opposing forces.

Number 2 is, by its very nature, negative and mental in its expression. Its element is Water. Two is emotional and is driven by the universal laws of attraction. Spiritually, Two seeks to develop wisdom and a love for knowledge. The Spiritual Lesson inherent in the number 2 is Love expressed through Harmony and Peace. The Keyword for number 2 is: Duality.

Astrological and Planetary affinities: The Number Two vibrates to the Zodiac sign of Taurus and to the planet Earth.

NUMBER 3

This number represents the artist, the writer, the creative visionary. Number 3 is Self-Expression, Manifestation, and Creativity in action. It has the aspects of Joy, enthusiasm, sociability and optimism. Three has the deep need to communicate with others, to share knowledge. In the ancient temples, the Number 3 taught priests and priestesses that their words of wisdom taken from the ancient books could bring harmony from discord or strife, if they were willing to experience what life had to offer in order to teach others of the choices available to them.

Number 3 symbolizes the pure radiant joy to be found in life. Through its own magnetism, 3 draws others to it as an inspiration, encouraging others to expand and grow. Three has the great power of Creative Imagination, of visualizing all potentials and possibilities as real. Because of its expressive creativity, 3 is involved with many different emotions and experiences, it has an intense need to drink long and deep from the Cup of Life. Negatively, 3 can scatter its creative energies wastefully, be impatient, and intolerant of others. Number 3 is, by its very nature, masculine and emotional in its expression. Its element is Fire. Three is also metaphysically a very Spiritual Number. It symbolizes the Holy Trinity. The number 3 seeks to communicate the Spiritual Wonders of the Universe it has experienced. The Spiritual Lesson inherent in the number 3 is to awaken the joy of the Soul. The Keyword for Number 3 is: Expression.

Astrological and Planetary affinities: The Number Three vibrates to the Zodiac sign of Gemini and to the planet Mercury.

NUMBER 4

This number represents foundations, stability and honesty. It is practical and patient and has the ability to organize. Number 4 has the aspects of a Builder of security and firmness on the Physical Plane. In the ancient Temples, the number 4 taught priests and priestesses that there were endless riches to be found in the realm of the Spirit; riches that far superseded what could be found on the physical material plane alone. Therefore, it was important to build foundations for the Spirit and the Physical, each supporting the other. Number 4 is also the symbol of law and order, or productiveness and industry. It is the builder whose tools are form and substance in the material plane. Therefore, the creativity manifested in the past must now serve a useful, practical purpose. The Number 4 is sincere and faithful, dedicated to the Truth, and willingly assumes responsibility for others. The fact that the Number 4 relates to the Earth and the biblical story of genesis which says that the formation of the Earth took place on the 4th day of creation, is an interesting esoteric tie. Negatively, Four can express itself in narrow-mindedness and rigidity and can be lacking the essential fluidity needed in life. It can be too stubborn and preoccupied with the material plane.

Number 4, by its very nature, is feminine in its expression. It is positive and mental. Its element is Earth. Spiritually, the Four is learning Self-Discipline over its artistic creative nature, taking the abstract and forming it into substance. The Spiritual Lesson for the Number Four is understanding the material plane before the Soul can raise itself higher on the Spiritual Evolutionary Spiral. The Keyword for the number Four is Justice.

Astrological and Planetary affinities: The Number Four vibrates to the Zodiac sign of Cancer and to the Moon.

NUMBER 5

This number represents changes in the life cycle of creation. It is versatile, and filled with adventure and curiosity. It has the aspects of freedom and resourcefulness deeply in-grained within its essence. In the ancient temples, the Number 5 taught priests and priestesses that choices must not be based on or influenced by fear. Instead, choices were to be based on Justice and the Universal Law of "Like attracts Like" or "Karma". This was considered to be the proper criteria to use in every circumstance of life.

Number 5 is symbolized as a pivotal point in the upward Spiritual Evolutionary Spiral. It meets with many different and diverse opportunities for experience and self-expression which will result in Spiritual Progress. Five has the need to communicate to others the variety of experiences it has, to share with others the wonders of the universe it has discovered on its Spiritual Journey. Therefore, Number 5 touches the lives of many, but is driven on, unable to settle long in one place. The quest of the number 5 will not let it rest for long, it must be free to change, to seek, to experience and to grow. Negatively, number 5 can express its gifts irresponsibly and act in a thoughtless manner. It can be plagued with too much changeability and long periods of procrastination, which has its roots in fear.

Number 5 is, by its very nature, masculine in its expression as well as negative and mental. It is both psychic and spiritual. Its element is Air. Five is in the process of learning how to utilize new opportunities, how to develop elasticity or flexibility of character. The Spiritual Lesson for number 5 is freedom from mental bondage, freedom from fear induced limitations. The Keyword for the number 5 is: Change.

Astrological and Planetary affinities: The Number Five vibrates to the Zodiac sign of Leo and to the Sun.

NUMBER 6

This number represents responsibility and service, it is the Teacher, the Parent, a creator of beauty and harmony. Six has the aspects of social consciousness deeply ingrained within its essence based on love and compassion. In the ancient temples, the number 6 taught priests and priestesses that the beauty of divine expression can be found in all things, however great or small. Six contains the ability to heal, to counsel others because of the understanding and love which emanates from it.

Number 6 symbolizes harmony, truth, balance, and love. It is domestic in its expression, willingly assuming responsibilities for others, learning how to adjust to different needs and requirements, bringing in the balance necessary for continued growth. Six is artistic and creative, driven to express the beauty within its soul, to share with others the bounty it has received. Six needs a commitment, a union with another, to create on the physical plane. Negatively, Six expresses its ability to bring balance into the world through interference rather than cooperation. It can be argumentative and jealous rather than understanding and accepting.

Number 6, by its very nature, is both masculine and feminine in its expression. It has a true Duality to it. Six is the Cosmic Guardian. Its elements are Air and Earth. Six is in the process of learning to live for others and not just for the Self alone, learning to take on responsibilities and learning to give selfless service to others. The Spiritual Lesson for Six is Soul Unfoldment. The Keyword for the number Six is: Harmony.

Astrological and Planetary affinities: The Number Six vibrates to the Zodiac sign of Virgo and to the planet Vulcan.

NUMBER 7

This number represents the Thinker, the Philosopher, it is the Mystic and the Seeker. Seven has the aspects of spiritual development through investigation. It is concerned with wisdom and study, with research and introspection. It is the vibration of silence and inner searching. In the ancient temples, the number 7 taught the priests and priestesses that the spirit of humankind could emerge victorious over any obstacle. That all trials or tribulations were Challenges to the Spirit, an opportunity to turn an obstacle into a stepping stone. Seven was considered the sacred number in the temples.

The Number 7 is a Seeker. It seeks for answers to the mysteries of life and of the universe. It has a hunger to know what its origins are, to penetrate the veils of hidden knowledge. Seven needs, even craves solitude, it needs to feel, intimately, its one-ness with nature. The Creator rested on the 7th day, as all things must have rest in order to assimilate, understand and digest the myriad experiences which is part of the life cycle. Seven is the master metaphysician. Perfect thinking and analysis are deeply ingrained in its nature, which is one of the many reasons that number 7 is called the sacred number. Negatively, the special gifts of number 7 are expressed as isolation, suppression of knowledge, and analysis made with a sense of detached coldness. The reclusive instincts are carried to extremes, causing it to be out of touch with reality.

Number 7, by its very nature, is negative and mental in its expression. Seven is also psychic and spiritual. Its element is water. Seven is in the process of acquiring understanding of the unseen or hidden realms. This number is also learning to develop patience and calmness in order to fully express its inner sources. The Spiritual Lesson for Number 7 is Development of the Spiritual Mind. The Keyword for number 7 is Intuition.

Astrological and Planetary affinities: The Number Seven vibrates to the Zodiac sign of Libra and to the planet Venus.

NUMBER 8
This number represents authority and leadership. Eight is the organizer with the aspects of self-reliance and discrimination. Its nature is one of responsibility and power. In the ancient temples, the number 8 taught the priests and priestesses that they must bring comfort to their fellow creatures and lead them toward a vision of exaltation and glory. The eight also taught that in order to retain prosperity for themselves, they had to share it with others, for only when they were willing to give the gift of prosperity to others did they truly possess it for themselves.

Number 8 symbolizes power and control, it is also a number which represents the laws of Karma. The double zeros, one on top of the other, which form the symbol of the number 8, represents the power of the Creator in manifestation on the material plane, it is the universal symbol of Infinity. Eight has the ability to see situations, people and opportunities in broad terms. It is steadfast in nature and has the qualities necessary to achieve the material goals it sets for itself. Expansion and growth on the material plane is part of the inherent gifts of the number 8. The eight will reap what it has sown in the past, be it for good or ill. Negatively, the number 8 can corrupt itself with intolerance, impatience, scheming, and a ruthlessness which is unmatched by any other number.

Number 8 is, by its very nature, positive, mental, and feminine in its expression. It is a number which vibrates to God. Its element is Earth. Number 8 is in the process of learning how to use wealth and material prosperity for the benefit of all creatures. It is learning how to dispense justice in all forms. Eight is also symbolic of the principles of material accomplishment. The Spiritual Lesson for number 8 is Material Freedom. The Keyword for number 8 is Leadership.

Astrological and Planetary affinities: The Number Eight vibrates to the

Zodiac sign of Scorpio and to the planet Pluto.

NUMBER 9

This number represents the Spiritual Teacher, the Sage. Nine is also the healer, the humanitarian. It has the aspects of self-lessness with a universal awareness. Nine is the Trinity of Trinities, the sign of accomplishment, achievement, and completion. In the ancient temples, the number 9 taught the priests and priestesses that each deed and word would be judged on the scales of Universal Truth. Number Nine also taught them the importance of balance, service, and of universal love for all creation.

Number 9 symbolizes compassion for all and a desire to give unselfish service to others. It is generous, patient, and benevolent, choosing to give unconditional love and acceptance to others, choosing to take a non-judgmental stance. Nine is aware that judgment is the realm of the Infinite Creator, not of humankind. This number also represents the artist, the writer, the deep philosophical thinker who, through many diverse experiences and learning opportunities is ready to share this knowledge, to teach what it has learned to all who are ready to listen. The Nine is driven by the passionate desire to give back to the universe some of the gifts it has so generously received. Negatively expressed, the gifts of number 9 are seen in waste and bitterness, in extremes of emotions and aimless dreaming.

Number 9 is, by its very nature, emotional and spiritual in its expression. Nine is masculine, mental, and negative in expression as well. It is the third power number and its element is Fire. Nine gives fulfillment of Self by giving of oneself. Nine is in the process of learning Love and Compassion for all, as well as Tolerance and Forgiveness. The Spiritual Lesson for number 9 is Forgiveness and the Development of Brother/Sisterhood. The Keyword for number 9 is: Universal.

Astrological and Planetary affinities: The Number Nine vibrates to the Zodiac sign of Sagittarius and to the planet Jupiter.

NUMBER 10

This number represents the diverse aspects of creation and the link between the God-Force and all creation. Ten is the door, it is a new beginning, a new chance under the direct guidance of the Creator. It also represents the Hand of God or the Creator stretched out to assist Humankind in their affair's. In the ancient temples, the number 10 taught the priests and priestesses that they were responsible to the kingdom of the spirit which was embodied in their own flesh.

The number 10 symbolizes opportunity, the Wheel of Karma turning once more. Ten combines the elements of 0 and 1 together, transforming these two energies into a totally new energy, with unknown potentials. The number 10 provides an opportunity, but it is up to the individual whether or not they make the most of this God-given opportunity, it is their choice whether to take the offer presented to them, or to turn their backs on it. A door can be opened, or it can be closed. It is a matter of personal choice or Free Will.

Number 10 is, by its very nature, intuitional and spiritual in its expression. It is a number which vibrates on a higher frequency than other numbers because of its transcendental nature. Its elements are Water, Air, Fire, and Earth.

Number 10 is in the process of learning how to leave behind physical limitations and transcend to the pureness of the higher realms. Learning how to leave behind the distractions of Illusions and accepting in their place Universal Truth is the Spiritual Challenge which faces the number 10. The Keyword for number 10 is: Opportunity.

Astrological and Planetary affinities The Number Ten vibrates to the Zodiac sign of Capricorn and to the planet Saturn.

MASTER NUMBER 11

The Master Number 11 symbolizes Intuition and Prophecy. The creative potential of the Number 11 is enormous, for it is comprised of the power of the Number One taken a step higher. In other words, the number 11 can be compared to the mathematical statement of 1 to the 2nd power. Eleven demands very high standards, it demands patience while at the same time, demands that quick decisions be made when the situation calls for action. This number bestows courage, talent and power, coupled with strong feelings of leadership. Recognition and/or fame is likely for an Eleven Vibration because of the brilliant inspiration and wisdom inherent in its nature. The number 11 is in the process of learning that true mastery is actually self-less service to others.

This vibration has been involved with the spiritual path for a long time and through its spiritual evolution it has learned a great deal concerning the mysteries of life and death. Master Number 11 possesses very acute psychic abilities which often manifest clairvoyantly. At times this master number seems to experience two "realities" at the same time, which can cause confusion and emotional turmoil. Because of the sensitivity of its psychic awareness, it becomes very important for this master number to learn how to deal with the unexpected and with abrupt changes. The master number 11's imaginative powers are increased and enhanced because of its ability to see the mysterious qualities of life. This number vibration can detach itself from distractions which gives its creative and inventive potentials the opportunity to develop more fully.

The Master Number 11 has a unique awareness of Reality despite the presence of Illusions which distract others. The priests and priestesses of the ancient temples regarded the number 11 as the symbol for the all-seeing eye; that which is Divinely Inspired and Divinely Guided, possessing prophetic power. The creativity displayed by this number has the capacity to affect the lives of others who come into contact with it. Number 11 has an unusual comprehension of diverse facts which helps them to grasp and utilize any situation to their advantage.

Other people see the Master Number 11 as a source of unusual inspiration. The artistic genius and creative flair inherent to this vibration demonstrates the visionary abilities the number 11 has. This vibration prefers to be different than others, to be unique and inventive. Negatively, the Master Number 11 can allow its idealistic, creative and artistic nature to degenerate into mere ego-centricity, resulting in a flagrant waste of talent, or when acting out its negative qualities, this master number can simply wallowing in laziness. When this happens, the Master Number 11 looses its higher power and reverts to its lowest expression as a number 2.

ASTROLOGICAL AND PLANETARY AFFINITIES: The Master Number Eleven vibrates to the astrological sign of Aquarius and to the planet Uranus.

NUMBER 12

Even though number 12 is reduced to the number 3 by adding together 1+2, the actual compound number 12 has certain special characteristics which must be taken into consideration when it occurs in a Numerology Profile or when it appears in dreams and during Meditations. Number 12 is special partly because of the Spiritual significance it has. There were 12 disciples of the Master Jesus; 12 Hebrew tribes who followed Moses from the Sinai; there are 12 months to a year, 12 Zodiac signs in Western Astrology, and it is the number which represents surrender to a Higher Force, of letting go and letting God.

The number 12 is an unusual vibration because it has learned how to accumulate inner strength and fortitude by undergoing a variety of experiences. This vibration has special presence, a quality of serenity which sets it apart from the mundane world, which tends to view this vibration with a great deal of puzzlement. The mental process of number 12 is focused in spiritual analysis rather than on judgmental analysis of others. The energies of this vibration are manifested in tolerance towards the various belief systems, philosophies, and life styles practiced by others.

The number 12 is aware of the great poverty and suffering in the world. It is aware of the problems people have with existing harmoniously with themselves and with their environment. This vibration knows of the difficulty people have in recognizing the difference between Reality and Illusion, but because of the unconscious intuitive link number 12 has with the Universal Mind, this vibration is also aware of the role "karma" plays in the lives of people. With infinite gentleness, the number 12 expresses the idea that afflictions, difficult circumstances, and challenges are the result of the "law of cause and effect". This vibration attempts to demonstrate to the world that what happens in an individual's life is partly governed by conscious and unconscious choices made by the individual, either prior to birth or as life presents options for choice.

This number embraces the philosophy that by reversing or changing one's thoughts it becomes possible to free one's self from limitations. The philosophy of number 12 is often laughed at by the world in general, who views this type of thinking as "unrealistic". Yet, by demonstrating this philosophy in a practical manner to the inhabitants of The Earth Plane, the number 12 has achieved this reversal, this freedom from limitation which enables it to understand and emphasize the beliefs of other people. Harmony, peace and serenity are not just empty buzz words to this vibration, these elements are part of its experience which grants freedom of the spirit.

The number 12 is a symbol of Wisdom gained through the sacrifice of personal ego, allowing the "true self" or "Higher self" to emerge. Others are drawn to the vibrations emanated by the number 12, vibrations which offer peace and guidance, faith and trust to the hungry hearts and minds of those who feel abandoned and lost on the Earth Plane. The number 12 teaches, by example, to have faith in oneself and in one's natural right to happiness and contentment. When this vibration is expressed negatively, it reverts to its lowest vibration of a 3.

ASTROLOGICAL AND PLANETARY AFFINITIES: The Number Twelve vibrates to the astrological sign of Pisces and to the planet Neptune.

NUMBER 13

Even though the number 13 is reduced to the number 4 by adding together 1+3, the actual compound number 13 has certain characteristics which must be taken into consideration when it occurs in different analysis techniques. Number 13 is special partly because of the spiritual significance it has. For example: There were 12 disciples, Master Jesus was the 13th. In the esoteric Hebrew teachings, it is written that originally there were 13 tribes of Israel, 12 of which settled the lands given them by Yahweh and one tribe that remained lost in the wilderness, doomed to restlessly roam the earth. There are 13 lunar months to a year, which shows the strong correlation between the number 13 and the "mysterious" and powerful phases of the Moon.

Since the "dark ages", when the Church suppressed knowledge and fostered superstition, the unenlightened have viewed the number 13 as the "death number", a number attracted the "devil" and his evil servants. Occult Masters and Metaphysicians know the number 13 actually symbolizes Change and Transformation. The legendary bird called the "Phoenix", represents the hidden meaning of the number 13 because it is reborn out of its own ashes every 500 years, ready to begin anew. Our lives on the Earth Plane are filled with a series of so-called "deaths" or transformations. Marriage, divorce, loosing one's virginity, the adolescent process, the rise from obscurity to fame or recognition, all of these and more are "mini-deaths" representing change and transformation.

It is unfortunate so many people allow fear to cloud their judgment which blocks their ability to respond to the higher vibration of the number 13. Instead, they respond to the mundane aspects of this number allowing their fear and superstitions to distort the true meaning of this vibration. To the unawakened, the number 13 represents death, bad luck, and the decay of the physical body. This negative and narrow view of the number 13 happens because too many people are preoccupied with overindulging the appetites of their physical bodies.

These "unawakened" individuals allow their desires and sensuality to rule their minds rather than channeling this energy into creative outlets. However, to those individuals whose awareness of the forces of the Universe has been awakened, the number 13 represents "Real" gratification and satisfaction achieved through the power of regeneration and transmutation. There are enormous potentials for ultimate achievement with this number which is balanced by an equally incredible potential for destruction if the powerful energies of this number is misdirected.

The number 13 is a vibration of constant change, each time one circumstance or situation is settled, others arose needing attention, creating a continuous cycle of transformation. Thirteen is a number of renewal and rebirth, and its function is to teach the inhabitants of the earth plane about the illusionary nature of material matter. This number helps us to understand the instability that is inherent in the essence of the Earth Plane and how important it is for us to build our foundations elsewhere. The number 13 does not consciously choose to lead or control others, but because of the strength and determination inherent in its nature, it tends to end up carrying the burden for others, or it will assume heavy responsibilities in order to get the results needed to bring about a satisfactory conclusion to complicated situations.

NUMBER 14

In the ancient temples, priests and priestesses considered the number 14 to symbolize the important function of the "Record-Keeper" or scribe. Scrolls or manuscripts containing the accumulation of occult and esoteric knowledge maintained over centuries were highly prized by most of the advanced ancient cultures. The artistic and creative talents of a scribe was considered to be a gift from the gods and those who possessed these talents were treated with respect and honor.

The number 14 possesses unique abilities which allows it to blend and harmonize diverse energy patterns. The mental processes of this number is in constant motion, seeking to find the perfect bridge between itself and the Universal Sub-conscious. The number 14 has equal amounts of feminine and masculine energy which it works hard to bring into balance. This vibration strives to be a channel for the forces of the Universe, knowing intuitively that it can serve as a conduit for knowledge needed on the Earth Plane.

This vibration has the potential to achieve a special attunement with the unseen forces of nature. When expressed negatively, this attunement can lead to an over-active sex drive and excessive indulgence in the sensual appetites of the physical body. When expressed positively, this attunement with nature manifests in profound sensitivity to the astral plane. The ability to communicate with "non-physical" beings is an inherent talent for the number 14.

The spiritual challenge for the number 14 is to blend the spiritual with the material, unleashing the creative potential of both. This vibration has the inspiration necessary to utilize its energy to build unique foundations of knowledge upon which others can build and grow from. This is a very creative number which needs an outlet for its expression. Mentally, physically, emotionally, or spiritually, the number 14 cannot tolerate limitations or restrictions of any kind regardless of the possible consequences. It must have the freedom to explore its universe and assimilate the knowledge it gathers along the way.

NUMBER 15:

This is an interesting compound number because of the ties it has to the Major Arcana of the Tarot. In the Tarot, the Number 15 represents "The "Devil" which symbolizes obsession with materialism and pleasures of the Earth Plane. "The Devil" is also concerned with temptations created by Illusions under the direction of the Ego. The number 6, which is the reduced vibration of number 15, has to do with responsibilities, the home, and security. When the number 15 is being expressed negatively, its energies can be used to manipulate other people's weaknesses to this vibration's advantage. This manipulation is motivated by the need for security and control.

Even though the number 15 is concerned with ambition and achievement, it can be expressed in a positive manner. The number 15 is in the process of learning how to let go of its obsessive attachment to material possessions and status. Part of the Spiritual Challenge inherent in the number 15 is the lesson that material attachments are really chains that bind and limit true expression. Bondage to the Earth Plane is not a worthwhile goal and causes only suffering and spiritual strangulation. Therefore, one of the important concepts the number 15 is in the process of understanding is that possessions can too easily become a prison for the creative spirit.

NUMBER 16:
The number 16 is a very magnetic and forceful vibration which can misuse its powers very easily. Because this number can attract other individuals to it without much effort, the temptation to manipulate others is a danger for this vibration. Number 16 has been given a talent to express its creative concepts, philosophies and ideas in ways that excite the minds of other individuals. Sixteen is a vibration of clarity and intellectual strength. This ability to see into the heart of most situations or circumstances can create a problem with overconfidence which may result in a temporary downfall. Periods of solitude and contemplation are absolute necessities for number 16. Without them, the energy of this number becomes scattered and chaotic.

Philosophy and meditation are important elements the number 16 concerns itself with. This number has the potential to become a powerful mystic, with fully developed psychic abilities such as: clairvoyance, prophecy, telepathy, and intuition. This potential has its roots in the deeply introspective nature of number 16, a nature which flourishes when allowed to retreat from the distractions of the mundane world. The Subconscious Mind has a great deal of influence over the actions and motivations of number 16. It serves to guide and teach, through practical experience, the lessons number 16 has need of learning.

Through the development of the mystical nature, number 16 awakens its spiritual self. Sometimes this awakening must come about through extreme pressure or a so-called "disaster" or "crisis", In the Major Arcana of the Tarot, the number 16 represents the "Tower" which symbolizes a flash of enlightenment from the "God-Head", the destruction and elimination of ego, and selfish ambition or materialism being ripped away. In Numerology, the number 16 has many of the same connotations as this tarot card, and because of this, the vibration of 16 can be expressed as a disruptive influence which brings, in its wake, enlightenment and true freedom.

NUMBER 17
As a special compound number, 17 is a natural seeker who desires to unravel the intricate knots of mystery in the universe. The unseen mysteries of the universe fascinate and enthrall this vibration which can easily become obsessed with finding the keys to the enigmas of the ages. The number 17 is fascinated with the occult and the secrets of the universal sub-conscious, intuitively knowing hidden knowledge can be tapped if one understands and harnesses the natural forces which permeate the universe.

The number 17 has achieved a "one-ness" with the Life-Force which endows it with great strength and fortitude. The enigmatic aura which surrounds the number 17 can cause fear in some and fascination in others. Therefore, the number 17 must be careful how it uses its inherent powers for many people can easily fall under the influence of number 17's charisma and can be led astray if this number is not living up to is spiritual potential. Number 17 must use its "spiritual gifts" wisely, or run the risk of self-destruction.

This number possesses a keen insight which can easily be applied to anything requiring concentration and mental application. There is a vibration of spiritual creativity ingrained in the essence of the number 17 which needs to be expressed. The compassion and understanding this number has developed allows it to help others who are caught in a web of illusion and need knowledge in which to free themselves. The number 17 has the ability to blend spiritual ideals into the frame work of the material world, an ability which needs more expression in today's world.

NUMBER 18

Intensity towards all aspects of life is the key characteristic of the compound number 18. The dream state is very active and filled with messages from the universal subconscious. The dreams of number 18 are extremely vivid and are often precognitive in nature. Because of this number's receptiveness and intuition it comes under the influence or guidance of the higher forces through its sleep-state. However, the receptive sensitivity of the number 18 can cause it to become bombarded with negative thoughts from others and needs to seek refuge in Nature which cleanses the negativity away.

The number 18 is a channel for the natural healing forces which vibrate through the universe. There is a tolerance and understanding of others which makes this number an excellent counselor or advisor. Eighteen is the compound number of 9 which is the humanitarian, born to offer selfless service to others. The thirst for spiritual knowledge and wisdom is unquenchable in this number expression. The need for completion and attainment motivates the majority of this number's actions and choices.

The mental expression of number 18 is limitless which creates the openness necessary for true "psychic" abilities to manifest. Foresight, predictions, clairvoyance, clairaudience, empathy and telepathy are just a few of the abilities the number 18 can channel when it is in attunement with the Universal Mind. The strong emotions and idealistic nature of this number could be directed toward the development of a new or better philosophy which would benefit all of humankind rather than just certain segments of the population.

NUMBER 19

This number is very unique, in that when added together, (1+9) it equals 10, another compound number. The number 19 has a special significance in that it represents one of the major transition points in a human being's life. At the age of 19, we are in a stage of transition. No longer an adolescent or simply a teenager, yet still not quite considered adults, this particular year of an individual's life has a very powerful influence. This is the year an individual sets into motion energy forces and karmic vibrations which will effect them for decades, and quite possibly for the rest of their life as well.

Number 19 is very independent and chafes against restraints of any kind. This restlessness must be channeled into positive manifestation or self-destruction could result. This is the number of a true individualist, one who could never accept the opinion of a group simply because it is the most expedient thing to do. There is a potent, dominant force which radiates from number 19 which can overshadow and, in some cases, even frighten, those who are less confident. Number 19 is, for the most part, a loner by nature.

When the number 19 is indulging in its negative vibration, the ego takes over creating an arrogant selfish demeanor. The ego also tends to make the number 19 extremely stubborn, often to the point of disaster. However, because the number 19 is a compound number of 10, the opportunity to be reborn, to turn the wheel of karma and make changes are constantly being offered this vibration. The ability to be regenerated from the depths of ego indulgence to the spiritual heights of self-realization is the power which motivates and directs the actions of this number.

MASTER NUMBER 22

The master number 22 symbolizes success and responsibility. This number is a master builder on the material plane. The need to take an inspirational idea and put it into practical use or manifestation, is a driving motivation behind the actions of the number 22. Self-Knowledge and Self-Control are very important issues concerning this number. The master number 22 is the number 2 taken, mathematical, to a higher plateau of spiritual power. The urge for attaining important accomplishments is important to the number 22, not for its own gratification, but for the benefit of large groups. This number feels a deep need to be of service to others, but in a practical manner. The master number 22 knows the importance of contributions to society as a whole, of serving as a unifying force. In many ways, the master number 22 can act as a Universal bridge-builder between two separate entities.

The power exerted by the master number 22 influences and touches many lives. Twenty-two is a creator on the material plane and is motivated by the desire to leave the physical plane in better condition then when it first encountered it. Because of its master number status, the 22 has higher expectations of its achievements and goals on the Earth Plane. It becomes necessary that the 22 learn how to keep a good mental and emotional balance when confronted with obstacles it needs to turn into stepping stone.

The 22 has such a deep nature that at times it doesn't even understand itself. Tact is an important element the 22 needs to cultivate, for it can be impatient with the slowness of others or of bureaucratic red-tape. As with all master numbers, the 22 is highly intuitive, a gift they don't always used. The master number 22 can become nervous and high strung so it is important that it learn the importance of perspective and balance. Negatively, 22 can become so caught up in the over-all picture that it becomes indifferent to the needs of separate individuals. The power that the number 22 has been gifted with can also turn into the temptation to be manipulative and exploit others rather than allowing themselves to be used unselfishly in service to others. When used negatively, the power of the 22 is reduced to its lowest vibration of 4.

MASTER NUMBER 33

The master number 33 symbolizes self-sacrifice and compassion for others. This is a difficult vibration for it has been called the number of the Christ

Consciousness, and therefore can be an extremely difficult vibration to live up to. The master number 33 is a visionary expression, compelled to reveal the Light of Truth to all who are willing to listen. 33 represents a teacher of teachers and must be willing to make sacrifices for others or for its ideals. This number is responsible for some special task on the Earth Plane, a mission it willingly assumed before entering the Physical Earth Plane.

The number 33 shows unusual courage and fortitude in the face of over-whelming odds and has the tendency to remain steadfast regardless of the consequences. This number accepts the burdens placed on it with patience and fortitude, without expecting rewards or even appreciation from others. Many times, the number 33 experiences what can be termed a "crucifixion" of its emotions, but despite that, the master number 33 remains ready to continue helping others even at the risk of its own emotional well-being. It would be helpful for the 33 to live more impersonally, with a detached but caring attitude toward others which would help it to handle the burdens placed on it more efficiently and serve as an example for others to follow.

Other individuals are attracted to the 33 because of its understanding and loving nature. These people know, instinctively, that they will receive the comfort and solace they need from the master number 33. By answering the needs of others, the number 33 fulfills its function on the Earth Plane. The very nature of the master number 33 is a generous and giving one. This is a very sensitive number, creative, artistic, and imaginative. Thirty-three appreciates and understands beauty, and can find beauty in anything.

Negatively, the master number 33 can be emotionally unstable and may try to sacrifice itself for any cause regardless of whether it be a worthy one or not. Because of this tendency, the master number 33 must learn not to become a convenient doormat for others. Fear and indecisiveness are emotions that can plague the 33 when depressed, especially when the need to reform and make the world a better place to live in is thwarted by outer circumstances. When used negatively, the powers of the number 33 are reduced to its lowest vibration of 6.

MASTER NUMBER 44

The master number 44 symbolizes perseverance, strength and self-disci-pline. It has the ability to make the best of any given situation it faces. The master number 44 is very resourceful, and has a great deal of common sense and can use its logical nature in constructive ways. This number is in the process of learning how to let the higher forces work through it mentally and physically. Serving as a Channel for the Will of the Higher Forces can be difficult, but the effort is worth the results produced by the master number 44.

Part of the Destiny of the number 44 is to serve the material and emotional needs of the world through productive and practical techniques based on metaphysical, esoteric and spiritual knowledge. It is the task of the master number 44 to translate or transform the ancient wisdom and the "new-age" metaphysical knowledge into "Tools" or "Keys" which can be used more easily by others. Practical spirituality is the keyword of the master number 44. If ideals or belief systems of wisdom cannot be used to help people in practical, everyday ways, those ideals have very little real value.

The master number 44 desires to find and share the universal prosperity that is available to all who seek. This number sets about to construct situations in which this prosperity can be shared with others. It seeks to better the world in a practical and physical way, or in other words, the master number 44 strives to unite the practical with the spiritual. This is a responsible number, often taking on heavy responsibilities concerning the welfare of the world because it can see practical solutions to the problems facing the world.

This number naturally inspires confidence from others because of the positive attitude it has. The master number 44 knows where it is going and how it is going to get there. This "knowing-ness" comes from the guidance of the inner teacher. Meditation and quiet are essential for the emotional and mental health of this number. It is through these times of quiet solitude and reflection that the energy levels are restored and new purpose and dedication is achieved.

MASTER NUMBER 55

The master number 55 is symbolized by communication, investigation, and freedom. The task facing the number 55 is learning how to separate Illusions from Universal Truth, and then to communicate that Truth to others. The number 55 is the champion of Justice, with high ideals and hopes which inspire others. This is a pioneering number, one whose curiosity and need to uncover what is hidden dominates and motivates their actions. 55 is an intense number and capable of extremes, but 55 is also a perceptive and innovative number.

Freedom is essential for the master number 55, it cannot tolerate limitations or narrow-mindedness and its restless seeking nature demands that it keep searching for knowledge, for answers to the questions that plague humankind. Because of this nature, the master number 55 is a traveler, one who has many varied experiences which will be digested and assimilated for any possible new knowledge and then communicated to others at the proper time. Change is natural to the number 55, giving it a versatile and adaptable nature which is necessary for the mission it is to accomplish on the Earth Plane.

Enhancement of the mind is very important to the master number 55. This goal is achieved through openness to knowledge, and the willingness to research and investigate ideas. The master number 55 is a number that demands actions, it is a warrior for Truth, and a protector of those less fortunate. 55 is a master number which brings a message of hope to those who are trapped in the Veils of Illusion. This master number has the unique ability to focus new sources of energy and vitality to those individuals who need the inspiration to carry on with their life's task. This vibration acts like a fresh breeze, happily whisking through the lives of others and shaking them loose from their stagnate positions.

MASTER NUMBER 66

The master number 66 symbolizes harmony, balance, compassion and symmetry. It possesses a thoughtful, responsible and idealistic nature which inspires the number 66 to do something concrete about the social problems it sees around it. Part of the Spiritual Mission of the master number 66 is to serve as a source of inspiration to others through its loving and giving nature. 66 also serves to guide and protect young souls who are placed under its care by the wheels of karma operating in the universe.

This number has the magnetism to attract what it needs into its life. As a result, the number 66 is very generous and willingly shares its resources and talents with those less fortunate. The master number 66 knows how to utilize its abilities in practical and useful ways. Integrity is an important characteristic of the master number 66, and this number demonstrates this principle in all areas of life. Therefore, whatever the number 66 has promised to do, it will strive with all of its energy and talent to deliver.

There is a romantic artistic side to the master number 66 that is balanced perfectly with an analytical and logical ability to solve problems. Others seek out the number 66 for counseling because of the capacity this number has for understanding, empathizing, patience and tolerance. 66 has no use for jealousy, and sees it as a destructive emotion that gets in the way of true happiness. The number 66 finds joy in the good fortune of others, knowing intuitively that all prosperity comes from one source which is limitless.

MASTER NUMBER 77

The master number 77 symbolizes the mystical and spiritual aspects of life. This number is one of silence, of allowing deep meditation and communication with the Higher Realms to be accomplished. The master number 77 represents the enlightened thinkers of the universe. Thoughts, even when not spoken, are a powerful energy which can be used positively to create, or negatively to destroy. The master number 77 has the insight and the mystical wisdom to understand the actions and motivations of others. This is the number of the Universal Subconscious and the subtle power it possesses. There is an imaginative and creative side to the master number 77 that can manifest itself in unique and unusual ways. This number has deep connections with the hidden mysteries of life and understands these "mysteries" with a mystical "knowing-ness" that is uncanny in its accuracy. The master number 77 is philosophical in its approach to life and to the challenges or obstacles which appear on life's path. This mystical and philosophical nature allows the number 77 to rise above the mundane aspects of life and to cut through the petty details which tend to obscure the real issue at hand.

The Master Number 77 has strong religious and spiritual ideals which it seeks to incorporate into its daily life. Self-discipline and dedication to the mission it has been given on the Earth Plane is one of the motivating forces behind the intense drive of the number 77. Introspective, but determined in its approach to the thinking process, the master number 77 uses the vast capabilities of its mind to reach unlimited mental and spiritual planes of thought available to those who have learned the necessary discipline.

MASTER NUMBER 88

This is a very strong power number, (the two figure 8's represent double Infinity signs). The God-power is emphasized by the 4 zero's which make Up the figure of the double eights. This power can be utilized either positively or negatively. The more power there is, the more temptation there is to be corrupted by it. There is an old saying which illustrates this maxim even better: "absolute power corrupts absolutely." Master number 88 rules the material world of business and high finance and the associated temptations to be found in these areas.

The number 88 is also the symbol of the esoteric scientist, the researcher and metaphysician who seeks out the unseen mysteries of life and reveals the discovered secrets to all humankind, allowing each individual to judge for themselves how to use this new knowledge. 88 is highly intuitive and desires Truth with a passionate zealousness. It seeks to solve the enigmas which have puzzled the world for eons. This number has a special relationship with the secret forces of the universe which gives the 88 a mysterious, even mystical, aura. The occult is a natural pursuit of the number 88 which uses its intuition and connection to the higher realms in order to understand the forces which have their roots in the occult.

The number 88 is very intellectual, but also very spiritual in an esoteric way. The challenge the master number 88 faces is in bringing spiritual principles into action in the business world. This is not an easy union to achieve, but the challenge is one the master number 88 relishes for master numbers need master challenges to motivate them to use their immense power. The 88 can achieve tangible and worthwhile results in the material world when using their unique abilities. This master number also needs solitude and time for meditation in which to germinate the seeds of innovative ideas. Once the germination period is complete, these seeds take form and manifest strong effects on the lives of many.

MASTER NUMBER 99

This is a very special and highly spiritual master number. Cosmic greatness is expected of this master number for its purpose is a very holy one. The 99 willingly assumes great burdens in order to ensure that highly evolved Spiritual Teachers and Avatars have the opportunity to guide and care for all the creatures of the Earth Plane. This vibration clears the path and paves the way for the Spiritual Masters, much like John the Baptist did for the Master Jesus. The master number 99 is rarely contained on just the physical earth Plane, it works its influence on several levels or "planes" simultaneously. The lower astral realms and the physical plane fall under the jurisdiction of the master number 99.

The master number 99 is the helpmate, motivator and guardian, the one who inspires other people to strive for a goal of spiritual excellence. This master number is a teacher of teachers, an advanced soul who has mastered almost all of the lessons to be found on the Earth Plane and now stands as a shining beacon of Light to guide other souls struggling to make the same journey. The master number 99 is extremely active and has a vivid creative imagination. 99 operates mainly on knowledge from the Universal Sub-Conscious Mind, it knows that the Earth plane is a plane of Illusion, trapped within a so-called "physical reality". But the Master Number 99 has long since realized it is not a physical body, it knows that it is not limited and knows how to see beyond the veils of illusion to the Light of True Reality.

This number is very emotionally oriented and is in tune with its feelings. The Dream State of the 99 is very vivid and serves as one source of rich inspiration and guidance. The 99 is intuitive and receptive to the energies that flow around it, giving it information about people and situations it comes into contact with. The 99 is a natural healer, both of the physical body and the emotional body. It is an accepting, non-judgmental vibration which instinctively knows the right thing to say to give comfort to those who are in pain or who are experiencing emotional turmoil.

The Master Number 99 is very patient, one of the most important lessons the Earth Plane teaches all souls on the Spiritual Path. The patience and understanding nature possessed by the number 99 serves as an excellent example for other souls, giving them a visible goal to strive for. Forgiveness and Love are two lessons the master number 99 is both teaching to others and learning for itself. Serenity and Balance are two personality traits inherent to the number 99. The hidden and powerful forces of nature are active and channeled through the master number 99, resulting in the gift of prophecy.

This is a very rare number to have in a Numerology Profile. It indicates great things are expected of the individual who possesses it. Even when reduced to its lowest denominator: 9+9=18 - 1+8=9, it is still a powerful number. 9's are the spiritual teachers, the guardians of the unawakened on the Earth Plane. This number symbolizes the Brother/Sisterhood of the Universe, of the entire Cosmos, One-ness with all creation, all life.

This chapter has been concerned with providing you with the basic symbolism of numbers and defining the components of a Numerology Profile so that you may experiment and explore the infinity possibilities concerning your own personality. Now we are ready to build on the bricks of this foundation. The next chapter is devoted to defining the separate meanings of each letter in the Alphabet, a necessary "key" in understanding the influences at work in your life.

CHAPTER TWO
SYMBOLISM OF THE ALPHABET

The purpose of this chapter is to help you establish an understanding of what each of the letters of the Alphabet mean on an individual basis. Cloaked with this knowledge, you can reveal many of the hidden influences in your life which may have eluded your understanding up until now. The letters in your name should be examined one by one and evaluated, on an individual basis, by their specific meanings as well as by the number vibration they correspond to. The first letter of your name and the first vowel of your name have a particular subconscious influence on the way you express yourself .

The more repetitions you have of the same letter in your name, the more intense the influence becomes. In other words, if you have more than two letter which are the same, the energies inherent in that letter become more pronounced, demanding an outlet of expression. The positive and negative qualities are also enhanced, and the temptation to misuse its power increases tenfold. By becoming aware of this phenomena, you will be able to control the energy much more effectively.

In each of the letter definitions I refer to letters being activated by the cycles of life. This can occur when you see a letter or series of letters in a dream or meditation. When this happens, most of the time the letters do not spell out any particular word or name. Sometimes only two or three letters will appear in a dream or meditation. In order to interpret what message is being sent to you via your subconscious, if you know what the individual meanings of each letter in the Alphabet are, you will be able to grasp the underlying significance of your dream symbols.

THE LETTER A
The letter A vibrates to the number 1 and is the first letter of the Alphabet, as well as the first Vowel. As the first letter, it is powerful and creative, filled with restless energy which needs positive outlets for expression. This is an innovative, pioneering expression possessing a great deal of self-reliance and will-power. The Letter A is a letter of ideas and plans, a metaphysical architect if you will.

When the Letter A is activated by a cycle, opportunities for new beginnings is greatly increased. The action motivated by the letter becomes a driving force behind the striving for leadership. The Letter A teaches important lessons in self-reliance and the need to get ahead through one's own efforts. The Letter A is both a mental and emotional expression which tempers its intellectual abilities with the intuitional.

As the first vowel in the first name, the Letter A is adventurous, original, progressive and has a strong independent streak. The Letter A is interested in new ideas and concepts, but prefers that they come from within themselves rather than from other sources outside themselves. This is because the letter A is very creative and must express this quality in a positive manner or this powerful energy will degenerate into aggressive behavior. The Letter A enjoys being unique, being different from others.

The Letter A will stand up for its own ideas and points of view even though the majority is in opposition to its stand. This letter wants to break away from the pack, to explore new territories and accept opportunities which create change in its life. The unknown calls to the Letter A with a siren's song it cannot resist. One of the major spiritual lessons for Letter A concerns a tendency towards arrogance and domineering traits. The negative trait of false pride and being obstinately opinionated are challenges the Letter A must face and overcome as part of their spiritual evolution.

THE LETTER B

The Letter B vibrates to the number 2 and is the second letter of the Alphabet. This is a letter of extremes: it can go to the heights of ecstasy and the depths of despair with equal ease. The division between the Spiritual and the Material is very pronounced in this letter. The nature of the Letter B is very torn between the forces of Light and the forces of Darkness.

On the positive side, there is a great love of nature and domesticity. The Letter B knows how to express a nurturing form of love as well as a selfish possessive love. This letter vibration can be hospitable, welcoming and warm to others, but it can also be demanding and tyrannical in getting its own way. Esoterically, the Letter B represents the descent of Spirit into Matter. The Letter B contains considerable potential for problems or trouble, but it also possesses considerable talents for understanding the "Hidden Laws" of the Cosmos. Whichever vibration is expressed depends on the Spiritual Maturity of the individual who is under the influence of this particular letter. When activated by the cycles of life, the Letter B is greatly influenced by subtle subconscious currents. There are many hidden actions and reactions occurring which are not realized until a later date.

The Letter B has a strong need for union with another, for partnerships, marriage, and commitments. Without a mate, this letter usually does not function at its true level of potential. Its energies have a tendency to become polarized and impotent without the steadying influence of a union or partner. Decisions are not easy for the Letter B to make, much vacillation between alternatives occurs unless someone can show the right path to take. The Spiritual Lesson for the Letter B is to develop serenity in regards to the emotions and the mental processes.

THE LETTER C

The Letter C vibrates to the number 3 and is the third letter of the Alphabet. Under the influence of 3, the letter C has very scattered energies which tries to take off in several different directions at once. When the Letter C is the first letter in the first name, it symbolizes a happy-go-lucky nature which also has a tendency to experience a tumultuous emotional life. Because of the excess energy possessed by this letter, it becomes necessary for it to have several projects going simultaneously, in this way, the scattering tendencies are harnessed in a positive manner.

The Letter C has positive influences on artistic and creative endeavors by generating the inspiration needed to manifest these expressions positively. This letter knows how to communicate and seeks interaction with others. The ability to promote the ideas and projects of others is a quality inherent in the letter C. This is considered to be a lucky letter to have in one's name, especially when it is the first letter of either the first name or last name. When the Letter C is not expressed to its highest vibration there can be impulsiveness, irritability and impatience.

When the Letter C is activated by one of the cycles of Life, it stimulates opportunities for success, growth and productivity. Prosperity and Happiness are also associated with this letter, especially during its most active phase. Since the number 3 is a marriage vibration, the Letter C has the potential to attract mates who bring rich emotional experiences into a relationship. Esoterically, the Letter C symbolizes harmony, perfect love, wisdom, tenderness and the Holy Trinity. In Christian Symbolism, the letter C vibrates to the three virtues of Faith, Hope and Charity.

THE LETTER D
The Letter D vibrates to the number 4 and is the fourth letter of the Alphabet. This letter represents stability and foundation. The Letter D is an "equalizer", bringing balance, determination and steadfastness to any endeavor it undertakes. It possesses the quality of practicality which allows the Letter D to express a sense of responsibility in the material arena of life. This vibration is attracted to the business world where its hard working nature can manifest results. Power and authority are the products of the energies expended by the Letter D.

Esoterically, the Letter D is considered to be dedicated to the service of the Creator. The ancients believed this letter possessed a superior grandeur because in most of the ancient cultures the name for their supreme god contained four letters. For instance, in Latin the name for God is "Deus", which contains four letters. Therefore, the Letter D is the symbol for immortality, endurance, tenacity and realization. This letter was used cautiously because the power it possessed was not easy to harness and utilize.

The Letter D vibrates to the Earth Plane and to the material concerns found here. When this letter is activated by one of the cycles of life, opportunities for building foundations for the future are revealed. During the active phase of the Letter D, there can be temporary setbacks or delays in one's plans in order to teach the individual the spiritual lesson of patience. Delays also occur as a karmic test to see if the individual can maintain a sense of hope and firmness of purpose despite apparent odds to the contrary.

THE LETTER E
The Letter E vibrates to the number 5 and is the fifth letter of the Alphabet, as well as being the second Vowel. The Letter E is a strong vowel which is very physical and relates to the five physical senses of the body. Astrologically, the

letter E is ruled by the planet Mercury, the planet of communication. Therefore, the Letter E is considered by the ancient masters to be a cosmic messenger whose mission is to bring knowledge to the masses from the Astral Teachers.

To achieve its mission in life, the Letter E must have freedom, emotionally, mentally, and physically. It is difficult for this letter to have any restraints placed on it for it is a true child of Change and must be allowed to express this urge when needed or its energy will become blocked resulting in volcanic-like explosions. Therefore, harmony is a necessity for the Letter E and is the quality which can harness the immense kinetic energy possessed by this vibration.

As the second Vowel, the Letter E represents personal growth through a variety of experiences, change and action. This is a very versatile vowel which attracts the unexpected to it like a magnet. Generally, the letter E is more interested in the activities and experiences found on the material Earth Plane than the discipline of spiritual matters. When this letter has gained the life experiences it needs in order to grow, it becomes drawn to the spiritual side of life which enhances its intuitive, "psychic" abilities.

When the Letter E is activated by one of the cycles of Life, it literally becomes a whirlwind of bundled energy as it is faced with many choices representing a multitude of possible changes and experiences. The active phase of this letter is filled with constant movement, new situations, new people, romance, and excitement. The Letter E, when in its active phase, is undergoing the spiritual lesson of learning how to overcome excessive indulgence in pleasing the senses. Sexual Temptations can be numerous and almost irresistible which can result in unstable relationships.

THE LETTER F

The Letter F vibrates to the number 6 and is the sixth letter of the Alphabet. Astrologically, this letter is ruled by the planet Venus which possesses the attributes of an affectionate and loving nature. Venus rules the emotions and the beautiful qualities of life. Under this benign influence, the Letter F emanates a loving aura, its kindness and caring attitude toward others gives this letter a great attractiveness. A peaceful and nurturing atmosphere in the home environment is a natural expression of this letter.

The Letter F possesses a compassionate and tender-hearted nature which others can take advantage of and cause this vibration much sadness. Luckily however, because of the loving influence of the planet Venus, this letter does not have to endure long-term sadness. The Letter F, vibrating to the number 6, is a fortunate letter in matters of heart. Esoterically, this letter symbolizes the "Two Paths" one may take in life. One may either become dedicated to Virtue or steeped in Vice.

Even though this letter represents union and great happiness, it also has a reputation for entanglements and strife, all of which serve to teach the lesson of "sacred" and "profane" love. When activated by a cycle of life, the Letter F is presented with opportunities involving the family and loved ones. As an expression who shoulders responsibility easily, the letter F offers willing service to others when it has been activated by the life cycles. During an action phase, this letter must learn how to make wise choices concerning their family obligations, otherwise problems could arise at a later date.

THE LETTER G

The Letter G vibrates to the number 7 and is the seventh letter of the Alphabet. Esoterically, the vibrations of this letter represent the triumph of Spirit over Matter and has a definite mystical aura surrounding it. The Letter G has an unusual depth of understanding concerning the mysteries of life which imparts a strong will that can withstand the capricious whims of fate. The intuitive abilities possessed by this letter coupled with its inventiveness creates a potent force on the Earth Plane.

Under the influence of the number 7, the Letter G possesses great promise, which can be manifested positively or negatively, depending solely on the level of spiritual growth attained. The Letter G can also be stubborn and dislikes interference from others even when it is in its best interest. This letter approaches the challenges of life with an ingenious and methodical thoroughness that is unequalled.

When activated by the cycles of life, the Letter G is given opportunities for expansion and growth in its affairs. During the active phase, this letter needs to express its energies toward productivity. When it does, material success, as well as emotional satisfaction results. The active phase of the letter G is a good period for the expression of creative arts such as music, writing, sculpture, painting, etc.

THE LETTER H

The Letter H vibrates to the number 8 and is the eighth letter of the Alphabet. This is a power letter because of its attunement to the number 8 which represents the God-Force and Infinity. The inherent power of this letter drives it to create and express its energies until fulfillment is achieved. The Letter H acts with a strong sense of compulsion in all of its undertakings. It possesses a restless and demanding temperament which is not altogether comfortable with others. The soothing beauty of nature is a source of real pleasure for the Letter H which does not need the company of others to make it feel complete or whole.

To the ancients, the Letter H represented the vibration of attraction and repulsion, life and destruction, separation followed by the promise of renewal. In esoteric writings, this letter symbolized the 8 punishments for the damned and the 8 blessings for the chosen. The Letter H could either experience great wealth or great poverty depending on the state of "soul grace" it possessed. Therefore, the powerful vibrations connected with this letter manifested according to the karma of the individual involved.

When the Letter H is activated by one of the cycles of life, the karmic wheel slowly turns and reveals a new path or doorway for the individual to take. Sometimes this karmic opportunity is disguised as an obstacle or barrier which forces the individual to make a choice. The active phase of the Letter H is deeply intertwined with the laws of Karma and the need to reap what has been sown previously. This is also a time when the sowing of karma begins for the cycles of life which have yet to manifest.

THE LETTER I

The Letter I vibrates to the number 9 and is the ninth letter of the Alphabet as well as the third vowel. To the ancients, this letter represented the Trinity of Trinities for it mathematically symbolized 3 times 3 equals 9. This letter is a law unto itself, powerful and intense with the spiritual challenge of developing compassion, universal love and understanding. This is not an easy task for this vibration because it does not like limitations of any sort and until it is spiritually awakened, it may see the concept of universal brother/sisterhood as a limiting factor.

The Letter I can be stubborn, even obstinate, wanting to express its energies when it wants to rather than when it is suitable for all. This is an artistic letter, creative and inventive. The Letter I can express its artistic creative talents in writing or designing, and through the use of a needle or chisel.

This letter has a moody temperament and is difficult for others to understand at times. Lecturing could prove to be a good outlet for this letter's energies.

As a vowel, the Letter I is a vibration of extremes, it can either be helpful and kind or self-centered and selfish. When being particularly negative, the Letter I can have a very quick temper. This letter is ruled by its heart and passions rather than by its mind or intellect. Possessed of many talents, the letter I does not like change and is not very quick to try new things. This letter has a tendency to stick to one thing and perfect it to the best of its ability rather than develop several talents at once.

When activated by one of the cycles of life, the Letter I has the potential to experience many ups and downs, delays and runs of luck which are both good and bad. During its active phase, the Letter I has an increase of intuition, sensitivity, and an abundance of vital energy. Important and powerful inspirations can be experienced during the active phases of this letter which can lead to Illumination and understanding of cosmic law.

THE LETTER J

The Letter J vibrates to the number 1 and is the tenth letter of the Alphabet. This letter has many of the attributes of the Letter A, except these attributes are more intensely expressed. The Letter J has set lofty goals for itself to achieve, goals which are both material and spiritual in nature. As the tenth letter of the Alphabet, the letter J represents a new beginning, karmic ties which have been severed and no longer serve to limit the expression of this letter's power.

Because of the influence of tenth position, esoterically, the Letter J represents the Hand of God granting protection, strength, and brilliance. This letter possesses occult powers that boarder on the mystical. Good fortune and blessings are experienced by this letter as it strives to achieve union with the Universal sub-conscious. More spiritually inclined than the Letter A, the letter J utilizes its inventive brilliance to benefit as many individuals as it can. Although selfishness is rarely manifested by the Letter J, a sense of self-righteousness can be a problem at times.

When activated by one of the cycles of life, the Letter J is presented with opportunities for promotion and gain. Offers of leadership roles tend to surface during this active phase. During this highly energetic time, the Letter J becomes even more motivated to assist those in less fortunate circumstances than itself. This quality of service to others brings good Fortune and happiness to this letter in unexpected and even mysterious ways.

THE LETTER K

The Letter K vibrates to the number 2 and is the eleventh letter of the Alphabet. Because of this dual influence of the number 2 and 11, the Letter K is highly intuitive and gifted with prophetic insight. Its versatility allows the idealistic side of its nature to be expressed in a great variety of ways. Esoterically, this letter possesses a hidden prosperity which reveals itself after experiencing difficult challenges which seemed insurmountable at the time.

The Letter K attracts the extreme in its experiences. There can be great achievement followed by great disappointment, and vice versa. However, even when it appears to be the darkest, the Letter K is rescued from total despair and led back into the light. The Spiritual Challenge for this letter involves service to others. The Letter K must learn how to channel its leadership abilities for the greater good of all rather than for its own ego satisfaction.

When activated by one of the cycles of life, the Letter K is given opportunities to express its spiritual idealism in creative and inspiring ways. It is important for this letter to choose a positive way of life, to aspire to a goal which can utilize the creative potential it possesses. If this letter allows itself to be drawn to the negative side of life, emotional and spiritual conflicts result. During the active phase of the Letter K, passionate emotional or romantic entanglements can arise as well as intense spiritual experiences.

THE LETTER L

The Letter L vibrates to the number 3 and is the twelfth letter of the Alphabet. The Letter L has many of the attributes of the Letter C except for the scattering tendencies the letter C possesses. The Letter L collects, synthesizes, and then completes any task it undertakes, a quality that is often lacking in the Letter C. This 12th letter of the Alphabet is a vibration of action, of taking charge and accomplishing set goals. It has a giving nature but does not allow others to take advantage of it.

The Letter L is very aware of the laws of karma and knows that what one gives out, one receives ten fold in return, whether it is good or bad. Esoterically, the Letter L symbolizes "grace" and "perfection", difficult qualities to live up to, but not impossible. When this vibration does not attempt to follow the direction of its higher potentials material problems, even suffering can result from entanglement with the Dark Path. It is easy to see how the ancient masters attributed such loft symbolism to this vibration: there are 12 Zodiac signs, 12 months of the year, 12 angels overseeing the divisions in heaven, 12 orders of holy spirits, 12 degrees of the damned, 12 tribes of Israel, and 12 Apostles.

When the Letter L is activated by one of the cycles of life, opportunities for selfless service occur. The chance for redemption through sacrifice of the personal ego is offered to this vibration which will grant profound spiritual knowledge and understanding of the grandeur of the laws governing the Cosmos. When in its active phase, the Letter L can bring tests or initiations in relationships or marriage. Much growth can be attained through the bonds of marriage for this letter, its creative potential is enhanced which brings lessons concerning the wise use of financial revenues.

THE LETTER M

The Letter M vibrates to the number 4 and is the thirteenth letter of the Alphabet. The Letter M has many of the attributes of the Letter D but is more spiritual and idealistic in its expression. This letter is highly intuitive and possesses a large range of "psychic" abilities. Because of the highly spiritual nature of the Letter M, it naturally assumes the burdens of others, offering itself in service, willing to sacrifice the needs of its personal ego to the greater needs of others.

Esoterically, the Letter M represents transformation, destruction of limitations, faith, hope and re-birth. Because of the receptive and understanding nature of this vibration, it is generally quite lucky in love for it has the ability to attract harmony and happiness in marriage or other similar relationships. This letter desires to create an environment which is nurturing and imparts a sense of security to those who dwell within its confines.

When activated by one of the cycles of life, the Letter M represents an important period of renewal and transmutation. During this time the old or useless ideas are either re-cycled or discarded. The active phase of this letter involves sweeping changes which can be unexpected or unsettling. However, these changes signal a new current for the future, new opportunities for achievement which need the freedom to develop without the limitations of the past. When properly activated, this vibration promises definite progress towards important goals and happiness.

THE LETTER N

The Letter N vibrates to the number 5 and is the fourteenth letter of the Alphabet. In the ancient temples, this letter was used to symbolize a scribe, the official recorder or historian of a ruler's court. The Letter N expresses itself with considerable imagination which has the power to inspire others with its creativeness. Writing is a natural outlet for the energies of this letter and helps it to maintain a sense of positive balance which it needs in order to avoid instability in its emotions.

Negatively, the Letter N can attract the energies of envy, jealousy and strife in emotional relationships. However, if this letter can balance its desire for personal pleasure and satisfaction with a desire to give these same qualities, the negative energies can be minimized, even eliminated. Esoterically, the Letter N attracts prosperity to it with very little effort, but this same quality can create antagonism in others if the personal ego is allowed to become inflated as a result of its good fortune.

When activated by one of the cycles of life, the Letter N represents continuous change and movement. A large variety of experiences ebb and flow, creating a sense of competition and striving for attainment. To the ancients, this letter represented revolution, sexuality, danger, and energy unleashed. During the active phase of the Letter N, excitement, touched with the spice of danger or the forbidden, seems to become more prominent than usual.

THE LETTER 0

The Letter 0 vibrates to the number 6 and is the fifteenth letter of the Alphabet as well as the fourth vowel. Teaching or counseling others is a natural expression of the energies of this letter. The Letter 0 is blessed with the qualities of patience and steadfastness which it puts to good use when dealing with the responsibilities it assumes. Like a sponge, this letter soaks up knowledge from books as well as from life's experiences.

This letter has an instinctive ability when it comes to parenting for it knows how to balance nurturing with discipline. Marriage and commitment is a natural expression for the Letter 0, without it, this vibration tends to feel lost and alone. Being very strong-willed, it is important for the Letter 0 to avoid arguing; even though there can be enjoyment in convincing others of the rightness of its point of view, there is a distinct danger that arguing will arouse antagonism rather than cooperation unless tact is carefully employed.

Jealousy can be a problem for the Letter 0 in relationships, causing disharmony and even breakups. Emotional control is one of the spiritual lessons this letter is in the process of learning. The Letter 0 prefers to establish a secure base of operations from which to build, gradually and steadily increasing its holdings. Natural beauty in the environment is a necessity for the emotional stability of this vibration which draws strength from the harmony found in nature's fertile growth.

When activated by one of the cycles of life, the Letter 0 is given an opportunity to be released from the limitations and illusions created in the past. During this active phase, hidden talents in music, poetry or the arts will surface, creating a new sense of purpose and radically altering the previous outlook on life. Through the expression of art or other creative outlets, this vibration releases the spiritual inspirational nature buried deep within. By touching the spiritual essence within, fears which have been limiting in the past are released into the light and their power to create havoc abolished.

THE LETTER P

The Letter P vibrates to the number 7 and is the sixteenth letter of the Alphabet. This letter possesses incredible gifts for creative expression which can be manifested through writing or lecturing, even some special forms of acting. The Letter P is an intellectual vibration, blessed with clear-thinking and logical analysis. Because of its mental gifts, this letter may appear emotionally cold or even indifferent due to its lack of physical gestures. The Letter P does have a tendency to rationalize its emotions rather than express them in a spontaneous way, however, this control over excess emotionalism enables this vibration to use its intellectual gifts more effectively.

When the Letter P misdirects its energies it can become a dominating force, filled with impatience at the slower pace of others around it. Others then see this letter as unsympathetic, even selfish in its demands. Learning to accept the different levels of others is an important spiritual lesson for the Letter P to assimilate. Fortunately for the spiritual growth of this letter when it is traveling down a path in life which is ego-oriented, divine guidance has a tendency to strike, like a bolt of lightning, illuminating the illusions and errors made, allowing corrections to be made.

When activated by one of the cycles of life, the Letter P is given special opportunities to use its creative talents, resulting in good fortune. During the active phase, wonderful prospects for the future are revealed giving this vibration the option of focusing on positive goals and attaining them. Wise use of the activated energies of the cycles will result in undreamed of achievements, but determination coupled with dedication is necessary first.

THE LETTER Q

The Letter Q vibrates to the number 8 and is the seventeenth letter of the alphabet. Although the Letter Q shares many of the same qualities as the Letter H, there is more intensity to this letter, an intensity which manifests itself in brilliant creativity. Emotions run deep in this letter, so deeply that it is in touch with the mystical realms where it has formed links to the Universal subconscious. The Letter Q is aware of the subtle forces at work in the Universe and allows itself to be directed by these gentle influences.

Communicating with others and with the spiritual realms is a natural expression for the Letter Q. This letter possesses a great intuitive ability which brings great fortune to it. The instinctive nature of this vibration is very attuned to the natural forces of the planet and under proper direction, has the capacity for prophecy concerning natural phenomena. Esoterically, the Letter Q symbolizes immortality, clairvoyancy, beauty and hope. This letter seems to have its own special lucky star guiding its actions, bringing rewards, recognition and even wealth.

When activated by one of the cycles of life, the Letter Q experiences a surge of mental and spiritual vitality which can be directed towards the achievement of life-long goals. Opportunities for attainment in creative and artistic endeavors occur during the active phase of this vibration. Leadership roles will be offered because of the increased personal and spiritual power unleashed by the active phase of this letter. Part of this letter's spiritual growth during this highly active time involves helping others to achieve their dreams without thought of personal reward.

THE LETTER R

The Letter R vibrates to the number 9 and is the eighteenth letter of the Alphabet. The Letter R possesses all the abilities which comprises the vibrational expression of the Letter I. However, the Letter R is stepped up nine degrees further and has a greater understanding and attunement to the Universal forces. This letter has a true, non-judgmental acceptance of other beings, and offers compassion wherever needed. The Letter R is not afraid to sacrifice its personal ego for the benefit of the greater good.

This letter has unique divinatory abilities which manifest through dreams or during periods of meditation. Precognition is very strongly marked in this vibration, although this talent can remain undeveloped by choice. The Dream State of the Letter R is very active and much guidance is received on a subconscious level during this state. This letter has the temperament of a teacher but must learn how to give knowledge and then allow the recipient to choose whether or not to accept it. It is part of the spiritual lesson for the Letter R to not allow the ego to become involved in the channeling of wisdom.

When activated by one of the cycles of life, the Letter R is offered opportunities for new directions on its path. Doors, which were previously closed, are opened during this active phase requiring thoughtful assessment and consideration. Many exciting new ideas and concepts demand further exploration at this time which can shed light on which direction this vibration needs to concentrate its energies. Recognition is very likely to occur during the active phase of this vibration if the way has been properly prepared in the past.

THE LETTER S

The Letter S vibrates to the number 1 and is the nineteenth letter of the Alphabet. One of the main attributes of this letter is its ability to endure the trials and tribulations of the Earth Plane. The Letter S is extremely intense both spiritually and emotionally, and that intensity can be used positively or negatively. The ability to charm or to inflict wounds has equal potential in this expression.

Esoterically, the Letter S symbolizes "Destiny", the power which twists and turns the path of life into a snake-like rope leading to enlightenment. In the ancient temples this vibration was referred to as the "symbol of surrender" which attracted happiness, success, honor, love, and money into the life of those who merited it. Under the influence of the number 1, the letter S is subject to many beginnings, some of which lead to fulfillment, and others which lead nowhere in particular but which grant experience and knowledge instead.

When activated by one of the cycles of life, the Letter S is blessed with the opportunity to triumph over any difficulties or obstacles which impede its progress. Although there are many twists and turns in the life experience of this vibration, ultimately achievement of long-cherished goals and ambitions are promised. The spiritual lesson the Letter S is striving to master concerns maintaining faith and a positive attitude in the midst of turbulent change.

THE LETTER T

The Letter T vibrates to the number 2 and is the twentieth letter of the Alphabet. This vibration has a need to control the circumstances and individuals in its environment, this quality can manifest positively in the building and conservation of what is important in life, or it can manifest negatively, resulting in the breakdown and destruction of what is fundamentally important. How the Letter T utilizes its energies in this matter is a difficult spiritual initiation which it will face over and over again until it masters the lesson.

If the Letter T chooses to express its energies positively, lofty spiritual heights can be reached. If it chooses to react in a negative manner to the challenges of life, this letter will be faced with constant emotional upheavals which leave a bitter taste in its wake. Esoterically, the Letter T is a vibration of life and impulsiveness. It represents important decisions to be made which can create or eliminate obstacles and limitations.

When the Letter T is activated by one of the cycles of life, a major period of reconstruction and transformation begins. There is a great deal of unleashed energy which needs to be directed into constructive projects or a self-destructive restlessness will grow and consume this vibration. During the active phase of the Letter T, spiritual growth and enlightenment becomes an important issue as this letter struggles to utilize its talents and abilities for the benefit of all rather than just for its own sake.

THE LETTER U

The Letter U vibrates to the number 3 and is the twenty-first letter of the Alphabet. Although the Letter U shares the attributes of the Letters C and L, there is a more intense universal and spiritual energy associated with the Letter U which the others letters do not share. The Letter U is the fifth Vowel of the Alphabet and expresses itself with an emotional creativity which has its source in the vastness of the Universal Sub-Conscious.

The very shape of this letter gives you a clue to its nature. Vessel-shaped, the Letter U collects and retains. It can be likened to a magic cup which holds good luck, charisma and prosperity. However, if the energies of the magic cup is misused, and greed or selfishness overwhelms one's good judgment, the cup will overflow and loose its precious gifts. Learning to share good fortune with others is an important karmic lesson for the Letter U to learn, it is not easy for the temptations are great, but the rewards are even greater.

The energy of the Letter U is very outgoing, carefree and happy. It possesses the ability to use words with inspired effectiveness. This vibration is very attractive to others and must watch a tendency to indulge in unconventional or unusual love affairs. The Letter U is a nature lover and has considerable talent with plants and flowers. Because of this letter's tendency to indulge its emotional appetites to excess, it can attract peculiar experiences to it which can be painful.

When activated by one of the cycles of life, the Letter U is given the opportunity for development of the subconscious nature, unlocking its hidden intuitive abilities. Obstacles and delays occur in order to guide this vibration in the right direction. Indecision is common when the Letter U is the in throes of excessive emotional situations, a habit they must learn to break or risk loosing out to others who are more emotionally stable. During the active phase of the Letter U, more responsibilities appear concerning family and loved ones. However, by gently assuming control, this vibration can substantially increase its need for security.

THE LETTER V

The Letter V vibrates to the number 4 and is the twenty-second letter of the Alphabet. By virtue of its master number position in the Alphabet, this letter has the potential to be a master builder, a master-craftsman. Esoterically, the Letter V is considered to possess deeply mystical powers which lie dormant, waiting to be tapped, until this vibration has elevated its state of consciousness to the proper stage in its Spiritual Evolution.

This letter has strong fixed opinions based on the knowledge it receives on an intuitive level. Once an offer of friendship has been extended, the Letter V remains loyal and steadfast through the good times and the bad. This quality makes the Letter V a valuable ally and a formidable foe. Committed relationships and marriage are important to this vibration because the responsibility assumed through a union with another brings out and enhances the building-securing instinct of this letter.

When activated by one of the cycles of life, the Letter V can become obsessed with a bad case of wanderlust, needing to "discover" new vistas, new experiences. This can cause a problem with finances. When young, this need to explore and experience new things can be a positive experience, building character and gathering knowledge for use later. When older, this obsession can manifest itself in a mid-life crisis where the need to completely re-route and re-structure one's life can cause a total reversal in the life style. When this need is activated towards the end of physical life, it manifests more in a preparation for a new existence after leaving the limitations of the physical body.

THE LETTER W

The Letter W vibrates to the number 5 and is the twenty-third letter of the Alphabet. Esoterically this letter is considered to be very lucky and assures success. If the Letter W follows the path of Divine Love and Acceptance, protection and assistance is promised. Unexpected help from superiors, from those in control is a special blessing granted to this letter. The creativity displayed by the Letter W surpasses the output of the other letters, E and N, who share the influence of the number 5, because of the spiritual quality inherent in this expression.

Seemingly born under a lucky star, the Letter W possesses many talents and has the gift of a magnetic charisma which can attract a great following and lead to fame. This letter is very persistent and refuses to allow obstacles to hinder its progress. It is ingenious in finding ways to utilize obstacles constructively and turn them into stepping stones to achievement. This intuitive understanding of the laws which govern the Universe allows the Letter W to make enormous contributions to society. If this expression slips into a negative behavior pattern, selfishness and greed are manifested.

When activated by one of the cycles of life, the Letter W is given the opportunity for deep, in-depth self-analysis, which reveals the untapped potentials it possesses. During an active phase, the Letter W experiences an emotional see-saw of ups and downs, that causes this letter to re-evaluate its goals and ambitions. This emotional fluctuation can bring marriage or divorce, depending on the circumstances. Whatever course is taken, it will be an important learning experience for the Letter W.

THE LETTER X

The Letter X vibrates to the number 6 and is the twenty-fourth letter of the Alphabet. This is one of the most intriguing letters of the alphabet because of the unusual potentials it possesses. The very shape of this letter reveals its distinct dual nature. The top half of the X indicates the receptive and retentive nature it has. The bottom portion of the X reveals the potential for Loss due to overindulgence in the sensual pleasures.

When the Letter X expresses its energies in a positive way it can make great strides in spiritual matters as well as material concerns. Attainment of important personal goals is achieved through the assistance of influential women. If this letter gives into the temptation of its negative nature, it wallows in sexual excess and amoral behavior. Unfaithfulness is a distinct problem for this letter when it operates solely on its negative vibrations.

When activated by one of the cycles of life, the Letter X enters an important period. The active phase of this letter represents a major crossroads. The decisions and choices made during this phase will have a profound and long lasting effect. If the Letter X can resist the seductive allure of its lower nature, the danger of deceit or deception by others will be eliminated allowing material and financial prosperity to develop unthreatened.

THE LETTER Y

The Letter Y vibrates to the number 7 and is the twenty-fifth letter of the Alphabet. This letter serves a dual role as both a consonant and a vowel. It is a strongly intuitional vibration which relies on "hunches" to make important decisions. The Letter Y is an introspective vibration which requires freedom to express itself.

Limitation, in any form be it physical, mental or spiritual, tends to create a dangerously volatile and unstable temperament. The Letter Y is greatly attracted to psychic phenomena and seeks to delve into the hidden mysteries of the ages.

This letter has a natural affinity for the beauty of nature and finds contemplative solitude a means of mental, spiritual and emotional renewal. This ability to renew its energies through meditative exercises helps this vibration to release bottled up emotions. Pythagoras, the Greek mathematician who re-discovered many of the "lost" secrets of numerology, considered this letter to be sacred. He also referred to this letter as the two roads, representing important choices or initiations on the spiritual path.

When activated by one of the cycles of life, the Letter Y is thrown into exciting situations where quick decisions and sudden change occur. During the active phase, this letter experiences obstacles in order to slow it down long enough to gain important benefits from observation. Even in the midst of strife, this vibration will achieve progress. The strength and passion possessed by this letter is an important element in the attainment of its goals during this active time period.

THE LETTER Z

The Letter Z vibrates to the number 8 and is the twenty-sixth letter of the Alphabet. This letter possesses the same attributes of the other Letters, H and Q, which share the vibration of the number 8. However, the Letter Z is a highly spiritually motivated expression. It has been blessed with inspiration, hope and guidance from the Universal Mind. The intuitive abilities of the Letter Z grants it the ability to understand human nature and through this understanding shows it the way to serve the needs of others.

Esoterically, to the ancients, this letter represented the power of "Jehovah", a power which could be misused by the unenlightened to manifest ruin and devastation due to greed and selfishness. The highly spiritual power inherent to the Letter Z is difficult to channel, especially when the ego has not be subdued. But this is part of the spiritual and karmic lesson the Letter Z has been challenged to learn. Through its unique brand of perceptiveness, this vibration can succeed beyond its expectations.

When activated by one of the cycles of life, the Letter Z is thrown into what seems to be a whirlwind of activity that darts back and forth, to and fro with a dizzying speed. However, even in the midst of this frantic time, definite progress is being made on the spiritual path. Opportunities for achievement and the attainment of personal goals are mixed in with a variety of experiences in order to teach the lesson of discernment and patience. During the active phase of this vibration it seems as though two steps forward and one step back becomes the normal way of life. What is important for this vibration to remember is that despite the air of confusion around it, advances are made which can not be taken away.

CHAPTER THREE

CHAKRA SYMBOLISM

It is our thoughts which are the magical `keys'
that have the power to unlock the hidden
Gateway poised between two planes of reality.
For deep within our being is an awareness, an intuitional `knowingness'
that is compelled to reach out,
to merge and become one
with the energy patterns that surround us.

One of the most important "Keys" in developing your awareness and intuitive gifts concerns the energy field, (aura), of your physical body and its seven centers of power. Physically and ethereally, energy is all around you and is absorbed into your body through power centers called "Chakras". When blockage occurs in one of the Chakras, an imbalance occurs in the physical body which can create "dis-ease" or other negative manifestations leaving you drained and fatigued as well as emotionally distressed.

Learning how to channel the flow of energy through the body's power centers or Chakras is an important step in our goal for self-realization. In the ancient temples of Atlantis, Egypt and Greece, the first lesson an initiate underwent concerned the proper maintenance of the Chakra system in their bodies. These ancient temples taught their seekers about the intimate correlation between the seven chakras, color, numbers and astrology. When you attain an understanding of this intricate relationship, you have taken the first step in mastering the inherent power you were gifted with.

All human beings possess seven chakras, even the planet earth has seven chakras or "power centers" that react and function in a similar manner to our own chakras. It is through our chakra centers that we channel the energy necessary to achieve personal growth, awareness and healing. With this in mind, the following information on Chakras is offered:

FIRST CHAKRA

Generally referred to as the "Root Chakra", this power center is located at the base of the spine and vibrates to the color red. The root chakra is the seat of the Kundalini Force which lies coiled three and a half times at the base of the spine. The Root Chakra governs physical strength, the expression of sexual energy, reproductive organs, desires, base instincts, warmth, and the "here and now". The 1st Chakra is a well of pure but raw energy needing direction. The Root Chakra is symbolized by a square.

The Kundalini is the energy which fuels our physical, mental, emotional and spiritual body. When the Kundalini is activated, but not channeled up through the higher Chakra centers, the energy released by this force results in an a raw sexual drive which demands gratification. If the Kundalini is not properly directed, the sexual instinct overwhelms all other instincts including the dictates of the Higher Mind. The Kundalini is a potent force that is not to be taken lightly or to be toyed with. It has great potential for destruction but equal potential for great strength and endurance if channeled properly.

When the Root Chakra is negatively stimulated or an individual wears too much red, problems with nervousness and egotism can surface. The "aura" will become infused with the color red, which will in turn, attract aggressive reactions from other people. The vibrations of the planet Mars has subtle influences on the Root Chakra. In astrology, Mars is considered to be the planet of sexual energy and reveals how we act out our sexual drive.

SECOND CHAKRA

This power center is referred to as the "Spleen Chakra", and is located just below the navel. the energy from the 2nd Chakra affects the pancreas and the bladder in the physical body. The Spleen Chakra vibrates to the color Orange and rules the emotions, appetite, energy levels, and openness to new ideas. Its symbol is the triangle.

Since the 2nd Chakra rules the appetite and is deeply associated with the color orange, I find it rather interesting that many fast-food restaurants have orange chairs, tables, or walls. By using this color, the appetite is stimulated by the 2nd Chakra which can cause cramps and depression if its needs are not gratified.

When the Spleen Chakra is negatively stimulated or an individual wears too much orange, they may have problems with feelings of laziness, inertia or depression. However, wearing a little of the color orange can attract thoughtfulness and consideration from other people. Vibrations from the Sun has subtle influences on the Spleen Chakra. In astrology, the Sun symbolizes our personality, the way we outwardly manifest our character traits.

THIRD CHAKRA

This power center is called the "Solar Plexus" Chakra and is located in the stomach area. Energy from the 3rd Chakra affects the stomach, liver, and cortex of the physical body. The Solar Plexus Chakra vibrates to the color yellow and rules clear thinking, joy, confidence, all learning and studying, decisions and personal power. Its symbol is the circle.

Yellow is not the color to use if you want to relax because the vibrations of this color activates the 3rd Chakra which, in turn, stimulates the mind and thinking process. However, if you are depressed or sad, yellow is an excellent color to use since it stimulates the 3rd Chakra to release negative emotions. It also aids in getting rid of bad habits and mental confusion.

When the Solar Plexus Chakra is negatively stimulated or an individual wears too much yellow, they could overstimulate their mental process which may result in migraine headaches. However, when used in moderation, the aura soaks up enough energy to give off waves of friendliness and good will which attracts other people of like mind to you. Vibrations from the planet Mercury has subtle influences on the Solar Plexus Chakra. In astrology, Mercury is considered to be the planet of intellect and curiosity.

FOURTH CHAKRA

This power center is called the "Heart Chakra" and is located in the central part of the chest, between the breasts. Energy from the 4th Chakra affects the Heart, chest and thymus in the physical body. The Heart Chakra vibrates to the color green and rules growth, love, peace, balance between the mind, body and spirit. Its symbol is a cross +, (not to be confused with the Christian symbol).

Green is a color which calms and soothes the vibrations from the 4th Chakra. Walking in the woods during spring or summer, when the trees are filled with thick green leaves, most people can feel a tingling in their chest from the energy the Heart Chakra absorbs from the plants. This occurs because of the rich variety of green shades to be found in nature. Living plants and flowers, radiant with multi-colored hues, have a profound effect on the human power centers or "chakra". Even atoms vibrate with an energy that gives off different colors, depending on their rate of speed and the chemical components the atoms interact with.

When the Heart Chakra is negatively stimulated or adversely affected by the energy around it, the physical body reacts with pain or tightness in the chest, difficulty in breathing and even heartbeat irregularities. The old saying "green with jealousy" actually means energy to the Heart Chakra has been closed off, which results in the aura being flooded with a sickly greenish-yellow or greenish-orange hue representing envy, jealousy and deceit. This happens because the 2nd and 3rd Chakra Centers have become overstimulated, blocking the "love" energy of the 4th Chakra.

It is interesting to note that vibrations from the planet Saturn subtly influence the Heart Chakra. In mundane Astrology, Saturn is considered to be the planet Restriction, but in esoteric or spiritual Astrology, the planet Saturn is referred to as the Karmic Teacher who demonstrates graphically that what you give out to others or the Universe, you get back tenfold. This applies to thoughts as well as deeds.

FIFTH CHAKRA

This power center is called the "Throat Chakra" and is located at the base of the throat. Energy from the 5th Chakra affects the nose, ears, mouth, thyroid and throat. The Throat Chakra vibrates to the color Sky Blue and rules communication, contemplation, self-expression, creativity, and healing. Its symbol is the crescent moon.

Sky blue is an excellent color to promote patience and understanding between individuals or groups who must settle negotiations, arguments, or conflicts. The Throat Chakra is activated by this color which allows clear communication to take place. It is interesting to note that humankind has always associated the color blue with heaven and it is through our throats and mouths that we say our prayers to heavenly entities.

When the Throat Chakra is negatively stimulated or adversely affected by environmental energies, the ability to speak clearly and thoughtfully becomes blocked. This can cause frustration and overly strain the delicate emotional balance of the individual. People who do a lot of lecturing, speaking or singing would find it beneficial to have sky blue around them or to actually wear the color. I've noticed in the waiting rooms whose walls are painted a sky blue, there seems to be less restlessness and impatience among the people who are waiting.

Of course too much sky blue would lead to problems with attention and alertness. Too much of any color tends to overload the sensory system rendering the positive energies of the color inert. Vibrations of the planet Jupiter has subtle influences on the Throat Chakra. In astrology, Jupiter is considered to be the planet of expansion and opportunity. The way Jupiter affects us is reflected in our creativity and in the way we assimilate knowledge.

SIXTH CHAKRA

This power center is referred to as the "Brow Chakra" and is located in the middle of the forehead just above the eyes. Energy from the Brow Chakra activates the power of the "third eye" and affects the activity of the Thalamus gland in the physical body. The 6th Chakra vibrates to the colors Indigo and deep Purple and rules intuition, higher comprehension, spiritual awareness, ESP or "psychic" gifts, and releasing. Its symbol is the six-pointed star or star of David.

When students first begin exploring the Spiritual Path, experimenting with different techniques, the "third eye" is gradually opened, allowing them to see past the veils of illusion. During meditation, especially when you first begin learning the techniques, you will experience a "tickling" sensation between your eyes, three fingers above the bridge of your nose. When you feel this "tickling" or "itching" sensation for the first time, it will distract you from concentrating on the meditation exercise you are attempting.

These weird sensations occur because most of us are not trained from childhood to use our "third eye". Therefore, the process of awakening and focusing the "third eye" is more noticeable. Some individuals, before getting a precognitive vision, will experience a sudden but brief sharp pain in their "third eye" which acts as a signal to their conscious mind of the message they are about to receive. Other people have reported a flashes of heat in their "third eye" instead. Since each person is uniquely different, how you experience the "awakening" of your "third eye" will naturally depend on the way you have established the lines of communication with your Higher Self.

When the Brow Chakra is negatively stimulated or adversely affected by surrounding energies the physical body generally responds with a headache or pain behind the eyes and sinuses.

Because this power center is intimately connected with releasing negative energy, a blockage in the 6th Chakra can have a painful physical backlash if we refuse to release anger or resentment. The more you fight to hold onto your negative feelings, the more afflicted the rest of the chakra centers become, causing stomach problems, difficulties with the heart, and so on.

The only problem with wearing or surrounding yourself with too much indigo or purple would be a lack of attention for material considerations. It might make you less inclined to deal with the mundane world and its egocentricities which could pose a problem in the business or corporate arena.

However, these colors act as a shield against the negativity of others, so the best advice would be to experiment for yourself to find the right balance.

When indigo or purple appears in the aura around the body, it indicates the individual is "seeking", either on a subconscious or conscious level, for enlightenment and wisdom. The higher vibrations of the planet Venus has subtle influences on the 6th Chakra. In mundane astrology, Venus symbolizes love, affection and relationships. But in esoteric or spiritual astrology, the planet Venus is defined in a slightly different way. Esoterically, Venus is concerned with "values" and "morals". What you value in life you are attached to. If you value the wrong things of people, you can have trouble "releasing" your attachment to them in order to grow in awareness.

SEVENTH CHAKRA

This power center is called the "Crown Chakra" and is located on the top of the head. Some metaphysicians will say it is just above the head, but others believe the 7th Chakra actually touches the top of the head. Energy from the Crown Chakra affects the pituitary gland in the physical body. The 7th Chakra vibrates to the color Violet and rules spiritual growth, self-realization and artistic expression. Its symbol is the lotus flower.

Using the color Violet is an excellent aid in stimulating the 7th Chakra which, in turn, activates the latent creative and artistic talents. Wearing this color promotes a calm peaceful spirit and helps you to maintain an emotional and mental balance as you go through your day. If you find yourself attracted to the color violet, it is a sign from your subconscious mind that you are seeking a spiritual teacher or guide who can help you attain self-realization.

When the Crown Chakra is subjected to negativity through the environment or through the individual's own actions, the Chakra will simply shut down, cutting the individual off from inspiration and guidance from the higher realms. However, when the 7th Chakra is stimulated with positive thoughts and emotions, an incredible glow of artistic and creative inspiration will fill the individual. Some of the greatest artists in history were able to clear their minds and open the 7th Chakra to divine inspiration, and it is reflected in their work.

Vibrations from the Moon have subtle influences on the Crown Chakra. In astrology, the Moon symbolizes the inner person, the you no one else knows. In many ways the Moon represents the "secret" you, the person you have spent several lifetimes creating and perfecting. The placement of the Moon in an astrology chart reveals the accumulated spiritual growth an individual has attained over many lifetimes and how much work still needs to be done. Therefore, the inner-connection between the symbolism of the Moon and the function of the 7th Chakra is clearly evident.

ADDITIONAL NOTES ON CHAKRAS

As I mentioned previously, the planet earth has seven chakras which correspond in function to our own chakra centers, although the earth's chakras do not line up in succession the way ours do. The physiological makeup of a planet is different from the physiology of a human body. It must be pointed out that our planet is alive, it is aware and has its own unique "sentience" and just like us, Earth is in a process of evolving and growing. We are the children of her womb, and like it or not, our destinies are intimately intertwined with mother earth for good or ill.

The Root Chakra of planet Earth is obviously located in the "Pacific Ring of Fire" for no where else on earth are the raw -fires of creation more active. The "plates" at the bottom of the ocean are constantly moving, heaving and shifting their location. A considerable amount of earthquakes and Volcanic activity is generated from the restless molten-hot magma underneath the ocean floor. The Root Chakra, ruling the awesome Kundalini force, also rules the Earth's instinctive nature to create on the physical plane. Like us, our mother the earth, possesses a Kundalini Force. The Earth creates new islands and land masses with the same overwhelming drive humankind has to pro-create offspring.

The Second Chakra of planet Earth is located in the middle of the Atlantic Ocean, between the Azores Islands and the Atlantis Fracture Zone. This area is commonly referred to as the Mid-Atlantic Ridge. This is where the "Tectonic Plates" are separating causing the North American continent and the European continent to physically move farther and farther apart. The 2nd Chakra deals with energy and this area of the planet is highly magnetized center which accounts for the "energy" expended to move the tectonic plates apart. You could call this power center the "belly-button" of the planet.

The Third Chakra of planet Earth is located in the Arctic Ocean between the North Pole and the Magnetic North Pole. Since the function of the 3rd Chakra is to clear away unwanted energies and vibrations, the Purity of the Arctic Ocean is maintained because of its frozen state. There are no land masses with an over-population of people to pollute the pristine pureness of this power center. This at least gives mother earth some breathing room in order to cleanse herself of the negativity we continue to bombard her with.

The Fourth Chakra of planet Earth is located in the continental United States in an area called "the four corner". This is the area where the boundaries of four states intersect to create a perfect cross, an ancient Native american Indian symbol for the power of nature. The states involved are Utah, Colorado, New Mexico and Arizona. Since the function of the 4th Chakra is love, peace, and balance, I find it interesting that this power center lies right in the middle of Native Indian lands. The American Indian has always revered nature and mother earth and it is fitting that they are the guardians of the planet's "heart" center.

The Fifth Chakra of planet Earth is located in the Caribbean region in the area of the notorious "Bermuda Triangle". This part of the planet is unpredictable and has a very powerful magnetic force centered there. Since the function of the 5th Chakra is concerned with communication, creativity and self-expression, it is interesting to note that the world's largest radio telescope is located on the island of Puerto Rico. Space craft launchings from the United States take place in Florida which is also under the influence of the 5th chakra. Although the Panama Canal is not directly under the 5th Chakra, it is close enough to be subtly affected by the energy of this power center. The Panama Canal was, (and still is), an important route of communication and interaction between the countries along the Atlantic and the countries along the Pacific rim.

The Sixth Chakra of planet Earth is located in the Himalayan region, encompassing Tibet and northern India. As with humankind, the earth possesses a "third eye" ruled by the 6th Chakra Center. It was the Tibetans who kept the knowledge of the "third eye" alive down through the millennia after Atlantis was destroyed. Since the 6th Chakra is concerned with Higher Consciousness and development of Intuition, it is no accident that the ancient civilizations of the region considered the Himalayan Mountains to be the sacred home of powerful Avatars and Spiritual Masters. the Ganges River, sacred to the people and religions of India, has its source in the Himalayas.

The Seventh Chakra of planet Earth is located in Antarctica, between the South Pole and the Magnetic South Pole. This part of the planet is extremely hostile to intrusions by humans or any other creature for that matter. Since the 7th Chakra is the seat of self-realization and spiritual growth, it is the most sensitive part of the planet. The ozone layer, which acts as a barrier to harmful radiation from the Sun, has a hole in it over Antarctica, allowing the planet to release its soundless pleas for relief out into the Universe. The more abuse we heap onto mother earth, the larger that hole will grow until the surface of the planet is saturated with deadly rays from the Sun. Where will we be then?

Our mother, the earth, has a right to expect her children to treat her with consideration and kindness. But modern man has done little more than violate and rape the planet. According to all spiritual teachings, we were meant to treat our bodies as "temples of the living spirit". Earth too, is a "living temple", destined to travel the spiritual path to enlightenment. The earth, like us, has a soul and is subject to the laws of Karma. What we give to planet earth, be it good or bad, will return to us tenfold. That is the Law. It is something to think about isn't it?

CHAPTER FOUR

COLOR SYMBOLISM

"Our lives are like a multi-colored tapestry, woven with the bright threads
of joy and sorrow, tragedy and triumph
which illuminates and enhances
the white radiance of the Universe."

Color is a very important and integral part of our everyday life which, when understood, reveals amazing "secrets" about ourselves and the world around us. The symbolism of Color is a vital "key" in unlocking the hidden messages which come to us during our Dream-state and when we Meditate. Understanding the energies generated by various colors can be applied when reading the Aura of others, or when working with Gems, Crystals and Minerals. The principles of color can be applied to Astrology, Counseling and the Tarot. Humans have a highly developed ability to perceive color that the other native creatures of Earth do not possess. It is a gift we take for granted, a gift many of us do not utilize fully. This chapter is devoted to giving you a strong foundation in Color Symbolism on which you can build further.

Most people have ignored the deeper meanings of color, unaware their own color choices reveals their subconscious state of mind. For centuries, artists have intuitively been aware of the Spiritual and Esoteric connotations of Color. I believe the time has come for all of us to become "consciously" aware of the true meaning of Colors and how to utilize them constructively in our lives. It is to this purpose that this chapter has been written.

Some colors are very bright, shimmering with a jewel-like brilliance. When this occurs, it is as though the energies or emotions if you will, are closer to the surface, more passionate and explosive. Other hues are very soft, very pastel in nature which indicates a more passive nature. The softness of the colors can indicate mastery over the emotions. Still, other colors are very muted in tone as though you were viewing them through a veil, which gives the colors a very mystical appearance.

Brilliant Jeweled colors indicate a vibrancy for life, an assertiveness and self-confidence that is well founded. However, because of the powerful energy generated by these radiant colors, the emotions are more difficult to control. Vivid colors are oriented to the Here and Now, accepting no limitation or restriction. They are stimulating and motivating, eager to experience the "High Drama" the Universe has to offer. Brilliant, jeweled colors are an explosive creative force, demanding expression in some form or another. This intense creativity can take on an artistic form or a negative form. It all depends on which choices an individual makes while working with these particular color hues.

Pastel colors are more passive, serene, attuned to the Unconditional Love of the Creator. These soft colors are more nurturing, giving one a sense of refuge, a haven from the frantic pace and kinetic energy of a full spectrum life. Pastel Colors indicate a control of the life-force and the ability to step back from an intense situation and allow compassion, not "passion" to be the determinating factor in their choices. Pastel colors have the ability to draw out the latent creativity in an individual and help the physical and mental body to open up the Chakra Centers to Divine Inspiration and to the direction of the Higher Intuitional Self. Pastel colors symbolize the virtue of Patience and Trust.

Muted colors are very special and call upon the collective unconscious of all life-forms in the universe and the Akashic Records where these memories are stored. They are mystical in nature and seem to vibrate to the ancient epochs of human experience, recalling distant lifetimes in long-forgotten civilizations. Muted colors represent the long lost heritage of the human race, and of other Sentient Races, both on this planet and on others throughout the Universe. When you see and experience the muted colors, they call upon these distant past-life memories of Atlantis, Lemuria, the lost civilization of the Tridents, and others. When you first see the Akashic Records during a dream or while in a meditative state, the records are cloaked in a veil of muted colors which draws upon the mystical nature of Life in the Universe.

To give you a few practical examples of how color symbolism can be applied in every day life, consider the business or corporate world. Many men and women in business tend to wear grays, beiges, browns, black and navy blue as their predominant color. Paying attention to the colors people choose to wear can tell you a lot about them, their mood and emotional state.

For example: Individuals who wear a lot of gray are usually in a state of transition or change in their lives. Perhaps they are striving to achieve a sense of balance amidst the emotional turmoil of a personal relationship which is not working out as smoothly as they expected. Gray indicates subconscious stress which may be eating away at the individual's mental and emotional well-being. When an individual is drawn to the color gray it may be due to an instinctive urge to be detached and aloof from the world and its problems. The color gray itself symbolizes a disciplined "Will" which is a necessary element to have in one's personality in order to "make-it" or be taken seriously in the business world.

The color Beige, (which is a blend of brown and white), shows an individual who does not wish to draw attention to themselves. There is a subconscious desire to be neutral, to work behind the scenes. Individuals who are drawn to this color do not want to be in the lime-light or to be exposed to the criticisms of others. On an instinctively level, the individual may have a secret desire to retreat from the painful intensity of life. When Beige is used as the predominant color in decorating a home, office, or place of business it shows a need for security and stability. It also represents a need for perfection and purity in the environment.

The color Brown gives the impression of reliability and practicality. For someone who wears a great deal of this color, it can indicate two things: first, they are a pragmatic, reliable person who has a very practical, down-to-earth personality; or, this is the image the individual is trying to project to others. Brown also indicates a need, (subconsciously or consciously), for recognition from others for services rendered. Next time you go into a bank, insurance company or real estate office, notice the colors the management people wear. You might surprise yourself at the impressions you pick up once you understand the symbolism of color.

Wearing Black can give the impression of Authority and Control, and a subconscious projection of latent power and mystery. In other words, there is much more to an individual wearing this color than what might appear on the surface or at first glance. These individuals are say subconsciously, "Are you willing to risk revealing my secrets?" "Are you brave enough uncover what is beneath my outward mask?" So, in many ways, wearing black can symbolize a Challenge issued by the individual on a subconscious or even conscious level.

Navy Blue is another "corporate" color that gives the impression you are in control, both of your emotions and of the situation around you. This is a conservative color indicating an individual who will not take risky chances based on half-baked ideas. The individual who is attracted to this color has a no-nonsense approach to life. Navy Blue is a color of Discipline and Superiority. It is a color of confidence and self-assurance. Wearing this color can also impart a sense of remote peacefulness and even a sense of detachment to the individual. Navy Blue imparts a non-verbal message of "don't waste my time" to other people. Here's a bit of information which you might find interesting concerning color. Blue Jeans have become quite popular in the last 25 years. The authentic blue-jeans range in color from medium blue to a dark royal blue, but the washed out, faded look of jeans are also popular. Dark royal blue indicates the promise of expansion, of substance and blessings from the Creator on the material plane. Pale blue, the faded color of jeans, indicates a willingness to deal with karmic situations, a preparation for a new existence. The medium blue is a color of healing, of learning to let go of possessive tendencies and attachments which distract the individual from their goals.

In the mid-sixties and early seventies, it was the faded look of jeans or denim which was the most popular. During that time a growing openness toward Spiritual Enlightenment was being experienced more and more by groups of people at an accelerated rate. But, as the mid-seventies and eighties proceeded, a more selfish attitude, the "ME" generation as it is called now, seemed to gain dominance. Their favorite color for jeans was the dark royal blue or black, indicating a desire for financial expansion, for more material substance in their lives rather than spiritual awareness. Now, there seems to be a trend back toward the medium blue, the healing of possessive and selfish tendencies.

Another example of the influence of color I want to share with you is a more personal one. A friend of mine, who has trouble getting motivated in the morning, has decorated her bathroom in soft peach, cream and pastel greens. But, because this is the first room she goes to when she wakes up, she has pasted large yellow bananas on the walls and mirror. Yellow is the color of the Active Mind, and the brighter the yellow, the more intensity there is in brain activity. She has come to realize that this subconscious choice of color was a deliberate one on the part of her Higher Self. The bright yellow of the bananas seem to "jump-start" her brain in the morning, giving her an infusion of much needed energy.

I firmly believe that the colors we wear and surround ourselves with strongly affect our emotions and moods; our state of mind if you will. Colors are the way we make statements about ourselves to other people, how we communicate with the world around us in a non-verbal manner. In other words, how we choose to "color" our world has a very deep, almost mystical effect on us, as well as on other people around us. Therefore, choose your colors wisely, the influence goes deeper than you are aware of.

THE SYMBOLISM OF COLOR

There are 3 Primary Colors: Yellow, Red and Blue. These colors when combined in twos, create the 3 Secondary Colors: Orange, Purple, and Green. There are 2 Colors I call the Alpha and Omega Colors, which are White, (alpha) and Black, (omega). When these 2 Colors are combined, they create a third color: Gray, the color of Balance between Alpha and Omega. These 3 Colors then form a special group which I call the Color Trinity.

The Primary Colors, Secondary Colors, and the Color Trinity are the base for all the colors in the Color Spectrum. It is these colors when combined in different groups which form the myriad colors we see around us. This is the secret to unlocking the meaning of colors. Once you identify the different "hues" which have come together in harmony to create something different from itself, you will have discovered the "heart" of that color.

With this information in mind, the following definitions on Color is offered to you.

WHITE: THE ALPHA COLOR

White symbolizes the Christ Consciousness. It represents Innocence, Purity and Perfection, a Union with the Supreme Being. This is a highly spiritual color which indicates the hand of the Creator guiding the individual in many unseen ways. White represents Truth, not personal truth, but Universal Truth. This color also represents the Transition of the Spirit from one level of being or knowing to a higher level. White is the color of Self-Mastery and wholeness.

When White is combined with other colors, as you will see later, it brings a special quality to that color. The vibration of the color shaded with White is raised to a higher, more spiritual level. It also helps to neutralize any negative qualities that color may have in its nature. Another interesting point about the color white is that to the ancient Egyptians, White symbolized Joy and Happiness.

BLACK: THE OMEGA COLOR

This color, when taken at face value or surface value, seems to represent Illusions, limitations, a closed mind, fear, doubt, depression, earthly bondage or bondage to the material world. It can also indicate misuse of psychic gifts and the reaping of negative karma. But there is much more to this color than what appears as surface negativity. Black represents a Cross-Roads on the path of a Spiritual Seeker. It also indicates a subconscious desire for a Teacher who will instruct you in Universal Law and Truth, who will instruct you in the Art of Transformation.

The appearance of Black is an indication that you need to accept your Karma, (good or bad), and learn to move forward with it. Black represents a Challenge or Initiation to be passed by you on your Path. This is where the Art of Transformation is involved. If you are afflicted with poverty, the "challenge" is to transform the negative into the positive force of prosperity. If you are experiencing sickness or illness, the "challenge" is to transform this negative energy into the positive force of health, and so on, these are but 2 examples.

Each of the negative connotations described in the first paragraph is a Challenge or Initiation in the Art of Transformation: Fear into Faith, Illusion into Truth, a closed mind into an open mind, depression into enthusiasm, doubt into certainty, and so on.

This is a multi-level color with many hidden meanings, but it is *not* a color to be feared in any way. Black is a color a Spiritual Teacher or Guide will wear to show their readiness to accept the Challenge of bringing Light from Darkness in their students. For the color Black represents the Cosmic Womb from which Life and Light is born.

An interesting and important historical note concerning the color Black has to do with the early Christian Church who associated the color Black with the so-called "Pagan" Mother-Goddess worship. The early Christian Church was very much an anti-feminine and staunchly patriarchal organization. The suppression of women and the shift of power from Matriarchal Balance to elitist male dominance was the main goal and focus of the early fanatics of the Church. Because of this, the Roman hierarchy of the Christian Church wished to discredit and abolish the worship of the "Mother-Goddess". The Priestesses and Priests of the Mother-Goddess wore black robes during certain festivals of the Moon, therefore, the Church associated the color Black with Heresy, Witchcraft and the Devil.

GRAY: THE BALANCE

This is the color of Change and Transition. It indicates a Testing for an individual. Gray also represents a disciplined Will, a detached aloofness. This color indicates analysis and mystical powers which affect the lower, psychic nature of a Sentient Creature. Gray is in the process of balancing, re-forming and expressing its newly combined energies due to the merging of White and Black.

The White energy is in the process of uniting with the Black energy in bringing forth new life from the Womb of Darkness, for out of Darkness is born Light but Gray, as yet, has no permanent form, it is in a state of constant Change, transiting from one level to another, learning to balance all the diverse elements the two parent colors possess. Therefore it is necessary for Gray to be detached and have a disciplined will in order to blend all the energies it has been gifted with.

It is also important to explore and understand the various "Shades" of the color Gray. This may seem to further complicate the issue of Color, But that is not my purpose. To understand Color, you must understand the complexity of elements which, blending together, create the aura of energy symbolized by a particular color. For example:

DOVE GRAY OR PEARL GRAY:

This shade of gray is very light in color, showing more of the White Spectrum than the Black Spectrum. Dove Gray is a tranquil color, it is harmony in the midst of change or subtle change which does not threaten to upset the balance already achieved. It is the peaceful acceptance of growth on a personal level. The outer circumstances may be changing for the individual, but on the inner levels, the individual, through the virtue of "Faith", sees the "changes" as fleeting or transitory and will not affect them in an adverse way. The "changes" represent "opportunities" for enrichment of the spirit.

CHARCOAL GRAY:

This shade of Gray is very dark in color, showing more of the Black Spectrum than the White Spectrum. Charcoal Gray is a color of frustration and impatience. The "changes" experienced with this color are more traumatic, giving the individual feelings of upheaval and a sense of being at the mercy of an unsympathetic universe. It is necessary to utilize patience when experiencing the effects of this color. Patience and steadfastness will help to alleviate much of the apparent negative energy of this color.

BLUE GRAY:

This shade of Gray with Blue overtones, represents the ability to analyze a situation while experiencing great inner and outer changes. Blue-gray symbolizes the ability to detach one's self from an experience and to use the logical analytical mind to assimilate this new information being received as a result of the "changes" occurring in one's life. Emotional Detachment and the ability to analyze are the qualities inherent to the color Blue-Gray.

SILVERY GRAY:

This shade of Gray represents Self-discipline and mastery over the subconscious mind, even in the midst of changing circumstances. This is a mystical color, conjuring up visions of mists, heroes and heroines, gods and goddesses, myths and legends. It is a color of meditation and quietness. There is an old adage which says: "The more things change, the more they stay the same." Silver Gray seems to symbolize this old saying.

OLIVE GRAY:

This particular shade of Gray is very muddy and drab, with touches of dull greenish-yellow, brown and gray, it is a mousy color. It is the color of chaos, of animalistic reactions. The intelligence has been over-ridden by base instincts which are ego-oriented. The changes taking place are violent and difficult. The veneer of civilization has been ripped away and the desire to survive or conquer at any cost has taken its place. This is not a very comfortable vibration, the negative energies unleashed by this color can be overwhelming and destructive. Jealousy and malice are two emotions which seem to be characterized very well by Olive Gray.

CRYSTAL GRAY:
If you are familiar at all with Rock Crystal or Quartz Crystal, you will understand what color I am talking about. A large cluster of Quartz Crystal has a misty cloudiness at the base of the cluster which gradually clears out to leave the tips of the crystals clear. This particular shade of Gray is seen more often in dreams and Meditation than in the Tarot, although there are new Tarot decks being created which incorporate crystalline colors and shapes. Crystal Gray represents the energy force used on Atlantis. This energy was used positively by the healers and light-workers, and negatively by the power-hungry and corrupt who saw themselves as the "Source" of power rather than accepting the fact they were the channel through which the "source" of all power worked.

Crystal Gray is a color that absorbs and collects negative energy and transforms it into pure energy, ready to be utilized at our discretion. Its potential for good is limitless, but the potential for misuse is also just as great. This is a color which symbolizes a very special Spiritual Challenge, it is an initiation color which presents many temptations to the initiate. How the initiate uses the power symbolized by Crystal Gray is their choice, but whatever or however they choose to act, a change or transformation will take place that is irrevocable.

THE YELLOW SPECTRUM

YELLOW:
Yellow is the color the 3rd Chakra Center which deals with clear thinking, studying, and all learning. It is called the "Solar Plexus Center". Yellow indicates intelligence, the Active Mind, and Joy. This color also represents Enlightenment and Integrity.

GOLDEN YELLOW:
This color symbolizes Soul-Grace or Soul-gift. The Active Mind has achieved union with the Creative Mind of the Universe, true Wisdom is now possible, true Knowledge is available for the individual to utilize. It is the color of Spiritual Blessings, of richness both materially and spiritually. This blessing is granted to those individuals who know how to use and share their Prosperity in positive constructive ways to help others to Achievement.

PEACH GOLD:
This color represents Enlightenment, Restoration, and Soul Advancement. It is the color of Attainment. It also indicates the power of physical and material manifestation in an individual's life, Peach Gold is the color of Rejuvenation on several levels: emotional, mental, spiritual and physical. This color also represents healing energies obtained from the Life-force itself.

PALE YELLOW:
This color has the same attributes as the other Yellow hues, but with a softer influence. Pale Yellow is a Pastel and has the characteristic of purity and innocence to it. The Active Mind has achieved union with the Christ Consciousness and has no need for aggression in its nature. This color is mystical and gentle in its manifestation. The mental activity generated by this color takes place on a Higher Intuitional Level rather than on a Conscious or Subconscious level.

GOLDEN BROWN:
This color represents the use of or the blending of Enlightenment with practicality and strength on the Earth Plane. It symbolizes one who is spiritual, but who has their feet firmly planted on the ground. The appearance of this color indicates one who offers themselves in selfless service to others. Golden Brown also represents a great deal of energy which needs to be utilized properly and expended on behalf of others.

AMBER:
This color absorbs negative energy and transforms it. It is a healing color and has the ability to stabilize energy fields. It is also a color of Good-luck and prosperity. Another unique quality of this color is its ability to draw dis-ease or negative energy away from an individual. Amber is the color of the "Life-Force", or "prana" energy.

BRONZE:
This is the color of unresolved Karma, both of the past lifetimes and of the present one. The unresolved Karma can represent merits or debts to be reaped or experienced. This color also indicates an initiation for the Seeker on the Path of Enlightenment. It is a sign to the individual to accept Grace for themselves, and by so doing, accept Grace for others. Bronze represents the law of Moderation on the Earth Plane and the rhythmic flow of the Universe. It is also the color of the lower subconscious mind.

BLOND:
This is a color which could belong more to the White Spectrum than the Yellow Spectrum, but it is a mixture of the two with a touch of golden brown. By Blond, I am *not* referring to what most people think of when it comes to hair color. Well...maybe a little. Let me explain. Most people know what color of hair a "Towhead" has. Its a white blond, a pale wheat color or straw color. This color symbolizes fertility, abundance and ripeness. Blond represents the harvest, the reaping of what you have sown previously, good or bad. It corresponds to the fall season and to the Astrological sign of Virgo.

ORANGE:
This color represents the 2nd Chakra center called the "Spleen Chakra". It represents physical healing, the balance of the physical and mental aspects of

human nature. Orange is a combination of Intelligence, energy, and good judgment. It also rules the emotions, energy and appetite.

DARK ORANGE:

This dark shade represents stubbornness, willfulness, and even, at times, arrogance. Pride, sarcasm, cynicism, and an inflexible ego are also attributes of this color. Dark Orange has a haughty unapproachableness to it. The passions are not under control.

ORANGISH-RED:

This shade of orange has the same meaning as pure orange, but with more passion, more energy. This is a color which charges you up physically, stirs your juices, so to speak. But because the emotions are closer to the surface and more intense than with plain Orange, they can overwhelm an individual more quickly and easily than you might expect. There is a possibility of uncontrolled passion and pride with this particular color. It takes a strong person to wear this dynamic shade, and represents a Challenge in balancing the increased energy and passion with good judgment when seen in Meditation, dreams, or the Tarot. This is also the color of racial pride.

THE RED SPECTRUM

RED:

One of the basic meanings to this particular color is new beginnings. It is a sign of many opportunities, many new chances or paths from which to choose. It is also the color of the 1st Chakra or "Root" Chakra which represents energy, sexual desires and physical passion. The Root Chakra is the area of the body where the "kundalini" lies coiled, 3 and a half times, at the base of the spine. One must gain mastery over the Root Chakra, (our desire nature), in order to advance along one's higher spiritual path.

The color Red indicates a healthy life force, strength, sensuality, the Here and Now, as well as temper and pride in one's possessions. The presence of this color indicates the opportunity to advance spiritually if we choose to accept the challenge. Red is also associated with the Phoenix, the mystical bird of rebirth and regeneration, in the cultures of the Middle East and in the Orient.

RUBY RED:

This rich, deep, jeweled color symbolizes Integrity and Authority that has been well earned by one's past actions. It is also a sign of approval from a Spiritual Master or Teacher. Ruby Red represents the Highest Personal Love Expression, as well as Selfless Healing. It is a rich and enduring color that gives instead of takes, it has the characteristic of discipline and control over the lower, baser nature of humankind.

ROSE:

This is the color of Mystical Love, of Empathy and Sympathy. Rose is also the color of Blessings from the Creator. It indicates responsive affection and affection that is reciprocal. For lovers, this color represents Soul Mates, or Twin Souls who have a bond that is far deeper than any physical bond could possibly be.

SOFT PINK OR SHELL PINK:

The Pastel shade of Pink indicates a Nurturing Love, Devotion, Tenderness, reverence, and sensitivity to other Life-forms and the needs they possess. This is a giving color, an unselfish color. The presence of this color may indicate this type of love is natural to the individual, or that the individual will receive this type of love from another, or, the individual is in need of developing these qualities in themselves.

DEEP OR DARK PINK:

What's interesting about this color is that it represents a lack of self-confidence, a type of insecurity possessed by an individual when it comes to the emotions. Because of deep seated fears of losing the love they crave, they tend to cling too tightly or "smother" the object of their desire or love. Possessiveness and jealousy are represented by the deep dark shade of Pink, which are strong emotions. However, these qualities can be elevated once an individual realizes they are worthy of love and have no need to "control" or "manipulate" others in order to receive love.

VIOLET PINK:

Self-Realization is the key word for this color. It represents artistic expression, creativity, and attainment. Violet Pink also symbolizes Intuitive Understanding of the way the Universe is structured and the laws which govern it. This is the color of a Seeker on the Spiritual Path.

VIOLET WHITE:

This is the color of the 7th Chakra Center referred to as the "Crown Chakra". It indicates Spiritual Growth, Wisdom, Universal Truth, faith, and humor. It is a healing color, life-giving and restorative. Violet White is also associated with the Christ Consciousness and Spiritual Understanding. This too, is the color of a Seeker on the Spiritual Path, but one who is even more dedicated and fixed of purpose. Many of the Saints had this color prominent in their Auras, although they are not the only ones who possess this color. Writers, artists, priests, priestesses, nuns, and others who have dedicated their life to spiritual pursuits also possess this color in their aura.

MAGENTA:

This color represents Spiritual Power, Mastery and Control. Because this color symbolizes such a High Spiritual Attainment, it is rarely used on most Tarot Cards, only a few decks have this color at all, and when they do, it is used very sparingly.

COPPER:
How do I describe this color? The best way would be to say Copper is a Pinkish Bronze, with a little Peach Gold mixed in. Copper is an electrical color in that it serves as a channel or conductor for energy. In Atlantis, many of the "Light Wands" were constructed of Copper Metal with crystals placed at both ends to focus the energy harnessed by the metal from the individual working with the Wand.

The color Copper represents Channeled Energy with limitless potentials and possibilities. How one uses that energy is, in itself, a Spiritual Test or Initiation.

REDDISH BROWN OR TERRA COTTA:
This is a karmic color indicating past-life violence, either committed to the individual or violence the individual committed to others. It is a Blood-Guilt Karma, reddish brown is the color of dried blood. Reddish Brown can also indicate jealousy directed toward the individual or that the individual is jealousy of the gains of others around them. This color can represent a difficult challenge or lesson ahead for the individual to face and deal with. It may even appear to be a restriction or limitation to the individual until they willingly decide to correct errors they have made in the past, and forgive the errors others have made concerning them. Once this decision is reached, the burden or limitation is lifted.

REDDISH PURPLE OR MAROON:
This color indicates Karmic Suffering or Testing in this life due to physical offenses committed to others in previous lifetimes. It represents difficult or harsh experiences which have or will temper an individual, teaching them discipline, as well as giving them maturity and generosity of spirit. It is often referred to as a color of sorrow, of tears, of heavy burdens, but leading to spiritual growth and release from karmic debts. Maroon represents Self-Awareness and teaches the lesson of Forgiveness.

THE BLUE SPECTRUM

SKY BLUE OR ROBIN'S EGG BLUE:
This shade of blue symbolizes Hope and Divine Assurance. Many paintings and sculptures of the Virgin Mary depict her with a Sky Blue Robe. Sky blue indicates the preparation for a new existence or new things in one's life. It also represents the healing of possessive tendencies and a passionless love. Sky Blue is the color of the 5th Chakra Center commonly referred to as the "Throat Chakra". It rules communication, creativity, and healing.

To the ancient cultures, which came centuries before the advent of Christianity and who worshipped the Mother Goddess, the priests and priestesses depicted their Goddess wearing a Sky Blue cloak as well. As a way to incorporate the ancient belief systems of converts to Christianity, the early church "borrowed" the idea of depicting the Virgin Mary wearing a Sky Blue robe. This shade of Blue is also the symbol of Spring and new growth.

MEDIUM BLUE:
This color indicates Serenity, Balance, and Blessings. It also indicates the subconscious and the flow of life, the Emotional and Mental Bodies are in balance within the individual. Blue is the color of Infinity and infinite peace.

SAPPHIRE BLUE:
The presence of this color shows that the emotional nature has matured, become more purified. It is the symbol of the Higher Mind. Sapphire Blue is a color which promises substance and expansion. On a more advanced level, Sapphire Blue, especially when prominent in dreams or Meditations, represents Mastery over the Ten Commandments.

TURQUOISE:
This is such a rich, lustrous color! It is the symbol of protection and good fortune. It is the color of power manifesting on the Earth plane. Both the color Turquoise and the gem stone of the same name have very strong karmic ties to Atlantis. The presence of this color shows a linkage between the individual and previous lifetimes in Atlantis where the individual possessed unusual "powers" and capabilities. The color Turquoise acts as a catalyst to re-awaken these memories and therefore, re-awaken the abilities the individual once possessed.

PALE BLUE:
This particular shade of blue indicates an emotional and mental distance from the frenzy of life. When this color appears it represents a mental attitude of willingness to deal with karmic situations in an impersonal manner. The ego is not in control, the individual has moved beyond the ego and its emotional fears. There is a neutrality or open-mindedness in dealing with karmic situations which occur and have subtle influences on the individual's life.

AQUA "BLUE-GREEN":
To better describe this color, I suggest that you visualize the sea or ocean on a sunny day; perhaps as it surrounds one of the tropical islands. The Aqua or Blue-Green, (sometimes referred to as "Peacock Blue" as well), is such a beautiful color for the ocean that it doesn't seem real when you first see it. The sea itself represents the womb of all life. It is rich, nurturing, and filled with unseen wonders. This color symbolizes the limitless bounty of Nature, of the Feminine aspects of the Creator. It is a color of joy and happiness, a color of love and security.

NAVY BLUE:
This color indicates stern control over the emotions. Detachment and Disciplined thoughts are also represented by this color. Confidence and Assurance, as well as a no-nonsense approach to life are attitudes symbolized by this color because this is a color which inspires and represents Authority. Navy Blue is ruled by the planet Saturn which is seen by some as the planet of challenge and

karma, but is also seen by others as the planet of Limitation and Restriction, representing an uncaring force which puts obstacles in their path. Too much Navy Blue can cause feelings of isolation, of being too controlled or narrow-visioned. It can have the affect of blocking out the Intuitional aspects of our nature, not allowing this Higher Source to have an input or influence us. There is also a fear of too much emotionalism inherent in the color Navy Blue which allows the repressive tendencies of this color to gain strength of expression.

PURPLE OR INDIGO:

This is the color of the 6th Chakra Center, commonly called the "Brow Chakra". It represents intuition, higher consciousness, the Christ Mind. It is a raw electric color, indicating karmic voltage, (the sowing of karma), tenderness and selfless love. It is the color of the Spiritual Life, the color of releasing, of letting go and letting God. This is the color of a Seeker.

THE REST OF THE COLOR SPECTRUM

GREEN:

The presence of this color symbolizes Growth, love, and healing. It also indicates material or monetary ease, peace, vitality, and abundance. Green is a channel color for healing love. It is the color of the 4th Chakra Center referred to as the "Heart Chakra". It brings balance between the Mind, Body, and Spirit. This color corresponds to the Spring season, and to the Astrological Sign of Taurus.

EVERGREEN:

There is a special meaning to this color for it represents the Evergreen Tree which is the highest evolved plant on the planet. The Evergreen Tree retains its color through all the seasons and does not have a dormant state which other trees have in winter. These particular trees store energy. If you stroke your fingers gently along the branches of an evergreen tree you will feel an unusual tingle begin in your hands and spread up your arms. When this happens, the tree is transferring some of the energy it has stored to you. What you do with this energy is your choice. The energy itself has limitless potentials, both of a positive or negative manifestation.

The color itself symbolizes creative energy, a power to be utilized in constructive ways. Evergreen is also the color of endurance, of generosity, of faith and strength against all opposition. It is the color of triumph and attainment.

EMERALD GREEN:

This shade of green has achieved a high level of purity. Its healing energies are entirely without self-interest. The heart is aligned to the "Logos" or Spiritual Truths and can, without being judgmental, offering healing to others. Jealousy and envy have been eliminated. Emerald Green has the ability to cleanse away the unwanted and the useless waste and distractions from our lives without pain. Emerald Green is the color of friendliness and trustworthiness. When seeing this color or the gem itself in a dream, it symbolizes an initiation in healing, the opening of the Heart Chakra in order that pure healing light can flow through you and outward to others. Once this initiation has been passed, the individual will be channeling a unique and special healing love which can center the mental, emotional, and physical bodies of other people.

MUDDY GREEN:

By this term I mean the sickly greenish colors that are nauseating to look at. I want to call this color "puke green", but that's too gross. This particular putrid hue of green is sometimes referred to as "pea green", "drab olive", or "bilious green". This shade of green represents self-deception, and deception on the astral levels. When this shade of green appears in dreams, meditations, or tarot cards, it is a sign of illusion and possible treachery. This color also symbolizes envy, jealousy, malice, and even hatred in some cases. It is the color of betrayal and selfishness.

BEIGE:

This is a neutral color, not wishing to drawn attention to itself. It is a color which represents those who wish to observe, but not actively participate in, the emotional arena of life. Subconsciously, those people wear this color or who surround themselves with it, are seeking to build a barrier between themselves and the emotionalism of other people. It is a color of non-commitment, non-involvement, a color of limbo. However, Beige is also a color of quiet efficiency, practical and hard-working.

The color Beige gives one a secured rest from the frantic pace of life, but, there is a possibility of too much isolation or neutrality inherent in this color. This is a non-threatening, unobtrusive color which symbolizes a desire to be seen as "harmless". Quite a few "business" people wear this color, especially those climbing the corporate ladder because it makes them appear to be "non-threatening" to those in higher positions. Beige can be used to hide ambition.

BROWN:

This color represents the Earth Plane. It is the color of security, steadfastness and material or physical power. When this color appears it often indicates a need for practicality and industry in an individual in order to reap the security they desire. Brown is the color of physical and mental satisfaction and receiving recognition from one's peers for physical services rendered.

BROWNISH ORANGE:

This particular color combination indicates a lack of ambition or drive, a "who cares?" attitude. It also is the color of repression, both of the self and others around them. Brownish Orange is the color of laziness and inertia.

BLACK AND BROWN TOGETHER:

This is a color combination not found very often on Tarot Cards, but it does appear on one or two Tarot Cards in certain decks and this combination will appear in Dreams or Meditations from time to time. The combination represents a karmic penalty to be paid, either to you, or by you to someone else. By accepting the need for correction of past errors, you are released from deep seated limitations which you may have carried with you through many lifetimes on the Earth Plane. Sometimes it is easier to be the one to pay a karmic debt than it is to be the receiver of a karmic payment. It is just as important to allow others to free themselves of karmic debt to you as it is for you to acknowledge your debts and repay them, but it is not always easy.

SILVER:

This color symbolizes Expanding Moods, Cool emotions, and Mystical Powers generating initiations for the individual. Silver is ruled by the influence of the Moon, whose Light reflects or mirrors what is around it. The Moon also symbolizes the powerful, nurturing and fertile Female Energy Force of the Universe. Silver is used to tap into that Intuitive, creative and artistic force which dwells within each of us. Silver is also the color of Self-Mastery and the unconscious mind.

OPAL:

The color Opal at first appears to be a cloudy milk-white, but if you look closely, you will see a hidden fire at its heart. Sometimes this heart of fire is composed of yellows, golds, reds, and oranges. In other opals, this heart of fire is composed of greens, blues, and golds, symbolizing a seething activity ensuing behind the scenes, hidden away from prying eyes. It is a color of gestation, where "seeds" are forming, changing shape, altering their molecular structure, getting ready to be transformed into something wondrous to behold. These "seeds" can be ideas or something artistic or musical being conceived. The color Opal provides the protection needed by these "seeds" from outside influence or distraction. This color or the gemstone itself often appears in Dreams or during Meditation. There are or two Tarot Cards which have this color on them which I will detail later on in the book.

BLACK OPAL:

This is a fantastic color. If you've ever seen the rare gem called a "black opal", you will understand what I mean. There is a silvery sheen to the black opal that is almost indescribable. The heart of the black opal is filled with fire, a swirling galaxy of colors creating tiny pinpricks of light that resembles the night sky filled with red, green, yellow, and blue stars. Astrologically, the black opal vibrates to the influence of the planet Pluto and therefore to the sign Scorpio.

When you see the color of the black opal or the gem stone itself, in dreams or meditation, it symbolizes the search for knowledge concerning death and karma. It represents an initiation or lesson involving the necessity of physical death in order to balance out the earth plane and lower astral planes. The Black Opal, either as a color or stone, shows one the transitory nature of the physical earth plane, and how a physical body is only one stage of "being" we experience on the path to our development as integrated spiritual beings.

NOTE TO READERS

Along with the explanations already given for color, the following chapters include the correlation between color and the Zodiac, and color as it relates to

Dreams and Meditations, and how it interacts with gems, minerals, and crystals. The planets used in Astrology are assigned a color or colors, as are each of the Zodiac Signs. These "Keys" will help you to understand the hidden beauty of your world and provide you with the tools you need to gain the goal of Self-Realization you are seeking. The next chapter is focused on the meanings of symbols as they appear in your Dreams or when Meditating.

CHAPTER FIVE

DREAM AND MEDITATION SYMBOLISM

VISIONS

"When the vision
was within my reach
I turned to grasp it---
But it vanished.

The ghost of unborn tomorrow
Hangs heavily around me
I reached out to touch
Reality and found it was but a dream.

Strange patterns upon the ink
A World no longer Real
Alone, lost in the mists
The Real world now hidden from me.
For I did not listen
to the Dreamweaver's Song
as it weaved its spell of enlightenment."
Lord Sargon of Voltar

    The use of Symbols in Dreams and Meditation is one of the oldest teaching devices known in the Universe. One symbol carries with it a meaning which would take hundreds, even thousands of words to describe. Up until our present millennium, language, as we know it today, did not exist. Hieroglyphics and other pictorial-symbols were used to convey complex ideas and philosophies by the Tridents and Lemurians, a practice continued by the ancient civilizations which followed. To the Lemurians, a pictorial-symbol was worth a thousand words, able to communicate a multi-leveled concept.

    In the Trident and Lemurian civilizations, the teaching and passing down of knowledge and wisdom to the next generation was the function of "Sages" or "Shamans", those individuals who created epic poems and songs, tapestries and paintings, (as well as using other methods), to pass on the accumulated heritage of their people. The "Teacher-Storyteller" was considered to be one of the highest functions for soul growth. Healers and Caretakers were also functions held in high esteem because of their extraordinary potentials for soul growth.

    During our dream-state or while under the freeing influence of a Meditation Exercise, our minds are released from physical limitations. During these states of altered consciousness we have access to the Akashic Records, to other dimensions, alternate realities, the collective unconscious and to our Higher Self which is in perfect attunement with the Universal Mind or God. Many of the world's greatest writers, musicians, artists, inventors and scientists have acknowledged the richness of their dream-state as one of the primary sources of their creativity.

There are many different categories of Dream Experiences. This is why it is important to keep records of your dreams. For easier reference, the following list has been compiled with different dream categories we will explore in this chapter:

1. Precognitive
2. Teaching-Counseling
3. Past Life Memories
4. Astral Traveling
5. Problem Solving
6. Nightmares--Fears
7. Fantasy--Allegorical

PRECOGNITIVE

This type of Dream Experience gives an individual a look into future events as they will eventually unfold. There are many documented cases dealing with "precognitive dreams" where individuals have dreamed of disasters which take place within days or weeks of the dream. Not all "precognitive" dreams have to do with impending disasters, quite the contrary. Many "precognitive" dreams concern happy events and joyful circumstances. Some "precognitive" dreams relate to an individual on a personal basis, revealing situations, people, or circumstances which will affect them in the future. Other "precognitive" dreams are concerned with events that will happen to other people, not necessarily the individual who has the dream.

There is some debate among researchers concerning the ability to change or influence the future because of revelations of "precognitive" dreams. Personally, I tend to favor the theory we can change future events when we have been warned through our dreams. Naturally, if one's precognitive dream concerns the safety or well-being of a famous individual we can't prevent it from happening unless that individual is willing to listen and it becomes important for you to remember you cannot force enlightenment or knowledge on anyone other than yourself. When it comes to natural catastrophes like earthquakes, storms, fires, etc., there is very little we can do to prevent Nature's actions. What we can do is minimize the potential damage through intelligent planning and cooperative effort.

TEACHING-COUNSELING

This type of Dream Experience varies from individual to individual. Some people actually see themselves in a classroom setting, with a "teacher" or guide giving instructions or offering knowledge. The "classroom" can resemble a University, College, or other "School-type" atmosphere. Other people have recorded the "teaching-counseling" dream taking place in ancient temples or in garden courtyard settings. These classroom settings generally are centered around a group session with the individual of the dream just part of a small "student" body.

Another setting for the "Teaching-Counseling" dream is a panel of several men/women dressed in white, seated at a bench which is very similar to a Judge's Bench in a courtroom. In this dream setting, the individual is being counseled on their actions and choices in life. This panel of "Counselors" is very rarely accusatory or judgmental, their purpose is merely to offer wisdom and assist the individual in reviewing their past actions and how to make future choices which will ensure spiritual growth.

There is another variation to the "Teaching-Counseling" dream which involves the individual and a wise man or woman on a one to one basis. In this dream experience, the "teacher" may appear in many guises such as a hermit, yogi, priest, priestess, etc., or even in an angelic form. Sometimes the "teacher" figure is the Spiritual essence of a family member no longer residing on the physical earth plane. The variations on this theme are as endless as your imagination.

PAST-LIFE MEMORIES

These Dream Experiences are usually triggered by a difficult or traumatic emotional situation or by seeing a movie, reading a book, or working with karmic astrology. However, there are special techniques which can be deliberately used to unlock the doors of memory in order to have "past-life memories" in a dream experience. Certain guided Meditations are very useful for this purpose and seem to have the ability to focus the awareness or sub-conscious on past life matters which are affecting the present life circumstances.

The only one who can really interpret whether a dream experience is a real past life memory or a fantasy episode is the individual themselves. Keeping a dream journal and recording as many experiences as possible is the only methodical and scientific approach one can take to establish enough data to accurately categorize, analyze and decipher the dream-state experience.

ASTRAL TRAVELING

This particular dream Experience is characterized by feelings of "flying" or "floating". Almost everyone can relate a dream experience in which they felt themselves hitting their bed with a jolt as though they had been levitating up to the ceiling. Deja vu experiences are usually the result of the "astral-traveling" dream experience or the "past-life memories" experience. Traveling to a unfamiliar country, state, city, or even a house which triggers a sense of "I've been here before," or "I've seen this before", is the signature response of astral traveling.

The "astral-traveling" phase of dream experience allows an individual to roam at will through the multi-dimensional levels of the astral plane. There is considerable speculation concerning the ability to reach alternate realities or universes through astral traveling in the dream state and through control experiments in astral travel while awake and fully conscious.

PROBLEM SOLVING

This is one of the most common type of Dream Experience and a very important one. Through the "problem-solving" phase of our Dream State we are able to confront emotional, mental and spiritual attitudes to the circumstances in our lives which are affecting us in a variety of ways and deal with the "feelings" generated in a constructive and positive manner. When we refuse to "deal" with problems during the Dream state, our dreams can, and usually do, degenerate into Nightmares.

Through the "problem solving" phase of the Dream-State we have access to higher guidance and the Universal Mind. Using parallel situations and mirror-situations, a problem solving dream can help to resolve mixed emotions or mental attitudes with common sense and practicality. Through the dream-state we can get a fresh or new perspective on our life situation and gain the insight we need to handle the problem effectively.

NIGHTMARES-FEARS

The most difficult of all dream experiences is the "nightmare". Nightmares are generated by fear; fear we have not faced on a conscious level. When an individual refuses to deal with the harsher realities of life they become buried in the subconscious and rise to haunt us while we sleep. The most overwhelming feeling in a nightmare is the sense of helplessness, of being at the mercy of whatever is pursuing us.

FANTASY-ALLEGORICAL

Whether you are creative, artistic, or inventive, this dream Experience is one of the richest sources of inspiration. Many writers and artists have received the special seeds of creative expression through a "fantasy" dream experience. "Fantasy" dreams serve another purpose other than as a source of inspiration. This type of dream experience is an excellent way enrich yourself on a mental, emotional, physical and spiritual level. Fantasy Dreams give you the opportunity for role-playing, for wish-fulfillment and can become a source of much needed physical release.

An "allegorical" dream experience is the most challenging dream to decipher and understand. In this type of experience, the emphasis is on symbols and situations which, on the surface, do not seem to make a lot of sense, and therefore the temptation to dismiss the dream as nonsense or unimportant is very strong. In actuality, an "allegorical" dream can, and very often does, contain elements of all the dream categories. Many Native American Shamans have visions or dreams whose symbols are taken from nature and the animal kingdom.

Having given you the basic outline of the different types of Dream Experiences, the rest of this chapter will be concerned with defining many of the symbols you may have during your "Dream-State" or while "Meditating". It is very important for you to remember that while the "universal" meaning for a symbol is given here, you must take into account what "personal" meaning a symbol has for you as well. All of us possess our own unique and individualized dream vocabulary. By combining the universal meaning of a symbol with your personal definition, the interpretation of your dream or meditation symbols becomes more clearly defined and possesses the unique characteristics which pertain to your life circumstances.

To help you organize the elements of your various dream experiences, try using the following check list to get you started in the process of breaking down the component elements of your dream.

1. First, make a list or summarize the major elements of the dream experience. Try to get as many details down as possible, even ones which seem inconsequential.

2. Is the dream in Black and White or in Color?

3. If the dream is in color, are the tones vivid and striking or soft and muted?

4. Are there any dominant or outstanding colors?

5. What is the setting of your dream?
    Morning?
    Afternoon?
    Evening?
    Dusk?
    Twilight?
    Night?

6. What is the overall mood of the dream? What emotions seem to dominate?

7. Did the dream leave you with a good feeling or a sense of dissatisfaction? Did it leave you with a feeling of anticipation or apprehension?

8. Were there any elements or symbols in the dream which make you uneasy? Which ones?

9. What is the most dominant or memorable image from the dream?

10. What category do you think your dream experience falls into?

SYMBOL DEFINITIONS

ABBESS: When this symbol is seen in Dreams or Meditation it usually pertains to a "Past Life Experience", either the individual's own previous incarnations, or the past life of someone they know or have recently met who has made a strong impression on them.

As a symbol of a past life, the Abbess represents a woman who was responsible, hardworking, authoritarian, highly disciplined, and wholly dedicated to her God and the women placed under her care. She served as a surrogate mother figure and an administrative agent for the Church. During the Middle Ages, an era where women were considered mere chattels of the dominant male society, an Abbess held a unique and powerful position. She administered the resources of vast estates held in the Church's name, her word was law in the Abbey and its land, and she was considered an "equal" to the nobility which also possessed vast estates and serfs to do their bidding.

Another "past-life" connection from this symbol comes from the late 1700's and during the Regency Period in England where the term "Abbess" was used as a reference to certain practices of prostitution. An "Abbess" was a madam, a woman who procured innocent virginal girls and boys for the jaded tastes of the nobility. She literally sold these victims into sexual slavery either in brothels or in private sales.

In a Dream-State which is focused on "problem-solving", the symbol of an Abbess represents the compulsion to submit to "authority" or "responsibilities" after a period of rebellion and refusal to accept the consequences of one's actions and choices.

If the Abbess is smiling and welcoming toward the individual it indicates that the individual has a true support system around them, with friends and/ or family who can be trusted and relied upon. A kindly Abbess represents unexpected opportunities leading to pleasure and happiness.

If the individual who dreams of an abbess has been ill or in pain, either mentally, emotionally or physically, the symbol of the abbess represents comfort, compassion and healing.

To actually dream of being an abbess personally means a fascinating future filled with achievement, ambition and unique experiences.

ABBEY: The symbol of an Abbey in Dreams or Meditation has a definite link to past life memories. Historically, an Abbey represented a distinct and regimented way of life dedicated to the service of God. Abbeys were also the places which kept alive the body of knowledge humankind had accumulated over the centuries. Religious manuscripts were created and copied by the monks using magnificent and fantastic calligraphy. During the Middle Ages, books were very rare, and only a select few even knew how to read and write. Illiteracy was extremely common even among the ruling classes. The flame of knowledge was carefully nurtured in the Abbey environment, knowledge which would have been lost to future generations.

To see an Abbey as a dream-symbol represents a place of retreat, of contemplation and protection from the hectic non-stop pace of the material world. Instinctually, your higher self is sending you a message to slow down, to take time away from the pursuits of materialism. There is a danger of illness or mental and emotional collapse if the individual does not change the pace of their life.

To actually dream of being inside an Abbey represents freedom from anxiety and worries. It indicates protection given by the God-Force of the Universe and the opportunities for joy, happiness, and recognition or fame. To be inside an abbey also represents great changes in one's life, changes which are needed and will lead to fulfillment.

To dream of an Abbey in ruins can be a warning of possible destruction of one's hopes or the feeling of being abandoned and without resources. This symbol would then be instructing the individual to rebuild their spiritual belief systems and to abandon a purely materialistic view of life otherwise they will see their plans fall apart.

ABBOT: The symbol of an Abbot has the same connotation as an Abbess, however, the emphasis is on the expression of masculine energy rather than feminine energy. An Abbot is also part of the "past-life memory" dream experience.

In a teaching-counseling dream-state the symbol of an Abbot is an indication the individual needs to pay more attention to the expression of their passions and sexual habits. In other words, a little celibacy is in order.

The appearance of an Abbot in a dream can also represent temptations which need to be resisted or difficult consequences will have to be faced. These temptations can be the result of plotting by envious individuals who wish to see the individual fail in their endeavors.

ABOVE: The sensation of having something above you has two distinct meanings. One of these meanings involves the feeling of protection, of having a shield. The other meaning implies impending disaster or sudden disappointment. The way to distinguish what this symbol means is to determine what emotions are triggered by the sensation of having something above you.

If the dominant emotions are danger and fear, then this symbol represents jealousy or envious friends and relatives. To dream of something falling near you from above implies a narrow escape from loss, either of money or some other material possession. This symbol is also a warning to carefully watch your conduct in business matters or in personal relationships.

On the other hand, if the dominant emotions surrounding this symbol are ones of safety or protection, this symbol indicates good news and opportunities for advancement in one's affairs, both personal and career.

ABYSS: This symbol occurs in both Dreams and Meditation. It represents difficult circumstances in one's life which have resulted in an impasse. Because of personal choices, the individual feels cut off or prevented from continuing on their path due to quarrels, unresolved problems, and heavy responsibilities which have become burdens to the spirit.

If the individual visualizes a successful crossing of the "abyss", it symbolizes triumph over adversity and the successful resolution of problems. If a bridge is seen spanning the "abyss", then the individual is the recipient of divine intervention, unexpected help, and a way out of current unhappiness.

If the individual dreams of falling into an "abyss", but is not hurt, it represents a warning to be careful how they conduct themselves in business or who they choose as partners, because the partners may not be honest and may drag the individual down.

ACORNS: To see acorns in a dream or in meditation represents opportunities to plant the seeds for future achievements, success and material prosperity. However, this symbol only indicates opportunities, and if the individual is not willing to make a commitment to a goal and/or is not willing to put forth the effort needed, they will not succeed. The "acorn" is a symbol of timing, indicating that the "time is ripe" to approach those in authority who will be receptive to your ideas. For creative and artistic individuals, this symbol is a sign to "go ahead" with creative projects for if they are willing to dedicate themselves to their craft, they will receive recognition and reward.

To see oneself gathering acorns is an omen of luck and prosperity. For lovers to gather acorns or hold them in their hands represents great happiness and joy. The symbol of an "Acorn Tree" is an indicator of a life filled with contentment, abundance, good recuperative powers from any illnesses, and the attainment of wishes and dreams.

AFTERNOON: This symbol appears in both Dreams and Meditation experience and has a variety of interpretations.

A rainy, cloudy or dreary afternoon denotes a gloomy mood or an unpleasant living and/or working environment which is affecting the individual's emotional or mental health. This generally represents temporary disappointments or unpleasant conditions which can be altered by the individual's actions.

A sunny afternoon indicates pleasant circumstances and times of joy ahead for the individual. Opportunities to establish enduring and valuable friendships will arise. If there is rain and the sun is shining in the dream or meditation experience it represents coming prosperity and/or gain in business dealings.

Another important aspect to point out concerning the weather conditions involves "Fog". If you see fog in a dream or meditation it represents a need to believe more in yourself and your talents, to trust your higher self for guidance or direction.

AGATE: When an agate appears in a dream or meditation, whether in a piece of jewelry or unset, it indicates movement and advance in business matters. It also represents a steady increase in income. (see Chapter 7--Geological Symbolism for more information).

AIR: To see--feel clear or pure air in a dream or meditation is a sign of release from the influence of the ego, a letting go and letting God. The individual is ready to allow the higher forces to guide and protect them without crippling limitations. Air is a symbol of spirituality and freedom, of hope for a better life because of renewed faith and trust. Air is the element of thought and communication, in the dream state or in meditation, air represents spiritual communication with Avatars and Masters.

If the air is not clean it indicates the individual is stilling holding on to materialism, anger, and negative emotions. Unclean air is a signal to the individual to let go of the past and accept the offers of help being extended to them.

ALARM: First, the alarm heard in a dream only has significance if there are no "outside" causes. If you dream of an alarm and wake up to find its your alarm clock just disregard it. However, if the alarm you hear in a dream comes from the dream itself, it symbolizes a big change about to come into your life. It also serves as a warning to quit procrastinating about people, situations, or career moves. An alarm in a dream represents a need to pay closer attention to details in order to avoid future problems.

ALLEY: The symbol of an "alley" represents a direction taken in one's life. How that "alley" appears in a dream can reveal whether or not the direction will prove to be a good choice.

If the "alley" appears dark, dangerous or has a dead end, it indicates a bad direction for the individual's life. The direction can be changed, but some loss or delays may occur in reaching the desired goal or destination. A dark alley can also represent friends who are in actuality hidden enemies from previous lifetimes or to whom the individual owes karmic debts. A dead-end alley is a warning to think twice about one's choices before taking action.

If, on the other hand, the "alley" appears well lit, or in good condition possibly lined with trees or other living-growing forms of nature, the direction the individual has chosen to take in their life will be a prosperous one and bring honor and recognition.

ALOE PLANT: To see an aloe plant in a dream or during a meditation symbolizes compassionate healing attained from Nature's bounty. To see oneself picking an aloe leaf indicates the willingness to initiate healing for oneself or to offer healing to others in need. Planting or harvesting aloe plants symbolize great joy and changes for the better.

ALPHABET: To dream of seeing or writing the alphabet represents unexpected good news on its way or something/someone you have been waiting for will arrive causing great happiness. If you are printing the alphabet on a tablet or piece of paper it symbolizes your worries and anxieties will soon be worked out to your satisfaction. For a foreign alphabet to appear in a dream represents a mystery solved or unknown forces at work in your life which will have very good results for you.

If one or more letters of the Alphabet appear in a dream or during meditation and do not form a recognizable word, the symbolism behind the letter itself has a special meaning. Sometimes letters will be carved into a rock or above a doorway in the fashion of runes. Unless the letters you see are initials of someone or something known to you, see Chapter Two for definitions on each individual letter to decipher the hidden meaning.

ALTAR: Symbolically, an altar represents a commitment to the Creator, a willingness to be guided by Divine Forces, and a surrendering of the demands of the Ego. This symbolism holds true for dreams and for meditation experiences. To see oneself kneeling at an altar denotes the fulfillment of an important wish or desire. To see oneself building an altar indicates the laying of a firm spiritual foundation which will bring great joy and prosperity.

If the individual dreams of an altar being destroyed, either by them or others, often indicates a past-life memory where the individual's faith was severely damaged or was a victim of religious persecution. By the same token, the individual could have been involved in persecuting others on religious grounds. In this case, the individual would have to do more research on their past-life activities in order to discover which scenario fit; victim or victimizer.

AMBER: Symbolically, in dreams or meditation, "amber" represents the powerful healing energies which radiate directly from the "life-force of the Universe". To receive a gift made of amber indicates coming wealth and prosperity, a gift that has been earned because of karmic merit. To give a gift of amber symbolizes abundance for the giver and the receiver. (see chapter 7--Geological Symbolism and chapter 4---Color Symbolism for more detailed information.)

AMETHYST: Symbolically, "amethyst" is a highly spiritual gem-stone with the ability to enhance and strengthen the "third eye" and psychic gifts. Amethyst symbolizes the power to dissolve karma, to heal the wounds of accumulated karmic debts, and is considered to be a metaphysical "key" to profound wisdom. (see chapter 7---Geological Symbolism for more detailed information.)

AMULET: The symbol of an amulet represents protection and intervention from the forces of Nature. An amulet is generally made of natural materials, copper, silver, gold, wood, or leather and is set with stones of power and etched with runic symbols. An amulet calls on the deep racial memories of past lives and of cultures shrouded in the mists of antiquity. To see this symbol in a dream can activate memories of previous lives, giving clues as to the "tribe" or culture an individual once participated in.

To see oneself wearing an amulet represents energies or thought forms activated in the past which the individual is bringing with them into their present lifetime. Perhaps the amulet serves to protect them from karmic enemies or serves to keep "alive" the talents and gifts the individual once possessed in a previous life. It is important to make note of what material the amulet is made of and what designs or stones have been incorporated into it. Where the amulet is worn gives further clues as to its purpose. For example:

An amulet worn on the breast represents protection of the "heart chakra", the emotional center. This location also indicates a shield against illnesses generated by an unhealthy emotional attitude.

An amulet worn on the wrist represents energy forces being directed through the hands, either to create on an artistic level or to defend and protect those placed under the individual's care. A wrist amulet also indicates the ability to make a good living through one's hands.

An amulet worn high on the upper arm represents a warrior caste which possesses unusual strength and stamina. It also vibrates to a male energy force and can be a challenge to direct properly. Warriors for the Forces of Light wore special amulets high on their upper arms signifying their covenant with the Divine Powers of the Universe.

An amulet worn around the neck--resting on the throat represents protection from mis-speaking or misrepresenting oneself and also serves to shield the "Throat Chakra". It also grants special abilities to communicate with the animal, mineral, and human kingdoms of nature. The ability to speak with a silver tongue, to reach out and touch with words those creatures who were "untamed" or wild, was part of the gifts incorporated into this type of amulet.

An amulet worn on a belt--circling the waist serves to protect the "Solar Plexus Chakra" and the "Root Chakra". This placement of an amulet gives the ability to channel the raw energies and passions of the "Root Chakra" into constructive areas. The sexual nature is under the conscious control of the individual which frees them from animalistic tendencies.

An amulet worn on a head-band--resting on the brow, above the eyebrows activates the "third eye" or "Brow Chakra". Prophetic abilities are enhanced and the raw electric power of the universe is channeled into manifestation by the "third eye". An amulet worn here strengthens and focuses the powers activated by the "third eye". Linkage to the "super-consciousness" or "Christ Mind" is formed by an activated "Brow Chakra", granting Self-Realization and awakening the latent wisdom the individual has gathered through many, many lifetimes.

To see yourself given an amulet in a dream or meditation means a special gift from the universe whose purpose is to protect you from the destructive forces of illusion and ego.

One important point about the "powers" of amulets must be mentioned. I have given you the positive interpretation or uses for amulets, however, the special energies of amulets have been used negatively in the past, causing great destruction. Some individuals have always sought personal power and prestige, disregarding the pure purpose behind the tools they used. The karma they have accumulated as a result is very heavy and burdensome, and they serve as a lesson to others not to misuse the gifts we are given to uplift and ease the plight of our fellow creatures.

ANCESTORS: Teachers, spiritual guides and mentors often choose to take on the form of an individual's ancestor in order to reach that person and be readily accepted and their words of wisdom heeded. This guise is a non-threatening one and allows the individual to listen with an open-mind. Many times an ancestor will appear in a dream to warn the person of impending disasters or potential problems, giving that person the opportunity to make changes in order to avoid the projected difficulties.

Ancestors also appear, especially in cultures of The Far East who practice ancestral worship, to offer comfort and love to their descendants. To dream of an ancestor is to experience the continuity of life, to feel the pulse of the universe firmly fixed within one's being. Many times ancestors will come to an individual in a dream just to visit, to exchange news and keep in touch.

AMUSEMENT PARK: This symbol, usually seen in dreams rather than Meditations, represents a healthy active sex life. It represents fun and relaxation, enjoyment and adventure. To dream of being at an amusement park is an omen of increased sexual activity in relationships. Symbolically, an amusement park can also denote opportunities to indulge oneself in pleasurable pursuits.

ANGELS: This symbol represents protection and guidance. Angels are a source of help and assistance to individuals on the Earth Plane. When an individual dreams of an angel it symbolizes a change of conditions for the better with increased opportunities for advancement, it also represents success in love relationships. To see an angel entering one's home indicates coming prosperity, well-being and happiness. There are many types of angels, each assigned to a specific task.

CHERUBS OR CHERUBIM ANGELS: These angels are channels of inspiration for music, art, poetry and masterbuilders. The majority of Cathedrals built in Europe were built by men who claimed to have received visions from heaven on how to build their masterpieces.

ANGEL OF DEATH: This angel is perhaps the most feared of all the angels because of its association with death. However, the real purpose of the "angel of death" is to assist an individual in leaving behind their physical shell or body and guiding them toward the Light so that they do not become trapped in the lower astral planes. This angel comes out of love and compassion with a genuine desire to ease physical, mental, and emotional suffering.

GUARDIAN ANGEL: This angel, specifically assigned to one individual at a time, serves to guide and help the individual in unseen ways. The angel is not allowed to interfere with the individual's choices unless specifically asked to do so, but is there to offer spiritual support and comfort when needed. To see one's "guardian angel" in a dream or meditation is an omen of protection and a sign to the individual of important changes about to occur in their life, changes which may be difficult, but will result in great accomplishment.

APPLES: The symbol of ripe apples in a dream or meditation indicates the time has come for the fulfillment of one's hopes and dreams. It serves as a signal to the individual to go ahead with their plans or ideas because there will be rich rewards. If the apples are not completely ripe, it represents a period of waiting is needed before reaping the benefits the individual is entitled to. However, the waiting period will be brief, and the harvest that follows will be a bountiful one. Naturally, if the apple is rotten, it symbolizes bad choices or actions which were not in harmony with the laws of karma.

AQUAMARINE: Symbolically, whether in dreams, meditation, or otherwise, the "aquamarine" stands for hope, courage, and a sharpened intellect. This stone vibrates to the "Throat Chakra" of the body and enhances creativity and communication skills. If the individual, in a dream or meditation, "see" themselves being given an aquamarine or buying this gem-stone it represents assured happiness in love relationships and in career vocations. (see chapter 7--Geological Symbolism for more detailed information).

ARCH: To see an "arch" in a dream or meditation symbolizes recognition and distinction gained by the individual because of their commitment and persistence to a goal. An arch is the symbol for achievement and wealth which has been earned because of karmic merit. To see oneself passing under or through an arch is a sign that other people will seek advice and favors from the individual because of their elevated position and accomplishments.

ARCHANGELS: These spiritual symbols are even more powerful in their effect for they rule the actions of the lesser angels. The "archangels" work to free humankind from karmic fixation, attempting to assist us out of karmic ruts. There are several archangels, however, most people are more familiar with the four Archangels; Michael, Raphael, Gabriel, and Uriel for they are the 4 archangels frequently mentioned in religious and mythological works.

ARCHANGEL MICHAEL: He rules the element of Fire and has dominion over the Summer Season. Some of the symbols of the Archangel Michael are: a diamond, a golden flaming sword, and golden armor. To see any of these symbols or the Archangel Michael himself in dreams or meditation indicates his presence in the individual's life. Through Divine Fire, the archangel Michael seeks to burn away obstacles created by negative karma. He is permitted to do this by the Creator under the law of "grace."

ARCHANGEL RAPHAEL: He rules the element of Air and has dominion over the Fall Season. Some of the symbols of the Archangel Raphael are a white horse, a white rose, the rising sun and a sapphire. To see any of these symbols or the Archangel Raphael himself in dreams or meditations indicates his presence in the individual's life. Through the use of the Divine Whirlwind, the archangel Raphael seeks to sweep away negative energies and thoughts which serve to impede the spiritual and material progress of the individual. The archangel is permitted to do this by the Creator under the law of "grace".

ARCHANGEL GABRIEL: He rules the element of Water and has dominion over the Spring Season. Some of the symbols of the Archangel Gabriel are: a golden horn or trumpet, a red rose and a ruby. To see any of these symbols or the Archangel Gabriel himself in dreams or meditations indicates his presence in the individual's life. Through the use of Sanctified Seas, the archangel Gabriel seeks to cleanse negative emotions and fears in order to free the individual from limitations created by the ego. The archangel is permitted to do this by the Creator under the law of "grace".

ARCHANGEL URIEL: He rules the element of Earth and has dominion over the Winter Season. Some of the symbols of the Archangel Uriel are: the aurora borealis, an emerald, crystals and an upside down tree. To see any of these symbols or the Archangel Uriel himself in dreams or meditations indicates his presence in the individual's life. Through the use of the Forces of Nature, the archangel Uriel seeks to eliminate and destroy the chains of pure materialism from the spirit of humankind in order to release their real potentials. The archangel is permitted to do this by the Creator under the law of "grace".

To see any of the archangels in a dream or meditation foretells of dramatic change in one's life, change that is needed and subconsciously desired. It is not always "easy" to experience change, especially when we fight against it. However, any changes initiated by the archangels will result in a better and more fulfilled life for the individual.

ARENA: The symbol of an arena represents a place of competition and conflict, a place of victors and victims. The image of an "arena" often conjures up bits of memories from previous lifetimes. Perhaps the individual was a gladiator or martyr sentenced to die in the arena, or merely a spectator. How the participants are dressed, the climate, what country and historical era, is it a modern day arena or does it appear to be an ancient Roman structure or something similar; all of these questions must be reviewed and answered in order to uncover the symbolism it has for you personally.

If the image of the arena is of modern design then symbolically the arena represents the "game of life", especially the material business world. It is filled with struggles, fears, envy, malice, need for revenge, need for dominance or success at any cost. To see this image in a dream can indicate the individual is feeling unusual pressures in the work environment, pressures which must be addressed before physical symptoms begin to take their toll on the individual's health.

ARK: This is an esoteric image that symbolizes the spiritual "covenant" the individual has with the Creator. A covenant that can never be broken or destroyed. It represents the unalterable unity humankind has with the powerful forces of the Universe. Deep within the essence of every being is a spark of the Eternal Creator, a spark that is the heart of the unity we share with one another and with the Divine Mind.

To see an ark in a dream or meditation is to be reassured of that Divine Covenant, to know that Pure Love stands ever ready to ease our troubled hearts and minds. As a dream symbol, the image of an ark signals very special events about to take place which will have a profound effect on the individual in a positive way. The ark promises abundance both spiritually and materially.

ASCEND: To feel yourself ascending in a dream symbolizes important spiritual progress. It also represents the overcoming of obstacles and challenges through the use of ethical and spiritual principles. The sensation of ascending symbolizes triumph over one's lower nature or ego. The upward path indicates a deepening attunement with one 's Higher Self and the development of intuitional gifts .

ATTIC: (see House)

AUTOMOBILE: In a dream, if an individual sees the image of a car and it belongs to them, it represents new circumstances and important news received. To see oneself driving a car represents a healthy, active sexual nature. If the car is speeding, it symbolizes an over-active sex drive which needs to be controlled, otherwise the reputation of the individual will be in jeopardy.

AUTUMN: Symbolically, the image of Autumn represents the harvest time, a time to reap what has been sown previously. When this symbol occurs in a dream or meditation, it signifies the time has come for the individual to accept the fruits of their "labors", or in other words, to reap the seeds of karma. If the individual has sown positive seeds, worked hard towards a visualized goal, and observed the laws of karma, their achievements will reflect this and result in fulfillment. However, if the individual has been sowing negative seeds through unethical behavior, they will "reap" their negativity tenfold. The image of Autumn symbolizes the spiritual truth: "The cost of giving is receiving". What you give out, your receive tenfold in return.

AVALANCHE: To see the image of an avalanche in dreams or meditation is to feel overwhelmed by obstacles, especially if the avalanche is made up of rocks. This type of image is usually a subconscious response to the individual's overall emotional and mental state, and can indicate a lot of pressures building up which will result in an explosion unless affirmative action is taken.

If the avalanche is one of snow, it indicates the defeat of obstacles and/or individuals who seek to impede your progress. The snow element of this image promises prosperity and good fortune.

BABY: Symbolically the image of a baby represents innocence and new beginnings. To see a baby in a dream or meditation is an omen of happiness and contentment ahead for the individual. The image of a baby symbolizes that part of ourselves which is still trusting, filled with wonder at the miracles of nature and the Universe. As symbols, babies represent success in love, relationships, and even in business.

BALCONY: Metaphorically, a balcony represents going out on a limb, taking chances without being totally sure of the outcome. Depending on the overall color of the dream, being on a balcony can indicate financial gains through daring and innovative actions on the part of the individual. If the overall tone of the dream is dark and forbidding, It indicates risks which can bring great difficulties to the individual's material security.

BAPTISM: Symbolically, the image of a baptism represents the surrender of the ego to the Higher Forces, the dedication of one's life to spiritual principles. To see oneself being baptized is an indication of a rich and prosperous life filled with joy.

BAREFOOT: To be barefoot in a dream or meditation indicates a special union with the forces of nature, a oneness with the living essence of the planet. To walk barefoot on snow is a sign of spiritual purity and innocence, it is also a symbol of an important initiation on the Spiritual Path. To see oneself walking barefoot through fire symbolizes a working through of karmic debts and the acceptance of "Atonement".

BARN: The image of a barn, whether empty or full, represents certain elements of ourselves, mainly the state of our emotions. Barns are used to store things. Symbolically, a barn stores mental, emotional and physical reserves. If the barn is empty, the individual's reserves are depleted and must be "restocked" or re-energized. In other word's, the individual has been so busy "giving" or "using" up their supplies, they didn't notice or would not acknowledge the diminishing effects of their actions.

On the other hand, if the barn is full and well-stocked, the individual has been using their resources well and not depleting their energies in wasteful ways. However, if the contents of the barn are stale or beginning to rot, the individual is being too miserly with themselves or their energies and the image of the barn is warning them about the wastefulness of their lives.

On the whole, a barn is a symbol of prosperity and well-being. The condition of the barn is a good indicator of what is really going on in the individual's life under the surface.

BATHING: Metaphorically speaking, the act of bathing symbolizes a cleansing away of guilt, a rebirthing process which renews the mind and spirit. To see oneself bathing in a dream or meditation is a symbol for the preparation of new things, ideas, people and situations in one's life. The act of bathing cleanses away the old and signifies the coming of success and accomplishment. If the water used for bathing is dirty or stagnant it represents difficulty in escaping from the consequences of past actions and/or karmic debts have not been fully dealt with.

BATHROOM: Symbolically, the image of a bathroom represents the elimination of waste and unwanted influence. Similar to bathing, the bathroom indicates a cleansing process involving the body, mind and spirit.

BATTLE: To see the image of a battle in dreams or meditation can be a flash-back to a past life memory. It depends on the scene of the battle, what forces oppose one another, what uniforms or armor the participants are wearing and if the individual has the "feeling" they are viewing a scene from history.

In and of itself, the image of a battle symbolizes internal struggles between the spiritual side and ego-oriented side of our nature. It also represents the struggles which occur in daily life, in one's work, relationships, career, etc. If the image of the battle pertains to the present life-time and circumstances and the individual is participating and winning the battle, it symbolizes overcoming opposition and obstacles to one's desires.

If the tide of the battle appears to be turning against the individual, this image symbolizes circumstances as well as other people are working against the interests of the individual. Beware of risky business ventures and unorthodox relationships. These other people are generally hidden enemies from previous lifetimes to whom the individual may owe karmic debts.

BASEMENT: (see House)

BED: The image of a bed represents rest and relaxation, giving one the means to renew and restore the physical, mental, and emotional body. To some individuals, the image of a bed calls to mind more "earthy" meanings such as seduction, sexual activities, romance, etc. With these two interpretations in mind, the following explanations are offered.

To see oneself resting or relaxed in bed represents a period free from anxieties and worries. It also indicates love and security. To see oneself making a bed represents important beneficial changes and/or a new love interest which will bring much happiness and contentment.

If the individual dreams they are in bed in a room unfamiliar to them they should be prepared for unexpected visitors and enjoyable times ahead. If the bed is outside in the open air and the weather is nice, it symbolizes unexpected opportunities for advancement and improvement in the standard of living. There is an "old wives" tale that says if you dream of sitting on the edge of your own bed you will be married soon.

BEING CHASED: The image of being chased in a dream represents a subconscious desire to escape or avoid unpleasant or difficult circumstances, relationships, or situations. This image indicates the individual wants desperately to avoid any confrontations in their life and as a result can end up running away from their own potential happiness. This "feeling" can degenerate into nightmare experiences if the individual does not learn to face their problems with a positive attitude.

BIRDS: To see birds flying symbolizes prosperity and happiness in the very near future. To hear them singing indicates disagreeable circumstances will he swept away and great joy is on its way. To see a bird with beautiful feathers with brilliant coloring symbolizes a coming marriage to a loving and generous mate who will bring great happiness to the individual.

To see a bird's nest with eggs indicates money from an unexpected source. If the eggs have hatched and the baby birds are alive and healthy it symbolizes good news the individual has been waiting for which will bring success, profits and important journeys. If the nest is empty, it represents the end of a burdensome situation and the beginning of new enterprises or pursuits.

BOOK: To see the image of a book in dreams or meditation indicates hidden knowledge or secret wisdom of the ages. A book is also the symbol of the "Akashic Records". To see a book represents time to be spent in preparation for important spiritual initiations. This image can also indicate revelations concerning the individual's karmic debts and merits and what path they have chosen to take in their present incarnation. Generally, the image of a book in dreams or meditation has a meaning which is tailor-made for each individual and cannot be fully defined in simple terms. The only advice I can offer is to try to explore what the book is about, if there is any printing on the pages and what that printing has to say. A book is definitely a message-symbol from the Higher Consciousness and the Universal Mind. What it means on a personal level can only be defined on an individual basis.

BRIDGE: The symbol of a bridge represents a way to surmount any obstacles which may be preventing the individual from realizing their desires. A bridge symbolizes safe passage through difficult circumstances. It serves as a uniting force, a way for opposites to come together on neutral ground without fear. The image of a bridge indicates a compromise made with honor and dignity which prevents difficulties or blockages to achievement.

BROTHEL: The image of a brothel in dreams or meditation can indicate a fragment of a past life memory. Either the individual worked in such an establishment or was a patron. A lot would depend on the rest of the dream-content as to whether or not it was a flashback to a previous incarnation.

In symbolism, a brothel represents the overindulgence of one's sexual and physical appetites. In which case, this image would appear as a warning to curb these excesses or risk material loss and/or disgrace.

BURNING: The symbolism of burning indicates a cleansing away of that which is decayed or no longer viable. By burning away the "deadwood", new growth has the room to grow and prosper. To see your own home or that of a family member or friend burning could be a precognitive or warning dream to check out any possible fire hazards, loose wires, etc. To see burning leaves or a bonfire in a dream is a sign of overcoming the difficulties and obstacles of the past and making preparations for a prosperous future.

BUTTERFLY: This image is an ancient symbol for reincarnation and transformation from one level to another. It is a sign of spiritual initiation and represents the deathless spirit of consciousness.

To see one or more butterflies darting about in the air or around flowers represents prosperity and attainment of wishes. The airborne butterfly is also a symbol of important news. To see a beautifully marked and colored butterfly is a symbol of a lasting love relationship for the individual which will bring great happiness and joy.

CASTLES: The image of a castle is a symbol of a desire, goal or wish that is not easily attained except through determination, dedication and commitment; yet when this goal or desire is attained, it brings a deep and intense feeling of inner security and fulfillment to the individual. The distance of the castle in a dream or meditation is an indication of how close the individuals goal or desire is. Castles with red or purple/violet topped towers symbolize these desires or goals have been attained or will be in the very near future. For the individual to actually see themselves inside a castle symbolizes great success and prosperity is theirs for the asking.

The image of a castle can also be a fragment of past life memories. The entire dream content has to be analyzed in order to determine its revelations concerning previous incarnations. Where there other people in the dream? What kind of clothing did they wear? What did the surrounding countryside look like? These questions and more need answering when working with a past life memory.

CAT: In most dream books the definition given about cats is very negative. The consensus seems to be that cats represent bad luck, disasters, evil enemies, treacherous friends and ill health. I do not accept this definition at all. However, I am giving you the negative as well as the positive interpretation so you can judge for yourself what the image of a cat means to you. One of the main reasons dream interpreters have given the cat such as negative role in dreams has to do with the attitude of the Church and Witchcraft.

To the Christian Church, which burned and/or tortured victims to death on trumped up charges of blasphemy, a cat was synonymous with Witches, the Devil and Evil doings. In this context, a dream involving a cat or cats could possibly have a link to deeply buried past life memories of execution as a witch, which would naturally disturb the individual on a sub-conscious level, evoking feelings of fear and/or trepidation.

Ironically, many of the cultures of the Far East as well as the ancient Egyptians, held cats in great reverence. Cat mummies have been uncovered in royal tombs or in tombs of the nobility, a testimony to the high esteem cats were held. Symbolically, a cat represents instinctive intuition and attunement with the forces of nature. Cats are generally independent in nature and are more than capable of surviving on their own, yet they still seek the company of humankind for affection and bonding.

To see a cat in a dream or meditation is an indication of a developing link between the individual and the intuitive forces of nature. Therefore, cats, as dream symbols, represent clairvoyant and clairaudient powers bestowed as gifts upon those individuals who respect and nurture nature's children. These "psychic" powers, along with psi-talents, are tools which, when used properly, can bring great abundance, success, happiness, and spiritual growth to the individual.

CATHEDRAL: The image of a cathedral represents the "house of God" a place where "God dwells or visits". To see or enter a cathedral in a dream or meditation indicates the individual is opening themselves up to Divine Light, allowing the Creator to touch their hearts and souls. A cathedral is a source of awe and inspiration, it touches the artistic and creative spirit of humankind, urging the spirit to continue its upward spiral climb. This symbol in a dream or meditation is a good omen, especially for those involved in artistic and/or creative endeavors for it represents Divine Inspiration.

CAVE or CAVERN: Symbolically, the image of a cave or cavern represents the womb of mother earth or the "Mother Goddess". In this respect, the cave offers shelter from the hostile elements of nature. The cave is a place of safety and refuge, a source of security. Caves and caverns vibrate with a special powerful energy which comes directly from the Mother Goddess or earth mother. To see oneself enter a cave is to be filled with this special energy force, a gift of love from the earth itself. This special power enhances one's intuitive abilities, hones the latent psi-potential. It is a gift offered unconditionally, a gift to be used as the individual sees fit. In this respect, the gift of this power becomes, in itself, a spiritual initiation. The individual who resists using the negative side of this power builds positive karma and eliminates the negative debts they have accumulated. Learning how to properly use the "gifts of the spirit" is one of the highest initiations on the earth plane school.

CENTAUR: These are creatures of myths and legends who symbolize profound ancient wisdom and arcane knowledge. Centaurs are also the astrological symbol of the zodiac sign Sagittarius. Half human and half horse, the centaurs were the product of genetic experimentation by the Atlanteans and remained in bondage to them until a secret underground group composed of healers and other psi-talents helped to free them.

Centaurs are teachers, philosophers and story-tellers. They are dedicated to Universal Truth and the Logos. Their gentle and benign nature made them ideally suited to work with children and young adults. They possessed the ability to channel the kinetic energy of the young into productive positive outlets. Centaurs are also very earthy creatures, revelling in their potent sensuality and the powerful rhythm of life that flows through them.

To see a centaur in a dream or meditation can indicate a fragment of past life memories concerning a previous incarnation in Atlantis. The individual needs to explore in depth all of the symbols found in an experience in which a centaur is seen. What is the overall picture? What other symbols are there? Are there any buildings? If so, what type are they? All these questions and more need to be explored in order to reveal more details of the past-life memory.

If this symbol is not a past-life memory fragment, it represents an important spiritual teacher or mentor about to enter your life. This "teacher" will not necessarily be someone the individual can actually see or touch, it could well be a spiritual entity without physical form. But whatever the form this teacher takes, the wisdom and knowledge they offer the individual is very important in the development of their own latent intuitive abilities.

CHAINS: The symbolism is obvious with this image. Chains represent bondage or limitations. If the chains are somewhat loosely wrapped around the individual, then the bondage or limitations they experience are self-imposed and can be removed with the power of positive thinking. If the chains are tightly wrapped, the individual feels at the mercy of an uncaring universe, they feel helpless and have lost hope. Tightly wrapped chains indicate heavy burdens for the individual, burdens they have little choice in accepting. This type of image can symbolize an extremely difficult emotional and mental period in the individual's life in which they must maintain their faith and believe that eventually these obstacles will become stepping stones.

CHILDREN: Symbolically, children represent the innocent, trusting side of our natures. Children do not, as a rule, manifest avarice, cruelty or prejudice. These are learned behaviors. To see children in a dream or meditation is a sign of great prosperity, abundance and blessings. To see oneself playing with children in a dream indicates great joy and happiness, a return of hope, faith and trust. To see a man, woman and child in a dream or meditation symbolizes the Holy Trinity, or the Trinity of Divine Power.

CIRCLE: The image of a circle in a dream or meditation represents the never-ending cycle of life, it is a symbol of completion. The circle is also the symbol of the Third Chakra Center called the "Solar Plexus" Chakra. This chakra rules clear thinking, all learning and studying, decisions and personal power. Its color is Yellow. To see this symbol in a dream or meditation indicates this chakra center is being activated and energized. This "activation" will lead the individual towards completion and self-realization.

CLIFFS: To see oneself standing on a cliff in a dream or meditation indicates a major turning point in one's life, a turning point in which the future outcome is unknown. To see this image represents an important choice weighing on the individual's mind. Feelings of fear, trepidation, even exhilaration are associated with this type of an image. The colors in the dream or meditation will give an important clue as to the possible outcome of this important decision. Check carefully for any other symbols which may seem to appear randomly; they are sent as signposts.

CLOUDS: To see the clouds in the sky during a dream or meditation indicates movement in one's affairs. The winds of change are beginning to stir in the individual's life, what type of change depends on the color of the clouds and the sky itself. Big black storm clouds indicate turbulent times ahead, there could be major disgrace involving the individual's associates which could back lash if the individual is not scrupulous in their dealings. If the sun is shining despite the black clouds, the individual will emerge triumphantly from the turbulent time ahead. Fluffy white clouds also indicate changes, but with a pleasant and happy outcome.

COMET: To see the image of a comet in dreams or meditation indicates unusual and unique opportunities for achievement and distinction for the individual. Comets represent a rise in fortune and status in the eyes of the world. The symbol of a comet can be an omen of fame or notoriety, the choice of outcome depends on the ethics and spiritual maturity of the individual.

CROSS: The image of a cross represents surrender to the Will of the Higher Beings or surrender to the Will of the Creator. It is a symbol of protection and self-sacrifice. The cross is also the symbol of the Fourth Chakra referred to as the "Heart Chakra". This chakra rules growth, love and the balance between Mind, Body and Spirit. It vibrates to the color Green. To see a cross in dreams or meditation indicates that the Heart Chakra is being opened and energized by the Forces of Light. When activated, this chakra center enhances growth, the potential to love unconditionally, and helps to create a much needed sense of "Balance" within the individual.

CROSSROAD: Symbolically, the image of a crossroad represents a major turning point in one's life. There are two paths to choose from, an important decision to be made which will drastically alter the life of the individual.

However, it is important to stress that neither path is a right or wrong choice. Which ever path the individual chooses to walk will contain the experiences and situations they need to encounter in order to grow and develop. It is true that some paths are easier to walk than others, but rarely do we know before hand which path is the easiest. This symbolism in a dream or meditation occurs so that the individual can be prepared for the changes coming into their life, so that they will not be completely overwhelmed by the choices they make either consciously or sub-consciously. In some dream interpretation books, the symbol of a crossroad is considered to be a sign of impending marriage for single people.

CROWN: The image of a crown in a dream or meditation represents attainment, fulfillment of a longed-for goal or personal wish. If the crown is close by the individual or held in their hands, if symbolizes attainment in the very near future, almost immediately. The further away the crown is, the longer the individual will have to wait for their achievements to be recognized or for the realization of their hopes.

If the crown is made of flowers it signifies great joy, abundance and fulfillment in matters of the heart. If the crown is of gold or silver, it represents attainment, honor, recognition, and advancement in one's vocation, artistic or creative endeavors or in the career. If the crown has gemstones embedded in it, make note of what kind of gemstones they are and look up their meanings in chapter 7--Geological Symbolism.

To see oneself being crowned is a sign of acknowledgement from the Universe that the individual has passed an important spiritual initiation and now is ready to utilize the gifts and talents they have developed as a result of the initiation.

CRYSTAL: To see oneself being given or finding a crystal in a dream or meditation represents a gift of love from the Universe. This crystal will enhance and amplify the individual's mental abilities and their psi talents. The history and meanings of crystals are tied to the ancient epochs of human experience. For further information on what a crystal symbolizes, see Chapter 7---Geological Symbolism.

CUPS OR CHALICES: The image of a cup or chalice is an ancient symbol of the Mother Goddess and the fertility of her womb. This symbol is associated with the emotional multi-faceted element of love. Love is many things, it is spiritual, mental, physical, sensual, sexual and compassionate. The expression "my cup runneth over", refers to a love which has been experienced in all of its aspects. It is important to note what the cup or chalice is made of and what condition it is in.

If it is bent out of shape, rusty or dirty looking, it symbolizes a subconscious negativity towards love, a cynicism based on past disappoints and old hurts. This negative attitude can involve sexual relationships, commitments, familial relationships, friendships, and so on. Subconsciously, the individual has feelings of betrayal and pain associated with any type of emotional involvement. This attitude is not only self-defeating, but it is self-destructive as well. The dream has occurred in order to draw the individual's attention to this problem and the need to deal with it on a conscious level.

If the cup or chalice is well cared for, polished and in good condition, the individual's subconscious attitude towards the multi-faceted aspects of love is healthy and vibrant. That doesn't mean the individual has not experienced disappointment in love or even pain, however, those experiences have not been allowed to sour and eat away at the individual's subconscious. A gold or silver cup or chalice represents the presence of Divine Love actively affecting the individual's life in positive ways. The individual serves as a channel for this Divine Love and in so doing, will experience many wonderful benefits.

DAWN: To see the breaking of dawn in a dream or meditation is to experience a renewal or birth of new opportunities. The Dawn symbolizes a new day, another chance to achieve one's goals and desires. There is a surge of hope and a feeling of newness associated with the dawn of day which energizes us and fills us with breathless anticipation for potential possibilities. Dawn is the symbol of Divine Intervention and unexpected assistance. It is an excellent omen for achievement.

DOG: To most people, a dog represents loyalty, faithfulness, and a true companion. Dogs offer unconditional love to those individuals who choose to share their lives with these animals. Symbolically, dogs represents the tamed and civilized instincts of humankind.

Dogs are also referred to as the benign representatives of Nature, willing and even eager to render service to humans. To see a dog in a dream or meditation is an omen of happiness and joy. The color of the dog is an important indication of the message it is bringing to the individual. Please refer to Chapter 4--Color Symbolism for further details on the meanings of color.

DOLPHIN: In the ancient past, Dolphins were seen as representatives of the Divine Essence of the Sea, as messengers, guardians of the oceans, and as protectors of humankind when traveling across the water. In many cultures of ancient times, dolphins were worshipped as Immortal gods and goddesses. Dolphins symbolize freedom, playfulness, protection, and light-hearted joy. Humans, as part of the evolutionary chain, share a special relationship with dolphins who possess brains larger than our own. To see a dolphin in a dream or meditation is a wonderful sign for it represents a "guardian angel" entity watching over us, monitoring our progress, and smoothing our path in life.

DOOR: The symbolism of a door is an obvious one, it represents a new opportunity, a chance to make a major change in one's life. To see the image of a door in a dream or meditation symbolizes prosperity, abundance, and the gift of "luck". To see oneself entering a doorway indicates a big change leading to material and financial security. To see oneself in a room with many doors which are all closed indicates temporary difficulties in getting one's goal established. With this image of the closed doors, the individual is being counseled to remain patient, continue to work hard, and have faith in themselves. This is a sign of a spiritual test or initiation.

DRAGONS: These mystical and magical creatures are guardians of the planet. They serve to protect the delicate balance of nature. Their strength is without equal. In the Far East, dragons are symbols of Ancient and Arcane Wisdom, and they have the power of Transmutation and Transformation. To see Dragons in a dream or meditation heralds an initiation concerning the laws of the Universe and to be imbued with the subtle energy of the planet itself. Once an individual experiences this unique initiation, they will feel a "one-ness" or "unity" with the forces of nature. Dragons are also symbols of material and emotional prosperity, the source of their wealth is the heart of the earth itself which gives generously of its gifts to a Dragon-Initiate.

DWARF: In countless myths and legends, dwarves have always been seen as "children of the earth goddess". They lived, worked, and loved within the "body" of their nurturing mother. Dwarves know how to harvest the gifts of the planet without destroying it. They are natural conservationists, dedicated to preserving the ancient earth magic. To see a dwarf in a dream or meditation is to come into intimate contact with the flow of "earth magic", to feel the power of transformation surge through the body.

A dwarf is a symbol of good fortune and prosperity as long as love and appreciation are offered to its mother, the earth. As a good omen, a dwarf represents distinction and honor for the individual having the dream. For an individual who exploits the earth, the image of a dwarf in a dream or meditation is an ominous one. In this case, the dwarf comes to warn the individual not to commit any further abuse. If the warning is not heeded, the wheels of karma will be set into motion and the individual will reap as they have sown.

EAGLE: The image of an eagle represents nobility of spirit, determination and strength in the face of any and all obstacles. To see an eagle soaring in the sky during a dream or meditation represents opportunities for fame, wealth, recognition and the realization of one's desires. To dream of riding the back of an eagle symbolizes the successful exploration of unknown territories, both mental and physical which will bring knowledge, achievement and satisfaction to the individual. (This interpretation also applies to a meditation experience.)

EARTH QUAKE: To see scenes of an earth-quake is usually a precognitive experience. This can be a disturbing dream especially if you are not sure where it will take place or when. Many individuals, after passing certain spiritual initiations which attune them to the vibrations of the mother earth, can "feel" on a sub-conscious and super-conscious level, the subtle shifts of the planet.

If the dream of an earthquake is not precognitive in nature, it represents outside forces causing disruption in the individual's life over which they have no control. Therefore, the dream comes as a warning to prepare oneself for difficult or turbulent times ahead.

EGYPTIAN ANKH: Symbolically, the Egyptian Ankh, by its design, represents the eternal life, reincarnation, the cycles and rhythms of a Changeless Universe. It also symbolizes the sacrifice of material ambition for a more spiritually oriented path in life. To see this image in a dream or meditation can be a memory fragment from a past life in which the individual lived in ancient Egypt. Otherwise, the appearance of this symbol in a dream or meditation occurs to remind the individual of the importance of their spirituality which must not be neglected in favor of material ambition.

ELF: In myth and legends, Elves are associated with the Forests and Great Woodland areas, mountain lakes, streams and deep still forest pools are their territory. They are the guardian angels of the plant kingdom, living in harmony with their environment, nurturing and sustaining the cycles and rhythms of life within Nature's guidelines. To see an elf in a dream or meditation indicates a very important event in the individual's life which will bring great benefits and undreamed of opportunities. The Elves are a source of "earth magic", and when they appear as symbols this special magic is being put to work for the individual.

EMERALD: The symbol of an emerald in a dream or meditation is a very good omen. This gemstone represents unique healing gifts, the ability to directly tap the Core Fire of the Cosmos and channel that power where it is needed. This power can never be misused, the individual who tries to corrupt this pure source will be consumed. It is not a gift to be taken lightly nor to be treated without respect. The Emerald symbolizes Molecular Fire, and this energy has the ability to affect the molecular structure of any cell, unleashing the power of "Transmutation". (For more information on the meaning of emeralds, see Chapter 7-- Geological Symbolism.)

EVERGREEN TREE: The evergreen tree is a symbol of loyalty, friendship, strength and faithfulness. It is the highest evolved species of the plant kingdom. To see the image of an evergreen tree in a dream or meditation represents limitless potentials for happiness and prosperity. This tree also stores energy and resources which are offered with unconditional love to the individual who is wise enough to understand the gift being offered. It is a wonderful symbol to see in a dream or meditation for it promises a joy and contentment in one's life which cannot be described, it can only be experienced.

FAIRY: A creature of ancient legend and myth, the fairy is a mischievous and fun loving creature with the gift of enchantment. The fairies are guardians of the creatures of the air; birds, butterflies, etc., for they are the winged essence of the "earth mother" or Mother Goddess. They serve to bring an element of merriment into the lives of all they touch. Symbols of laughter and happiness, the fairy seeks to lighten the dark places of our minds, to sweep aside the cares which prevent us from seeing the beauty around us. To see a Fairy in dreams or meditation is a sign of contentment and indicates the burdens we may be carrying will soon be lifted from us so that we too, may dance with joy in flower filled meadows.

FEAST: To see the image of a feast in a dream or meditation is a sign of unexpected and happy surprises in store for the individual. A feast is a time of celebration, it is a symbol of rewards for past labors. To dream you are eating with others at a feast is a sign you will soon achieve the realization of an important goal or desire.

FEATHER: The image of feathers in a dream or meditation can be symbols of a past life as an American Indian. Feathers have a powerful significance in Indian rituals and ceremonies. To see many feathers in a dream or meditation represents a life which has little burdens or burdens which are easy to cope with and do not drain the spirit. Eagle feathers in a dream is a power sign representing attaintment of important goals.

For the individual to dream they are gathering feathers indicates rapid advancement and success which will lead to great joy. To see oneself wearing feathers is a sign of great honor and recognition to come. To see black feathers in a dream or meditation indicates a big change coming that will bear a special challenge for the individual to face. This challenge is neither positive or negative, the way it affects the individual depends on their previous actions or karma.

White feathers represent incredible luck which seems to always save the individual at the 11th hour of need. Red feathers symbolize the successful beginnings of new enterprises, a good start in achieving one's goals and ambitions, boundless opportunities. Brown feathers represent material success and security. Gray feathers symbolize wealth that is material, spiritual and emotional in nature. It is a wealth that goes beyond mere money. Light blue feathers or violet feathers represent the realization of desires, of hopes and dreams. Tan feathers symbolize important journeys, meetings, and messages.

FENCE: Symbolically, the image of a fence represents limitations and obstacles to be overcome. The limitations represented by this image are usually self-imposed in some way because the individual does not have faith in their own abilities or their right to happiness. Subconsciously, feelings of guilt have the ability to build fences around the spirit as a form of self-punishment or self-martyrdom.

However, if the individual climbs over the fence or cuts the fence down in their dream or meditation, it represents the overcoming of obstacles and limitations leading to ultimate victory and success.

FIRE: This element cleanses, purifies and Warms. It also consumes, destroys and reeks havoc if unchecked or uncontrolled. Fire is another symbol for the activated Kundalini or raw sexual energy. In a dream or meditation to see oneself kindling or starting a fire indicates unexpected and pleasant surprises. This image can also indicate an important and powerful sexual encounter which can cause great change in the individual's life. It may represent the beginning of a major relationship which can last a lifetime or more. Because of the nature of Fire, this relationship can seem to consume the individual at times, but it will also serve to cleanse and purify the individual as well. Sexual energy can be easily misdirected, so in essence, the individual is challenged by this "union" or love-relationship to raise it to a higher level through the proper use of the Kundalini.

FLOOD: Symbolically, the image of a flood represents a feeling of being at the mercy of an uncaring universe, of being swept up by unknown forces beyond the individual's control. This image in a dream or meditation usually indicates an unsettled state of mind which has been suppressed on a conscious level. Therefore, the subconscious mind sends the image of a flood as a way to express the pent up emotional state of the individual. This dream symbol comes as a warning to the individual to start dealing with their emotions in positive ways before it begins to take its toll on their physical well-being.

FLOWERS: The presence of flowers in general in dreams or meditation represent the bountiful gifts of Nature. They symbolize the final outcome, the "flowering" of achievement, a goal that has been reached, or the attainment of a heart's desire. Flowers are also symbols of beauty, they please the eye and other senses as well as indicating great happiness and joy. To see oneself picking or gathering flowers in a dream or meditation represents a coming union with another person, a loving commitment leading to emotional fulfillment.

FLYING: Many dream analysts equate the sensation of flying with sexual expression and orgasmic experiences. This interpretation may be valid for many people in certain dream experiences, however, it depends on the individual and the total content of the dream experience. Generally, the sensation of flying is associated with astral traveling or "out of the body" experiences. It imparts a sense of freedom to the individual, it allows them to sense their true nature which has no limitations. "Flying" in a dream or meditation allows the individual to reach other dimensions--other realities without being restricted by a solid physical body.

FOREST: Symbolically, a forest is alive, a feeling/thinking entity, pulsating with myriad forms of life, a physical manifestation of the "earth mother" or Mother Goddess. Forests are magical places, the energy patterns are intense and unique. To see oneself in a forest during a meditation or dream symbolizes prosperity, pleasure, protection and an unmistakable feeling of being loved. This feeling of love may be an omen of an important romantic union, a special mate, possibly the appearance of one's soul-mate. For people involved in artistic and creative endeavors, the image of a forest in their dreams or meditation indicates coming fame and recognition of their creations. The public will be very receptive to the individual's "work", bringing a great deal of success and real achievement into the individual's life.

FUNERAL: This is one of the most unsettling images to appear in a dream or meditation and it has the capacity to frighten, even terrify most people. However, the image of a funeral is not a sign of death or disaster. A funeral represents a "putting to rest" or "laying to rest", old conditions, situations and circumstances in the individual's life. When one experiences the ending of a difficult phase in life, subconsciously, the mind needs to "bury" the experience, to finalize and compartmentalize the emotions and attitudes associated with the experience. A funeral symbolizes the ending of an old cycle and the preparation for a new one.

To see oneself in a coffin and the object of a funeral indicates a new life or new beginning without chains and burdens from the past to limit one. To see someone else as the object of a funeral can be interpreted literally or allegorically. In other words, the influence of the person in the funeral will no longer be as active or part of the individual's life. It does not represent physical death for the person who is the object of the funeral.

Occasionally, a precognitive dream concerning the death of someone you know may occur, but this is a rare occurrence.

GARDEN: The image of a garden represents fertility, both of a physical and a creative nature. To see oneself in the midst of a flower garden in dreams or meditation symbolizes happiness and joy in one's romantic endeavors, or a union or marriage for those who are uncommitted. A bountiful garden represents increases in material prosperity and success in financial matters. To see oneself working in the garden indicates unexpected rewards or money. To see oneself walking through a beautiful garden with another person of the opposite sex is a definite omen of love and marriage in the near future. A neglected or barren garden represents struggles or difficulties ahead in the future, however, if the individual works hard to sow the right seeds, they can avoid these problems.

GATEWAY: To see the image of a gate or gateway in a dream or meditation indicates an important change in the individual's life which will have far-reaching consequences. Gates also symbolize decisions, choices to be made, opportunities being offered. Gateways are the symbols of adventure, a new frontier, a chance to explore and experience new things, people, and situations. However, the individual does not have to accept these changes, they have the option to close the gate, and remain at their present level.

GIFT: Symbolically, to receive a gift in a dream or meditation is to reap the ripened seeds of karmic merit or "good" karma. This gift will bring good luck, abundance, success, happiness, joy and love into the individual's life. To see oneself receiving a gift in a dream or meditation indicates a proposal of love and marriage in the near future. Receiving gifts in a dream or meditation is a wonderful omen for good. To see yourself giving a gift to another indicates a generous, loving nature which will be rewarded in turn. To dream of giving to others symbolizes the realization of one's hopes and desires for what you give, you receive tenfold in return, but not necessarily from the source you give to.

GLASS: This is an ancient symbol for good luck, prosperity, and good news. Glass also symbolizes protection from the lower astral forces and from unseen enemies or those who wish to bring disgrace or bring about the downfall of the individual. To see glass or hold glass in a dream or meditation indicates a transfer of knowledge to the individual concerning the effects of karma and universal laws on the inhabitants of the earth plane. Glass is used to represent spiritual teachings and arcane wisdom.

To see oneself breaking a glass object indicates possible actions or choices which are not very wise and could bring problems and/or difficulties at a later date.

GOLD: To see gold in a dream or meditation is a symbol of spiritual power and strength. Gold represents rewards from the Universe due to "grace". Gold objects symbolize abundance, success and prosperity. (For more information on the meaning of Gold see Chapter 4 Color Symbolism.)

HALL: The image of a hall or corridor represents the passageway from the physical earth plane to other dimensions and to the astral realms. This is a common symbol in both dreams and meditation. If the hall or corridor is dark or dimly lit, it indicates exploration of the lower astral realms which is not always a pleasant experience. If the hall or corridor is well lit or has a bright white/blue/violet light at the end, it indicates exploration of the higher realms and other dimensions or realities. The bright light promises protection and guidance during the individual's "journey".

HARVEST: Obviously, the image of a harvest is symbolically related to the law of karma: "as you sow, so shall you reap." To see oneself harvesting alone in a dream or meditation indicates steady and sure progress based on the individual's own efforts. They will achieve success entirely on their own merit. To see oneself harvesting with others in a dream or meditation indicates prosperity, fruitfulness, and abundance which comes from a cooperative effort. In other words, the individual will succeed in their endeavors through the assistance of loving friends and important or powerful people who believe in the individual's vision. If the harvest itself is not very bountiful, it indicates small successes and much work that still needs to be done in order for the individual to succeed in their aims.

HAWK: The image of a hawk is considered to be a power symbol for many American Indian tribes and for the ancient Egyptians. The hawk is a hunter, strong, intelligent, determined and very successful in its ability to provide for itself and its family. To see a hawk in a dream or meditation indicates the individual possesses many of this bird's qualities. The hawk can also represent a past life memory fragment of ancient Egypt or a previous lifetime as an American Indian.

Traditionally, the symbol of a hawk represents victory and triumph in personal and professional affairs. It is an indication of productive results which will bring the individual recognition and financial security.

HEAVEN: The image of heaven is a very personal and individualistic experience. No two visions of "heaven" are the same, nor should they be. Heaven represents the ultimate attainment, the ultimate destination which results in a total union with the Creator. Therefore, the image of heaven in a dream or meditation is an experience to be treasured because it represents the active--loving presence of Divine Forces in one's life. Forces which seek to bring joy, happiness and contentment to the individual.

HELL: As with the image of heaven, the image of hell is a very personal and individualistic experience. To the ancient scholars, the concept of "hell" represented the lower astral realms where the newly dead resided as well as "souls" who refused to let go of the earth plane. Sometimes when an individual sees the image of "hell" in a dream, they are astral traveling in their sleep and have not taken the proper precautions to protect themselves from being drawn into the lower astral realms. When an individual has a dream experience of "hell" it indicates the misuse of "psychic" gifts which gives off negative energy that attracts the inhabitants of the lower astral planes.

HERMIT: To see the image of a hermit in dreams or meditation is a symbol of a spiritual teacher or angelic entity who has come to offer the individual special wisdom and guidance. The presence of a hermit in one's dreams indicates opportunities to learn and grow which will have direct and beneficial effects on the individual's life circumstances. It would be a good idea for the individual to heed the messages the hermit has to offer because they will serve to greatly aid the individual in achieving their goals.

HOSPITAL: Symbolically, a hospital represents a place to be healed physically, emotionally, mentally and spiritually. To see a hospital in a dream or meditation indicates a need for personal healing, a need to slow down and take a rest from the frantic activity of everyday life. The symbol of a hospital is a message from the individual's super-consciousness indicating a need to change the pace of their life in order to avoid potential problems and stress which could easily lead to physical illnesses.

Occasionally, the image of a hospital in a dream can be precognitive in nature. If this is the case, the individual will have to use their own "intuitive" feelings for the proper guidance.

HOUSE: The symbol of a House represents the mind, or more specifically, our three states of consciousness: the basement of a house represents the sub-conscious, the first or main floor of the house is the conscious mind, the attic represents the super conscious mind.

In a dream or meditation experience which involves the image of a house, it is important to determine what condition it is in. If the individual visualizes themselves entering the basement of the house, it represents confronting or examination of the contents of the sub-conscious mind. If the basement is dark, cluttered with junk or debris and creates feelings of trepidation, it signifies many sub-conscious fears which work to undermine the conscious efforts of the individual.

Usually when an individual sees the first floor or main floor of the house it contains furniture and other home-like decorations. Since the first floor represents the conscious mind, the items seen on this floor represent thoughts, ideas, people, situations, etc., which the individual deals with on a conscious level, usually on a daily basis. If the main floor of the house is too crowded with furniture, it symbolizes a life which has become too "cluttered" with details and needs some re-evaluation.

The next floor or the Attic represents the super-consciousness, that part of our minds which has links to the Universal Mind and to the Creator. To see an attic symbolizes the exploration of one's super-conscious. If the attic is stuffy, has little light and is dark, it represents a super-consciousness which has not been developed. If the attic is large and roomy, with windows letting in the light, it represents a super-consciousness which has established its links to the Universal Mind and therefore, is able to channel inspiration and guidance from the Creator to the conscious mind.

ICE: Symbolically, ice represents a frozen state, a state of suspended animation, nothing is moving, going forward or backward. In this respect, Ice symbolizes limitations, usually self-imposed. Since Ice is composed of the element Water and Water symbolizes the emotions, the image of ice in a dream or meditation is a strong indication of frozen emotions. The individual is not dealing with their emotions, instead they have chosen to bottle them up and compartmentalize them, sealing the emotions off so the individual does not have to confront them.

INSECT: The image of insects in a dream or meditation is a symbol of industry, hard work and cooperative effort. This image sends a message to the individual that by working with others rather than against them or in competition with them, the individual will achieve a much greater success and in a shorter period of time than if they wasted their energy and effort fighting against other people. However, if the individual dreams of insects attacking their garden or fields, it indicates outside forces seeking to undermine the individual's hard work.

JEWELS OR GEMS: The image of jewels or gems in a dream or meditation represent qualities or "talents" an individual possesses. They represent treasures of the soul, rewards an individual has earned through karmic merit, (the sowing of good deeds). If the jewels or gems are taken away from the individual in a dream, it indicates the misuse of talents and abilities. If they are stolen from the individual by a thief, it represents a warning to be more diligent or careful about the people the individual chooses to be intimate with. For more details on the meanings of jewels or gems, see chapter 7---Geological Symbolism.

JURY: The image of a jury in a dream or meditation is a symbol of karmic review by one's spiritual teachers and mentors. Usually, the individual is undergoing a point by point examination of their actions and choices while being counseled on the karmic effect these actions have had. This type of "karmic review" happens every time the individual is ready to make another upward step or initiation on their spiritual path of evolution.

KEYS: The image of a key or keys in a dream or meditation represents the "tools" or knowledge the individual needs in order to achieve their goals. The key serves to "unlock" the door of opportunity, to "free" one from limitations. The symbol of a key is a gift to the individual from the Universe. What the individual chooses to do with that key is up to them.

KISS: To feel a Kiss on one's forehead or cheek during a dream or meditation is a sign of approval and acceptance from one's spiritual mentor or "angel". This "experience" is a message to the individual that they are doing well on their spiritual path. To see oneself kissing another person in a dream indicates coming success and happiness that the individual will want to share. Sometimes the experience of a "kiss" in a dream is a sign of an exciting romantic relationship about to enter the individual's life, a relationship the individual is ready for.

KITTEN: The image of a kitten in dreams or meditation has the same connotation as a cat, however, a kitten is a more youthful manifestation of this energy force and needs time to mature and develop discipline. Kittens are playful, mischievous and very much involved in the "here and now". To see a kitten in a dream or meditation indicates the individual is in the beginning stages of a growth and learning process, a time of adventure and exploration which will lead to mature talents and abilities. A kitten is a symbol of learning through play and experience. It is an excellent omen of happiness and fun.

LABYRINTH OR MAZE: The image of a labyrinth or maze in a dream or meditation symbolizes a state of confusion, the individual's life has become extremely complex. Situations, people and circumstances all seem to come together to create a chaotic state of which the individual has little idea on how to proceed. Labyrinths or mazes are symbols of puzzles, of mysteries which need to be solved. This image in a dream also indicates surprises, some which are not pleasant, and some which are. This type of image is a sign from the subconscious mind, revealing the internal stress it is experiencing.

However, if the individual dreams of a labyrinth or maze which is made of green plants, flowering shrubs, and vines, it symbolizes unexpected advancement and success arising out of a situation which seemed hopeless.

LAKE: The image of a lake symbolizes the subconscious mind and the element of Water which rules the emotions. If the lake in the dream or meditation is clean, it represents success and achievement for the individual in whatever endeavor they are undertaking. It is a good omen for business, financial affairs and artistic and creative projects. If the lake appears muddy or discolored, it signifies delay in achieving one's goals. If the lake is calm, smooth and reflects the rich color of the sky, it is a sign of happiness in love.

LIBRARY: The image of a library in a dream or meditation symbolizes the "Akashic Records". To see oneself inside a library represents the ability to tap into the stored knowledge and wisdom of the Akashic Records. This image also indicates unexpected help and assistance from spiritual teachers or mentors. A library in a dream or meditation indicates rapid advancement of one's goals and desires. It is a positive sign of achievement.

LILIES: These flowers are symbols for "inner" hearing, the ability to hear "voices" of teachers from the higher astral realms. Lilies are also symbols of purity and resurrection and they also represent gifts of the soul. To see lilies in a dream or meditation is a sign that happiness and contentment will come into the individual's life very soon.

LOTUS: The real origins of this symbol is shrouded in the mists of antiquity, mists what reach back through time and space to the Age of the Lemurians. In recent millennium, the symbol of the Lotus Flower has been used by Tibetan monks for thousands of years. In the religions of the Far East, the Lotus is considered to be a symbol of "Nirvana", and represents the 7th Chakra Center or "Crown Chakra". The Crown Chakra vibrates to the color Violet.

The Lotus represents spiritual perfection--growth and Unity with the God-head, the primeval force of the Universe. This flower is considered to be the symbol of Self-Realization and is a source of powerful creative inspiration. To see this symbol in a dream or meditation is to be touched by this powerful force, to become one with the Universal Mind.

MASK: The image of a mask in dreams or meditation is a warning of possible deceit by those the individual trusts. A mask is a symbol of concealment, a means to hide Truth from others. If the individual sees themselves wearing a mask in a dream indicates they should be very careful to be honest and above-board in all of their dealings, whether it is in business or on a personal level. The image of a mask represents the temptation to take the easy way out, a temptation the individual is being warned to resist.

MOON: The image of the Moon in a dream or meditation is a symbol of the Mother Goddess. The Moon represents the feminine principle or energy force of the universe. The Moon also symbolizes the Universal Subconscious Mind, a consciousness that deals in the complex range of emotional responses. Dreams and visions are ruled by the influence of the Moon which has the capability of tapping or triggering latent psychic or intuitive gifts.

A brightly shining moon in a dream or meditation represents good luck and success in love affairs and relationships. To see oneself bathed in moonlight indicates unusual assistance and favors from important or prominent women. The moon as an image in dreams or meditation is a symbol of growing feminine power, a power that operates on a covert level rather than in a blatant manner.

CRESCENT MOON: The symbol of a Crescent Moon is used to represent the Fifth Chakra Center or "Throat Chakra". This Chakra Center rules communication, self-expression, creativity, and healing. It vibrates to the color Sky Blue. The Crescent Moon is a sign of steady increases, the climb to success and achievement.

FULL MOON: The symbol of a Full Moon is used to represent the fertility of women and nature. It is a sign of intense enjoyment and a stimulated sexual drive. The Kundalini is more active under the influence of a Full Moon which is why ancient cultures practiced fertility rites under a Full Moon.

MOUNTAIN: The image of a mountain in dreams or meditation symbolizes a challenge, not an obstacle or difficulties, but a training ground on which the individual is allowed to exercise and develop their natural talents and abilities. A mountain is a symbol of achievement, of attaining a long-cherished goal. To see a tall mountain with snow-capped peaks in a dream or meditation indicates an opportunity to succeed beyond the individual's wildest dreams if they are willing to accept the challenge.

OAK TREE: The image of an oak tree in a dream or meditation symbolizes great prosperity and abundance now and in the future. The Oak tree is a symbol of strength, honor, integrity, endurance and personal power. To see oneself sitting under an oak tree in a dream or meditation indicates a happy life with much contentment and joy. If the oak tree has acorns on it or on the ground, it is an indication of unexpected gifts and promotion in the world. Acorns are also the symbols of the fruit of one's labor.

OCEAN: The image of an ocean represents the vast collective Unconscious Mind of the Cosmos or the Universal Mind. It is here, in the collective unconscious, that the memories of all lifetimes, past, present and future, are to be found. The ocean is a source of limitless prosperity and abundance, it is never empty of gifts and is constantly renewed by Universal Forces. To see a rough or stormy ocean in a dream or meditation is an indication of struggles caused by hidden enemies from former lifetimes. However, once the balance of karma has been satisfied, the ocean promises restoration and achievement. To see a calm ocean with moderate waves in a dream or meditation is an indication of fascinating adventures and good fortune in personal and business affairs.

OWL: In the ancient cultures, an Owl was the symbol of the goddess Athena, the goddess of Wisdom. The goddess Athena was also a protector of women and ruled the defensive side of war. To see an owl in a dream or meditation is an indication of an important message or letter which the individual can use to their advantage. The image of an owl in dreams is also a sign of protection from the "Mother Goddess" aspect of the Creator.

PALACE: Generally, the image of a palace in dreams or meditation is a fragment of a past life memory. How the individual "feels" about this palace will give important clues as to what type of past-life associations they may have had with a palace and what era in history this experience took place. If the individual "feels" no ties to previous lifetimes with this image, then the symbol of the palace is a warning to avoid temptations and to avoid people who choose to waste their time and talents pursuing constant pleasure.

PALM TREE: The image of a palm tree calls to mind visions of tranquil south sea islands where the living is easy and unhurried. Therefore, the symbol of a palm tree in a dream or meditation indicates a need to relax and step aside from the frantic pace of the material world. The individual is subconsciously feeling the effects of a stressful lifestyle and would benefit greatly from a "time-out". It is important to pay attention to these subtle messages or symbols the subconscious sends us for, if we do not, we pay for it in physical, emotional and mental distress which can lead to major health problems in the future.

PEACOCK: There are a lot of legends and myths surrounding the peacock;

some are beautiful stories, some are quite negative. In some cultures, a peacock or its feathers are considered to be omens of good luck in business and love. In other cultures, a peacock is considered to be a sign of avarice, conceit and jealousy. When you see the image of a peacock in a dream or meditation, it is very important that you stop and think what a peacock means to you personally. If your culture teaches you peacocks are negative symbols, then consider the dream experience as a warning you are involved with people who could lead you astray or who are living a lifestyle devoted to frivolity. If, on the other hand, your culture teaches you that peacocks are positive symbols, the consider the this image to be a sign of riches and completed ambition.

If you are not culturally indoctrinated toward either direction, then consider this; The colors of a peacock's feathers are emerald green, royal blue, indigo, gold, golden brown or copper. These are colors which vibrate on a highly spiritual level and they represent self-realization and achievement. (For more information on the meaning of color see Chapter 4---Color Symbolism.)

PEGASUS: The image of a winged horse, or "pegasus" is a symbol of artistic and creative freedom. The winged horse is an ancient symbol for the active imagination, a powerful tool of the mind. Without imagination the human race would not have evolved as far as it has. Imagination is an essential ingredient to success and fulfillment. To see "pegasus" in a dream or meditation represents a flow of creative inspiration which can be utilized by the individual to their advantage. To see oneself riding "pegasus" in a dream or meditation is a signal from the Universal Mind to open oneself up and channel this powerful energy into some form of artistic or creative manifestation. Write that book, paint that painting, create that sculpture, compose some music, write a song, poem, or story, design a house or clothes, stop saying no to your own talents, remove negative programing, let loose and create!

PENTACLE: A pentacle is a circle with a pentagram, (five-pointed star), in the middle. It is an ancient symbol of the Mother Goddess and Her arcane powers. Pentacles are feminine in nature, depicting Unity with the forces of the Earth Plane and an attunement with Nature. In the Tarot, Pentacles are one of the Minor Arcana suits which represents the element of Earth.

To see a pentacle in a dream or meditation indicates action in one's material affairs. This refers to business, career, and financial matters. The key to interpreting the meaning of a pentacle in a dream or meditation lies in the "number" of pentacles you see. Using the basic information on numerology provided in this book, look up the number and read its meaning. Then apply the definition of that number to your material concerns, such as business or career.

PHOENIX: This mystical bird is a symbol of Resurrection, Rebirth and Eternal Life. The legend of the phoenix says this bird arises from the ashes of its own funeral pyre, renewed, cleansed and purified. To see a phoenix in one's dreams or meditation indicates an initiation of Divine Fire, a fire which cleanses the spirit and renews the soul. The phoenix is a symbol of wonderful potentials for the individual, whether they utilize these potentials is part of their initiation.

PIT: The image of a pit in a dream or meditation indicates subconscious problems with an important decision. The individual is unsure of the results their decision or choice will create and an element of fear has manifested itself. A pit symbolizes failure or what seems to be insurmountable obstacles and problems. It indicates a great deal of risk associated with the decision the individual must make. Sometimes this decision can concern a relationship and commitment, sometimes this symbol will refer to decisions in business, finances, even partnerships that the individual is not sure of and therefore is worried about the outcome.

POLICE: Depending on your personal feelings towards policemen and women, the image of a police officer in dreams or meditation generally represent one's "guardian" angel or spiritual mentor. A police person, whether male or female, represents an authority figure and protection. To see a policeman or woman in a dream indicates turbulent times ahead in which the individual will need guidance and assistance from the Universal Mind. It does not necessarily represent tragedy or negative experiences. It represents a time of dramatic change which will affect the individual's sense of stability.

POPPY: This flower is a symbol of bad habits formed in previous lifetimes which may surface on the subconscious level in the present incarnation. The poppy appears in a dream or meditation as a warning against addictive behaviors, it is a sign the individual will feel a strong temptation to indulge in this negative side of their personality. By addictive behaviors I am referring to drugs, alcohol, gambling, even sex.

PRECIPICE: (see Cliffs)

PREGNANT: The image of pregnancy in a dream or meditation can refer to actual child birth or of being pregnant with "ideas" or creative talents. Pregnancy indicates fruitfulness and fertility. The time is right to "give birth" to artistic and creative ideas or projects, the right people will be ready to assist the individual in the manifestation of their creative endeavors. The right doors will open, the opportunities for recognition and achievement will be provided for the individual.

PRIEST: The interpretation of this symbol depends on what kind of priest is seen in a dream or meditation. If the priest is obviously of Christian orientation, such as Catholic, Episcopalian, Greek or Russian Orthodox, the interpretation depends largely on how the individual feels about priests in general. If they feel negative or intimidated by a priest, it indicates disapproval of the individual's actions or choices.

However, if the image of the priest is not of Christian orientation, it indicates subconscious "ties" to religions or belief systems which are nature oriented. The image of a priest can also be a fragment of a past life memory in which the individual participated in rituals celebrating the forces of nature. Or, depending upon the content of the dream, the past life memory could be about a very brutal religion like what the Aztecs practiced. The individual may have been a sacrificial victim or the priest who committed human sacrifices.

PRIESTESS: The image of a priestess in dreams or meditation calls upon memories of past lifetimes in which the individual was initiated or dedicated to the Mother Goddess. In the earlier epochs of human culture, especially in the Lemurian Civilization and to some extent the Atlantean Civilization, (in the very early stages of development), worshipped the feminine aspect of the Creator whom they called the Mother Goddess. Women were the main source of spiritual guidance because of their attunement to the cycles of nature, cycles their own bodies obeyed.

To see the image of a priestess in dreams or meditation symbolizes an attunement to Nature and the rhythms of the Universe. Quite possibly, the individual was once a priestess who served her people and her "Mother" through healing, nurturing and teaching. These qualities or abilities are still present in the individual in their present lifetime regardless of their sex. Therefore, the message of the priestess is to develop and utilize one's intuitive talents and healing abilities to their fullest potential. The world has need of them.

PUPPY: The image of a puppy in a dream or meditation has the same connotation as a dog, however, a puppy is more youthful manifestation and needs time to grow and develop discipline. The symbol of a puppy indicates a lack of maturity, which is not a negative image at all. Therefore, a puppy merely represents the process of growing and learning, of youthful zest and energy, and a precious gift of joyousness.

PYRAMIDS: The image of a pyramid in dreams or meditation symbolizes a storehouse of secret ancient and arcane wisdom which is available to the individual. To see oneself entering a pyramid in a dream or meditation is a sign of success and prosperity. The pyramid represents the mysterious and ancient civilizations of Egypt, Atlantis, and Lemuria. They represent the mysteries of life and the universe. Pyramids are considered to be energy collectors and this energy can be used in unique ways, such as regenerating living tissue and activating the Intuitional Mind.

QUICKSAND: The image of quicksand in a dream or meditation is a symbol of distractions and temptations created by the Earth Plane and the Ego. It is a warning to beware of Illusions, to be careful not to get suckered into situations or commitments that will lead to misfortune and disgrace. This is a strong message from the super-conscious to be wary of people posing as friends who seek your downfall or who seek to deceive you for their own purposes.

RAIN: Symbolically, rain is a blessing, a benediction from the Creator because it nurtures and renews the earth and the lifeforms which abide on it. Rain is a symbol of cleansing, of washing away that which is no longer needed in order to prepare the way for abundance and fruitfulness. Without rain the crops will not grow, nor would trees, flowers, or other plants. Our lakes, streams and rivers are revitalized by rain. Therefore, rain also represents an energy force which inspires growth and prosperity.

However, uncontrolled rain such as a storm with lightning and/or hail, indicates difficult changes ahead. If the individual's goals in life have been based on personal greed and the methods they have used to achieve these goals have not been ethical, the image of a violent rain storm in a dream or meditation is a clear warning of karmic retribution, a violent upheaval which will cleanse away the individual's achievements.

To see a brief rain-shower while the sun is still shining in a dream or mediation represents the realization of one's wish or hopes. To "see" or "feel" a brief rain while walking in a forest or garden in a dream or meditation is a symbol of unexpected gifts or opportunities.

RAINBOWS: The image of a rainbow is a symbol of Divine Intervention and Divine Protection. Rainbows are harbingers of good-luck, happiness, and prosperity. Biblically, rainbows are the symbol of the Covenant God made with the creatures of the earth after the great flood, symbolizing His promise never to unleash his anger on the planet in that way again.

To see a rainbow in a dream or meditation represents important changes for the better, it is a blessing to you from the Universe. To be in love and see a rainbow in one's dreams or meditation is a sign of assured happiness and joy in the relationship. It is also a symbol of commitment and marriage to those individuals who are not already married. If the individual is married and sees a rainbow in their dreams it indicates a deepening joy and contentment through the years.

RING: The image of a ring, (which is, in essence, a circle), is a symbol of completion and commitment to a greater whole. A gold ring is symbolic of Solar Power or "Star" energy, it is a masculine energy. A silver ring is symbolic of Lunar Power or "Earth" energy, it is a feminine energy. Receiving a ring as a gift in a dream or meditation indicates a gift of power from the Universe for the individual to use in the best way possible. If the ring has one or more gem stones or precious stones, refer to Chapter 7--Geological Symbolism for information on the stone.

RIVER: Symbolically, a river represents the many streams of consciousness found in the universe. It is a sign of inspiration and the "psychic" senses or talents. Rivers are emotional and mental roads for the mind. They represent paths an individual can take in life. These river paths can indicate emotional commitments, relationships, or feelings about life. One has the power to choose how to respond on an emotional level. A winding river in a dream or meditation symbolizes a life path with many turns and changes. A swiftly moving river is an indication of a life which is continually active. Pay attention to the color of the river, the color can give you more information on the circumstances your life has created.

ROSES: The image of a rose in a dream or meditation is a symbol of devotion, joy, and happiness. To smell a rose in a dream or meditation is a sign of good news, important news which can change the life of the individual. Roses are considered to be symbols of Divine Healing and Forgiveness. It is a fact that rose hips contain Vitamin C, one of the most important elements the physical body needs to maintain good health.

RED ROSE: A red rose is a symbol of desires, hopes and wishes. It also represents selfless sacrifice and a willingness to surrender to the Will of the Higher Forces.

WHITE ROSE: A white rose is a symbol of desires which have been purified through a union with the Creator or Universal Mind. It is also a symbol of purity. The chains of the ego have been severed.

BLUE ROSE: A blue rose symbolizes the impossible dream. It also represents the creative nature seeking manifestation, the individual has the gift to inspire others, to communicate on many different levels. A blue rose is used to symbolize soul grace.

GOLD ROSE: A golden rose symbolizes the attainment of the impossible dream. It is a sign of achievement and accomplishment. The gifts of the spirit have been channeled into positive manifestation.

BLACK ROSE: A black rose is used to symbolize the blood-ties to the ancient "Wicca" religion. It represents one of the highest spiritual initiations of the earth plane. Black roses are a gift from the Mother Goddess to those individuals who show an unusual affinity and attunement with the forces of Nature. To receive a black rose in a dream is a sign of prophetic powers being bestowed upon the individual.

   If you see any other color of rose in a dream or meditation, please refer to the definitions on color in Chapter 4--Color Symbolism for more information. If the rose you see in a dream or meditation is withered or dying, it indicates an absence of hope or disappointment.

SACK: The image of a sack or satchel in a dream or meditation represents the "gifts" of the Intuitional Mind and the memories of previous lifetimes. To see a sack or satchel in a dream symbolizes luck and prosperity created by the individual's own talents and abilities, fortune smiles upon them. To see oneself filling a sack is a strong indication of material gain and abundance.

SATAN *(a.k.a. Lucifer or the Devil)*: The image of the devil or satan in a dream or meditation symbolizes obsession with the earth plane. It is a sign of temptations and illusions. The individual may be too immersed in materialism and is neglecting their spirituality. The image of satan or the devil appears in dreams or meditation as a warning to the individual not to have a closed mind or to be judgmental with others. This symbol is not a sign of death or disaster, it appears in order to jolt the individual back into "awareness".

SATYR: The image of the mythical satyr is a symbol of fertility and an extremely active Kundalini Force. To see a satyr in a dream or meditation is an indication the individual's sexuality and sensuality has been rising, demanding an outlet for its energy. If the individual wishes to get pregnant or impregnate another, the image of a satyr indicates the realization of this aim. For some people, the image of a satyr in their dreams has been a positive sign that they were the object of someone else's sexual desire. The appearance of a satyr in dreams or meditation serves as a warning not to allow one's sexual appetites or "needs" rule them.

SCEPTER: The image of a scepter in dreams or meditation is a symbol of power and responsibility. Through this symbolism, the individual is being singled out for a position of leadership which will bring them honor and recognition. To see the image of a gold scepter in dreams or meditation indicates a position of power and influence as a figure of authority. This leadership position could be in business or in politics. The image of a silver scepter in dreams or meditation indicates power and influence used behind the scenes in subtle but dramatic ways and is often referred to as the "power behind the throne" syndrome.

The image of a crystal scepter in dreams or meditation is a symbol of trust and great power channeled from the Universe. The individual is being given the heavy and important responsibility of using astral forces in positive and beneficial ways on the physical earth plane. A crystal scepter is also a symbol of a High Initiate, one who has been a High Priest or Priestess in another lifetime, a lifetime in which they served the Creator with honor, respect and faithfulness. Because of the dedication the individual possessed in that previous lifetime, the talents and abilities they developed are still with them, waiting to be tapped. The crystal scepter is the conduit or signal to "awaken" and "revive" those abilities.

SCHOOL: The image of a school in dreams or meditation represents a place of learning, of gathering knowledge. This image generally appears in "teaching" dreams when the individual is being counseled and given instructions concerning their life on the physical earth plane. An "astral" school is a symbol of wisdom and the exchange of ideas. It serves to inspire and guide the individual in their everyday life as well as during the major points of change and choice.

SEA: (see Ocean)

SEASONS: There are four Seasons: Spring, Summer, Fall and Winter. Each season represents or embodies certain symbolic elements. Spring symbolizes new beginnings, the sowing of seeds or the sowing of karma. Springtime lays the foundations for future achievements and honor. Summer symbolizes a time of rejoicing and renewed commitment. Patience and nurturing will culminate in abundance during this season. Some of the "seeds" sown in the spring will be ready for "reaping" in the Summer. These seeds can be ideas, proposals, choices, actions taken, partnerships, etc.

The Fall season symbolizes accomplishment, fulfillment, and reward. This is the time to "harvest" all the results of previous plans and endeavors. Fall represents the natural outcome of what has been sown in the past. Winter is the season of rest, relaxing and contentment. The time has come enjoy the fruits of one's labor. Winter is also a time of preparation for a new cycle, a time to "recharge" one's energy. As you can see, the time of season in a dream or meditation gives important clues that contribute to defining the meaning behind a dream or meditation experience.

SEEDS: The image of seeds in a dream or meditation represents a time of "sowing" or planting karma. This can be good or bad karma. Seeds symbolize a time of industry and work towards one's goals or aims in life. Opportunities will arise for advancement, the individual is being guided to prepare for future prosperity, success, recognition and abundance. Because seeds represent beginnings, it is very important that the individual "plant" the right seeds so that the harvest they reap will be a sweet one. The final outcome depends on the individual's integrity and honor, after all, the Universe has given the individual the chance to succeed, the rest depends on the way they utilize these opportunities.

SERPENT: The image of a serpent is a symbol for the Kundalini Force which lies coiled three and a half times at the base of the spine, the "root" Chakra. The Kundalini is the raw unchanneled creative force or power which must be directed by the Higher Mind. If it is not, the unchanneled Kundalini activates the sexual and physical appetites to a fever pitch. The desire nature must be controlled and channeled up through the Chakra Centers by the individual.

Serpents are also very ancient symbols of secret wisdom, a wisdom which is dangerous in the wrong hands or if used improperly. The type of secret knowledge embodied by the serpent symbol can devour the person who does not know how to use it. It would be like putting the secrets of nuclear power in the hands of primitive or fanatical people.

Serpents or snakes have also been used as ancient symbols of the healing arts.

SHIP: The image of a ship in dreams or meditations symbolizes hopes, wishes and desires we have sent out into the Universe. A ship is a sign of prosperity and realization. To see oneself on board a ship symbolizes the individual is in control of their own destiny or "life circumstances" and has the power and ability to make manifest their goals in life. If the sea is rough, it indicates some obstacles which are really challenges to the individual's ingenuity. To see a ship coming to dock is a sign of good news, of opportunities the individual has been waiting for.

SIX-POINTED STAR: The symbol of a six pointed star is more commonly known in esoteric circles as the "Seal of Solomon". This symbol has also been referred to as "The Star of David", an emblem representing the Jewish Faith. It is considered to be a symbol of great power, a key to ancient hidden knowledge. Esoterically, the six-pointed star symbolizes the perfect blending of matter and spirit. It is a marriage or union between the emotional and mental elements. The image of a six-pointed star shows the polarity between masculine and feminine energy and how both energies magnetize the other.

The six-pointed star is also used to symbolize the Sixth Chakra Center or "Brow Chakra." This chakra center rules intuition, ESP, higher comprehension, and releasing. It vibrates to the color Indigo or Purple. To see this symbol in a dream or meditation signifies the opening and energizing of the Brow Chakra. When the Brow Chakra is activated, the "third eye" becomes open and focused. The "Third Eye" is used to see through veils of illusion, to penetrate the astral realms and to processes non-physical visions.

SILVER: The color of silver in a dream or meditation symbolizes the feminine energies of the Universe. Silver deals with the Hidden Intuitional nature of humankind. To see oneself wearing silver clothes in a dream or meditation indicates good fortune and happiness. Silver is the metal and color of the nurturing Mother Goddess. It is a mystical ore that has the ability to protect the wearer from negative influences of the night. To find silver in a dream or meditation indicates prosperity and luck in emotional matters. To receive a gift of silver in a dream or meditation is a sign of coming joy. (for more information on the meaning of the color silver please refer to Chapter 4---Color Symbolism.)

SMOKE: The image of smoke in a dream or meditation indicates attempts are being made to deceive or mislead the individual. Smoke obscures the Truth, it hides reality and creates a medium for Illusions to take hold. If the smoke is coming from burning incense or candles in the dream or meditation, the individual should be wary of the visions they see. To see smoke swirling around one in a dream or meditation can indicate difficulty in seeing the path of life clearly. Decisions and choices are hard to make because the individual is having problems with self-deception.

SNAKE: (see Serpent)

SNOW: The image of snow in a dream or meditation indicates purification of the emotions. It is a sign of abundance and good luck to the individual who has undergone an initiation of purification, one who has surrendered their ego to the Will of the Creator. Snow is a blanket of protection for the earth when the bitter cold winds blow. In the spring, the snow melts to provide nourishment and assistance to the earth in bringing forth new growth. Snow on a mountain top in a dream or meditation indicates achievement. Driving or walking through snow in a dream or meditation represents good news regarding one's goals or ambitions in life.

SPEAR: The image of a spear in dreams or meditation is a phallic symbol representing the power of masculine energy. It is a sign of assertiveness and leadership. However, because the spear symbolizes such raw power it can be misused or degenerate into war-like actions and aggressiveness. When used properly, the power symbolized by this image can manifest success, rewards, and abundance. When used negatively, the power is corrupted and used to enslave others, to dominate and create quarrels or fights which lead to disaster.

To see this image in a dream or meditation shows this power is available to the individual to use at their own discretion.

SPIDER: The image of a spider in dreams or meditation is a sign of industriousness and determination to succeed in one's endeavors. The color of the spider will give important clues in defining the meaning behind the dream or meditation. To see a spider spinning and creating its web indicates the individual will build or buy a home for themselves, a home filled with constructive energy and security. The image of spiders and webs in a dream is a fortunate omen for happiness, abundance and the realization of one's desires. To be bitten by a spider in a dream indicates spite or jealousy from one's acquaintances or friends.

SQUARE: The image of a square in dreams or meditation represent a firm foundation, a basic structure on which to build. A square symbolizes "karma", both the positive and negative aspects. It is the raw building material from which great things can be constructed. The symbol of a square also represents the First Chakra Center or the "Root Chakra", where the Kundalini Force lies coiled 3 and a half times at the base of the spine. The Root Chakra rules physical strength, sexual energy, reproductive organs, warmth, and the "here and now". It vibrates to the color Red.

To see the image of a square in dreams or meditations signals the activation of the Root Chakra, to be charged up by the Forces of the Universe. What is done with this activated energy is up to the individual. It can be directed positively, or negatively which will cause this energy to be focused on the sexual appetite to the exclusion of all other considerations. It is one of the first initiations a seeker on the Spiritual Path encounters.

SQUARE WITH DOT IN CENTER: As stated above, a square represents karma and the ties it has on an individual, both positive and negative. A square with a dot or circle in the center symbolizes release from karma, freedom to rise beyond what one has been in the past. This image is seen in dreams and meditation, usually as a sign etched somewhere on a building, an object or even as a solitary image on the mind's canvas.

STAG or DEER: The image of a stag or deer in a dream or meditation is a sign of important news and messages leading to wonderful opportunities for the individual. Stags or deer are symbols of manifested power and majesty in Nature. They are strong and enduring, swift and beautiful. To see a herd of deer in a dream or meditation is a sign of an abundant Future.

STAIRS: The image of a staircase leading upwards symbolizes honor, recognition and fame. Stairs are symbols of achievement and the realization of one's goals or ambitions in life. To see oneself climbing stairs is a sign of an important event or opportunity in one's life which will result in a dramatic change for the better. To see oneself at the top of a staircase indicates unusual success and prosperity in the very near future.

Stairs are also symbolic of the Spiritual evolution of an individual. The higher one goes on the stairs, the more negative karma the individual has erased from their soul. Descending stairs indicates communion with the collective unconscious. It is also a sign of active prophetic talents guided by the Intuitional Mind.

STALLION or HORSES: To many dream interpreters, the image of horses or riding horses in a dream has strong sexual overtones. Whether or not this is true depends on your own experience. If after dreaming of riding horses you feel a release of sexual tension, then this dream has been a way for the sub-conscious mind to safely take care of your sexual needs. Only you, the dreamer, knows for sure what this dream experience means to you.

Symbolically, a stallion represents a raw and pure power. It is a leader, guiding the lives of others through the sheer force of his will or charismatic presence. The appearance of a stallion in one's meditation or dreams indicates a position of power and/or affluence will be within the individual's reach. The color of the stallion or horse will give important clues in the interpretation of this experience.

STARS: The image of stars in a dream or meditation symbolize the realization of one's hopes, wishes or desires. It is a sign of great prosperity and achievement. To see shooting stars in a dream or meditation symbolizes unusual honor and recognition. Stars are symbols of hope, happiness and joy. The brighter or more brilliant the stars, the sooner one will experience their good fortune. To see stars falling to earth is a universal sign of a natural disaster or war, events the individual has no control over.

STEPPING STONE: The image of a stepping stone in a dream or meditation symbolizes unexpected help or assistance during times of great change or in a time of challenge and uncertainty. To see oneself barefoot and crossing water by using stepping stones indicates success and advancement in all personal endeavors, including business or career. The appearance of stepping stones indicates the individual will rise above attempts to prevent them from achieving their goal.

STREET or ROAD: Roads, highways, streets, etc., have the same basic symbolic meaning. They represent the individual's path in life, the course they have chosen to take. The condition of the street or road in a dream or meditation is very significant. If the road is rough, not well preserved, filled with pot holes and the like, it indicates many of the circumstances in the individual's life will have setbacks, detours, and delays. To see a wide open street in a dream or meditation represents prosperity and good will directed toward the individual, a period of "smooth sailing" where everything seems to develop the way the individual wishes it to.

To see a street or road in a dream or meditation which is not well traveled or appears to be a little-used path, it indicates the individual has or will choose to pursue a different or unique way of life. This image is explored in Robert Frost's poem, "The Road Not Taken", in other words, the individual will or has chosen to take the road others usually do not take. This path or life-style will lead to great inner discoveries, to the development of an unusual philosophy, it is the "road" of a Spiritual Seeker. One who refuses to accept "society's" limitations and illusions.

STRING: To see strings in a dream or meditation is a warning to be careful about any business deals or proposals the individual is involved in. There could be hidden restrictions or ties which could hamper the individual's plans and progress. To see oneself wrapping string around an object indicates the power to attract what is needed into one's life. The color of the string can provide insights into the meaning of the symbol. Red string would indicate the power to attract new beginnings or opportunities. Gold string indicates prosperity and abundance. (see Chapter 4--Color Symbolism for further information on color.)

SUN: To see the image of a beautiful sunrise in a dream or meditation symbolizes success in new endeavors or creative/artistic projects. A beautiful sunset symbolizes contentment, joy and prosperity. The sun symbolizes Pure Solar Energy under the direction of the Universal Mind. It has a masculine nature in its expression or vibration. As the Moon represents the manifestation of the Mother Goddess, the Sun symbolizes the presence of the Father God.

To see a golden sun in a dream or meditation indicates the power of Love and Attraction at work in the individual's life. The opportunity to make a commitment in a relationship will arise leading to a special bonding with one's "soul mate" or spiritual complement. To see the sun breaking through clouds is an indication that troubles and vexations will pass away and no longer have the power to complicate the individual's life. A red-gold Sun is a symbol of the activated Kundalini Force. Intense physical, sexual and sensual experiences are ahead for the individual when the sun gleams a golden-red color.

SUNFLOWERS: The image of a sunflower in dreams or meditation symbolize the presence of Divine Fire, of inspiration from one's higher self. Sunflowers represent courage and obedience to the Forces of Light. It is a sign of well-being and prosperity when seen in dreams or meditation. The appearance of sunflowers in a dream or meditation is a sign for the activated power of the Sun. These flowers are symbols of the Highest Attainments or Achievements possible on the physical earth plane once the individual has surrendered themselves to the benign Love of the Creator.

SUNSHINE: The image of sunshine in a dream or meditation is a sign of Divine Blessings. It represents good news, acknowledgement of one's creations or efforts, and fulfillment of hopes. The sunshine is the harbinger of joy and prosperity. To dream or have the experience of being bathed in sunshine during a meditation, is a clear indication of honor and fame. To see oneself and others enveloped in the embrace of sunshine is a sign of love and affection from a special and important person in the individual's life. To see or feel sunshine in a dream or meditation represents a long and happy life filled with contentment and joy for the individual.

SURGERY: To feel oneself undergoing surgery in a dream or meditation indicates something or someone in the individual's life needs immediate attention. It is a warning to pay closer heed to one's actions and choices. There is a mystery involved or unknown--unseen forces are at work that could have a dramatic effect on the individual's life. Sometimes, this symbol in a dream is used to warn the individual about an enemy who seeks their downfall. To see oneself performing surgery on someone else indicates the individual's services will be required by others.

SWAMP: The image of a swamp in dreams or meditation indicate difficulty and misleading circumstances ahead for the individual. All is not what it appears to be, there are many hidden undercurrents at work, seeking to undermine the individual's efforts. Swamps are dangerous places, full of deadly secrets and traps for the unwary or unenlightened. To see oneself in a swamp is an omen worth paying attention to. The circumstances and people around the individual are not to be entirely trusted. Extreme caution should be taken in forming any partnerships or in signing agreements.

SWAN: Symbolically, swans represent gracefulness, loyalty, faithfulness, and good fortune. Swans mate for life and grieve themselves to death if they loose their mates. Because of this, in ancient times, swans were considered to be symbols of "soul mates" or soul compliments. To see a swan, or several swans, in a dream or meditation indicates great joy, happiness and contentment. To see the image of a pair of swans swimming in a lake or river represents a lasting relationship based on love and mutual need. This relationship is one that brings out the best in both partners.

SWORD, DAGGER or KNIFE: The image of a sword in a dream or meditation symbolizes a tool or means for penetrating the veil of illusion, allowing the Light of Truth to shine forth. In this sense, the sword represents the mind or intellectual awareness of a human being. It is, however, a two-sided sword which can be used to distort the Truth through the use of hatred or prejudice. The Sword represents Great Hate and Great Love, (its two-sided nature), how the energy of the sword is manifested depends on the integrity of the individual. A flaming sword seen in a dream or meditation is a symbol of the Logos and of Divine Intervention in one's affairs. To see swords in a dream or meditation is also an indication of honor and distinction for the individual.

The image of a dagger or knife in a dream or meditation represents a cutting away or releasing of something or someone from the individual's life. Daggers are also ceremonial symbols used in ritualistic religions which the Aztecs practiced. Therefore, the appearance of a dagger in a dream or meditation could be a past life memory fragment from that civilization or other similar cultures. To see oneself wounded by a dagger or knife in a dream indicates possible destructive action taken by one's enemies. However, forewarned is forearmed and the consequences of negative actions by others can be prevented or its power blunted.

TABLE and TABLECLOTH: The image of a table in a dream or meditation represents the enjoyment of life. To see people seated at the table is a sign of prosperity and joy. A table is where we partake of sustenance, therefore a table symbolizes one of the ways we get our needs met in life. If the table appears scarred or mutilated in some way, it indicates that our "needs" are not be taken care of properly or are not manifesting the way we hoped. To see oneself repairing a broken table in a dream is a sign the individual is taking charge of or responsibility for their life and, through positive and construction action, will see to it their "needs" are met.

To see a cloth on the table in a dream or meditation represents material gains for the individual. A table cloth with gold and/or silver threads symbolizes fulfillment of one's desires. If it is solid gold or silver it is a sign of abundance and contentment. If the tablecloth appears dirty it indicates problems or difficulties created by the individual's own actions. An embroidered tablecloth represents an important event will take place which will change the individual's life. The color of the tablecloth will give important clues to the events or meaning of the dream experience.

TALISMAN: The meaning of a talisman when seen in a dream or meditation has the same definition as an amulet. It can be a ring or a stone with engraved figures, mantras, or pictures. A talisman acts like a shield against negative vibrations, absorbing and transforming the energy. To see a talisman in a dream or meditation indicates protection from disturbing or negative energies around the individual. To see oneself being given a talisman in a dream or meditation indicates the fulfillment of one's wishes.

TAPESTRY: The image of a tapestry in a dream or meditation is another reference symbol to the veils of illusion which cloak the Astral Realms from the earth plane. Tapestries also represent luxury and wealth, qualities highly sought after on the physical earth plane. The presence of a tapestry in one's dreams or meditation hints at hidden mysteries just beyond our grasp. They arouse our curiosity and need to explore the unknown. Therefore, the appearance of a tapestry in a dream or meditation symbolizes the "need" for further seeking, a need to make a commitment to the path of enlightenment. To see oneself creating a tapestry in a dream or meditation indicates the individual's involvement with "unseen" forces who are providing inspiration and guidance in the individual's creative or artistic pursuits.

TEACHER: The appearance of a teacher in dreams or during meditation represents a messenger from the Universal Mind which seeks to bring enlightenment and knowledge to the individual. To see oneself as a teacher in dreams is a sign the individual is being prepared as a channel for wisdom and inspiration. Perhaps through writing, music, painting, speaking, counseling, etc., the individual will offer channeled knowledge to those hungry people who have verbally or subconsciously requested the presence of a teacher in their lives. To be a channel for the Divine Mind is a heavy responsibility and can arouse many temptations. The individual always has the choice whether or not to accept this responsibility.

TEMPLE: Symbolically, a temple represents the home of the Soul, that part of us which has remained pure and in complete union with the Supreme Being or

Creator throughout all time. The temple of the soul is a place of renewal and rejuvenation. It is a place to let go of fears and worries, and allow ourselves to be bathed in a healing glow of love from the Universe. Temples are places of incredible healing, a healing that goes beyond the physical, reaching deep within to restore and revitalize the spirit. Temples are the storehouses of Pure Energy direct from Universal Forces of Light.

Sometimes, the image of a Temple in dreams or meditation are fragments of past life memories. Perhaps a lifetime in ancient Greece or Egypt, even Atlantis or Lemuria. Temples have been a part of the human experience for eons and can be found in almost every culture. If the appearance of a Temple in your dreams or meditation is related to a past life, carefully study the people around you, the artwork, and your emotional feelings about the temple. This will help you to determine where and possibly when this lifetime took place.

TEPEE or TENT: The image of a Tepee in a dream or meditation is a direct reference to the Native American Culture. If the experience is not related to a past life memory, the tepee symbolizes a need to get back to basics, to get rid of excess baggage and learn to live within nature's laws. By no means does a tepee represent a simplistic way of life, on the contrary, it symbolizes a way of life which is harmonized and balanced. It is a "focused" life, one without clutter and distractions. It is extremely difficult for "modern man" to acclimate himself to the rhythms of nature, to "listen" to the voices of the wind and earth. The "tepee" symbolizes a respect for Nature that transcends cultural barriers.

The image of a tent in a dream or meditation indicates temporary conditions affecting the individual. To see oneself living in a tent represents great changes to come, a complete alteration of one's life-style. Whether these images represent positive or negative events to come depends on the integrity of the individual and the choices they make.

THREAD: To see a silver thread or cord in a dream or meditation is a symbol of the "non-visual" attachment between the physical body and the astral body. When you see a silver thread on your body in a dream it is a sure sign of astral travel and not just an ordinary dream experience. The silver thread or cord protects us from danger and from permanent separation from the physical body. It absorbs shocks or negative energy while we are astral traveling.

To see gold threads in a dream or meditation is a sign of advancement concerning one's career or desires. Copper threads indicate the presence of kinetic energy being channeled into the individual, an energy which can be used for many purposes, including the manifestation of one's goals. Broken or cut threads indicate a parting of ways between friends or partners. Sometimes this parting can be motivated by anger or the faithlessness of other people.

Silk threads represent happiness and contentment in a life filled with many twists and turns of fate. Silk is very soft and sensuous to the touch, but it is very strong and durable despite its delicate appearance. Silk threads in a dream or meditation carry with them a touch of mystery and anticipation, indicating a life-path that may be filled with unusual adventures if the individual is willing to open themselves up to the experience.

Threads made of cotton or wool are more practical in their meanings. These types of threads are more centered in everyday affairs or the mundane material world. They indicate steady and reliable progress in the individual's affair's. The color of these threads will also give important clues as to the interpretation of the dream experience. To see oneself unraveling tangled threads in a dream or meditation indicates important revelations and enlightenment to come. Knotted threads indicate challenges for the individual to address. This doesn't necessarily mean problems or obstacles to overcome. It represents opportunities for the individual to develop undiscovered talents and abilities which have lain dormant within them.

THRONE: Traditionally, the image of a throne in a dream or meditation symbolizes power, authority and responsibility. A throne also represents prestige and honor. For the individual to see themselves sitting on a throne in a dream or meditation indicates rapid advancement and realization of ambitions. To see a friend, family member or even an, as of yet, unknown person sitting on a throne during a dream indicates unexpected help from that person in achieving one's goals. In some dream interpretation books, an empty throne is considered to be an omen of bad luck, indicating disappointments. However, I prefer to think of an empty throne as a sign of possibilities, if one is willing to strive for one's goals. It is a promise of rewards to come, of recognition for one's labors.

THUNDER: Symbolically, to hear/see/feel thunder in a dream or meditation is a power sign from the subconscious which is trying to jolt the individual out of a complacent attitude. The sound of thunder is used to get the individual's attention, to prepare the way for an important message from the Universal Mind. Sometimes, because of stubbornness or whispers from the ego, we do not pay attention to the Voice Within. Thunder and/or lightning is an effective means to awaken our awareness and focus it in the direction of the Universal Mind. The effect of Thunder is not used to frighten or subdue us, it is merely a tool used to break through limitations created by the ego.

TOOLS: The image of tools in a dream or meditation symbolizes the ways and means of achieving one's ambitions. "Tools" represent our spiritual gifts, talents and abilities which aid us in every facet of our lives. Without "tools" we could not make advancements, nor could we take advantage of the opportunities for prosperity that come our way. To be given tools as a gift in dreams or in meditation indicates the potential for great happiness and abundance. The keyword here is "potential", for we must use the "tools" or talents we are given in order to experience success and fulfillment. The "tools" will not operate on their own, they must be guided and utilized with creativity and inspiration.

TORNADO: To see the image of a tornado in a dream or meditation could be a precognitive sign from The Universal Mind concerning a real disaster. Tornadoes are the raw unleashed forces of Nature capable of complete devastation. If the dream or meditation is not precognitive in nature, the tornado represents a powerful sweeping force loose in the individual's life which could cause great difficulties. Circumstances are out of the individual's control and tremendous change is in the air.

TOWER: Symbolically, the image of a tower indicates isolation from the world. This type of isolation can be beneficial to individuals who choose creative and/ or artistic expression as their path in life. Isolation also aids serious scholars who seek to unravel the secrets of the Universe. Towers are symbols of high achievement that comes from dedication and commitment to an ideal. However, the tower can also indicate feelings of loneliness in the individual, feelings of being cut off from the rest of the world.

TOYS: The image of toys in a dream or meditation symbolizes the "child" essence within us. Children represent innocence, enthusiasm, boundless energy, joy, and trust. If the toys appear dusty as though they haven't been used or played with in a long time, it signals the "child essence" of the individual has not been allowed to express itself and they find it difficult to trust in the goodness of others. In other words, the individual has lost much of their enthusiasm for life and are imposing self-made limitations on themselves. They need to re-learn the importance of simple pleasures, of relaxing and expressing themselves in a playful--joyful manner.

If the toys appear in good condition or as though they are used on a fairly frequent basis, it indicates the individual has not completely lost their joy and innocence. In other words, the individual still possesses an innate wonder of the universe and even if they cannot completely or totally trust other people, the individual still trusts in the Love the Creator has for them. To receive a toy in a dream or meditation symbolizes an unexpected gift or pleasant surprise. To give a toy as a gift to another person in a dream or meditation is an act of love which will be rewarded tenfold.

TREES: To the priests and priestesses of ancient cultures, trees were sacred talismans and represented protection, comfort, nurturing and a healing love. In many ancient writings and myths the symbol of "the Tree of Life" is used with great consistency. The Christian and Jewish religions are not the only spiritual doctrines which use the symbolism of the Tree of Life in their creation myths and in their esoteric books of knowledge. The Tree of Life represents Universal Wisdom which lies hidden from the material mind.

The Tree of Life shows the pattern of the life-paths which are available to us. Some scholars say there are ten paths, others say there are twenty-two paths which lead us back to one-ness with the Creator. There are 22 Major Arcana cards which symbolize the 22 keys which opens the gate to the 22 life-paths. However, there are four Minor Arcana suits which contain fourteen cards per suit. Therefore, there could be many more life-paths than what the ancient mystics divined.

With this information in mind, when one see's a tree in a dream or meditation it indicates important revelations for the individual. To see a fruit or nut tree filled with fruit in one's dreams indicates rewards, abundance and satisfaction ahead. A flowering tree represents a gift of love bringing joy and happiness. A decorated Christmas tree in a dream or meditation indicates a time of contentment, the enjoyment of friends and family, and relief from anxiety or worries. An oak tree represents strength and perseverance. A willow tree symbolizes the ability to bend with the wind without loosing one's identity. A willow tree is wise in the art of compromise. Maple trees indicate unexpected advances and opportunities.

To see the image of a tree in a dream or meditation, regardless of what species it is, is a symbol of spiritual and emotional progression. Trees represent honor and recognition for one's achievements in growth and awareness. The taller the tree, the higher we have evolved on the spiritual path. If the tree appears dead or has fallen to the ground, it indicates an "unawakened" state in regards to Universal Truth and spirituality. The individual is taking a "vacation" in this lifetime rather than striving to overcome or correct mistakes made in the past. ·

TRIAL: To experience a "trial" in a dream or meditation indicates an assessment is being made of the individual and of their actions. It represents a period of reflection in the individual's life, a time to evaluate what has happened in the past and to set the agenda for the future. It is important to stop and take time out to reflect on one's direction in life. If the path taken seems to be leading away from one's goal, changes can be made, alternative options can be taken to bring oneself back into "focus". To see a "trial" in one's dreams or meditation is not an omen of negative events or problems, it is merely another spiritual tool or subconscious message that assists the individual in "awakening" their own intuitional guidance.

TRIANGLE: The image of a triangle in dreams or meditation is a symbol of the Holy Trinity or Triad of Power. The triangle is also a symbol of the Second Chakra Center, referred to as the "Spleen Chakra". The Spleen Chakra rules the emotions, appetite, energy and openness to new ideas. It vibrates to the color Orange. To see the image of a triangle in dreams or meditation is a signal to the individual that this Chakra Center is being opened and energized by the Higher Forces. When the Spleen Chakra is activated, the energy level is
raised higher and the emotions are made clearer or more focused in positive ways.

TRIDENT: A trident is a three pronged spear, very similar to a pitch-fork and is associated with gods and goddesses of the oceans. The image of a trident relates to a very early epoch in human evolution, to pre-Atlantis days. The trident was the symbol used by a civilization of the same name which spawned the Lemurian Civilization. To see a trident in dreams or meditation is a sign the individual will begin to experience karmic consequences of the actions and choices of a previous lifetime spent during the reign of the Trident Civilization.

This "karmic" reaping can be positive or negative, its manifestation depends solely on the individual's level of growth during that life time. It is very important to examine other symbols or images in the dream or meditation experience in order to determine what type of changes are being wrought in the individual's life. On a purely symbolically level, tridents represent honor, recognition and respect. However, the symbol of a trident is very rarely seen in dreams or meditation unless the individual has major ties to the Trident Civilization and is about to undergo sweeping changes in their life.

TRUMPET: The trumpet is a symbol of the Archangel Gabriel and its sound is used to awaken the righteous to justice. The sound of a trumpet is a battle call to the Forces of Light. It has the power to dispel the mists of darkness, to rend the veils of illusion and allow Truth to be set free. To see/hear a trumpet in one's dreams or meditation is a sign of karmic justice being activated on your behalf. Its power will not be used against the individual, but for the individual's spiritual and emotional wellbeing. It is Divine Intervention, the Universe stepping in to right a wrong.

Trumpets herald new beginnings and the end of circumstances or situations which have served their purpose and no longer have meaning. It is a symbol of spiritual awakening, opportunities to experience the Logos will be presented to the individual. These important and major changes in the individual's life will lead to self-realization and fulfillment. The individual's life will never be the same, it is progressing to a new level. In many ways, this symbol can be likened to a "rebirthing" process for it awakens the latent talents and abilities the individual has always possessed, but never utilized.

TUNNEL: The image of a tunnel is usually associated with out of body experiences or near-death experiences because the tunnel represents the passage from the physical plane to the higher astral planes where the Light resides. One generally sees the tunnel during times of great stress or trauma. It is meant to be a reassurance of continued existence and of the Pure Love which awaits our acknowledgement. Some people have reported going through a tunnel in their dreams when they communicate with relatives or friends who have already left the earth plane and their physical bodies. Therefore, the image of a tunnel in dreams or meditation must be evaluated on an individual basis. The tunnel itself merely represents the passageway from one level of existence to another.

UNCOVER: To uncover something in a dream or meditation symbolizes an important revelation, a mystery solved or the "root" cause of a problem unearthed. To see oneself taking the "lid" off of something represents exposure. This "exposure" could be of illegal dealings in business or politics, it may indicate the exposure of lies or false representation, or it could be the discovery of one's own motivations. What you "uncover" in a dream or meditation has a great deal of importance in defining the message of your experience. The individual could be "uncovering" something positive or negative. Understanding this experience depends on the overall tone of the experience, what colors are prominent and what other symbols are present.

UNDERGROUND: In general, to be underground is to hide or take refuge from the pressures of the world above. There could be a high level of stress associated with the individual's career, relationships, financial concerns or physical problems which activate a need in the individual to escape or get away. The sensation of being underground can indicate a positive or negative attitude in life. For example: Escaped slaves used the "underground railroad" system from the south to freedom in the north. This represents a positive example, even though it meant secretive but usually selfless aid to desperate people.

Negatively, the term "underground" can refer to anarchist groups seeking to undermine governments or societies in violent but secretive ways. If the individual is operating on a negative level, the image of being underground can indicate deceitful practices or subversive tactics used to get one's own way regardless of the cost or outcome. If the individual is operating on a positive level, the image of being underground can indicate hard work behind the scenes without the desire for recognition or anonymous contributions made to aid others toward achievement.

UNDRESS or NAKED: To see oneself undressed or naked in a dream or meditation symbolizes vulnerability and innocence. Sometimes, and for some people, to be naked in a dream indicates exposure and revealment. Usually though, to be undressed or naked in a dream or mediation is a sign the individual has nothing to hide and is not trying to deceive anyone. To other people naked in a dream or meditation represents acquaintances, friends or family whom the individual can trust. To see oneself undressing in privacy is a sign of material satisfaction and happiness to come. Undressing oneself or others can also be a fantasy dream experience with strong sexual overtones. In which case, the experience is meant to be for simple pleasure and release.

UNICORNS: These magical and mystical creatures are warriors for the Forces of Light. They cannot tolerate hatred, cruelty or that which is false. They are pure of heart, united with the Creator through love and obedience. Unicorns guard the defenseless and the innocent. They are also considered to be unmatched in the healing arts. To see a herd of Unicorns in a dream or meditation is a sign of material and financial gains. The Unicorns trust the individual to use this abundance and prosperity to help others and to uplift the consciousness of the planet. To kill a Unicorn in a dream or meditation symbolizes loss created by the selfish actions of the individual.

VALLEY: The image of a valley in dreams or meditation symbolizes peace, fertility and contentment in emotional and material issues. If there are animals and/or lush plant life in the valley it represents abundance and prosperity for the individual. A barren valley in a dream or meditation indicates bottled up emotions, the individual is subconsciously suppressing their needs for love and commitment. Valleys generally possess a feminine energy linked to the Mother Goddess and therefore are able to manifest creativity.

VAMPIRE: The image of a vampire in a dream or meditation symbolizes people or situations which suck the vitality from the individual. I'm sure many of you have had experiences with "psychic vampires", those individuals whose negativity drains you dry just to be around them. They have the ability to sap your strength leaving depression and weariness in its place. When you see the image of a vampire in your dreams or during meditation, your subconscious mind is trying to warn you to build a Shield of Light around yourself for protection against this barrage of negative energy. Of course, it is entirely possible that seeing a Vampire in your dreams merely means you've been watching too many horror movies.

VEILS: The image of veils in a dream or meditation refers to the barriers the world of Illusion would place on an individual. The world of illusion would confine and define us as mere physical bodies. The veils shimmer between two worlds of possibility: The world of Illusion and the Planes of Reality The world of illusion, created by the Ego, serves to separate and isolate us from one another and from our Source. The world of Reality serves as a beacon of Light to guide us to Truth, it serves to demonstrate all living things share a common bond, all living things carry a spark of the Creator's Fire within them. Although the world of Illusion seeks to use the Veils to hide the Truth from us, the Veils themselves beckon us to penetrate the "secrets" they conceal.

VINEYARD: The image of a vineyard in a dream or meditation symbolizes comfort, ease, and abundant prosperity. To see green vines beginning to bear fruit or vegetables indicates success will be achieved soon. If the vines are already laden with ripened fruit or vegetables, attainment is at hand ready for the individual to reach out for or acknowledge. Withered vines indicate vain hopes or wrong choices made. Green vines who have not yet bore fruit or vegetables represent healthy new beginnings, strong friendships and a bright future. Flowering vines symbolize attainment of wishes or desires.

VIOLETS: I'm sure many of you are familiar with the phrase "as shy as a violet" or that violets represent modesty. I prefer to see violets as discerning, with a discriminating awareness, not shy or fearful. A violet will only grow or prosper in peaceful conditions, in areas where harmony is found. It chooses not to struggle or fight for advantage or supremacy, instead it thrives in places others would not consider "optimum" or "advantageous" enough. Therefore, to see violets in a dream or meditation is a sign from the super-conscious to be more discerning about one's friends and associates as well as one's choices concerning the material world.

VOLCANO: The image of a volcano in a dream or meditation, whether it is erupting or not, symbolizes raw untamed power. Volcanos are the crucibles of creation, they process the raw material, minerals and ores needed to sustain life on the planet. To see a volcano erupting in a dream or meditation could be a precognitive warning; or, it could represent events and situations over which the individual has no control. To see a quiet, non-active volcano in one's dreams or meditation indicates latent forces at work subtly bringing about important changes in the individual's life. To see a volcano whose crater is filled with water, creating a lake, represents the taming influence of the Super-consciousness on the raw energy of the Kundalini. (even planets possess the Kundalini Force.)

VULTURES: The image of vultures or other birds of this nature in dreams or meditation indicate a person, society, or institution that preys upon the weaknesses of others. To see this image in a dream or meditation is a warning to the individual to be careful of their associates or any business dealings they may be involved in. To see oneself trapping or killing a vulture in a dream or meditation indicates the elimination of negativity from the individual's life or the defeat of rivals whose methods are reprehensible. Vultures serve an important role in nature, but they have no place in human affairs.

WALL: The image of a wall in a dream or meditation symbolizes a barrier between the individual and what they seek. Sometimes this wall represents the barrier to past-life recall or it serves to protect the individual from unpleasant memories. Many times the appearance of a wall in one's dreams or meditation indicates an obstacle that needs to be seen as a challenge. An obstacle can become a stepping stone with the right attitude and action.

To see oneself climbing or jumping over a wall indicates success and achievement of one's goals. To see a wall being built in a dream is a sign the individual should take care not to become stingy with themselves or their material gains. To see a wall being torn down in a dream or meditation is a sign of opening up, of reaching out to others and allowing them to "touch" the individual's life in various ways. To see oneself walking on top of a wall symbolizes indecision and uncertainty concerning which way to direct their life-path.

WALNUTS or NUTS: The image of walnuts, or any kind of nuts for that matter, in a dream or meditation symbolizes the "fruit" of labor, material and spiritual riches or rewards. Nuts are gifts from Nature, they are blessings which sustain and nurture us. The special quality of nuts lies in that we can eat them just as they are, or we can use them as seeds to plant future growth. In other words, we can enjoy and savor our abundance and prosperity in the here and now and still have the means to provide for our future or the future of our children. To receive a gift of walnuts or other kinds of nuts in a dream or meditation symbolizes satisfaction, success, and achievement.

WATER: This element cools, soothes and refreshes. It also overwhelms, floods, and sweeps away everything before it if uncontrolled. Water is the symbol of the Sub-Conscious and the Universal Sub-Conscious. It represents emotions and intuition. Clear water is a sign of prosperity and abundance when seen in a dream or meditation. To see oneself drinking clear water represents a willingness to be guided and inspired by the Universal Mind. It also symbolizes balance in the emotional and mental bodies.

WATER FALL: The image of a waterfall in dreams or meditation symbolizes spiritual power that the individual can harness and utilize under the direction or guidance of the Universal Mind. To see oneself standing under a waterfall is to be cleansed of negative karma and anointed with grace. To see a waterfall at night, under the light of the moon is a sign of acceptance from the Mother Goddess, a symbol of approval from Her. To see a waterfall during the day, under the rays of the sun is a sign of acceptance from the Father God aspect of the Creator. A waterfall seen in a beautiful nature setting represents happiness and joy. A waterfall seen in a building or city represents recognition and honor from one's peers. In general, waterfalls seen in a dream or meditation represent attainment of the individual's deepest desire or wish.

WATER LILY: The image of a water-lily in a dream or meditation symbolizes the blossoming of awareness in the Subconscious Mind. The water-lily indicates "talents" of a spiritual or psychical nature the individual has developed in previous lifetimes which can be put to good use in the present. If the pond or lake where the water-lily rests is a muddy color, it indicates the individual will have the opportunity to redeem the errors or mistakes made in the past. The color of the water-lilies can give important clues in defining the over-all meaning of the dream or meditation experience.

WEDDING: The image of a wedding in a dream or meditation symbolizes the union of two polarities, the coming together and binding of forces. A wedding is a sign of happiness and success for the individual. Opportunities will arise for partnerships or for working in concert with another person to achieve personal ambitions. Of course, to dream of a wedding or see this ceremony during a meditation could be a precognitive experience as well. Whatever the case may be, a wedding serves to unite and blend two halves into one whole or one entity. A wedding can also symbolize the harmonizing of our three states of consciousness with the Universal Mind.

WHALE: To see a whale in a dream or meditation is a portent of unexpected, but beneficial changes in one's life. A whale symbolizes good luck and steady, reliable friends who seek to further the individual's aims in life. To see a whale in a stormy ocean indicates fortunate happenings in spite of a chaotic environment. To see several whales in a dream or meditation represents many happy events or reasons to celebrate in the near future .

WHARF or DOCK: The image of a wharf or dock in a dream or meditation represents a state of waiting, a time when preparations are made to guarantee receptiveness. Ships, which represent our hopes, wishes and desires, bring their treasures to the wharves or docks. Therefore, wharves and docks are the recipients of abundance and prosperity, a place where long-awaited rewards are collected. To see oneself standing on a wharf or dock is a signal to the individual to practice the virtue of patience and using affirmations or prayers in regards to their desires for the individual will attain what they want if they show their worthiness by having faith and trust. If a ship is nearing the docks or wharf, it indicates the realization of one's hopes and wishes is close at hand.

WHEEL: The image of a wheel in a dream or meditation symbolizes the "Wheel of Karma" or "Destiny". Each turn of the wheel signals the end of old situations and circumstances as well as release from heavy burdens of the past. The turning wheel also indicates the beginning of a new cycle and progressive change. Wheels are also used as symbols of opened Chakra Centers. When the wheels are rotating, the chakra centers have been activated and have awakened the

Kundalini Force, bringing it up through each of the seven centers, creating balance and harmony.

The Wheels represent a tremendous force at work, a force fueled by Divine Fire. To see these wheels in action in a dream or meditation indicates the individual is in the process of an important spiritual initiation which will alter their perception of the Universe. To see oneself turning a wheel in a dream or meditation is a sign the individual is taking responsibility for their destiny and is willing to accept the consequences of their actions and choices.

The wheel also has a rich Native American heritage as the "medicine wheel", a tool used by Shamans for healing the mind, body and spirit. The spirit animal or totem of each of the astrological signs are represented on the Indian Medicine Wheel as are the flowers and colors of each of the signs. The spirit animals of the zodiac are used in addition to one's personal vision of a spirit animal. In essence, the individual possesses two or more spirit animals which protect and assist in the attainment of one's goals.

According to Native American symbolism, the following information concerning spirit animals and flowers are found on the Shaman's Medicine Wheel and vibrate to the astrological signs as given here:

Aries: spirit animal is the Buffalo and the flower symbol is the Corn Flower.
Taurus: spirit animal is the Llama and the flower symbol is the Violet.
Gemini: spirit animal is the Hummingbird and the flower symbol is the Magnolia.
Cancer: spirit animal is a Cat and the flower symbol is the Red Rose.
Leo: spirit animal is the Red Fox and the flower symbol is the Lily of the Valley.
Virgo: spirit animal is the Peacock and the flower symbol is the Sunflower.
Libra: spirit animal is the Blue Jay and the flower symbol is the Gardenia.
Scorpio: spirit animal is the Mountain Lion and the flower symbol is the Carnation.
Sagittarius: spirit animal is the Coyote and the flower symbol is the Dahlia.
Capricorn: spirit animal is the Squirrel and the flower symbol is the Daisy.
Aquarius: spirit animal is the Eagle and the flower symbol is the Orchid.
Pisces: spirit animal is the Turtle and the flower symbol is the Narcissus.

WHIRLPOOL: Symbolically, a whirlpool represents conflicting emotions biding their time to overwhelm the individual at the most inopportune moment. These emotions have been gradually building in strength because they have been ignored by the individual for a long time. If these emotions are not dealt with promptly, they grow in strength and can engulf the individual before they realize it, dragging them down into an emotional abyss which is difficult to escape. The image of a whirlpool in dreams or meditation can indicate an emotional relationship which threatens to overwhelm the individual's good sense. Care should be taken in any physical bonding or sexual activities.

WHIRLWIND: Symbolically, a whirlwind has many of the same connotations as a whirlpool, however, rather than emotional issues, the whirlwind represents conflicting mental attitudes and confusion. The image of a whirlwind in a dream or meditation can indicate chaotic conditions in professional or business concerns. Be careful of any agreements signed or partnerships formed, for this image is a warning of possible deception or devious actions of others. The individual's reputation could be badly damaged by envious and secretive foes posing as friends.

WILD ANIMALS: In Native American mystical rites, a shaman guides a student in a meditation exercise in order for the individual to discover their "animal brother" or "kindred spirit" in nature. I believe the same principle applies to animal images in dreams. When the Native American Seeker underwent their "vision quests" under the guidance of their Shamans, the animal they saw in their vision represent qualities they, themselves, possessed. For example: A Running Wolf symbolized endurance, good hunting instincts, and the ability to survive the odds, etc. A Deer symbolized swiftness, adaptability, and the ability to provide for the needs of its family, etc. The Shamans taught their students that each animal had positive qualities to be admired and respected, even rabbits and squirrels, animals which were not commonly thought of as cunning.

A grizzly bear is a symbol of raw power, wild and untamed. Where as a black or brown bear, still a symbol of power, has a gentler nature or a more understanding nature. A polar bear, by contrast, is a killing and eating machine that has no conscience in regards to killing and eating its own female counterpart after mating. The best advice I can give you concerning the interpretation of a wild animal image in your dreams or meditation is to study what that animal represents. What are its habits? How is it seen by other animals? What kind of nature does it have? All of these questions and more must be answered and explored to understand the nature of the wild animal that appears to you. Remember; the wild animal represents positive qualities you possess or have at your disposal if you will only develop them. The choice is yours.

WHITE: To see the color white prominently in dreams or meditation represents great joy and happiness. It is the color of innocence and purity, of Union with the Supreme Force of the Universe. To see white furnishings in a dream or meditation indicates successes in business ventures. To see oneself wearing white clothes is an omen of contentment and satisfaction in love relationships. White walls, carpets or flooring, or even a white house or building represents attainment in financial and material affair's.

WIND: The wind is a force of Nature which sweeps away the debris that clutters our lives. The presence of wind in a dream or meditation symbolizes great changes about to take place, changes that not only affect the individual but their environment as well. To see oneself walking in the direction the wind is blowing indicates success and happiness because of changes in the business climate or professional world. To walk against the wind indicates resistance to change which could lead to missed opportunities.

WINDMILL: The image of a windmill in a dream or meditation is a sign of steady progress and movement in one's affairs. The windmill moves because of actions taken by the forces of Nature. These actions bring opportunities for achievement and realization of one's goals if the individual is willing to accept it. To see a windmill turning in the wind in a dream or meditation represents material and financial gains. If the windmill suddenly changes direction in movement it represents a warning of possible reversals in business for the individual.

WINDOW: The image of a window in a dream or meditation symbolizes protection from negative astral forces. Windows are also symbols of once in a lifetime opportunities. If the window is open in a dream or meditation it symbolizes the attainment of success in one's ambitions. The bigger the window, the more abundant and quicker the success will materialize. If the window is closed in the dream it indicates the individual is not taking advantage of the opportunities the Universe is providing them with. A broken window represents promises the individual has not followed through on.

WINGS: To dream you are wearing wings indicates honor, recognition and happiness. To see the symbols of wings in a dream or meditation represents good news and happiness in love. To be given wings in a dream or meditation symbolizes the passing of a very important spiritual initiation. It signifies the individual has gained mastery over their Kundalini and has triumphed over their cravings of their lower nature or ego. Because the symbol of wings represents high achievement on the spiritual path, one does not see this image very often.

WIZARD or SORCERESS: The image of a wizard or sorceress in a dream or mediation symbolizes prosperity, change and transformation. To see oneself greeting a wizard or sorceress in a dream indicates important events to come which will change the individual's life for the better. To see oneself as a wizard or sorceress in a dream or meditation indicates the individual has the power to channel the forces of nature, the individual has a special rapport or attunement to the energy patterns of the earth itself. This symbol could also be a fragment of a past life memory from Atlantis or from the early Druid Priesthood.

WOLF: The image of a wolf in dreams or meditation symbolizes luck and abundance. A wolf also represents a guardian spirit sent by the Mother Goddess to protect the individual from hidden enemies who claim to be Friends. Wolves also serve as guides through the treacherous abyss between the earth plane and the astral realms. To see a wolf come toward you and lay down at your feet in a dream or meditation is a sign of high honors and fame. The wild spirit of Nature, embodied within the wolf, has chosen to serve you in achieving your goals. A very special gift, one which must be earned through karmic merit or through Grace.

WREATH: To see a wreath in a dream or meditation symbolizes success in attaining one's wishes and desires, Wreaths are symbols of happiness, joy and triumph. They represent victory over opposing forces, over the lower nature and over the plane of illusion. To be given a wreath in a dream or meditation indicates enriching relationships and contentment in love affairs, it is also a sign of respect and honor from one's peers.

YARN: (see Threads or String)

YELLOW BIRD: The image of a yellow bird in a dream or meditation symbolizes a Soul-Gift or Soul-Grace. It is a sign of spiritual blessings which are manifested materially and spiritually. The yellow bird is a special omen to the individual indicating their mind has achieved union with the Creative Mind of the Universe and because of this, True Wisdom--True Understanding is now possible. To have a yellow bird fly up to you or sit on your hand in a dream or meditation indicates that joy and enlightenment are being offered to you. Since the color yellow symbolizes the Active Mind and a bird represents mental freedom, the yellow bird image in a dream or meditation is showing the individual they have been blessed with the gift of clear thinking and integrity.

ZODIAC: To see the image of the zodiac in a dream or meditation symbolizes good fortune in the near future. The Zodiac represents achievement and financial gains. To see your own zodiac sign in a dream or meditation is a sign of extraordinary good luck and prosperity. It indicates you will succeed in your goals beyond your wildest dreams. To see other signs of the Zodiac, other than your own, in dreams or meditation, is a sign of opportunities to realize your deepest desires. Your potentials are unlimited and your present and future have been blessed.

NOTE TO READERS

Naturally, there are many more Dream "Images" or symbols than what I have covered in this chapter. My intent has been to give you a basic working foundation in symbolism. The best source for defining symbols in dreams and meditation comes from your own Higher Consciousness, heed your "Inner Voice" and the visions you see in dreams and meditation will become clearer and more understandable.

I cannot stress enough the importance of keeping a dream journal and meditation journal. The information you will amass through this practice will be invaluable to you.

You will also notice that I have not defined meanings for "emotions", like fear, anger, jealousy, anticipation, excitement, and so on. I have omitted definitions of emotions because I don't feel there are any "pat" answers or slick definitions for our emotions. Emotions are very complicated and need to be worked out on an individual basis. The purpose of dreams, after all, is to attune you to Divine Guidance. The emotions your dreams arouse in you must be carefully examined in concert with the total content of symbols in the dream.

Remember, trust your own instincts or "inner voice", do not just blindly accept *anyone's* definitions for dreams or meditation. For further information on dream symbolism I recommend reading the following books along with any books you discover on your own:

Watch Your Dreams, by Ann Ree Colton
Zolar's Encyclopedia and Dictionary of Dreams, by Zolar
10,000 Dreams Interpreted, by Gustavus Hindman Miller
The Complete Dream Book, by Edward Frank Ellen
Man and His Symbols, edited by Carl G.Jung
The Inner Eye, by Joan Windsor

I would also like to recommend reading the book titled: *Angel Fire* by Father Andrew M. Greeley. It is a fiction-fantasy about angels and humankind which will change, forever, your perception of "angels". This story literally "ignited" my imagination and altered my concepts of the Angelic Kingdom. There is a golden thread of truth which runs through this story, a truth which comes from the esoteric and religious writings only a privileged few in the Church's hierarchy has had access to.

Of course, you may find the story unacceptable, which is perfectly all right. But I hope you will at least give the story a chance to touch your heart, you won't regret it.

SPECIAL NOTE

This note is for those readers who believe or at least have an open mind about the existence of UFO's and/or alien visitors. To some individuals, a few who can be considered experts, believe certain images in our dreams are due to "alien" contact. If you are unfamiliar with this viewpoint, allow me to recommend the following two books: *Communion* and *Transformation: The Breakthrough*; both written and experienced by Whitley Strieber. If this concept catches hold of your imagination, or you believe you may have some experiences along these lines, there are other authors of UFO encounters whose books would be of interest to you. Just ask your local librarian or bookseller for books concerning UFO experiences and/or abductions.

I have brought you this point concerning "alien contact" because the images brought into a dream experience could possibly be tied to subliminal visitors from other dimensions, alternate realities or even other planets. As a Spiritual Scientist and Seeker, I cannot, in good conscience, overlook an idea or concept just because it doesn't fit into "normal" or acceptable parameters. A closed mind is the weapon of the Ego, used to entrap us in the world of illusion. To allow the Ego to dictate to you is a sure way of closing off your path to Enlightenment. Having an open mind is one of the greatest gifts we can give ourselves. However, having an open mind is not synonymous with gullibility. Therefore, keep your mind open, but develop a healthy skepticism as well.

CHAPTER SIX
ASTROLOGICAL SYMBOLISM

As part of the foundation of knowledge we are establishing together, it is important for you understand the unique inter-connectedness between the "Keys" outlined in this book. Although the study of Astrology, Numerology, Color, Gems, Minerals, Crystals, and Dreams can be pursued without any working knowledge of the Tarot, it is almost impossible to work with the Tarot without studying and developing an understanding of these "Keys". This is because the Tarot is comprised of a mixture of these different "Keys" or symbols.

Not all of the references on Gems, Minerals, and Crystals defined in this chapter and in Chapter Seven are directly involved with the Tarot. However, new decks are being created all the time, and more and more references are being used that pertain to Crystals, Gems, and Minerals. Perhaps you, the reader, will design your own Tarot deck based on the information given you in this book. I hope so. I hope that you will take the information in this book and expand on it further, adding your own unique touch to this body of knowledge.

ASTROLOGICAL PLANETARY COLORS

SUN: Gold, bright yellow, and sometimes yellow-green are the colors ruled by the Sun.

MOON: Silver, white, emerald green, and sometimes evergreen and light shades of gray are colors ruled by the Moon.

MERCURY: Yellow, orange, and sometimes lilac and off white are the colors ruled by the planet Mercury.

VENUS: Blue, blue-green, and turquoise are the colors ruled by the planet Venus.

MARS: Red, crimson, scarlet, and other shades of red are the colors ruled by the planet Mars.

JUPITER: Purple, indigo, and sometimes violet are the colors ruled by the planet Jupiter.

SATURN: Olive green, the various shades of Gray, Navy Blue, Evergreen and Black are the colors ruled by the planet Saturn.

URANUS: Electric blue, pale green, citrine, and other light bluish-green colors are ruled by the planet Uranus.

NEPTUNE: Dark or Royal Blue, indigo, gray, green, colors of an opalescent nature along with pink and coral colors are ruled by the mystical planet Neptune.

PLUTO: Yellow, Opalescent Blacks, pale green, aqua, and rose are colors which are ruled by the planet Pluto.

EARTH: Terra Cotta and Lavender shades of blue or white are the colors which are ruled by the planet Earth.

NORTH NODE OF MOON: Peach Gold and Silver are the colors which are ruled by the North Node.

SOUTH NODE OF MOON: Bronze and Reddish Purple are the colors which are ruled by the South Node.

PART OF FORTUNE: Sky Blue and Copper are the colors which are ruled by the Part of Fortune.

The following section contains a summary definition for each of the 12 Zodiac signs plus their correlating colors and the gem, mineral or crystal which vibrates to each individual sign. The information pertaining to the Spiritual and Esoteric Aspects of Astrology are necessary elements which give a deeper understanding of the mysterious universe around us. Comprehending the ancient science of Astrology is one of the "Keys" necessary to unlock and expand your awareness, a goal well worth achieving.

ARIES THE RAM

KEY PHRASE: "I am."
KEY WORD: "Action."
ELEMENT: Fire.
TRADITIONAL RULING PLANET: Mars
ESOTERIC RULING PLANET: Mercury
BASIC NATURE: "The pioneer or warrior."
KARMIC CHALLENGE: "To learn Patience."

Aries symbolizes "Self-Realization". First to emerge from the Cosmic Womb of Life, the Arian realizes they are, at last, an individual, a separate entity who is still joined, in essence, to the Universal Consciousness. Filled with the "fires" of life, the Arian desires to blaze the trail into the unknown, forming a passageway for others to follow. Stimulated by new experiences, the Arian begins the process of creating a unique personality, of developing depth of character to sustain their vibrant warrior spirit.

Independent, inspired, and enthusiastic, it is difficult to contain, let alone control the fires of the Arian spirit. Impulsive to a fault, the Arian must learn how to direct and channel their energies rather than allowing selfishness or a "me first" attitude distract them from their spiritual goals. Arians are natural leaders who are attracted to positions of authority and command. They see obstacles as challenges to the spirit and relish the opportunity to exercise their talents in conquering the difficult. Impossible is not a word an Arian has in their vocabulary.

As the first "fire" sign of the Zodiac, the Arian mind is ablaze with a multitude of ideas and creative projects they feel compelled to begin. With so many "irons in the fire", it can be difficult for the Arian to complete all of their projects. The Arian initiates so that others can bring the project to completion. It is difficult for an Arian to work under the direction of another person. Aries is self-motivated and must be allowed to find their own methods of doing things through trial and error. Any other way is emotionally and mentally repugnant to them and if forced, the brilliant creativity of the Arian is greatly diminished.

The Esoteric planetary ruler of Aries is the planet Mercury. This is because the sign Aries rules the head and the planet Mercury rules the brain. Once the Arian becomes aware of their higher function, they are able to channel their thoughts and actions with a disciplined will. The "fires" burning in the Arian mind have the ability to purify their thinking process and elevate their awareness. A spiritually oriented Arian realizes they are a "pilgrim" on the steep and rocky road to Enlightenment.

When the Arian turns the course of their life toward the spiritual path, they seem to continually face "initiations" geared to increase their self-awareness. As the Arian allows the esoteric influence of Mercury to flood their being, they tame the "martian" energy of their ruling planet, creating new opportunities for self-expression. When they channel their fiery nature mentally, Arians are uniquely brilliant, developing ideas which benefit their cosmic family in positive ways. Once the Arian learns to focus their mental energy on a higher vibration they truly become inspired by the Universal Forces.

Aries, "the Ram", is an ancient symbol of sacrifice. In the Judeo-Christian Old Testament there are many stories which refer to the sacrifice of a ram on the altar. In the Christian New Testament however, and especially in the Book of Revelations, Jesus, after he became the Christ, is referred to as the "Lamb of God" who takes away the sins of the world through his self-sacrifice. According to ancient texts, Jesus was born on April 7th which falls under the Astrological sign of Aries the Ram. His rising sign or ascendant was Libra.

The lesson which the element of Fire teaches humankind is the lesson of Love, and for Aries the lesson is the wise use of love. Arians are in the process of learning to put aside the old self, which was caught up in the pursuit of vain personal desires, and is creating a new self which understands and uses the real miracle of selfless love. This "new" self uses the ambition and drive of the Arian spirit for people or causes rather than for personal gain.

The truly enlightened Arian is a "warrior" for the Forces of Light.

PRIMARY COLORS: All shades of Red and Rose tones.

SECONDARY COLORS: Greens and blues used in small amounts.

STONES WHICH VIBRATE TO ARIES: All red stones, rubies and garnets. Tourmaline, Zircon, Fire Opal, Topaz, Jasper, and Feldspar are also stones which vibrate to the influence of Aries.

METALS: Gold, Bronze and Iron.

CHEMICAL AFFINITIES FOR ARIES: Kali Phos., (potassium phosphate). The stones containing these biochemic salts are Turquoise and Moonstone.

PRIMARY STONE FOR ARIES: Topaz. The clear yellow shade of Topaz is ruled by the vibrations of the planet Mercury, esoteric ruler of Aries. Mercury rules the intellect and yellow is the color of the active Mind and clear thinking. Topaz also is found in shades of light blue and white. These shades of Topaz enhances creativity and communication abilities, traits the spiritually oriented Arian seeks to develop. The unusual hardness of this stone, only two points lower than a Diamond, demonstrates the determination of the mind to rule the impulses of the lower nature. The energy vibrations of the Topaz has the power to "tame" the fiery nature of the individual wearing it.

Traditionally however, Topaz is considered to be under the influence of the planet Mars. The word Topaz means "Fire" in Sanskrit, showing the relationship between this stone and the qualities of the planet Mars. Ancient cultures called the Topaz "fire stone", believing it contained the mystical fires of creation. In India, the Topaz is considered to be one of the gemstones that symbolize the Kundalini Force. Because of this association, this stone was used to aid the desires of lovers who believed the Topaz had the power to "ignite" the fires of the Kundalini.

To the ancient Atlantean civilization the Topaz represented the power of the Sun offering wisdom to those adepts who were willing to commit themselves. The energies of the Topaz also symbolized fidelity, friendship, love and divine goodness. Because of these qualities, the Topaz was often used in the construction of "Light Wands" as one of the 7 points of light. This stone was also worn on a copper, silver, or gold band around the head, resting on the 3rd eye because it was thought to aid in the visionary qualities of the 3rd eye.

TAURUS---THE BULL

KEY PHRASE: "I have."
KEY WORD: "Stability"
ELEMENT: Earth
TRADITIONAL RULING PLANET: Venus
ESOTERIC RULING PLANET: Vulcan
BASIC NATURE: "The builder and accumulator."
KARMIC CHALLENGE: "To learn Detachment."

Taurus represents "Self-Reliance". They have an intense desire for possessions and material things. Through possessions they achieve a sense of security they lack, and it is this drive to achieve possessions which propels the Taurean to the great heights of productivity. Taurus has the ability to give others a feeling of security, even though they often feel they lack it themselves. During a time of crisis, Taurus is a rock to be relied upon, whose calm practical advice is a great asset.

It takes a great deal to disturb the tranquility and steady temperament of a Taurus. However, they can be extremely stubborn and fixed in their opinions, if they are pressed too hard, they will become obstinate. There is a danger that if pushed too hard or too far, Taureans can become enraged to the point they no longer consciously realize what they are doing. But, the majority of Taureans, and especially the Spiritually Enlightened ones, go out of their way to avoid confrontations or find other peaceful means to solve difficult situations.

The lesson which the element Earth teaches humankind is the lesson of service, and for Taurus the lesson is of practicality on the physical plane. We cannot be of true service to others unless we have something of practical value to offer them. Learning how to deal with business and finance in a positive manner that benefits not only ourselves but others, is one of the primary lessons all souls must learn on the physical plane.

Taurus, who comes after the pioneering Aries, settles and cultivates the territory the Arian discovers and explores. The Taurean is filled with the potent forces of Springtime, the urge to create is very strong. This creative urge manifests itself in a variety of ways. Agriculture, pro-creation, artistic creation, and material building are just a few of these ways to express the Taurean need for practical creativity.

In Esoteric Astrology, Aries represents Adam and Taurus represents the Garden of Eden, symbolizing the manifestation of creation on the physical earth plane. This sign has an intuitive rapport with Nature, a deeply developed sense of attunement with the forces of the Universe which produces the fertility in Nature. This aspect of the Taurean temperament is represented by the esoteric planetary ruler of Taurus which is the planet Vulcan.

In the ancient myths, the god Vulcan symbolized the ability to produce the implements and inventions need to promote continued creative productivity. Vulcan was also noted for his ability to create things of beauty and artistic instruments which enabled others to gather the material objects and the seeds of ideas spawned by the Arian required to create abundance. Like the mythical god Vulcan, the Taurean is a powerful force for working magic or miracles with the potent elements of the earth, creating practical and beautiful objects which provides true assistance to their fellow beings.

The influence of Vulcan causes the "Awakened" Taurean to transform their "Desire nature" into spiritual "Will" under the guidance of the Higher Forces. Rather than wallow under the earthy influence of Venus by pursuing mere sensual gratification, the spiritually motivated Taurean chooses to prove their worth by offering service to others. This transformation is an important Initiation on the Path of Spiritual Enlightenment. Therefore, this gift demonstrates, on a practical level, how others can achieve the same tangible results.

Taureans have the inherent power to utilize their strong, stubborn natures to straighten out the confusion created by others. Using their iron-clad determination, the Taurean bears emotional and physical burdens without comment or complaint for years. Ironically, the more difficulties or problems which occur in a Taurean's life, the more reserves of strength and faith they seem to find. Family and friends are highly treasured and shown incredible amounts of loyalty and devotion by the Taurean, no matter how much time and energy it requires.

PRIMARY COLORS: All shades of Blue except for the darkest shades.
SECONDARY COLORS: The light tints of any color when used in small amounts.
STONES WHICH VIBRATE TO TAURUS: All light blue stones, especially Lapis Lazuli and Turquoise.
METALS: Silver and Copper.
CHEMICAL AFFINITIES FOR TAURUS: Nat. sulph., (sodium sulphate). The stones containing the Taurean biochemical salts are Lapis Lazuli, Feldspar, and Jadeite.
PRIMARY STONE FOR TAURUS: Lapis Lazuli. In some of the ancient esoteric texts concerning the era of the Old Testament, there are references made to the tablets that Moses brought down from the Mount being carved of Lapis Lazuli. In Biblical history the word "Sapphire" often meant Lapis Lazuli and was held almost in mystical awe by the tribes of ancient Israel as well as the Egyptians and Assyrians of that era.

Lapis Lazuli is a stone with strong ties to Venus because of the lustrous blue color of the stone speckled with flakes of gold. These "gold flakes" are really tiny pieces of Iron Pyrites and not real gold. The blue color of this stone is what makes it such a good representative of Venus since it denotes, peace, beauty, and ease, qualities the higher nature of the mythical Venus was reputed to possess.

GEMINI THE TWINS

KEY PHRASE: "I think."
KEY WORD: "Variety."
ELEMENT: Air
TRADITIONAL RULING PLANET: Mercury
ESOTERIC RULING PLANET: Venus
BASIC NATURE: "The communicator."
KARMIC CHALLENGE: "To learn how to channel and control their mind and energy."

Gemini represents "Mental Exploration". A Geminian mind hungers for knowledge and intellectual stimulus. They have a wide network of communication which incorporates different mediums in order to satisfy their fierce desire for information. A Geminian is intuitive, perceptive, but also logical and they thrive on the stimulation of new situations, new people, new environments. Their minds operate at a highly accelerated rate, ideas practically tripping over themselves in their heads. Since Logic and reason is the criteria with which Gemini's judge their world, they can appear to be detached and impersonal when it comes to emotional situations. A Geminian individual is to learn how to channel their immense energy potentials in positive outlets.

The lesson which the element of Air teaches humankind is about the unfolding of mental vehicles, and for Gemini the lesson concerns the ability to reason and experiment in order to discover that which is harmonious in life. Conscious co-operation with others or "brotherhood" is important for the Geminian to experience and understand on an intellectual level. Gemini is a dual sign and symbolizes the dual cosmic forces of positive and negative, light and darkness which the individual must experience and understand before they can achieve true Enlightenment and be taught the Logos of the Universe.

Gemini is the first Air Sign of the Zodiac and therefore, represents the development of ideas, thoughts and other mental processes. Without this development, comprehending the complexities of the world of matter would be impossible, nor would the experience of harmony and balance be possible. Only through mastering the mind can one learn how to work in cooperation with the forces of the Universe, and through this cooperative effort, learn how to master the realm of the physical.

Gemini is in the process of learning to mentally distinguish between Truth and Illusion. This process increases sensitivity, the intuitive faculties, and promotes enlightenment. The Geminian consciousness is being expanded by the development of intricate mental processes, an expansion which results in an understanding of the physical plane and the relationship it has with the other, higher planes of existence. In other words, Gemini comes to intellectually experience the unity of the subconscious mind with the superconscious mind which results in "Spiritual Awareness" or "Divine Wisdom."

However, before this lofty goal can be achieved, Gemini must explore and accept the dual nature it possesses. This "duality" encompasses the positive and negative energy polarity, the "light" and "dark" cosmic forces of this multi-leveled universe. Gemini embodies the principles of Yin and Yang, and must learn how to balance these forces mentally, emotionally, and spiritually. Once they have begun this journey of self-awareness, they leave a legacy behind for others to follow.

Part of Gemini's Earthly task or function is to examine and explore as many ideas and thoughts as they can uncover. Through a process of checks and balances, the Geminian keeps or discards those ideas or thoughts which will contribute greatly to the spiritual and physical evolution of humankind. Gemini communicates the ideas and philosophies needed to form a solid foundation for the growth of civilization.

One of Gemini's greatest gifts from the Creator is the mind, a mind which is geared to rationalization. In this respect, Gemini is highly intellectual, possessing the abilities of the "scientific mind". But they also possess, but rarely use unless spiritually awakened, a highly intuitional mind capable of channeling universal knowledge and ideas. These two sides of the Geminian mental capabilities illustrates the duality of nature this sign possesses. The greatest Challenge the Geminian faces on the physical earth plane is the challenge of going beyond the limitations of the rational mind and reaching out for the knowledge and wisdom available from the higher realms.

The biggest pitfall the Geminian faces is their use of personally created logic.

Trying to rationalize logically the input of information that flows from the Universal Subconscious tends to throw them off their mental stride. Unfortunately, Gemini has to come to the realization, through personal trial and error, that the mind is meant to be used as a tool and servant of the spirit, not its master. Faith and Trust are difficult concepts for the rational logical mind to accept, but accept these concepts Gemini must or they run the very real risk of limiting the potential for understanding.

As the Esoteric Planetary Ruler of Gemini, the planet Venus embodies the concept of "duality". Venus has the ability to attract what it needs, thereby bringing together mental and emotional factors which must be intertwined and balanced in order to function properly. Venus teaches the Geminian not to be so detached in their approach to life, knowledge, and relationships. Creative and Artistic expression are ruled by Venus and many Gemini's find fulfillment through writing or the arts such as painting, sculpting, handicrafts, etc., which allows them to beautify their environment and the environment of others.

PRIMARY COLORS: White, all of the Yellow shades, and blue-grays.
SECONDARY COLORS: Iridescent colors which appear to be woven with silver threads.
STONES WHICH VIBRATE TO GEMINI: Topaz, Agates, Carnelian. All pale Yellow stones, especially the yellow and golden variety of Crystal, Sapphire, Sphene, Tourmaline, Beryl, Zircon, Amber, and Pearls.
METALS: Silver, Silver-gilt and Mercury.
CHEMICAL AFFINITIES FOR GEMINI: Kali Mur, (potassium chloride). The stones containing the Gemini Biochemic Salts are Amber, Moonstone, and Amazonite.
PRIMARY STONE FOR GEMINI: Tourmaline and Sphene. The light and vivid sparkle of these stones reflect the rulership of Mercury. These stones have a dual nature when well cut and polished, which harmonizes with the mental vibration of Mercury. The Tourmaline has a pyro-electric influence which blends with the magnetic influence of Mercury. These powers attract and channel free-flowing energy which recharges the mental "batteries" of the individual wearing this stone.

Sphene is a rare stone and symbolizes the ability to overcome the negative nature of Gemini which can be flighty and too-changeable. The energies of this stone serves to "balance" the mental merry-go-round of a Gemini, allowing them to process in-coming information in an orderly fashion. The word "Sphene" in Greek means "a wedge". Highly evolved Geminians can serve as "a wedge" between materialism and open the passageway for Divine Light to flow unobstructed.

CANCER THE CRAB

KEY PHRASE: "I feel."
KEY WORD: "Sympathy".
ELEMENT: Water.
TRADITIONAL RULING PLANET: The Moon.
ESOTERIC RULING PLANET: Neptune.

BASIC NATURE: The patriot, the protector, and the sentimentalist.
KARMIC CHALLENGE: "To learn discernment."

Cancer represents the "Intuitive Nurturer". Individuals with a strong placement of Cancer are very vulnerable to the phases of the Moon. They deal with life based on their emotions and feeling rather than with their mind or intellect. It is extremely difficult for a Cancerian to control their emotions because they are like psychic sponges soaking up the environment around them, often without being aware of what they are doing. Cancers are born worriers and with the constant bombardment of emotional stimuli on their psyche it is easy to see why they are susceptible to mood fluctuations.

Cancers are extremely tenacious and what they have, they hold onto regardless of whether it is good for them or not. Part of Cancer's karmic lesson is to learn how to let go and let God. This means letting go of negative emotions, relationships, and influences, a very difficult concept for Cancers to implement. By drawing negative emotions from others and creating added burdens for themselves, Cancers become susceptible to a wide variety of physical disorders. Once they have suffered enough from this particular character trait, the emotionally wounded Cancer will attempt to "harden" their hearts against others.

While under constant bombardment of the senses, a Cancerian feels compelled on a subconscious level to create a "shell" which they feel will shield them. The downside of this subconscious desire for refuge creates barriers to understanding and awareness rather than the simple protection they were originally seeking. This need to control their environment can lead to isolation in unawakened Cancerian souls. Attaining an inward serenity releases the Cancerian need for self-protection.

The lesson which the element of Water teaches humankind is Control of the emotions and for Cancer the lesson is to learn serenity in the midst of emotional chaos. Cancerians are so sensitive, receptive and impressionable, that they are often overwhelmed by the harshness of the material world. Learning how to rise above the chaos and maintaining a calm sense of peace without isolating themselves is a major challenge for the emotional Cancer. Cancerians must find an active positive expression for their feelings and emotions despite their extreme sensitivity.

Neptune, the Esoteric Planetary ruler of Cancer, was the god of the sea in ancient times. The planetary influence of Neptune on the emotional sensitivity of an individual has been well documented in Astrology. Neptune is associated with the Universal Womb of Creation and has an "attunement" with the force of light which activates cellular function in all life-forms. This deep sensitivity produces an acute affinity for the Astral Realms, making communication with other dimensions automatic. The Enlightened Cancerian is then able to gather and comprehend all of the experiences and emotions of many previous lifetimes stored in the subconscious.

Under the influence of the higher vibration of Neptune, a Cancerian has an instinctive knowledge of the Mother-Goddess Force of the Universe and can channel that powerful nurturing energy to all living and growing creatures. Through selfless nurturing, the Cancerian gains mastery over the turbulence created by their receptiveness to any type of active psychic energy. No longer at the mercy of every emotional vibration pulsating around them, an enlightened Cancerian, under the benign influence of Neptune, can collect all this emotional energy, whether positive or negative, and channel it towards the Light to be transformed into useful and beneficial energy.

PRIMARY COLORS: White, cream, and all shades of Green except for the darkest or drabbest shades.
SECONDARY COLORS: Pastel shades of any color can be used in small amounts along with colors that are Opalescent in nature.
STONES WHICH VIBRATE TO CANCER: Pearls, Moonstone, Crystals, Milkstone, and the white variety of Chalcedony, Sapphire, Topaz, Jade, Opal and Meersham.
METALS: Silver.
CHEMICAL AFFINITIES FOR CANCER: Calc. Fluo., (calcium fluoride). The stones containing the biochemic salts for Cancer are Flour Spa and Topaz.
PRIMARY STONE FOR CANCER: Rock Crystal

Rock Crystal or Quartz Crystal is a stone that is uniquely suited to the sensitive vibrations of the Moon. In sunlight or artificial light, the clear cool, crystalline beauty of this stone absorbs the energy around it and amplifies it. When you look at a piece of crystal, it appears to be a piece of Moonlight that has found solid shape and form. Some pieces of crystal appear to have different colored lights trapped within its geometric shape. This is caused by cavities within the crystal which contains liquid or gases, showing the natural affinity crystal has to the Water element.

For many millennia, Crystal has been associated with the enhancement of psychic abilities and the development of intuitive precognition. Long regarded as a healing agent, medicine cups and other drinking containers were made of Crystal in the ancient eras of humankind. It was believed that crystals, when dipped in water or other liquids, had the power to discharge magical healing properties. In Atlantis, huge crystals harnessed the power of the Sun to create a source of efficient energy for the Atlanteans. Machines of all types were powered by the energy of the Crystals. Healing wands, used as channels to direct energy into the body, were also constructed of crystals. Crystals are used in the modern world as well, in computer chips.

LEO---THE LION

KEY PHRASE: "I will."
KEY WORD: "Faith."
ELEMENT: Fire.
TRADITIONAL RULING PLANET: The Sun.
ESOTERIC RULING PLANET: The Sun.
BASIC NATURE: "Affectionate, generous and domineering."
KARMIC CHALLENGE: "To learn True Humility."

Leo represents "Self-Development". Their creative nature demands expression in some form or another. Leo's optimism and joy of life brings sunshine into the hearts of others. They are, by nature, noble, passionate, good-natured, courageous and big-hearted, however they do have a negative tendency to run, even take over other people's lives because lordly Leo firmly believes they know what is best for the person involved. Leo's are also noted for their stubbornness and persistence in clinging to their opinions against all opposition.

When a soul incarnates under the sign of Leo, it has reached a stage in its evolutionary development where the Super-Consciousness or "Christ" Consciousness begins to exert more of an influence in the individual's life experiences. Many challenges arise in a Leo's life where they must choose to act either in an enlightened manner or revert to Ego-directed actions. The choices Leo makes will guide them to experience the "Heart Light" of the Universe. Leos seem to be compelled to follow their hearts and when they do so, they create many opportunities for creative and artistic self-expression.

This "gift of the Spirit" possessed by Leo, this ability to be attuned to the Life Force of the Universe, enables Leo to have a deep sense of self-worth, self-confidence, and security. This can be a double-edged sword however, for with this type of self-confidence it is extremely difficult for a Leo to bow to human authority. The expression of their personality demands that they operate on their own initiative, and for the most part, this is how they should conduct themselves. But, if Leo allows their Ego to take control and disregard the wisdom of the soul, they create disaster for themselves and often times for others as well.

When Leo is stimulated to action by motivation from their heart center, they are filled with a joyous contentment which gives them a needed sense of self-control and inward calm. In the process of discovering their own soul potentials or power, Leo is being taught obedience to the Laws of the Universe and to the Creator. Through this obedience, Leo learns how to rule the "self" or "Ego" by bringing themselves into harmony with the creative forces of the earth plane and the Higher Realms. With their mental and emotional natures nurtured by Divine Love, they become open to Divine Wisdom and Understanding.

The element by which Leo is ruled is Fire, and Fire teaches humankind about the intricacies of Love. Leo's are in the process of learning to express Love on many different levels, but most importantly, Leos are experiencing opportunities for creative self-expression, developing a love for the process of creating whether it is pro-creation or artistic creation. Part of the lesson of Love is learning to obey the Voice of the Creator within oneself, because it is only through obedience to Divine Will can an individual truly unite with the Creative Forces of the Universe. The mind of humankind, when under the influence of Divine Love is guided by Divine Wisdom.

Leos, when they have learned the true meaning of Love by experiencing many diverse challenges, recognizes the Divine Spark within each person that is constant and trustworthy. The enlightened Leo also realizes that the ego can and does undermine this Spirituality inherent in all humankind. With this knowledge comes the realization that they, Leo, have a function as a true leader and they must search for and encourage the good or Divine Spark in others. Leos must show, by example, how the higher nobler nature of humankind triumphs, in the end, over the vain posturing of the ego inspired lower nature.

PRIMARY COLORS: All shades of Orange and Gold.
SECONDARY COLORS: Emerald Green, Azure, and Royal Blue used in small amounts are also good colors for Leo.

STONES WHICH VIBRATE TO LEO: All colors of Diamond and Topaz. Yellow and golden varieties of any stone, but especially Tourmaline, Beryl, Citrine, Sapphire, Zircon, Sphene, Aventurine, and Spodumene.

METAL: Gold

CHEMICAL AFFINITIES FOR LEO: Mag. Phos., (magnesium phosphate). The stones containing these salts are Peridot, Nephrite, Serpentine, Soapstone, and Meerschaum.

PRIMARY STONE FOR LEO: Sapphire. The word "Sapphire" comes from the Sanskrit which means "beloved of Saturn." Strength, endurance, and wisdom are attributes the ancients saw in the planet Saturn and in the meaning of the gem stone Sapphire. The Sapphire is second only to the Diamond in hardness. The white and gold hues of the stone Sapphire correlate to the Sign Leo, while the more deeper mystical blue hues of the stone are related to the planet Saturn.

One of the interesting physiological aspects of a Sapphire stone, one that clearly demonstrates its relationship to the Sun as well as Saturn, is the fact that all Sapphires, regardless of color, are susceptible to rays of radium. Even the dark blue Sapphires, when exposed to radium rays change color, turning green first and then finally turning yellow. This change in colors shows the power of the mind, (yellow), when linked to the heart, (green), is transformed into Spirituality, (dark blue or indigo). Leos are in the process of learning how to link the heart and mind chakras in order to achieve spiritual awareness.

Sapphires also symbolize Universal Truth, meditation, devotion, protection from evil, chastity and heavenly qualities.

VIRGO THE VIRGIN

KEY PHRASE: "I analyze"
KEY WORD: "Service"
ELEMENT: Earth
TRADITIONAL RULING PLANET: Mercury or Vulcan
ESOTERIC RULING PLANET: The Moon
BASIC NATURE: "The critic or craftsman."
KARMIC CHALLENGE: "To learn Tolerance and Patience."

Virgo represents "Analytical Service", and teaches its natives how to discard the "chaff from the wheat" or to classify and analyze what is worthwhile and rid themselves of what is stagnate and useless. To the ancient Greeks and Romans, Virgo was the goddess of Justice, and expected perfection from humankind. When humankind disobeyed her edicts, she returned to the heavens in disgust at the bestiality displayed by humankind.

Virgoans have restless inquiring minds and the ability to analyze situations and data which they enjoy. Their memories are extremely efficient. Their logical, scientific mind demands to know what, why, where, when and how. Virgos are hard workers with an abundance of nervous energy. It is this restless nervous energy which makes it difficult for them to relax or take it easy. Another Virgoan trait is the constant seeking of perfection, oftentimes on a subconscious level.

Virgos are very sensitive to mental, psychic, and atmospheric conditions, their minds are so fine tuned that they have learned to use their physical bodies like barometers. Some Virgos are so adept in this trait they can even sense changes in the weather before it happens. Because they are so sensitive, the environment around them, people, places and weather conditions subtly influence their ability to think and concentrate. If surrounding conditions are negatively charged, the Virgoan can actually suffer physical and emotional pain, creating depression, fear and melancholy to the spirit.

One of the major spiritual Challenges facing Virgo is how to harness the power of their minds, master the complexities of the mental process and turn it into a servant of the Spirit. Virgo constantly seeks knowledge, even the most minute bits of information, to analyze, classify, and organize for later use. Because of this trait, Virgo is drawn towards scientific analysis and study. Their minds are well suited for debate, comparison-analysis, and criticism. It is the last of these qualities, (especially nit-picking criticism), that tends to get a Virgo in the most trouble, for diplomacy is usually not one of their developed attributes.

The back-lash of energy caused by Virgo's criticisms leaves them quite bewildered. This confusion helps to spur the Virgo to seek a solution, which leads to the lesson of discernment. Once Virgo has embarked on the path of discernment, they can will learn the difference between what is essential and what is trivial. True discernment, under the guidance of the Higher Forces, directs the mental activity of Virgo to distinguish between what is Illusion and what is Reality and eliminates the need for destructive judgement or criticism. This is a very necessary step for Virgo because they are not just overly critical of others, they are overly critical of themselves as well, an attitude which is extremely limiting if not actually self-defeating in the long run.

Virgo is an Earth Element, and the Earth Element teaches humankind the lesson of Service, and a Virgoan is learning this by gaining knowledge through investigation, which will in turn lead to wisdom in service to others. Discrimination or discernment is extremely important to all souls on the physical plane. Because of the emphasis placed on the mind and logic by the Virgoan, it becomes even more important for them to develop the skill of discernment. By developing this quality, mental arrogance is laid aside and the individual will surrender to Divine Wisdom and Light in order to truly "know" how to be of service to others.

Esoterically, Virgo symbolizes the fruitful and ripe harvest which has not yet been taken from the fields. Therefore, it contains the potential abundance needed to nurture and sustain life. Virgo contains latent power waiting to be unleashed by the proper stimuli. Not always consciously aware of vast potentials it possesses, Virgo waits for an internal signal to release the immense creativity that has built up within over several lifetimes. If Virgo waits too long to release the "fruits" or gifts it has nurtured on a subconscious level, they can become stagnant and useless.

PRIMARY COLORS: All Yellows, and all but the darkest shades of gray.
SECONDARY COLORS: Full red and reddish brown in small amounts, as well as Heather mixtures, and spotted or striped color blends.
STONES WHICH VIBRATE TO VIRGO: Topaz, Chrysolite, all of the Agates, Amber, Citrine, Chalcedony, Carnelian, Feldspar, especially Labradorite and Sunstone.
METALS: Silver, Silver-gilt and Mercury.

CHEMICAL AFFINITIES FOR VIRGO: Kali. Sulph., (potassium sulphate). Lapis Lazuli and Feldspar are the stones which contain the Virgoan bio-chemical salts.

PRIMARY STONE FOR VIRGO: Amber

Although Amber can be considered part of the treasures of the sea, it has characteristics and historical connotations showing the influence this gem has over Virgo individuals. Amber is absorbent by nature, and many unique fragments and unusual creatures are found fossilized within it, trapping the essence forever. This rather bizarre quality shows a strong connection to Mercury, ruling planet of Virgo. The planet Mercury rules intellectual curiosity and the need to dissect and ingest knowledge. And Virgos are definitely interested in the detailed analysis of objects in order to classify the knowledge they gain.

In ancient times, Amber was one of the first natural stones to be carved into pieces of jewelry and other artistic items. The mental, spiritual and psychical affect of Amber on highly evolved minds made humankind instinctively form it into amulets and talismans, a fact which again demonstrates the influence of Mercury.

The ancient cultures of Mesopotamia believed that Amber was incapable of transmitting infection and therefore, used Amber in various ingenious ways, as mouthpieces, eating and drinking vessels for the sick, and so on.

Amber was considered by the Atlanteans to be a sacred receptacle of light. They felt that it symbolized courage and strength. Other ancient cultures, especially in the Middle East and Far East believed that Amber gave magic power and protection against negativity. The Vikings believed Amber was the goddess Freya's tears.

LIBRA THE SCALES

KEY PHRASE: "I balance."
KEY WORD: "Harmony"
ELEMENT: Air
TRADITIONAL RULING PLANET: Venus
ESOTERIC RULING PLANET: Uranus
BASIC NATURE: "The diplomat or moderator."
KARMIC CHALLENGE: "To learn Decisiveness."

Libra represents "Idealist or Peace-Maker". Balance is a major focus for Librans which creates a problem with indecisiveness. The ability to completely see both sides of a problem or situation makes it very hard for Librans to choose one or the other. They would prefer to compromise and find a middle ground, incorporating both sides of an issue into one larger, more integrated whole. Companionship and partnership is a vital necessity to a Libran native.

Librans need peace, harmony, affection and beauty in their lives. Subconsciously, they know how to smooth ruffled feathers, and pour calm into an intense confrontational situation. This subconscious ability as a peacemaker comes from the intense Libran desire to avoid Friction and imbalance. The Libran is here to learn how to weigh every problem in the scales of Truth and to follow that guidance regardless of the cost. In other words, Librans must "dare" to be committed to Truth, Justice, and Mercy.

The element of Air teaches humankind the lesson of "Brotherhood", and in Libra, the lesson is learned through action. The lessons of give and take, of balance and harmony in human relationships come under the rulership of Libra because the Libran instinctively feels the unity of all life. Through a union with another person, the Libra learns and experiences the important qualities of mercy, justice, cooperation, tolerance, gentleness, acceptance, dispassion, and sometimes suffering at the hands of a mate.

Love is extremely important to the mental and emotional well-being of Librans. Until the Libran awakens their spirituality, they often undergo a "crucifixion" of the body through their need for gratification of the senses. This desire for physical fulfillment must be refined and elevated to fulfillment of the spirit. When the Libran accepts this ultimate truth, they gain the pure state of love they so desperately sought in the flesh. Thus enlightened, the Libran becomes "aware" of the law of love and the proper way to channel this gift to others.

Librans possess the ability to transform human relationships into true unions of the spirit. At first, the Libran manifest this ability on a personal plane by pleasing others, but once "awakened" to their true function, the Libran raises the relationship to a higher level, one of spiritual devotion. When enlightened, Librans can use the power of the sexual urge to balance the male and female energies within its own being before physically joining with another. To blend, merge and unite two into one is the true meaning of marriage, the real consummation Libra seeks from the power of love.

Metaphysically, Libra is considered to be the sign where karmic law is administered based on actions or results of actions. Uranus, the Esoteric planetary ruler of this sign, is called the "Awakener", a powerful force which promotes liberation from bondage to the earth plane through Enlightened Understanding. The planet Uranus issues a challenge to the "justice" conscious Libran to rise above fatalistic judgments and karmic law to embrace the spiritual concept of "Atonement" and "Grace."

From the viewpoint of Universal Consciousness, Libra's biggest spiritual challenge is to unite, through the building of a bridge, the polar electrical forces of the Father-God and the Mother Goddess, the marriage between Spirit and Matter. Libra must demonstrate to the dense earth plane the true equality between male and female energies. Without this equality, the exchange of life-forces between individuals becomes sporadic and erratic, draining the individuals rather than invigorating them.

PRIMARY COLORS: All shades of the Blue spectrum, including the Blue-green shades.
SECONDARY COLORS: Rose tints and golden rose used in small amounts.
STONES WHICH VIBRATE TO LIBRA: Turquoise, Lapis Lazuli, Blue Diamonds, Opals, Malachite, Rose Quartz, Jade, all but the darkest blue of any stone.
METALS: Silver and Copper.
CHEMICAL AFFINITIES FOR LIBRA: Nat. Phos., (sodium phosphate). Lapis

Lazuli, Turquoise, and Feldspar are stones which contain Libran Bio-chemical salts.

PRIMARY STONE FOR LIBRA: Jade. There are nine shades of Jade, each vibrating to a Universal Truth. The Chinese, with their profound inner wisdom, have revered Jade above all other precious stones since before recorded history. The Chinese altars to the Earth and the Moon are made of Jade, as are the statues of their various deities, especially the goddess *KUAN YIN*. This Chinese goddess embodies all the purest and highest spiritual virtues of the planet Venus. KUAN YIN is a nurturer and protector, willing to be self-sacrificing for the good of others, loving and forgiving. She is considered to be the "perfect" example of womanhood to many Chinese.

The Chinese symbol for Jade is YU which means "Precious" in relation to the virtues of Justice and Wisdom, courage, charity, and modesty. Imperial Dragons, (the only ones to have 5 toes), were carved of Jade because according to Chinese tradition, the imperial dragon personified the qualities of Wisdom and Justice. Experts of Jade can distinguish one type and color of Jade from another merely by touch. An interesting note since the planet Venus rules the sense of touch and Jade has an affinity for the vibrations of Venus.

One other interesting note; it is considered to be unlucky to buy Jade ornaments for yourself. To receive the infinite blessings associated with this stone, it must be given as a gift to others. To receive it as a gift from someone else is considered to be extremely lucky for the recipient, blessing both the giver and the receiver.

SCORPIO THE PHOENIX

KEY PHRASE: "I desire."
KEY WORD: "Fortitude"
ELEMENT: Water
TRADITIONAL RULING PLANET: Pluto
ESOTERIC RULING PLANET: Mars
BASIC NATURE: "Resourceful, determined, and transforming."
KARMIC CHALLENGE: "To learn Forgiveness."

Scorpio represents "Magnetic Intuition" and Scorpio ruled people seem to relish and even enjoy tackling impossible tasks. They thrive on work or situations which demand intense concentration and very strong determination. Scorpio is considered to be one of the most powerful signs in the Zodiac because of their strong will and determination to accomplish whatever they set out to do. One of Scorpio's strongest and weakest points is their capacity for extreme self-sacrifice on behalf of their loved ones.

Scorpios have a high level of functioning intuition which allows them to understand the motives and actions of others, and this makes it very hard to deceive them. However, when their own emotions are involved, their objectivity is thrown into a tailspin, creating chaotic impressions they cannot accurately sort out. Scorpios tend to be deep and mysterious, much like their element, Water. The intense seething emotions churning beneath the surface is rarely seen due to the calm strength they have and project outward. People strongly influenced by Scorpio have an intensity of feeling or emotion about them which they channel into what ever they are doing.

Scorpio is a sign which has so many spiritual challenges to face, it is difficult to complete all in one single incarnation. Scorpio is deeply involved with the mysteries of generation and regeneration, of creation and destruction. Understanding these mysteries relentlessly compels the Scorpio, which will ultimately result in obtaining the Spiritual Wisdom our ancient ancestors knew and celebrated. It takes an enormous amount of self-discipline in order to achieve this objective because before the Scorpio can begin the journey to knowledge, they must first learn how to control their turbulent emotions and transform the selfishness of the Ego into the openness of the Spirit.

The Phoenix, the highest evolved form of Scorpio, has learned to master the art of Transmutation and Transformation. The Phoenix has gained mastery over the Ego and transformed the self-oriented desire nature into a desire to serve the Will of the Creator. Because the heart of the Phoenix is tranquil and serene, what was once mysterious begins to dissolve, revealing the True Wisdom of the Universe. The Phoenix aspect of Scorpio intuitively knows the true meaning of physical joining with another person. Sex or sexual intercourse has been raised to its highest level under the direction of the Phoenix influence.

Sex and death, two experiences which dominate the subconscious and conscious mind of Scorpio, are phenomenons of change. The physical act of sexual joining causes subtle shifts in the spiritual essence of the two beings engaging in sexual intercourse. This sexual act results in an exchange of "Life-Forces" between the two people involved. Because of the cosmic implications of sexual energy, Scorpio must learn to be careful in their personal use of this energy and in their selection of mates or partners.

Metaphysical scholars have long instructed their students that each sexual encounter results in taking on some of the partner's karma along with the life-essence. The exchange of atomic structures which takes place causes an enormous psychic metamorphosis within each of the individuals involved. This is because the sexual act itself acts as a transformer for the electrical energies being merged together. Scorpio is fascinated with this process and seeks to understand the power that is unleashed when this sexual union takes place. The Phoenix aspect of Scorpio instinctively understands the "supernatural" effect of this energy and respects its power as a reflection of the divine creative forces of the Universe.

As the esoteric planetary ruler, Mars reveals the hidden, elusive nature of Scorpio. Mars, the greek god of war, represents a real "battleground for the soul", a battle Scorpio valiantly accepts even though they intuitively know this will generate challenge after challenge for them to face and master. Trials and initiations on different levels constantly surface in a Scorpio's life. Conflicts and crisis are intense, especially for those individuals who have chosen the Path of Enlightenment. However, at the same time, Scorpios are gifted with the ability to seize any obstacle and turn it into a stepping stone for the power of transmutation runs hot and strong within them.

PRIMARY COLORS: Reds and Greens of all shades.
SECONDARY COLORS: Yellow, Orange, and Brown in small amounts.
STONES WHICH VIBRATE TO SCORPIO: Coral, Ruby, Emerald, Tourma-

line, Garnets, Fire Opal, Jasper, Feldspar, Topaz, Red and Green shades of other stones.
METALS: Silver, Gold and Iron.
CHEMICAL AFFINITIES FOR SCORPIO: Calc. Sulph., (calcium sulphate). Coral, Lapis Lazuli, Flour Spa, Hessonite and Demantoid Garnet, Nephrite, and Sphene are stones which contain Scorpio Bio-chemical Salts.
PRIMARY STONE FOR SCORPIO: Ruby. Ruby symbolizes Self-Mastery and Control, it is considered to be the purified fire of the Kundalini raised to its highest level, which correlates to the karmic function of Scorpio. Even in the days of antiquity, the Ruby was used to enhance the positive beneficial aspects of love and friendship, again demonstrating this stone's affinity to the deep intensity of Scorpio's nature. In the East, the Ruby is considered to be antagonistic to all forms of evil, spiritual, mental, and physical.

The Atlanteans were aware of the power the Ruby had to transform and discipline the energies of the individual who worked with it. The vibrations of the Ruby were used to amplify sympathetic and emphatic abilities as well as to stimulate passion. Warriors embedded rubies in the hilt of their swords to ensure invulnerability. Priests wore rubies because of the attributes of dignity and longevity reputed to be stored in the essence of this stone. Like its twin, the Sapphire, the Ruby is next in hardness to the diamond.

SAGITTARIUS THE ARCHER

KEY PHRASE: "I see."
KEY WORD: "Freedom."
ELEMENT: Fire
TRADITIONAL RULING PLANET: Jupiter
ESOTERIC RULING PLANET: Earth
BASIC NATURE: "Philosophical, friendly, and honest."
KARMIC CHALLENGE: "To learn Restraint."

Sagittarius represents "Enthusiastic Expansion" and possesses a zeal for Truth unmatched by any other sign. The volatility of the element, (Fire), which rules them, is demonstrated in the outspoken bluntness characteristic of Sagittarius. Enthusiasm, optimism, and a philosophical nature are also characteristic of individuals strongly influenced by this sign. Restlessness is a major battle for Sagittarians to wage since it is difficult for them to maintain a constant output. They need occupations where foresight and a willingness to take a chance is offered because of their love for exploring the unknown.

Because of Sagittarius' restless seeking mind and fiery nature, they feel a continual pull between their higher and lower intuitional mind. This fluctuation occurs so that Sagittarius will strive to develop the resources of the Higher Mind. The constant tug of war occurring mentally between exaltation and despondency slowly but surely awakens the Sagittarian to the knowledge of Divine Love which surrounds them at all times. It is this awareness of Eternal Love that gives the Sagittarian their optimistic attitude regardless of the circumstances.

When on the Spiritual path, Sagittarius comes to realize their demand for physical and emotional freedom does not provide them with the security they desire. With this realization, Sagittarius begins to channel their energy into a search for spiritual freedom, the only real freedom there is. Their exploratory nature ceases to drive them in a physical search around the earth and instead, focuses inward in a search for the Spiritual Self and the connection with the Divine Mind of the Universe.

The planet Earth is the Esoteric ruler of Sagittarius because it not only represents a heavenly body, but also a state of mind, i.e., the "Earth Plane". The Earth Plane is were humankind is learning to expand its awareness in an upward spiral. Earth is a "school" where souls incarnate to learn the laws of the Universe and to experience the consequences of their choices and actions, or "Karma". The ability to prophesy is a talent Sagittarius develops while being exposed to various situations on the Earth plane. Situations which occur to demonstrate the need for Wisdom and Understanding, the need for Spiritual Enlightenment.

Sagittarians are in the process of learning how to blend human love with Divine Love. The restlessness that is such an integral part of their character, is what spurs the Spiritually evolved Sagittarian to search for true freedom of the Spirit. In the process of this "search" the Sagittarian develops a genuine love for wisdom, for scientific, philosophic, and metaphysical studies. While pursing a union with their Higher Self, the Sagittarian awakens their Intuition and abilities as a prophet. Once this has been accomplished, the higher vibrational influence of Jupiter comes into play and the individual is taught that working in harmony with the Law of Life on all planes is the way to True Freedom.

The true function of the spiritually enlightened Sagittarian is to be a teacher, philosopher, friend and law-giver to their companions. When the Sagittarian has found Truth for themselves, they will speak words of wisdom and inspiration, and the light of Love with shine through them to help others along the spiritual path.

PRIMARY COLORS: All shades of Purple, Mauve, Violet, Lavender, and Lilac.
SECONDARY COLORS: Soft Greens and Silver Grays in small amounts.
STONES WHICH VIBRATE TO SAGITTARIUS: Amethyst, all purple and violet shades of any stone, especially Spinel, Zircon, Almandine Garnet, Spodumene (Kunzite), and Feldspar.
METALS: Silver, Silver-gilt and Tin.
CHEMICAL AFFINITIES FOR SAGITTARIUS: Silica, (silicic oxide). Quartz and Amethyst are stones which contain the Sagittarian bio-chemical salts.
PRIMARY STONE FOR SAGITTARIUS: Amethyst. Amethyst, part of the "crystal" family, has a mineral composition, (silicon dioxide), which allows it to be a transmitter of light in the same manner as other "crystal" specimens. Considered to be a stone of prophecy by the ancient cultures of Lemuria and Atlantis, Amethysts were worn on the Brow Chakra to encourage dreams and visions. Atlantean healers used Amethysts in their "Light Wands" because of the healing energies these stones generated.

Because of the unique energy patterns possessed by the Amethyst, this stone became associated with the ability to curb self-indulgent excesses. Large Amethyst clusters were used in Atlantean homes to ensure peace of mind, protection from evil and benevolent energies. The Amethyst is associated with the virtues of wisdom, truth, and humility, qualities which are also considered to be under the dominion of the planet Jupiter, ruler of the sign Sagittarius.

CAPRICORN THE MER-GOAT OR UNICORN

KEY PHRASE: "I use."
KEY WORD: "Attainment."
ELEMENT: Earth
TRADITIONAL RULING PLANET: Saturn
ESOTERIC RULING PLANET: Persephone
BASIC NATURE: "Self-discipline, compassion, and wisdom"
KARMIC CHALLENGE: "To learn Sociability."

Capricorn represents "Practical Social Foundations", yet because of their thoughtful, self-contained demeanor, they appear to be loners. This is due to the walls Capricorns build around their sensitive vulnerable emotions, for they are prey to worry, pessimism, doubt and a strong fear of being hurt by others. Capricorns are tactful, warmhearted, compassionate people. Their own personal suffering help them to identify with the sufferings of others. The reason for so much personal suffering in a Capricorn's life is so that they will seek spiritual attainment rather than personal attainment. Once they are aware of this important lesson, the constant setbacks, delays and obstacles diminish.

Capricorn, like a few other Zodiacal Signs, has more than one "symbol" which identifies different aspects of its character. Capricorn has been called the "Mountain Goat", the "Mer-Goat" or "Sea-Goat", and the "Unicorn". The Mer-Goat and the Unicorn aspects of Capricorn are very spiritually oriented and are under direct and constant Divine Guidance. Mer-Goats, who are mythological sea creatures, possess all the vast material riches of the sea. They have no need to strive for security and material possessions. Mer-Goats, loving and compassionate, leave the safety of their oceans for the difficult adjustment to land in order to be of service to humankind. The Mountain Goat, on the other hand, seeks only to serve itself, to accumulate riches and power for its own use, not realizing what the Mer-Goat already realizes; that true prosperity, true wealth cannot be found when directed by the Ego.

Down through the vast epoch of the planet, the dissolving properties of the oceans have worn away the stones and mountains of land, reveal the riches locked within the earth itself. The Mer-Goat, heir to the abundance of the Ocean, has the Divine Wisdom and Understanding needed to use the riches of the sea for the benefit of all, not for self or a few select individuals. The Mer-Goat has the gift to create form and substance from raw materials. In this way, the Mer-Goat serves the needs of humankind while the Mountain-Goat manipulates others to serve them.

The Unicorn symbol for the Astrological Sign Capricorn is a very ancient one and refers to those rare individuals who have the special task of being "World Saviors." This aspect of Capricorn is an "initiatory" one. The phrase, "Many are called, but few are chosen", aptly describes the difficult spiritual tests the Unicorn must face in order to achieve the goal of "World Savior." Many fail the test, only a few are strong enough to triumph over the temptations which occur. Only when the initiate has undergone sufficient grief and suffering experienced through the "Heart Chakra", do they become aware of the Light within them which radiates outward and transforms them into the Unicorn, a relentless and tireless seeker of Truth.

When a soul incarnates under the strong influence of Capricorn, they have reached a point in their spiritual evolution where they must meet and master the temptations of matter, or the material world. Capricorn is the last of the signs governed by the Earth Element, and under this influence, power and understanding of the laws of matter or the material world can reach its peak. Then the real task begins, taking this knowledge and putting it to work in service of others who are less fortunate or less evolved. When true awareness is gained, the Capricorn can act as the Spiritual Counselor, the Teacher to whom others are sent for instruction. Enlightened Capricorns help others to see the choices available in life, thus fulfilling a karmic obligation to serve.

Astrologers from ancient times onward have taught that the sign of Capricorn was one of extremes. Capricorn has a range of potential from the "black" magician to the most selfless Master, the highest expression of this sign. This is a very Karmic sign who must learn self-discipline, accept challenges, and experience struggles in order overcome the trials and temptations of selfishness. When these lessons have been mastered and the heart has been filled with Pure Love, the Capricorn has successfully prepared to become a focus or channel for the Wisdom, Love and Power of the Creator. In accepting this Spiritual Challenge, in accepting the Role they chose before incarnating, the Capricorn fulfills the highest function and obligation of a Spiritual Teacher or Master.

PRIMARY COLORS: Dark Blues, Magneta, Wine-Red, Browns, Grays, and Black.
SECONDARY COLORS: All the deepest shades of colors, except for Orange, in small amounts.
STONES WHICH VIBRATE TO CAPRICORN: All shades of Coral, Pearls, Amber, Diamonds, Jet, Smoky Quartz, Brown Tourmaline, Soapstone, Sphene, Aventurine, Haematite, and Obsidian.
METALS: Gold, Silver and Lead.
CHEMICAL AFFINITIES FOR CAPRICORN: Calc. Phos., (calcium phosphate). Coral, Nephrite, Sphene, Flour Spa, Hessonite and Demantoid Garnets are stones which contain Capricornian Bio-chemical Salts.
PRIMARY STONE FOR CAPRICORN: Coral. Although Coral is considered to be a treasure of the sea, it has strong affinities with Capricorn and the planet Saturn. The Mer-Goat, a mythical creature of the sea, is one of the esoteric symbols of Capricorn. In the ocean, the natural home environment of the mergoat, Coral is the primary component of this mythical creature's abode. Coral is a symbol of the rich bounty of the sea, but also of the delicate beauty that is easily destroyed by greed. Rather than destroy or exploit the beauty so selflessly offered to him, the Mer-Goat willingly leaves behind these riches in order to serve the needs of humanity with wisdom and gentle understanding.

An even more ancient esoteric symbol for Capricorn is the Unicorn whose purity and goodness are legendary. The Unicorn's horn, the symbol of its uniqueness, shows the Capricornian and Saturnian influence on crystallized structures. Saturn, ruling planet of Capricorn, deals with calcification, a mineral process which forms and destroys both bones and horns. The single horn, symbol of the Divine Path of Truth, is also formed in an upward spiral, which represents the Spiritual Evolutionary Spiral of the Soul.

Coral, which is the bony structural part of the Polyps which it supports in life under the sea, lives on as a permanent rock-like material when the Polyps have decayed. This action vividly demonstrates the planet Saturn's work under the water mirroring this planet's reactions on stones, rocks and the bones of animals on dry land. Coral is composed mainly of Calcium Carbonate, (or carbonate of Lime), Saturn's most important symbol in the astro-chemical world.

To the ancient Atlanteans, Coral was considered the sacred Sea-tree of the Mother-Goddess. It symbolizes longevity, fertility of the waters, ideas, and aspirations. In ancient times Coral was also famous for curing the "dis-eases" and problems which come under an afflicted Saturn placement in an Astrology Chart that was cast for medical purposes.

AQUARIUS THE WATER BEARER

KEY PHRASE: "I know"
KEY WORD: "Truth"
ELEMENT: Air
TRADITIONAL RULING PLANET: Uranus
ESOTERIC RULING PLANET: Saturn
BASIC NATURE: "Broad-minded, original, and eccentric."
KARMIC CHALLENGE: "To learn Warmth."

Aquarius represents "Idealistic Reforming" and under the influence of Uranus, Aquarians are determined to change the "old order" with new electrifying philosophies. Aquarians have the determination and persistence to get ahead once their intellectual fervor has been aroused. The influence of Saturn and Uranus gives Aquarius the ability to expand their thinking process in unique and varied ways, which can sometimes result in stunning breakthroughs. However, they can be very stubborn and no amount of persuasion or pressure will get them to change their position.

The symbol for the sign of Aquarius is the "Water Bearer", which is shown pouring water from an urn. This represents the flow of knowledge from the Universal Subconscious to an individual to use in service of humankind. In Christian lore, the waters of Aquarius represents the baptism and atonement of the Christ, offering us the opportunity for spiritual awareness. This selfless, loving "act" of brotherhood symbolizes the purpose of the Aquarian who seeks to establish true equality of the heart and mind on the Earth Plane.

Aquarians are intuitively aware of the important role they play in the advancement of the "new age" for humankind. Their brilliant minds have the capacity to understand and even predict future patterns of human destiny. Under the stable influence of Saturn, Aquarius has the depth and power of concentration necessary to study problems concerning science, philosophy, and sociology. Aquarians are ideally suited to work on such concerns for they have the self-discipline required to maintain an open-mind until all the facts have been presented.

Aquarius rules electricity which is symbolic for the "electric" Personalities of individuals born under the influence of this sign. They have a strange "instant" type of intuition which enables them to "know" what type of character or inner motivation another person has. Spiritually oriented Aquarians have a true insight into the reality of other people, able to easily slip past the "masks" most of us wear as protection for our vulnerabilities.

This unique insight into human character and behavior, gives the enlightened Aquarian an uncanny understanding on how to handle all types of people, granting each individual the right of dignity and respect. The Spiritually Evolved Aquarian has the power to "see" through the veil of illusion the Ego utilizes to hide the true spiritual essence of an individual. This power to perceive Reality in the midst of Illusion is a talent the Enlightened Aquarius treasures and intuitively knows must be harnessed in the service of the Forces of Light.

Aquarius is the sign of brother/sisterhood giving the personality of an individual born under the influence of this sign gentleness and creativity and the ability to understand and even empathize with the problems of others. Aquarius loves to debate and challenge intellectual or emotional issues, but they do not like to argue unless they are defending something, in fact, arguments make them physically and mentally ill. Nor do Aquarians engage in gossip about others, to Aquarians, gossip is a wasteful use of time and energy.

Since Aquarius is under the influence of the Air Element and the lesson Air teaches humankind is one of "brotherhood", Aquarians generally are among those rare individuals who treat others as they would like to be treated themselves. True Brother/Sisterhood can only be established through an outpouring of compassion and non-judgmental acceptance. People born under a strong influence of Aquarius have special responsibilities towards the Spiritual advancement of Humankind.

An individual who incarnates under the influence of Aquarius has a special ability to stimulate changes in humankind which uplifts their state of consciousness. Aquarians have an intense awareness, an instinctive understanding or self-knowledge of the duality of Wisdom and Love. This sign also possesses a sensitivity which manifests mentally, psychically, and spiritually which they use in service to others. The Spiritually Evolved Aquarius carries the "Logos" within them which illuminates their "Heart Chakra", drawing people to them who need the Aquarian's inspiration and knowledge to stimulate them into action.

Aquarians are high-strung, very sensitive and have a delicate nervous system. Because of these traits it is imperative for Aquarians to have periods of quiet, solitude, meditation and retreat from the distractions of the everyday material world. Silence enables the Aquarian to quiet their conscious mind and open up to the input of their Higher Consciousness which channels direct wisdom from the Life Force of the Universe. This capability grants the Aquarian the distinction of being ahead of their times, of knowing what patterns or trends will take shape and how those patterns should be directed so all may benefit.

PRIMARY COLORS: Electric Blues and Greens, banded and striped blends of Yellow and Brown as well as striped blends of Yellow and Red.
SECONDARY COLORS: All striped, banded or Tartan mixtures of any colors

used in small amounts.

STONES WHICH VIBRATE TO AQUARIUS: Topaz, Crysoberyl (Alexandrite), Cymophene, (Cat's Eye), Tiger-Eye, Carnelian, Crysophrase, Sard, Agate, Onyx, Labradorite, Aventurine.

METALS: Platinum, Silver, Uranium, and blended Metals.

CHEMICAL AFFINITIES FOR AQUARIUS: Nat. Mur, (sodium chloride). Amber, Lapis Lazuli, Sunstone, Jadeite, and Labradorite are stones which contain Aquarian bio-chemical salts.

PRIMARY STONES FOR AQUARIUS: Chrysoberyl, Alexandrite & Cymophane. These 3 stones are very unique in that they do not alter their color or character when subjected to outside pressure, i.e., heat or acid, a characteristic of Aquarius temperament, which is bound and determined to go their own way regardless of the outside influences or consequences. Chrysoberyls, due to their extremely unusual appearance, have an obvious tie to the sign Aquarius, which is often thought of as avant garde. The ties to Uranus is easily perceived too, for the influences of Uranus are often considered to have unpredictable effects on people's lives.

The rare and uniquely beautiful Alexandrite, was seen by the ancient cultures as a magic stone because of its weird ability of being green by daylight and rich red by artificial light. This unusual quality clearly demonstrates the correlation between Aquarian originality and inspirational mental processes and the attributes of the rare Alexandrite.

Cymophane, commonly referred to as Cat's Eye, has soft feline lights and bars of color that shift and change as the stone is moved, giving it a unique kinship to the Uranian temperament. There is a superstition among some cultures of the far east that the red and white Cat's Eye causes or promotes domestic strife. What is even more interesting is that those who have Uranus in the First or Seventh house in their Natal Astrology Chart are frequently subjected to turmoil in marital relationships. This astrological fact clearly demonstrates the uncanny ties between the Cymophane Cat's Eye and the planet Uranus, ruler of Aquarius.

PISCES THE FISHES

KEY PHRASE: "I believe."
KEY WORD: "Unity."
ELEMENT: Water
TRADITIONAL RULING PLANET: Neptune
ESOTERIC RULING PLANET: Pluto
BASIC NATURE: "Imaginative, mystical, and self-sacrificing."
KARMIC CHALLENGE: "To learn Perseverance."

Pisces represents "The True Mystic" and is blessed with the gift of prophecy when awakened to their true nature. Learning to listen to their strong inner intuition is a major challenge for a Piscean since they have a tendency to doubt their own conclusions. Believing in themselves, having "faith" in their abilities and their ties to the Creator will go a long way in assisting Pisceans to accept their unique qualities.

The picture symbol for Pisces is two fish, swimming in opposite directions. This symbolism refers, on the one hand, to the limitations and restraints of the physical body on the earth plane, and on the other hand, to the unlimited spiritual essence of humankind whose natural place is the astral realms. The astral realms is where the subconscious and collective universal subconscious dwells. These are planes of emotion, imagination, and mental vibrations. Pisceans who develop their "psychic" gifts are able to easily transport themselves mentally and astrally to these other planes of existence. Edgar Cayce, a Pisces, was one such individual who easily slipped in and out of the astral realms and brought back needed information.

Anatomically, the sign of Pisces rules the feet, that part of our anatomy which is constantly in contact with the earth. The feet absorb the subtle vibrations of the planet and transmit these vibrations to the rest of the body. This constant stimulation of the senses causes the Piscean to be extremely sensitive and receptive. This sensitivity is emotional in nature which causes the Piscean to "feel" the entire spectrum or range of emotional responses. It also can affect them to the point they feel entirely responsible for the comfort and happiness of those they love or to feel it necessary to carry the whole weight of responsibility on their own concerning any projects they are involved in.

In the Spiritually Evolved Piscean, there is an almost desperate yearning to merge with the souls of others and with the vast Creative Life Force of the Universe. This need for Unity or Union with the Divine essence enhances the emotional sensitivity of Pisceans to the point where they can empathetically experience the emotions and thoughts of others. This emotional sensitivity can make the Piscean prey to manipulation by others.

The constant psychic stimulation a Piscean is bombarded with helps them to break the limiting bonds of reason or logic, so that the individual has inner experiences which teach them that more things exist in heaven and earth than material science or philosophy dream possible. Of course, this process also accentuates the vague dreamy state Pisceans are prone to which often causes them to neglect the practical details of life and have to be brought back into focus from time to time.

Pisces is under the influence of the Water Element which is related to the emotions and psychic energies. Individuals who are in the process of learning the lessons of the Water Element are exceptionally sensitive and responsive to thoughts, feelings and astral surroundings. Pisceans are so receptive that they often unconsciously absorb the ideas and mental outlook of others whom they contact. Luckily however, it is rare for a Piscean to completely lose faith through depression and other outside stimuli.

PRIMARY COLORS: All of the shades of Greens and Greenish Blues except for the darkest shades.

SECONDARY COLORS: Opalescent or Pale rainbow mixtures of all colors used in small amounts.

STONES WHICH VIBRATE TO PISCES: Opals, Iris Quartz, Emeralds, Green Beryl, Aquamarine, Bloodstone, and all other green stones, especially Jadeite and Nephrite.

METALS: Silver and Tin.

CHEMICAL AFFINITIES FOR PISCES: Ferr. Phos., (ferric phosphate). Haematite, Peridot, Almandine Garnet, and hemantoid Garnet are stones which contain Piscean bio-chemical salts.

PRIMARY STONE FOR PISCES: Opal. Neptune, ruler of Pisces, is considered by Astrologers to be an elusive, mysterious planet whose vibrational influences are not always completely understood. It does have a mystical influence on us, perhaps because Neptune is associated with the "astral realms". Its spiritual energies usually act to ignite our imaginations with inspiration for the effect of Neptune's vibrations are generally internal. To the ancients, Neptune was the god of the sea, who ruled over all liquids, even oil. In astrology, Neptune is associated with visions, dreams, psychic phenomena, "other world experiences", and negatively, this planet is also associated with drugs and alcohol.

When acting out of its highest vibration, the planet Neptune is highly spiritual, using its power to help us achieve a higher consciousness. Neptune has a highly spiritual significance, and is reputed to have strange healing and anti-healing qualities, according to its aspects with other planets. If positively aspected, the individual will receive unusual and unexpected blessings. If negatively aspected, the individual will have unexpected problems that are not understood by other people.

The Opal has been associated since ancient times with mysterious happenings and strange fatalities, and has been endowed with almost physical powers of movement and influence. Many cultures consider the Opal to be a stone of bad luck since this stone does react to the aura of the individual who wears it. If the individual is selfish, materialistic, or greedy, somehow the opal amplifies and attracts negative or "like" energy which usually results in some calamity befalling the owner. The Healers of Atlantis considered Opals to have remarkable healing properties if used properly. Opals are non-crystalline silica, containing varying amounts of water or other liquids and gases. These characteristics clearly mark the Opal as the property of Neptune.

When cleaned and polished, the Opal glows with the color harmony of Neptune. Each Opal is unique, no two stones are ever exactly alike in color. Some Opals reflect the rich varied colors of the sea, others appear to have captured the heart of a flame within their opaque essence. I have even seen some specimens of Opals which were a deep dark blood red, shot with veins of golden yellow. They are beautiful stones, but easily cracked and chipped if not handled properly.

SPECIAL NOTE

In this next section, the Astrological Historical Eras or Epochs of human development will be outlined. I am including this information because when an Astrology Portrait is constructed for an individual, the astrologer uses various means to chart previous incarnations and the behavior patterns established in those previous lifetimes which affect the individual in their current life. Knowing the historical ages one has lived in previously and understanding the socio-religious cultures that prevailed during that time period helps you to understand parts of your personality which may have mystified you.

An Astrology Portrait contains many different elements which reveals some of the details of previous lifetimes which affect you in the here and now. The Moon, the Nodes of the Moon, the 12th house, the 7th house, the Nadir or 4th house, the Earth Sign Placement, the Waxing and Waning Phases of the Moon along with the angles of the chart itself, all serve as indicators to the Spiritual Astrologer who is constructing a Multiple-Life Profile using an individual's Natal Chart Data. These elements are used to probe into the hidden facets of the individual's personality which has taken, literally, hundreds even thousands, of years to develop.

In an Astrology Portrait, the zodiac sign the Moon is placed in at birth represents a Sun Sign of a previous life and contains elements of many personality traits developed over many, many past lifetimes. Using the Moon's placement for Karmic and Spiritual Analysis reveals behavior patterns, habits and experiences from other lives which are combined, on a subconscious level, with our personality in this lifetime. The Moon is like a reflective Crystal Ball or Mirror which has collected and stored our emotions ("Feelings"), thoughts, ideas, and experiences from our previous lives and echoes these experiences to others through the subconscious expression of our personality.

Needless to say, the personality of every individual has some negative elements to it which need to be transformed and reshaped. It is our Natal Sun Sign which takes on this particular task. Regardless of the sign our Sun is in, the positive traits we possess are "imprinted" on our Subconscious by our Higher Awareness which seeks to blend the positive patterns with the patterns already stored in the memory banks symbolized by the Moon Sign. It then becomes our task to sort through the behavior patterns and habits we have experienced and developed in previous lifetimes and eliminate that part which is negative and self-defeating. Then the positive energies stored in our Subconscious from previous lifetimes must be blended and harmonized with our present personality. You don't have to be an astronomer or an astrologer to realize the Moon constantly changes its shape in relationship to the Sun and to Earth, just the way our personalities change and develop over the years. The Moon reveals the different levels of awareness and understanding we are in the process of assimilating from the past and from the present. Therefore, the Moon is a karmic indicator of the spiritual growth we have attained in previous lives and what we have to work with, (along with other planetary factors), in this life time to increase our Spiritual Awareness by utilizing the potential growth periods which occur.

The North and South Nodes of the Moon are Karmic Indicators, both for this lifetime and for previous lifetimes as well. The Zodiac Sign of the North Node of the Moon represents "potential" soul growth for the present life time. The North Node reveals the area where we can achieve the highest spiritual expression, what new things we need to learn or experience which will assist us on our Path of Enlightenment.

The South Node of the Moon represents the effect which attitudes, events, behavior patterns and habits from previous lives have on us in our present life. It is a karmic foundation on which this present life is built and reveals the weaknesses that need to be eliminated in order to continue on the Path of

Enlightenment. The South Node represents Personal Growth through karmic situations and Challenges. With this spiritual insight, one can help others to face their karmic challenges with understanding and divine guidance.

Another Karmic Indicator of an Astrology Profile is the Sign and Planets of the 12th house. The 12th house rules the subconscious mind and the emotional responses one has. In this house, the accumulation of subconscious memories from previous lifetimes can surface as blockages or automatic responses to outside stimuli which has a self-defeating result. Therefore, it is extremely important for individuals to deal with the backlog of stored emotional and mental experiences before they create more difficulties or obstacles.

On the other side of the coin, the subconscious impressions of the 12th house can lead to a spiritual awakening and a new understanding of the mysteries of the universe. The 12th house can serve as a channel for mystical inspiration because it causes an individual to be more receptive to the higher states of consciousness. Through the 12th house our subconscious minds have a direct link to the Universal Consciousness which we can tap into for Wisdom and Divine Guidance when we choose to do so.

The 7th house or Descendant is also a Karmic House that reveals both positive and negative behavior patterns established in previous lifetimes. However, these patterns affect our interaction with other people in partnership situations. Whether that partnership involves business, romance or marriage. This house shows what type of people we attract into our lives as a result of our own subconscious energy patterns and the messages we send out into the Universe. Because of the Karmic Nature of this house, the Descendant shows us that what we do to the world, the world does back to us tenfold.

The 4th house of a chart, commonly called the "Nadir", represents our Astrological Foundation for the Soul. The Nadir reveals your "Roots" or the "Real" you which is not always revealed to others. The 4th house shows the traits or strengths which we have developed in previous lifetimes which we are bringing with us in the present incarnation. These traits or strengths help us to achieve the goals we have set for ourselves.

The Earth Sign Placement reveals spiritual gifts from previous lifetimes which need to be utilized in the present incarnation. These gifts of the past must be integrated with the abilities and talents of the present life so that one can experience a wholeness of Unity. The sign in which the Earth is placed also reveals any Karmic debts or merits from previous lifetimes which must be faced before we can progress in our search for Spiritual Enlightenment and Self-Realization.

At some point, if you don't already have one, it would be a good idea to have a Natal Chart constructed for yourself. It would be an extremely useful tool and you would then have more information to use with this section of the book. By knowing what zodiac sign is on the cusp of the 12th house, and the sign of the Moon, Earth, Nadir and Descendant, you will discover what historical eras you once lived in during previous lifetimes.

Now, with this background information on some of the Karmic Elements of an Astrology Portrait, I will go into the descriptions of the Astrological and Historical Eras of humankind. I would like to stress however, that the given "years" are approximations. It is very difficult to be precise when "looking" or "remembering" that far back in time.

THE AGE OF THE TRIDENTS

This period in time occurred from 57,000 B.C. to 17,380 B.C., and was called the Age of the Tridents. This is an era shrouded in mystery, filled with myths and legends concerning the original entrapment of the spirit in the flesh, "god-like" men and women, time travel, bridges between alternate universes and visitors from distant star systems. This was the Age of Expansion and Discovery. At this time it is unclear whether the Tridents who came to rule much of the settled areas of earth during the period from 52,000 B.C. to 50,000 B.C., were humans who had evolved on the planet Earth, or humanoid creatures from the Star System of Sirius or from another system. Regardless of the origin of the Tridents, they would be considered ruthless Manipulators by our standards today because of the absolute power they possessed over the inhabitants of Earth.

Land masses during this era would not be recognizable to the modern world. The magnetic poles and the polar ice caps of this era were not where they are today. During this period of ancient history, great earth changes took place. What we call Siberia had a tropical climate as did Antarctica which was joined to Australia and New Zealand. The Caribbean Sea was very cold, its waters frigid in temperature, but rich in plankton. It did not become a warm-body of water until approximately 12,000 B.C. Very little of the North American continent was above water, except for portions of Montana, Wyoming, Utah, Colorado, New Mexico and Arizona.

Great Ice Ages occurred forming huge land-eating glaciers which would periodically retreat only to form again. Volcanic activity and great earthquakes continually added stress to the unstable tectonic plates of the ocean floor. The shifting of the Poles back and forth created bizarre and fascinating weather patterns. Souls, never before embodied in the flesh, were attracted to the magnetic energies of the planet Earth and the seemingly endless new experiences available for exploration.

The planet Earth, along with many other worlds, were filled with irresistible beauty. Nature, wild and free, was abundant with her gifts. Fruit laden trees, vines full and ripe for picking, a profusion of edible plants and roots, and luxuriant grasslands with magnificent flowers of all kinds weaved a spell of enchantment impossible to resist. Observing the bounty of nature and the pleasant playful actions of the animals, these non-physical androgynous beings were fascinated with the sexual activities of "separate" sexes in animals.

Becoming overwhelmed with the "desire" to experience, to taste, to feel, the "pleasures" available to the animal kingdom, these beings began to exercise their "free will" and creative expression to fashion strange shapes out of physical matter to house their curious spirit. When this experimentation began to loose its newness, these beings of energy devised a more "intimate" way to gratify their appetites for pleasure. Without permission of the host animal, they started flitting in and out of different animal bodies in order to experience more intense "physical sensations" available on the earth plane.

Once these beings of pure energy interfered in the natural order of the earth plane by temporarily usurping the physical bodies of the earth's creatures, they put into motion the powerful law of Karma and became "entrapped" in the density of matter. They did not like being trapped within a heavy physical body, forced to experience pain and suffering instead of continual pleasure. But they had abused their power of co-creation and no longer had the option of leaving the earth plane unless the physical body they inhabited "died". This was living purgatory to the formerly light beings. They had never experienced pain, suffering, or death before. They sent out a cry for help to those of their kind who had not given into the temptation to "play" in the density of matter on the earth plane. However, their pleas would not be answered for several thousand years.

Earth was not the only planet that attracted non-physical beings of energy. A multitude of different planets in other solar systems and galaxies also experienced many of the same events. For a certain percentage of planets, the occurrences discussed here occurred much earlier in time, and for others, the time frame is very similar perhaps differing by a few thousand years one way or the other. I bring this point up because of "visitors" our planet has had over the millennia and the "changes" they invoked. "Evolution" occurred at different rates of speed on other planets, many were greatly accelerated compared to Earth.

These "other" worlds had mastered the mysteries of time and space travel, bringing galactic exploration to the same level as a sea voyage from one continent to another. More technologically advanced than the newly enfleshed creatures of earth, the "travelers" were greeted like angels of deliverance. The arrogant erring children of light, who still had not learned their karmic lessons, were certain rescue from "entrapment" was at hand. Nothing could have been farther from the truth.

At first the entrapped spirits of the formerly androgynous beings welcomed these more "perfect" travelers. The physical appearance of the travelers were nothing like the cross-bred monstrosities the entrapped beings had created in their insatiable desire to experience sensual pleasure. In fact, the majority of these creatures were little more than freaks whose bodies had been designed strictly for enjoyment rather than for practical existence on the dense material plane. There were two major land masses on which the star-travelers set-up outposts which eventually would become known as Lemuria and Atlantis. Once the travelers had established a base to work from, enslavement of the entrapped beings quickly followed. Finding the physical appearance of their new slaves repugnant as well as inefficient, the travelers used sophisticated techniques to begin transforming the fleshly forms into more acceptable shapes. It must be mentioned that the travelers generally appeared to the earthbound creatures as nebulous forms of light rather than in a solid form.

When a massive earthquake struck one of the land masses on which the travelers had created an outpost, deadly gases were released from the heart of the planet which forced many of the travelers to retreat back to their star-ships. The earthquake had triggered enormous volcanic activity making the habitable surface of the planet unstable for their purposes. Using highly advanced instruments, the star-travelers discovered another ice age approaching and decided to leave this world and continue their voyages of exploration through inter-galactic space. A few travelers, drunk on the power they had acquired over the pitiful creatures they had enslaved, decided to remain on Earth.

The travelers who remained behind to rule earth were called the "Titans". Many cultures have references in their mythology to these giants, gods and goddesses of immense power and even greater cruelty. But one of the Titans, a man gifted with prophecy, was not cut from the same cloth as the others. He had a vision of the lowly creatures of earth rising up and attaining the "spiritual awareness" they once possessed. He was determined to help them gain that goal. He has been called many names, but the most famous name was Prometheus.

Surreptitiously and with great cunning, Prometheus managed to gather small groups of enslaved earthbound creatures and hide them in safe pockets, usually caves. Concealing his activities from his fellow Titans, Prometheus began the painful process of altering the creatures into humanoid form using his own precious essence as the transforming agent. Changes which would have taken thousands, even millions of years to evolve through the natural selection process, were accomplished in a few short years.

Unaware of Prometheus' secret work, the other Titans were becoming bored and restless with a planet-bound life-style. The decision was made to leave Earth and travel once again through the star-filled heavens seeking adventure. Confident of their own power and superiority, the Titans had no fears of leaving their back-ward slaves behind. If they decided to return, they were certain the creatures they had left would not have sufficiently progressed to oppose their "right" to take control once again. In their arrogance, the Titans assumed no earth creature would ever be able to challenge their combined strength, let alone stop them from assuming their rightful place as gods.

To protect the spark of awareness he had stimulated in the earthlings, Prometheus decided to leave with the other Titans so as not to stir up any suspicions. Having foreseen the events of the future, Prometheus left behind teaching "crystals" which would greatly enhance the rate of evolutionary changes within his small band of humanoids. Prometheus gave many technological "secrets" to his group, carefully concealed within the teaching crystals. His last gift to his transformed "children" was an intense desire to achieve enlightenment and the need to share this gift with their fellow beings. This "desire" became a fierce driving motivation which completed the transmutation of Prometheus' "children". Filled with the burning need to "know", they emerged from their transformation as the Tridents.

THE AGE OF SCORPIO:
SUB-AGE OF TAURUS

This period in time occurred from 17,380 B.C. to 15,220 B.C., an Age of great power and change. Pluto, the ruling planet of the Zodiac Sign Scorpio, symbolizes the tremendous forces which were at work during this Era; forces which transformed atomic structures in nature, causing enormous changes and releasing energy particles into the biosphere. The effects of this transformation unleashed vast explosive volcanic activity which served to regenerate the surface of Earth and allowed the planet to release precious minerals and ores needed to sustain more life. Volcanic activity enriches the soil when rain and wind are allowed to mingle their essence with magma of the Earth's interior.

The goal of the Tridents was to stimulate and then cultivate the "Desire Nature" of Earth's Creatures towards the attainment of Self-Awareness and Spiritual Enlightenment. Some Tridents accomplished this through annihilation and the destruction of old forms. Others, more compassionate, accomplished their purposes through transmutation and regenerative means, such as the elimination of stagnate material by breaking down the sub-atomic structures into energy which could be transformed into viable and useful forms.

To some Occult Scholars and Researchers, the Age of Scorpio refers to the Serpent in the Garden of Eden. The Serpent, also referred to as the "Kundalini", was activated in Humankind, a change which resulted in the level of their awareness and stripped away their veneer of ignorance or innocence. However, in order for humankind to advance along the path of spiritual enlightenment, they had to be "jarred" out of their cocoon of blissful ignorance. With Knowledge came the awareness of action and reaction, or, "the Law of Karma", the law of cause and effect.

During the Age of Scorpio, the Forces unleashed by the Tridents caused infinite refinement of all levels of life on the planet through a constant process of transmutation and transformation. These very Forces, although controlled at the beginning by the Tridents, soon grew so overwhelming that not even the Tridents could control them any longer. As a result, the Tridents too, were effected by the laws of transformation they had activated.

The main body of the Trident Civilization was underground, possibly due to unstable weather conditions or an instinctive desire for secrecy programed into them long ago by Prometheus. Elaborate Tunnels, Labyrinths and Mazes opened into beautiful Grottos with dwellings carved out of living rock. The Tridents were masters of growing a vast variety of mushroom type fungi, their primary source of food, supplemented occasionally with fish or other aquatic life-forms such as crab, oysters, shrimp, and other shelled creatures.

The Tridents, under the influence of the Sub-Age of Taurus, developed sophisticated techniques of farming underground and under water which, unfortunately, we, even in our so-called "high-tech" civilization, do not possess. These highly advanced techniques were lost to us during the fall of the Trident Civilization, although most of the methods were retained by the successors of the Tridents, the Lemurians, who continued the practices of underground living and farming. It is believed by some Occult Researchers that the Lemurians were the offspring between the backward humans of earth and the powerful Tridents. Other clairvoyant researchers believe the Tridents retreated to life in the oceans due to the genetic mutations and sub-atomic alterations in the DNA which drastically altered the physiology of the Tridents.

THE AGE OF LIBRA:
SUB-AGE OF ARIES

This period in time occurred from 15,220 B.C. to 13,060 B.C., and considered to be one of the high-points of the Lemurian Civilization. This was the Age of the Active Intellectual and of Unity through shared goals and outlooks. The emphasis was on developing mental and spiritual strengths rather than on manipulating the environment. The Lemurians did not continue on the same path as their predecessors, the Tridents. Instead, the Lemurians focused their attention on harmonizing themselves with Nature and balancing their own psyches.

The Age of the Tridents was so turbulent that peace became the most important asset to the Lemurians. The Scholars of this civilization delved into the workings of Karma to better understand the laws which were unleashed on them by the actions of the Tridents. Various centers were established throughout the settled lands which were dedicated to gathering Knowledge and increasing Wisdom. Simple but effective systems of justice were evolved, for the Lemurians were determined not to repeat the same mistakes that brought down the empire of the Tridents.

Lemuria was a matriarchal society which had a mystical understanding of the rhythms and effects of the Moon Phases. Under the gentle guidance of Wise Women or High Priestesses, the Lemurians endeavored to learn the true meaning of sharing and giving. This society was a communal one, everything was shared equally between the members. Selfishness was expressed very rarely by the Lemurians because they knew all too well from the legacy left to them from the Tridents the consequences of such negative expressions.

Rather than one large society or civilization, the Lemurians established many smaller communities or "Clans" which supported and encouraged the communal living style they initiated. Both the Feminine and the Masculine aspects of the Creator were worshipped and each community or clan had both a male priestess and a female priestess who worked in conjunction with each other to maintain the harmonious balance with Nature. During this Historical era there was no competition between the sexes. Each served the Creator in his or her own unique way and were equally valued for the abilities they developed.

Artisans were supported by each individual community, for beautiful creations were highly prized. Even though the Lemurian Civilization was focused on mental and spiritual development, they chose to honor their connection to the Life Force of the Universe by creating beautiful objects which served useful purposes, but which also beautified the environment. The art work of this civilization reflected the harmony and grace of a unity with Nature and with the Universe.

The Lemurians were excellent organizers, knowing how to blend diverse personalities and talents into functioning, cooperative and coordinated communities. This was the era where Soul Mates were able to find each other with ease, a situation which is no longer possible in our present era. The Lemurians, through conscious communion with the Creative Life Force intuitively came to understand certain spiritual laws which made union between male and female an enlightening experience.

Males in this society understood they possessed a feminine psyche within their essence, just as the females realized they possessed a male psyche within. Therefore, the males were able to develop their intuitional abilities and could express the gentle, nurturing side of their natures without losing their essential masculinity. Females were able to develop a deeper sense of self-confidence and could blend their innate intuitive natures with an assertive creativity without losing their sensitivity or their femininity.

Unlike the Tridents, the Lemurians realized that the planet Earth was a living entity with a consciousness and capable of "feeling". This sensitivity to the living vibrations of the planet itself allowed the Lemurians to gain unique knowledge concerning the structure of the Universe. The Lemurians regarded the Earth as their Mother and respected her for the bounty she selflessly offered them. With this deeper understanding and love for the planet, the Lemurians took great pains not to exploit the planetary being which nurtured and sustained myriad forms of life.

THE AGE OF VIRGO:
SUB-AGE OF PISCES

This period in time occurred from 13,060 B.C. to 10,900 B.C., and was the Era which witnessed the splintering off from the Lemurians of a new civilization which later became known as the Atlantean Civilization. This was a critical age, and age of clashing idealogies that caused a rift in the Lemurian Society. The two groups which emerged from this split were very different. The group which maintained the Lemurian Ideals retreated to the mountains seeking spiritual purity and perfection and became dedicated to manifesting these qualities in themselves.

The second group, later to become known as Atlantean, used their inquiring minds to delve into the mysteries of science. Chemistry, physics, bio-engineering, crystal energy, all these subjects and more, fascinated the fledgling Atlantean society. Subconsciously seeking perfection in Nature rather than in themselves, the Atlanteans worked tirelessly to eliminate what they judged to be crude or coarse from Nature. These early Atlanteans possessed the same thirst for knowledge as their predecessors the Tridents, but without the regenerative and transforming qualities.

The Atlanteans developed into practical, hard workers who relished the challenge of analyzing and solving problems. They had a flair for details and organization, relishing their own standard of order and harmony. Their minds were constantly active, seldom at rest, always seeking new ways and methods of dealing with problems and challenges. Seeking perfection in Nature, they became a very critical and faultfinding society, convinced they alone had the right answers.

Unlike the Lemurians, the Atlanteans viewed the living sentient planet Earth as a commodity to be harnessed and enslaved to their will. They saw themselves as superior beings who had a right to exploit the Earth and force this living entity to obey them. They took for granted the nurturing of the planet, viewing this unselfish giving as the proper service due them. As their technological knowledge grew, so did the arrogance of the Atlanteans.

However, even though the majority of Atlanteans held the belief the planet owed them servitude, there were those spiritually oriented individuals who began to subtly fight this type of attitude. Always critical of Nature and other creatures who were children of the Earth, the Atlanteans, feeling dissatisfaction, began criticizing and faultfinding among themselves which caused them to slip into smaller "Clans" or "Families", each claiming superiority in some scientific field.

This split within the Atlantean society created a civilization without checks or balances. Some clans, drunk on power and ambition, had no higher authority which could curb their ego-oriented impulses. Each "Clan" had autonomy within their own group and answered to no one else. Marriage was a tool to create allegiances between different "Clans." The Atlantean society was more Patriarchal in structure than the Lemurians, although women were able to head certain "clans", especially those involved in the healing arts.

THE AGE OF LEO:
SUB-AGE OF AQUARIUS

This period in time occurred from 10,900 B.C. to 8740 B.C., during an era in which humans worshipped the Sun and the Sphinx, (a creature with the body of a lion and the head of a human being), became the symbol of royalty and power. The Sphinx represented a deeply-buried racial memory of the mistakes made during the Age of the Tridents. In their arrogance, the Atlanteans were certain they could avoid the pitfalls made in the past, yet continue the manipulation and misuse of creative power they once so recklessly and thoughtlessly indulged in.

Great earthquakes which had occurred in the previous "ages" had broken up the continent of Atlantis into several islands, the largest one being the seat of power in the Empire. At the center of this island a huge crystal was enshrined, a source of immense power. It was shaped like a diamond, though half of it was buried in the ground leaving the portion above ground in the shape of a giant pyramid. This crystal had the power to tape into the magnetic field of the planet itself for islands of Atlantis were situated on the 2nd Chakra or "Spleen Chakra" of the planet.

This was an era referred to as the Golden Age of Triumph, a pinnacle for Self-Expression. It was the major high-point in the Atlantean Civilization. The inhabitants of Atlantis lived in grandeur, with magnificent palatial city-states as physical evidence of their achievements. Many Atlanteans felt they were the source of "Power" rather than being mere channels for Universal Power. Having mastered so many technological wonders, Atlantean scientists were beginning to manifest the same character traits of their former hated masters the Titans. Perhaps to prove to themselves they were no longer easy prey for tyrants like the Titans, they ended up becoming a carbon copy of what they hated so passionately.

Explorers by nature and conquerors by choice, the Atlanteans established many outposts in various parts of the world. The Yucatan Peninsula was a particular favorite as were the lands to the north, across the gulf which are part of the southwestern states we know today. Southern England and Wales was another area Atlantean explorers were fascinated with. There are legends of Atlantean attempts to conquer the lands of the Mediterranean, which were finally abandoned due to a brewing turmoil within the Atlantean power structure.

Two major factions of power rose up, each challenging the other for supremacy. Unfortunately, neither of these factions were dedicated to the pursuit of spiritual awareness. At this point in Atlantean growth, the majority of the people followed a religious doctrine geared to the Path of Darkness. Edgar Cayce refers to these people as the "Sons of "Baal". Continually seeking more and more outrageous physical and sensual gratification, the followers of the Path of Darkness constructed elaborate temples dedicated solely to pleasure.

Human sacrifice was routinely practiced by this religious sect with the complete approval of the Atlantean majority. The excuse used to justify such actions was a need to purify the planet of the "monstrosities", descendants of the original entrapped beings of light who were now considered the outcasts of society. The outcasts were treated like "things", devoid of any rights. Used for the most menial, disgusting manual labor, the majority of Atlanteans did not believe the outcasts possessed a soul, let alone a mind which could think and feel pain.

The "children of Light", a minority group composed mainly of healers, teachers and enlightened scientists, worked very hard to change the prevailing attitude of their fellow Atlanteans. The children of Light knew that all creatures possessed a soul and were one with the Creator, deserving of acceptance. This was not a popular belief. The children of Light sought to achieve spiritual unification with the Creator and tried desperately to help the brutalized outcasts.

But the sons of Baal, determined to keep the reins of power firmly in their grip, proclaimed a "Golden Age of Reason", dedicated to science and the mind of man. Who needed spirituality? It was pure superstitious dogma not worthy of consideration. Many brilliant minds, corrupted by the temptations provided by the sons of Baal, were deeply involved in experimentation. They considered themselves "all-powerful", and with extreme arrogance, assumed they had the right to experiment on any creature they judged was not physically or mentally evolved as they were. During this so-called new golden age, genetic experimentation in the altering of animals was a universally accepted practice by the Elite governing body of Atlantis. The "Sons of the Elite" consisted of scientists and researchers in all fields who had splintered off from the sons of Baal seeking to become the sole source of power on Atlantis. Science and technology was their religion, their "dogma" and they began spreading their knowledge through conclaves, travel by air, and in undersea laboratories. The Atlanteans, who had long ago re-discovered how to release the forces of the atom, began dangerous experimentation which would lead to a cataclysmic upheaval.

THE AGE OF LEO:
SUB-AGE OF AQUARIUS

This period in time occurred from 10,900 B.C. to 8740 B.C., during an era in which humans worshipped the Sun and the lion became the symbol of royalty and power. This was an era referred to as the Golden Age of Triumph, a pinnacle for Self-Expression. It was the major high-point in the Atlantean Civilization. The inhabitants of Atlantis lived in grandeur, with magnificent palatial city-states as physical evidence of their achievements. The Atlanteans felt they were the source of "Power" rather than being channels for Universal Power.

The inhabitants of Atlantis had discovered the secret of concentrating the rays of the Sun through specially constructed and mined crystals in such a manner as to harness its power for practical purposes. These "forces" were used for many purposes including the propulsion of vehicles through space and the regeneration of human and animal bodies. There are also legends and deeply buried memories of the ability to leap through time and the ability to transfer between dimensions. Spacial distances between the stars was conquered originally by the Tridents, and this knowledge was "rediscovered" by the Atlanteans making them able to "conquer" the challenge of space. There are some intuitive clairvoyants who "feel" that it was to the stars that the Atlantean's fled when the final cataclysm occurred which destroyed the continent of Atlantis.

During this age, humankind were assigned the "Karmic" task of searching for the Light of the Creator within the human heart instead of relying blindly on the decrees from the head of their clans. To assist in this quest for enlightenment, highly evolved spiritual teachers and guides manifested on the Earth Plane. These spiritual teachers and guides are known to us in the present era as figures from legend and myth, such as: Prometheus, Athena, Isis, Osiris, Diana, Vyasa and others. But because of the stubborn ego-oriented resistance to their teaching, these teachers began to ease themselves out of the mainstream of Atlantean life.

To compensate for the withdrawal of the spiritual teachers and guides, the creative and spiritual evolution of certain gifted individuals was increased which resulted in the arts of music, poetry, painting, sculpture, and architecture being removed from the apprenticeship stage to true mastery. Humankind had mastered crafts and other practical creative expressions in the Age preceding this one. But now, in the Age of Leo, more emphasis was being placed on the fine arts and the further development of more highly technical skills. Wondrous "High Tech" advancements were achieved during this Age, advancements we, in our present period, have yet to re-discover.

Towards the end of the Age of Leo came the Sub-Age of Aquarius which saw arrogance and Ego begin to dominate the inhabitants of Atlantis. It was referred to as the Golden Age of Reason, a major high-point in the Atlantean Civilization during which humankind worshipped Science rather than the Creator. The inhabitants of Atlantis during this time period were deeply involved in experimentation. The people felt "All-Powerful", and, with extreme arrogance, assumed they had the right to experiment on any creature they judged was not as physically, mentally, or spiritually evolved as they were.

It is this so-called "Golden Age" which is the source of many of the legends concerning creatures who were half animal and half human. Genetic experimentation in the altering of animals was an universally accepted practice by the Elite governing body of Atlantis, which consisted of scientists and researchers in all fields. Because manual labor was considered to be beneath the dignity of an Atlantean, experimentation on animals to make them capable of doing the so-called "dirty work" was implemented. As a result, these genetically altered creatures were virtually slaves to the Atlanteans who considered these creatures as freaks designed for their amusement.

Science and Technology became their religion, their dogma, and they began spreading their knowledge through conclaves, travel by air, and in undersea laboratories. Different concepts, active mental ideas were applied to electronics, magnetism, and wave theory. Unfortunately, they became corrupted by the use of Power and began to feel *they*

were Creators instead of co-creators with God. The Atlanteans discovered how to release the forces of the atom and consequently engineered their own destruction. Plato, the Bible, and legends of many other lands, tell how these early people, having used their power selfishly, upset the balance of Nature until the very elements themselves rebelled against their oppressors and produced cataclysmic upheavals.

It is very possible, not to mention quite likely that many people incarnating today are meeting some of the Karmic Results of the unwise actions they generated in their previous Atlantean personalities. Psychic investigators, like Edgar Cayce, have been able to reveal considerable new information about this turbulent era in human history. Therefore, it becomes a vital issue for all of us to search within for pieces of memory which could help to shed new light on how we can deal with the energies science has unleashed on our present era; an issue which could have disturbing ramifications if not dealt with before its too late.

AGE OF CANCER:
SUB-AGE CAPRICORN

This period in time occurred from 8740 B.C. to 6580 B.C., during the final days of Atlantis. Trouble and Turmoil erupted everywhere as the once "Golden Age" dissolved into an Age of Chaos. There was massive flooding in unexpected places, increased volcanic activity, the rising and sinking of land masses altering forever, the face of the Earth. It is unclear to science, at this time, whether or not a pole shift took place during this era or whether one took place during the era of the Tridents. Further examination of the fossil records is needed to determine a more exact time placement.

During the decay and decline of the Atlantean Civilization, the inhabitants of Atlantis were deeply involved in experimentation on other human beings, no longer confining themselves to the animal kingdom. The arrogant egotism of the Atlanteans led them from experimenting on helpless creatures to actual alterations of human beings on a mental, physical and emotional level. The "Elite" conveniently "forgot" the karmic consequences of such alterations for they considered themselves to be at least as powerful, if not more so, than the Creator.

Genetic experimentation was a universally accepted practice by most Atlanteans and it wasn't long before this experimentation progressed to "lower" class humans. Mer-men and Mer-maids were the results of such genetic mutation and experimentation. These "sea" creatures were useful in working the underwater cultivated gardens and in the research laboratories situated under water. But with the eventual sinking of the Atlantean continent, and the mad scramble of the Atlanteans to reach a safe haven, these sea-creatures were released from their bondage.

Powerful male Clan Leaders rose to take charge of the crumbling empire. They possessed a stern, stoic attitude, arrogantly assuming they could reverse the powerful forces they had unleashed. The common people desperately needed their leaders to be sensitive and caring, but this need was not fulfilled by the powerful clans. Unfortunately, these "leaders" were merely physical bodies without true spirit for their egos prevented them from "hearing" the gentle guiding Voice of the Creator. This was an era which vitally needed Nurturers and Healers, not war-lords with aggressive natures. The "Sons of Baal" still held the majority of Atlanteans in a death grip, refusing, in their arrogance, to see the errors of their ways.

There is an overlap between each of the Astrological Ages which naturally precipitates the unleashing of chaotic energies. However, the transformation between the energy of the Sun to the energy of the Moon was extremely disruptive. Finding the balance between the element of Fire, (symbolized by the Sun) and the element of Water, (symbolized by the Moon) is close to impossible because the two elements are exact opposites in nature. When these diametrically opposed "forces" are combined with the arrogant tampering of the Atlanteans, disaster could be the only consequence.

Many metaphysical scholars feel it was the energy forces of the watery sign Cancer which was the major factor in creating the deluges which overwhelmed the last remnants of the Atlantean Civilization. These massive floods have been written about in connection to many legends, but we now have proof of the floods through the geological and archaeological records which have revealed the magnitude of destruction caused by the massive floods. Since Cancer is ruled by the Moon, the drastic changes on the ocean floor due to the misuse of the "crystal" of power embedded on the main island of Atlantis could have reversed the magnetic field of the planet causing a drastic shift between the planet Earth and the Moon, resulting in an altered orbit around the Sun.

The children of Light, true descendants of the Prometheus spirit, gathered small bands of bewildered men, women and children for evacuation. Each band of refugees were guided by a "healer" and a "visionary", individuals who were dedicated to the forces of light. Taking only those supplies and materials which would make settlement in other lands easier to accomplish, these brave people abandoned the "old ways" of selfishness and greed. They were determined to rebuild a civilization based on unification with the Divine aspects of Nature.

The old ways of worship in the great Temple of Atlantis,complete with ritualistic human and animal sacrifices, were abhorrent to the children of Light. The over-indulgence of sexual appetites and physical gratification encouraged by the sons of Baal in the Temple was no longer accepted by the bands of refugees who chose to follow the direction of the "children of Light". All the myriad forms of Nature, which represented the nurturing and forgiving nature of the "Mother Goddess" became an integral part of the belief system of the refugees. Fantastic creatures such as fauns, dryads, nymphs, satyrs, fairies, elves, and gnomes, seeing the genuine sincerity of the children of Light, came forward to help in the transition.

In some cases, certain bands of survivors of the Atlantean devastation had to retreat to the safety of caves and caverns, (symbols of the womb of the Mother Goddess). This allowed them to make a new beginning starting from the womb of their "mother" the earth. Under these conditions, the children of Light were able to demonstrate how to re-establish the link between the Higher Self and the Forces of Light. In order to do this, the refugees from Atlantis were forced to set aside their arrogance and constant striving for superiority and had to accept the fact their continued survival was dependent on the nurturing instincts of the great Earth Mother.

AGE OF GEMINI:
SUB-AGE SAGITTARIUS

This time period occurred between 6580 B.C. to 4420 B.C., during which the Twin Concepts of the Life-Force were re-introduced. The philosophy of Yin and Yang, (the Twin Life-Forces of opposite polarity), were studied and explored in depth. The descendants of the Atlantean Catastrophe were wanderers, traveling in tribes seeking adventures and excitement while looking for the ideal place to settle and begin to build new civilizations based on memories of former, more illustrious times.

During this time, humankind began to once more domesticate animals and establish agricultural societies. Dependence on hunting alone was no longer necessary. This allowed the rootless wanderers to abandon their vast migrations for a more settled community type of existence. However, the migrations had served a useful purpose in the exchanges of personal histories, ideologies, knowledge and goods. As the awareness in the rhythms and cycles of Nature grew, the survivors of Atlantis began to plant the necessary seeds for the future foundation of knowledge in the cultures they touched and sometimes merged with. The climate of the settled areas of land during this era was very warm and temperate, similar to the present day Mediterranean. A great deal of traveling and socializing occurred during this time which resulted in the establishment of ambassadors and representatives. Humankind began to turn its energies toward the intellectual arena. Learning how to channel the emotional drive along creative lines resulted in the exercise of logic and reason. The development of schools and systemized learning processes became increasingly necessary to insure material success in trading.

Egypt, once an outpost for Atlantis, became a mecca to the survivors of the destruction of Atlantis. Although not all of the advanced knowledge accumulated by the Atlanteans had been saved, enough survived to create a civilization far in advance of its neighbors. Using Atlantean technology, the Great Pyramid was constructed for sacred rites of initiation. Unfortunately, enough followers of the sons of Baal had survived the preceding cataclysmic era to cause friction during this pivotal reconstruction period.

A new class of people rose during this time, they were Scholars and Sages who took it upon themselves to gather knowledge from every possible source and to see to it this knowledge was passed on from one generation to another, establishing a line of continuity in the classifying of diverse types of information and the labeling of concepts and ideas which reside in the abstract. Craft-work such as the weaving of cloth, rugs, tapestries, as well as the art of working with clay and the use of kilns required considerable skill and hand-eye coordination, revealing the influence of Gemini on this Era.

The subtle influence of the Sagittarius, (polar opposite of Gemini), was manifested in the renewed exploration of religious philosophies. Priests and Priestesses became dominant figures in society during this Era. The establishment of libraries to house scrolls with metaphysical and religious knowledge were constructed in beautiful buildings. Enlightened seekers sought to bring forth from the subconscious minds glimpses of ancient memories concerning the sacred duality of their own natures. This intuitive insight resulted in the eager exploration of their higher and lower selves. The Karmic concepts of "good" and "evil", or "right" and "wrong" became incorporated into religious doctrines and debated endlessly by philosophers.

Certain archaeologists have come to the conclusion that it was during this particular Era when the modern forms of writing we use today had their beginnings. The steady growth of trade between diverse groups of people necessitated the formation of universal signs and symbols which would allow adequate records to be made and communication to take place. Sacred pillars, appearing in pairs to represent the concept of the Twin Life-Forces, began appearing in the temples of Egypt, the Yucatan, South America, Babylon, Assyria, Crete, Thrace, and other developing civilizations.

The seeds of China's illustrious culture and civilization is believed to have begun during this Era. The cradle of civilization for China was in the Yangtse-Kiang river deltas, later to be known as the Szechwan Provence. Tibet, the land which gave refuge to the ancient Lemurians who had not had any contact with the Atlanteans responsible for the catastrophic destruction of their continent, had flourished in isolation high amid the Himalayan Mountains. The temples, culture and art work of the Tibetans continued to evolve along spiritual paths.

China, India, Cambodia, and the Far East in general, flourished under the influence of this Era. Many Eastern Masters lived and taught during this period of time, offering their knowledge and wisdom to the hungry minds who were desperately in need of spiritual direction. However, there was also a great deal of frivolous pursuits and mental game playing during this period as well. The so-called "privileged classes" were mainly divided into two groups: One group was interested in spiritual knowledge and the development of spiritual gifts. The other group was caught up in physical development and athletic and competitive pursuits, choosing to ignore the development of their mental and spiritual potentials.

AGE OF TAURUS:
SUB-AGE SCORPIO

This time period occurred between 4420 B.C. and 2260 B.C., during an era which witnessed a return to productive use of land and a big increase in agriculture techniques. The use of oxen and other beasts of burden became a widely used practice in farming. The majority of the Priests and Priestesses, concerned more for material abundance and continued fertility than simple cerebral spirituality, concentrated on practical sacrifices in the Temples to their gods and goddesses. Life for the majority of people revolved around the growing seasons of crops and the fertility cycles of domesticated animals.

The cultures of the Orient, the Near East, Middle East, Central and South America, Babylon, and Egypt flourished and grew prosperous during this time. The Temples served an advisory role to the common people on how to conduct their daily lives as well as offering the elite class schools for their children.

Metaphysical knowledge was expanded and implemented in practical ways. The people of this time were either nomadic herders or settled into communities focused around farming or the trading of goods and merchandise.

In the more advanced societies, agricultural settlements developed into large cities where a new class of merchants and traders sprang up. The building of huge monuments, pyramids, fortresses, palaces and temples in these cities proclaimed to the world their prosperity, and the power of their traditions and religions. Artisans created sculptures, paintings, and mosaics as an outward expression of their inner feelings of beauty but also to serve practical and religious purposes. However, the emphasis was on the beauty of these items, with a need to appeal to the senses as well as the need for useful service. Through the visions of the Artisans, pictures and sculptures gave expression to ideas and concepts, but also served to decorate the temples, palaces, tombs, homes, and gathering places of the people .

The progress towards established civilizations was helped by the "Rediscovery" of Copper, a metal under the rulership of the sign of Taurus and the Planet Venus. With the value of copper established, other ores such as gold, silver, tin, iron, etc., were mined and then processed into farm tools, jewelry, weapons, and coins. By establishing coin money, efficient systems of taxation could be implemented enabling the ruling class and the class of the priesthood to gather the wealth needed for building magnificent temples, palaces, and monuments. Hand in hand with the accumulation of wealth came an increase of jealousy and greed and the desire for the conquest of other societies in order to loot their wealth.

The Age of Taurus---Sub-Age Scorpio greatly influenced the style of architecture erected in this era. Many of the tombs and monuments contained secret passageways, secret crypts, hidden treasure rooms as well as secret but efficient death-traps for those who dared to violate the sanctity of these monuments. One of the principle traits of a Taurus-Scorpio ruled individual is that what they have, they keep. This applies in life as well as death and unless the Taurean or Scorpio gives of their own free will, they will find a way to extract revenge from those who do not honor their wishes.

The influence of Taurus's Polarity Scorpio, as the natural ruler of the 8th house which, among other things, rules death, influenced this era in the treatment and rituals for the dead. During this influence, mummification of the dead, (humans and animals included), was implemented as a way to preserve the physical integrity of the body and to honor the passing of the Soul from one stage of existence to another. No other culture came close to the sophisticated Egyptian techniques for mummification, (taken from sacred scrolls left by the Atlanteans). These techniques allowed the Priests of Egypt to amass a great deal of medical and anatomical knowledge.

Under the influence of the Scorpio Polarity of this Age, small pockets of secretive societies turned to underground gods with ritualistic and sacrificial rites. Worship of the Bull grew to Cult Status in secret societies all over the settled world and had some influence in almost all of the developing cultures of this time. Bull worship incorporated many strange customs and bizarre rituals in its practice. Images of Bulls began to be carved in stone walls of temples and into golden statues during this era. It was a common practice for fanatical members of these early bull cults to stab a bull to death and then cover themselves with its blood. The Minoan Civilization, where the majority of the people were devoted to the Bull Cult, "celebrated" their religious fervor with "Bull Dancers". It was not uncommon for a young beautiful virgin to be "sacrificed" to the horns of a bull, thereby insuring continued fertility and abundance.

The influence of the sons of Baal gained a secret prominence in many societies during this era with the re-instatement of the practice of ritualistic human and animal sacrifices. Rites of sexual perversion with animals and virgins were one of the manifestations of the influence of the "sons of darkness". Embracing the concept of jealous gods who possessed violent appetites, gave these "priests" the excuse needed to indulge the baser side of their natures. These materially and physically oriented individuals also did their very best to encourage a system of "privileged classes" and "lower castes" into society.

In contrast to the indulgence in the lower vibrations of Scorpion energy, enlightened individuals, still faithful to the spiritual laws they had been given, created two magnificent temples; The Temple of Harmony and the Temple of Healing. The Temple of Harmony was dedicated to preserving and adding to the accumulation of spiritual wisdom handed down through the ages. Within this Temple, many "aware" men and women sought to raise their levels of spiritual guidance so they might, in turn, teach the masses the importance of Universal Truth.

The Temple of Healing was dedicated to transforming the physical appearance of these descendants of the Atlantean "outcasts" or monstrosities as well as awakening within these creatures an "awareness" of their own innate divinity. Correcting physical and mental deformities was accomplished through electrical therapy, color therapy, musical vibrations, surgery, medicine, chanting and the use of meditation to establish their link with the God force within. This purification process took several years to complete but it was well worth the effort, for the majority of these creatures were transformed into near physically perfect human beings, ready to begin the next phase of the spiritual evolution.

AGE OF ARIES
SUB-AGE LIBRA

This time period occurred between 2260 B.C. and 100 B.C., during an era which witnessed the widespread formal proclamation of laws for the sake of the self-preservation of the "Tribe" or community. This age saw the rise of Greek influence. The Trojan War took place during this era which served to unite the warring Greek City-States for a short time. After the Trojan War, while Greece was preoccupied with its classical period, the Egyptian Empire continued to expand and grow. Artisans gained more appreciation and recognition for their beautiful creations.

This was a very active war-filled era, with civilizations rising and falling in Mesopotamia, in India and the Far East. The Age of Aries, ruled by the planet Mars, the god of War, saw continued military conquests taking place all over the globe. Barbarians and so-called "civilized" men were eager for the spoils which were the result of their aggressive acts. This age saw the beginning of the end for women's rights. The shift of power once more swung towards a patriarchal society except for a few isolated pockets here and there which clung to the concept of the Mother Goddess.

During this era, Egypt became more feudal and the "nobility" began to assert itself in governmental policies. According to many historians, this was the time period when Moses led his people out of bondage to Egypt and the culture of the Hebrews began to coalesce and grow in influence. It was the Age of the Sacrificial Lamb---the Messiah, a "World Savior" who would lead the people into a time of peace, joy and plenty. This represented an important change in consciousness for many people. Eventually, the Hebrew culture grew to influence the Egyptians and the scattered nomadic tribes of Mesopotamia. The Ram and the Lamb were religious symbols of great significance to the ancient Hebrews, and many other cultures of this era as well.

There are stories in the Old Testament reveal how the blood of the "lamb" was used in ritualistic practices. One such ritual was called the "Passover", which had to do with smearing the blood of a lamb on the door posts so that the Lord would "pass-over" that house and spare its occupants. The sacrificial lamb, called the "Paschal Lamb" comes from the Hebrew word "pesah" which means to pass and protect. The Paschal Lamb was considered a sacred animal and was regarded as the "Lamb of God", who willingly offered himself up for sacrifice every year at springtime to herald man's entrance into a new life, a new season with the opportunity to renew one's commitment to God.

This concept of the Sacrificial Lamb or the Messiah, was later adopted into the Early Christian religion because of the symbolism of Jesus's death and resurrection during Passover, which occurs during the influence of the astrological sign of Aries. Jesus was called the Lamb of God and the Christian expression "washed in the blood of the lamb", stems from this ancient Hebrew symbolism. Even as early as 2000 B.C., the people of Egypt were turning away from religious worship of the blood-hungry Bull god named "Apis" to a more benevolent, just and loving Sun god called Amen-Ra.

The determined and single-minded pursuit of material rewards, the growth and prosperity of city-states and the jealous greedy need to amass wealth and possessions which symbolized the major focus for the preceding Era, was the leading cause for organized warfare during the Age of Aries. The men of this Era had no scruples to prevent them from marching off to war, from conquering their neighbors, literally slaughtering anyone or anything that stood in their way and taking by force what they lusted after. Iron, the metal ruled by the planet Mars and the astrological sign of Aries, took the place of copper, the metal of Venus and Taurus, and was used to create more effective and deadly weapons.

This was the Era of the mythological mortal "human" heroes, celebrated in epic poems, legends and stories throughout the civilized world. Ordinary mortals whose intelligence, cunning, and special abilities to face enormous odds and win, were revered by the common people. Tired of the endless exploits of silly gods and goddesses, the common man needed someone they could relate to, to aspire to emulate. Thus, the "age of the hero" was conceived.

The human qualities of leadership, courage, idealism, individuality, and physical prowess were qualities any man could develop if he tried hard enough and was dedicated enough. The ability to lead others in battle, to inspire others to deeds which seem impossible to mere humans and the willingness to challenge the will of the gods, were qualities considered to be the ultimate virtue of a Hero regardless of the long-range consequences of the Hero's actions.

Religious teachers and prophets also emerged in an attempt to guide humankind toward obeying the spiritual laws of God. Laws, based on religious teachings, formed the cornerstone of many cultures in the Middle East. Rules and regulations, checks and balances were instituted in society in order to instill a sense of security to its citizens by spelling out clearly what their rightful place and duties were to the community. Many enlightened leaders or philosophers such as Moses, Hammurabi, Plato, Socrates, the Judges of Israel, and several others rose up to lead their people away from simple "self" interest to a new sense of national pride.

Towards the end of the Age of Aries, the Roman Empire began its climb to power. Although the Vestal Virgins, (symbols of Libran ideals) were highly revered by the people of Rome, the martian influence of Ares, god of war would come to be the most widely worshipped "god" of the people. Originally, Rome was built on republic ideals, a senate composed of learned wise men were chosen to establish the laws which would govern this nation. Unfortunately, very few women were even considered to have the capability of understanding the fine intellectual ideas flourishing during this era. Equality between the sexes, women in positions of power and authority died, for the most part, with the collapse of the Atlantean Civilization.

The metaphysical and spiritual truths concerning the importance of balance between male and female energies was viewed with contempt. Even with the influence of the ideals of justice and fairness from the Libra Polarity, women still were not considered to be individuals in their own right. As mere extensions of their fathers or brothers and then of their husbands, women had little input into the structure of society during the Age of Aries, nor were they allowed to make any intellectual contributions. Their use was strictly for breeding purposes, for male pleasure, and as bargaining tools. Even with the succeeding Age to follow, with its symbol of the Virgin Mary as an object of worship, women were still severely limited in what they could contribute to society.

AGE OF PISCES:
SUB-AGE VIRGO

This time period occurred between 100 B.C. and 2060 A.D., during an era which saw the formation of ideas and principles around the concept of the "Brotherhood of Man". It was called the Dawn of New Man---initiated by the birth, death, and resurrection of Jesus, called the Christ. The spiritual ideal of Compassion, Forgiveness and Brotherhood between all races and creeds was a principle that had difficulty in being accepted. This was a time of great change, the shifts in awareness for masses did not come easily, nor did it come without negative side effects.

The negative influence of the sign Pisces can be detected in the debauched actions and hedonistic activities of the Greeks and the Romans. Time after time, the cycle of obsession with the physical gratification of the body continued to surface with clock like regularity. Humankind, after all these millennia, were still absorbed in the temptations of the material plane. Even after the early Christian Church was established in Rome, the decay of Roman civilization continued unabated, ushering in the ignorance of the Dark Ages,

The Circus Maximus in Rome is a prime example of the state of debauchery and cruelty which existed during this Era. Torture of animals and people, alcoholism, drug use, sexual promiscuity and sexual deviations were behaviors which could almost be considered the "norm" during this Age. Even later, when the influence of Virgo began to manifest itself, the actions taken during the Crusades were hardly "brotherly" in nature, nor was the actions of the Spanish Inquisition, which was nothing more than a zealous religious sanction for torture and maiming. The growing influence of the Islamic Faith, was also spread through war and conquest just as were the ideals of Christianity, exhibited the negative effects of this Age as well.

The spiritual influence of the Age of Pisces was to make humankind aware of the need for mental and spiritual purity which necessitated destruction of the "Ego" and dependence on, or worship of, the physical body. Jesus demonstrated that sacrifice and suffering is sometimes the catalyst needed to break the stranglehold of one's Ego, to make one aware of the Illusions created by the Ego. Through the example of his own life, this simple, loving man strove to bring spiritual awareness back to the people.

On a more positive note, after the destructive warring Age of Aries, the influence of compassion and understanding did manifest itself in various areas of the globe. Charity, courtesy to strangers, generosity of spirit, and forgiveness were qualities that became important in society due to the influence of the Age of Pisces. Some governments began to realize the importance of taking responsibility for the welfare of those less fortunate. The influence of the Virgo Polarity during this age accounts for the improvements made in hygiene and the healing arts. The Virgoan fetish for cleanliness and neatness manifested in improved use of water in sanitation and plumbing.

However, the negative side of Pisces was demonstrated as well during this era. The use of food, alcohol, and drugs to escape from reality were common, it is still common today and we are, after all, still under the influence of the Age of Pisces. Neptune, ruling planet of Pisces, has two sides to it. One side is the highly compassionate and loving spiritual energy as epitomized by the Christ in the form of Forgiveness and Unconditional Acceptance of others. The other side, is one of illusion and deception, as epitomized by Roman Emperors and their cohorts who were afraid their power and control over the people would be lost due to the influence of this new religion.

The mass executions of early Christians was due to the overwhelming fear in the hearts of the unenlightened, a manifestation of the negative energy found in the planet Neptune. What is ironic is that the early Christians, once they had begun to acquire power, also acted out the negative vibrations of Neptune, destroying the library at Alexandria and other centers of wisdom out of fear that the knowledge contained there would be a threat to their new religion. Even the Emperor Justinian, who was a converted Christian, destroyed or attempted to destroy the metaphysical teachings of Christ in order to maintain a more direct control over the people, encouraging their dependence for spiritual knowledge and guidance on a select few rather than encouraging the people to explore their relationship with the Creator independently.

The early influence of the Age of Pisces resulted in new religions, new philosophies and the growth of new ideals. Religious orders, monks, nuns and the Church of Rome had its roots in the early period of the Piscean Age. The early Church waged a cruel and relentless battle against those people who still worshipped the "Mother Goddess" and celebrated their intimate ties to nature in joyous rites of song and dance. In the end, the early church fathers incorporated many of the celebrations of the Mother Goddess into the Christian religions. In fact, St. Bridget of Ireland is really the Celtic version of the Mother Goddess.

Healers who still faithfully followed the ways of the Mother Goddess were tortured and burned even though their talents were desperately needed and the church did not have any healing knowledge to replace what was destroyed. The simple country peasants realized that this new Christian God was a jealous one, and they were too afraid to openly practice their old ways, so they devised ways of remaining true to their original faith while paying lip-service to the demands of the new god who had conquered their lands. Luckily however, enough of the new converts to the Christian religion balked at having their Healers murdered that secret societies sprang up to protect the "wise women" from those who sought to wipe out the influence of the Mother Goddess.

The middle period of the Age of Pisces also witnessed the idealistic "age of chivalry", the epitome of Neptunian influence. King Arthur and the Knights of the Round Table, Merlin the Magician, the Isle of Avalon, Gastonbury, Morgan le Fey, quests for the Holy Grail, the legends of Lancelot and his mysterious ability to bring the dead back to life. The "Code of Knighthood", one of the noblest ideals to be devised, made manly compassion and protection for the weaker members of society a virtue worthy of achievement.

Women were to be placed on pedestals and worshipped from afar. Knights were eager to prove their worthiness for their ladies through heroic deeds and unselfish sacrifices. Unfortunately, only the women of the "nobility" were treated with respect and consideration. Women who belonged to the serf class fared much worse at the hands of pious "knights". As usual, the notion of "equality" between the classes was not even remotely considered.

Yet, in the early days of chivalry, a sincere attempt was made to treat the "serfs" with a sense of justice and fair play. In return for working the lands, planting the crops, and tending the animals, the serfs were promised protection from marauding bands of cut-throats, homes to live in and raise their families, and most importantly, food to eat. The "lady of the manor" saw to the medical needs of the serfs, ensuring health so that the manual work could be done. In the beginning, this was an equitable division of labor for how could a "knight" till the fields, plant crops, harvest the yield and still have time to hone his skills as a fighter?

After the medieval period, filled with superstitions and deadly plagues, a new era came to light. The "renaissance" period, born in Italy but quickly spread to the rest of Europe during the 1400's, is clearly linked to the mental discipline of Virgo. A return to reason was desperately needed as an antidote to the fanatical religious zeal exhibited by the Church of Rome. Too many "good" and pious people had died during the great plagues for the masses to continue to accept these events as "God's Will".

The subjects of science, astronomy, mathematics and literature, once strictly the domain of the Catholic Church, were studied and researched by men who were not part of the elite Clergy of the Church. Even as the boundaries of knowledge were stretched, these dedicated men had to be careful not to arouse the ire of the Church for heretics were still burned at the stake or imprisoned and tortured. Gradually however, divisions within the body of the Church forced the bishops and priests to turn their attention inward on their own problems.

Since we are still experiencing the Age of Pisces, these early roots affect us in a variety of ways. Even now in the 20th century there are fanatical religious sects who seek to force the rest of the world to their way of belief. Drugs and alcoholism are still problems facing us needing compassionate solutions. The influence of the Sub-Age of Virgo manifests in the scientific strides and commercial materialism which began in the 15th century and continues to the present day. Yet we are still plagued with wide-spread selfishness, greed and people who lust for power. Whole countries starve while other countries waste the food which could feed millions.

How far have we come since the Age of the Tridents? Will the Earth rise up again to shake us from our current state of complacency? Will another Pole Shift occur altering the face of the Earth beyond recognition? How much of our civilization will survive the earth changes foretold by the Native American Indians, Edgar Cayce and others? Will some madman unleash nuclear weapons or chemical warfare on the world causing death and destruction for millions, even billions of people? Will we endure another Ice Age? Or will we destroy the Ozone layer first, ending life as we know it? These are questions which face us now. The year 2000 is not very far off and time is getting short.

CHAPTER SEVEN
GEOLOGICAL SYMBOLISM

In this chapter we will explore, in depth, the Metaphysical and Esoteric aspects of the Mineral Kingdom. When working with crystals, gems, and minerals, it is important that your intentions be honorable, pure, humanitarian, and in harmony with Divine Laws. The time is ripe for enlightened individuals to accept the responsibility to be a part of the positive transformations occurring on the planet. All that is required or necessary is an openness and willingness to listen to the silent voice as it speaks to your inner self. Crystals, gems and minerals have an "awareness" similar to our own and they want to be utilized in accordance with Divine Will.

Most Crystals, gems and minerals have evolved to a state of pure acceptance. They "feel" a need to be of service to others, to give Love and healing, a need that spiritually evolved humans share. Together, humans and crystals create a harmonic resonance which soothes the jagged energy patterns which permeate the planet. Negative emotions and energies can be transformed by the loving vibrations that crystals, minerals and gems emit.

Minerals, gems and crystals also have strong Esoteric, Metaphysical, and Astrological affinities to humankind. As I have described before, each sign, with its ruling planet, vibrates to particular minerals, gems and crystals. Part of the reason for this is the Biochemic Salts contained in these stones and because of color and relationship to the astrological ruling planet of the sign. All the colors and stones have particular meanings and qualities which, when worn or used properly, can be of great benefit to the Seeker.

The Gems, Minerals, and Crystals are listed here alphabetically for easier reference. I have tried to research and gather as much information as possible on each of the stones or minerals discussed in this chapter, however, not every mineral or gem on the planet is listed. If there are certain stones not mentioned or defined here, I urge you to work with that particular stone and find out for yourself, through practical experimentation, what meaning or significance that stone may possess.

AGATE VARIOUS COLORS:
BLACK: courage, victory in games.
BROWN OR TAWNY: anti-reptile, protects against fever, epilepsy, madness and dropsy. Used to promote Victory in war. It also promotes happiness, intelligence, longevity and riches. It corresponds to the 12th year of marriage.
GREEN: protects and guards against blindness.
GREY: protects against colic, diarrhea, and stiff neck.
RED: promoter of calm and peace. It protects against scorpions and spiders.
BLUE LACE AGATE: This stone is a powder blue with lace white streaks of

color. The blue lace agate greatly assists in developing inner peace and serenity. It also stimulates artistic expression.

BOTSWANA AGATE: This stone is a soft gray and pink in color. It assists you in finding positive creative expression in the business world.

TURRITELLA AGATE: This stone is black with fossilized sea shells. Good for deep inner healing. It is also associated with courage and victory in games.

MEXICAN LACE AGATE: This stone is a multi-colored brown, red, white and yellow. It is an all purpose healing stone. Especially good for healing eyes.

MOSS AGATE: There are strands of green moss in a clear or milk colored stone. It is an all purpose healer. It is also an agricultural talisman worn by humans and animals. It corresponds to the 14th year of marriage.

Above and beyond these meanings, the Agate also bestows upon its wearers wisdom, eloquence, and protection from accidents.

ALEXANDRITE (also see Chrysoberyl)

Alexandrite is a form of Chrysoberyl and is a very rare and strangely mystical gemstone. It has the extremely weird ability to be the color green in daylight or under direct sunlight and to change its color to a deep wine red in artificial light. The most powerful Adepts in Atlantis who worked closely with magnetic energy utilized the unique and powerful properties of the Alexandrite in their "Light-Wands". This gemstone was believed, by the Atlanteans, to have direct ties with the awesome influence of the planet Uranus, a planet which was referred to as the "Awakener". Alexandrite is considered to be an "awakener" of latent psychic abilities, and to create the opportunities for great and dramatic change. It is further reputed to have the ability to open the "third eye" and to grant the gift of prophecy to the wearer.

AMAZONITE

The color of this stone is a light blue-green. It is similar in appearance to Turquoise. It is calming and also good for financial prosperity. Tradition has it, this stone was held in reverence by the Amazonian women who valued it for its ability to balance the emotional body with the spiritual body, granting them the power to transform their sexual energy into creative-artistic manifestation.

AMBER

Amber is considered to be a jewel of the sea. It is absorbent in nature and many strange creatures and unusual fragments can be found fossilized within it. In ancient times, amber was one of the first stones to be carved into jewelry and other artistic creations. The special mental, spiritual, and psychical effects of Amber was recognized by the Atlanteans who utilized it in amulets, talismans and in "Light Wands". In the ancient civilizations of Mesopotamia, priests and priestesses of the temples believed that Amber was incapable of transmitting infection and they counseled their followers to make mouthpieces and eating and drinking implements for the sick out of Amber.

This stone is used to draw disease from the body. It absorbs negative energy and helps the body to heal itself by activating the immune system. Amber has the peculiar ability to stabilize and "ground" an over-stimulated emotional nature. From ancient times to the present, amulets of amber are made in India and the Far East to protect the wearer, (male and female), from ill-luck and/or sterility.

To the Atlanteans, amber symbolized the miracle of congealed light and courage. They felt that Amber gave a special magic power to the wearer. The Vikings considered Amber to be the goddess Freya's Tears. The ancient Greeks considered Amber to be sacred to Apollo, god of the Sun.

AMETHYST

This beautiful crystal is found in various shades of purple from the lightest translucent violet to a deep rich purple. The energy of Amethysts are very spiritually oriented. This stone works to sharpen the intuitive senses and is good for headaches and for the relief of stress and tension because its energies promote peace of mind. Many people have used the Amethyst as an aid to conquer addictive behaviors, including overeating. I know of a few people who have put amethyst crystals in their refrigerator to help them maintain the will power to loose weight.

This crystal also guards against sorcery and promotes luck, good memory, and pleasant dreams. It also symbolizes the change of consciousness. It reflects the essence of magic and the ability to change from one reality to another. The color of Amethyst and/or the stone itself, placed over the third eye can quiet the mundane thought process and instill tranquility. It teaches the lesson of humility by initiating wisdom and understanding.

To the Atlanteans, amethysts were considered to be the stones of healing, a bringer of dreams and visions. It was also used as protection against over enthusiasm. Amethyst is often referred to as the "Bishop's Stone", because this stone is still worn today by bishops of the Catholic Church. It symbolizes humankind's moral victory over world pleasures and temptations. Amethysts clearly relate to setting ideals and of achieving them. It corresponds to the 17th marriage year.

APACHE TEARS

This stone releases repressed emotions and the build-up of negative energy which creates dis-ease. It is a very smooth translucent smoky brown or gray stone which feels incredibly soothing to the touch. Just holding it in your hand and rubbing it with your thumb or finger almost immediately creates an aura of calmness and relaxation.

APATITE

This is considered a stone of the future. It brings knowledge by clearing away and helping to eliminate confusion. It awakens the finer inner self we all possess, that part of us which has always been and always will be in a state of Unity and constant harmony with the Creator of the Universe.

AQUAMARINE

Aquamarines stimulate the "Throat Chakra" and bring forth energy needed for creative inspiration and expression. This stone also helps the wearer to communicate with others in a harmonious and balanced way. Aquamarines promote hope, health and youth. Aquamarines also represent courage and are reputed to protect the wearer from the hazards of the sea and helps to sharpen the intellect. They have a cooling and tranquilizing effect on the human psyche.

AVENTURINE

This stone is forest green in color with tiny flecks of mica which has a beneficial effect on the pituitary gland. The energy from Aventurine helps to stimulate the compassionate nature of an individual and can affect, in a beneficial manner, the healing energy emanating from the Heart Chakra.

AZURITE

This stone aids in stimulating the "inner eye" and helps in recalling past life behavior patterns carried over into the present which need correction or adjustment. The energies of the Azurite aids in transferring the thoughts of the subconscious mind into the conscious for examination, healing and releasing. The Lemurians used the transforming qualities of this stone to cleanse the subconscious. Azurite has the uncanny ability to penetrate and move blockages to the flow of energy through the Chakras.

BLOODSTONE

What is so fascinating about this stone is its color. It is actually a dark green variety of quartz which is spotted with red drops of Jasper that looks like blood. The energy of the Bloodstone seems to have a very good effect on men. This stone was used in the Temples of Healing in Atlantis and Egypt as a cleanser for the physical body. Its energies have a special affinity for the kidney, liver and spleen. Temple Healers used its powers to purify and detoxify the blood. It also helps the body to carry greater amounts of light and energy which promotes rapid healing. Bloodstone is reputed to give courage and wisdom.

There is an old legend about this stone that says it was placed at the foot of the cross, where it received the precious drops of blood which fell from Christ's wounds. The stone, thus endowed with mystical and divine qualities, is said to arrest hemorrhaging from wounds and to stop nosebleeds.

HAEMATIE

A form of Bloodstone, this mineral, though black in appearance turns a deep blood red color when held up to the light. During ancient Babylonian times it was used as a seal to help its owner destroy their enemies. In the days of Lemuria and Atlantis, Haematie was considered to be a powerful energy source. Unfortunately, most of the time its energies were used in negative ways rather than in a positive healing manner.

CARNELIAN

This stone balances the power of the sexual drive and improves concentration. It is a symbol of strength and beauty, with the ability to harness and "ground" powerful energy fields so they can be utilized in an efficient manner. Carnelian enhances personal power and stimulates a deeper love and appreciation for beauty and gifts of the earth. It also was used in ancient times to give perpetual protection. Carnelian also promotes friendship and guards the wearer against dangerous bleeding, rage and the evil-eye.

CATOCHITES

Commonly called "Corsican stones" these stones are said to protect the wearer against enchantment or fascination and mesmerism. During the ancient epochs when powerful "wizards" or "magicians" walked the earth Catochites were worn by these wizards to protect themselves from the powerful energies of their rivals. In the dark ages, where men saw witches under every bush, these stones were jealously guarded and used for protection from the "evils" of the devil. Basically, Catochites have certain properties which neutralize or absorb psychic energy. They also have the capacity to store this energy until an individual with special knowledge and skill releases the stored energy for personal use.

CHALCEDONY

This stone is considered a generally lucky stone. It is used as a guard against fever, temper and the evil eye. The ancients used this stone as an amulet for milk producing cows. In humans, the energy of the Chalcedony has the ability to stimulate the lymph node system and the glandular system of the body. This stone is also considered to have very soothing, beneficial effects on the emotional and mental bodies, to keep them in balance, avoiding excesses which can have harmful effects.

CHALK

This mineral and other minerals and stones which are white in color are considered protection against fire and witchcraft. Chalk has the ability to absorb and retain energy. It was also considered to be a talisman for stomach ailments and corresponds to the "Spleen Chakra". Chalk can also help to balance the Kundalini Force with the intellectual nature of an individual.

CHRYSOBERYL

This stone is very Aquarian in nature in that it maintains its own integrity regardless of outside influences, even heat or acid will not alter its color. Chrysoberyl helps to awaken one's intuition through bringing forth the unconscious urge for awareness of true inner individuality. Chrysoberyl, in stimulating one's intuitive awareness, gives the energy needed to obtain new knowledge to break down old ideas and behavior patterns from previous lifetimes. The influence of the planet Uranus strongly stimulates the energies of the Chrysoberyl and, as a result, these released energies manifest in unique ways.

CHRYSOCOLLA: "Gem Silica"

This unique mineral is used to develop virtues of patience, kindness and tolerance, compassion and humility. It inspires the soul to surrender to the latent divine forces of ones own nature. Chrysocolla possesses a powerful feminine energy which helps to heal feminine disorders. This mineral also acts as balance to the emotions, bringing comfort and ease to an unquiet heart and mind. Chrysocolla was used by Atlantean and Celtic healers to lower fevers, heal burns, neutralize anger and to calm frazzled nerves.

CITRINE

This yellow crystal is good for any kind of mental activity. Many executive types like it because they say it clears their offices of bad energy. It stimulates activity in all of the physical systems. The energy vibrations of the Citrine is warming, comforting, penetrating, energizing and life giving. It was used in the ancient temples to channel pure Crown Chakra energy to the Solar Plexus Chakra for manifestation of the conscious will. Citrine also stimulates the creative process. This stone has the power to re-energize the body and align the solar plexus chakra with the heart chakra by removing blockages created by the emotions. It is very useful for business, learning, studying, relationships or family matters which need to be brought out into the open. Citrine channels a "refined" spiritual power.

COPPER

This was a highly prized metal to the Atlanteans and the Egyptians. Its conductive properties smooths and enhances the flow of blood within the body. Copper creates an aura which allows the emotions of an individual to flow with life, helping them to release old grudges and resentments. This metal greatly assists in the development of self-awareness, emotional calm, and spiritual self-confidence. Cooper's unique energy vibrations stimulate the letting go of old patterns and beliefs. Copper, although not a stone, is a mineral which acts as a channel for energy. It facilitates and augments patterns of energy so they can be utilized creatively.

CORAL

All colors of Coral are reputed, in some cases, to turn pale when its constant wearer becomes ill or afflicted. Once the individual's health begins to improve, the coral will resume its original color. In India and Italy, Coral of all colors is still looked upon as a "ward" or talisman against the evil spirits which hover around in life and after death. To the Atlanteans, Coral was considered to be the Sea-Tree of the Mother-Goddess and endowed the wearer with longevity, ideas, and aspiration. Coral, of all colors was considered to be the antidote to an afflicted Saturn placement in an Astrological Chart.

BLACK CORAL

The Lemurians considered Black Coral to have the power to prevent suffering. This shade of Coral is also considered to be the esoteric symbol of the mythical Mer-Goat, a self-sacrificing creature, motivated by Pure Love and a compulsion to Serve those who are struggling and bound up on the Earth Plane.

To the ancient Lemurians, Black Coral represented the Divine Path of Truth. Black Coral symbolizes the vast riches of the ocean and the nurturing qualities of the Mother Goddess.

RED CORAL

Red Coral contains animal and mineral substances. The Romans used to hang coral beads around the necks of their babies and on their cradles to preserve their teeth and as a protection from fits, poisons and sorcery. It was also regarded as a amulet against fire, winds, shipwreck, and lightning. Red Coral was used as a medicine and given for bladder trouble and gripping pains, and as an antidote to sterility once it was crushed and heated, turned to powder and mixed with water.

CRYSTAL CATEGORIES

CLEAR QUARTZ CRYSTAL (Also known as Rock Crystal)

Rock Crystal has the ability to amplify, blend and synchronize a diversity of energy, such as light, electricity, magnetic fields, and the even more subtle vibrational patterns which scientists are just now beginning to work with and understand. The unusual electrical properties of Quartz may be what is responsible for the power of the quartz to align our consciousness with the electromagnetic forces of the Universe.

Quartz Crystal has been regarded since the beginning of the earliest civilizations on the planet to be the magic stone of Divination and Clairvoyance. The ancient Greeks called this stone as "the ice of eternity". To mystics quartz crystal was known as the "philosopher's stone". It has very unique properties for it is capable of dispersing white light into the seven color rays of the rainbow.

Crystal gazing is a unique and timeless tradition dating back to pre-Atlantean times. The ability to explore the past and the future, to see visions and to gain special insights which otherwise may not be available to us, is part of the mystical traditions of the Celtic Race, of Oriental philosophers, and of mystical civilizations which preceded the fabled time of Atlantis.

Quartz Crystal is uniquely suited to the ultra sensitive vibrations of the Moon. In sunlight or in artificial light, the Quartz Crystal has the ability to absorb and amply the energy around it. The appearance of a Quartz Crystal can be likened to a piece of Moonlight that has found solid shape and form. Crystal has long been associated with the enhancement of psychic abilities. Medicine cups and other drinking vessels were made of Crystal in the ancient epochs of earth because of the healing qualities this stone possesses. It was also believed that crystals, when dipped even in water, had "magical" healing qualities.

Many of the ancient cultures used the quartz crystal as a general, all-purpose remedy. It is widely believed that if you wear a crystal around your neck it will increase your natural resistance to "dis-ease" and the influences of negative energy. Quartz Crystal has the power to increase "psychic" or intuitive abilities. It was the Clear Quartz Crystal or Rock Crystal which was used by the Atlanteans to tap the core of the Earth's magnetic field. Rock Crystal absorbs, stores, and transforms energy.

In Atlantis, huge Quartz Crystals harnessed the power of the Sun to create a source of efficient energy for the Atlanteans. Machines of all types were powered by the energy of Crystals and Magnetic Fields. Healing Wands and Light Wands, used as channeling devices to direct energy into the body, were also constructed with crystals. Crystals are used in the modern world as well, in computer chips.

LEAD CRYSTAL

The scientists of Atlantis were the first to work with Lead Crystal to amplify energy patterns in Nature. Many of the palaces and beautiful homes of Atlantis were decorated with Lead Crystal. It was used in windows, walls, floors, and many other areas. Lead Crystal works harmoniously with other Quartz Crystals and helps to focus the powerful energy forces of the Quartz Crystal. Because Lead Crystal acts like a prism, capturing the rays of white light and acting as a transformer to release the 7 rays of color within the white light, this human-made element is a very powerful implement when working with the Chakra Centers. Crystal Balls and pyramid forms made of Lead Crystal are useful tools in psychic development and experimentation.

ROSE QUARTZ

This particular type of crystal has the fantastic ability to make you feel good just by holding it. People who wear Rose Quartz seem to attract love and romance into their lives. It has the power to comfort and heal wounds the heart has accumulated, even wounds that have festered for many years. The Healers of Atlantis considered Rose Quartz to be an essential aid for self-fulfillment and inner peace. Because of its dynamic intensity, the powerful vibrations emitted by the Rose Quartz manifests an energy that non-verbally teaches the power of forgiveness. The Temple of Healing used the Rose Quartz to reprogram the heart chakra of the so-called "monstrosities" to love the spark of Divine Light within them.

RUTILATED QUARTZ

This stone has cross currents of electrical charges that amplify healing and balance. It is a very powerful crystal with a great capacity for regeneration and transmutation. In this aspect, Rutilated Quartz has a strong affinity for the planet Pluto. Rutilated Quartz works on an unconscious level to transform repressed desires created by the ego.

SMOKY QUARTZ

Smoky Quartz stimulates and "awakens" the Kundalini Force and purifies the root chakra. It inspires you to accept the challenge and responsibility to change the quality of your life and helps you to come to terms with the demands of the physical body. Smoky Quartz works very well to reverse depression and fatigue of the emotional, mental and physical aspects of the body. This is a good crystal for people who have high ideals/aspirations but are unable to live up to their own standards. Smoky Quartz was used in Atlantis to purify and dissipate negative energy and auric debris. The energy vibration of this stone can shift levels of consciousness from the lower planes to the higher. The healing properties of this crystal can remove drug-related stress.

SNOW QUARTZ

It is white in color. The stone itself assists in the purification process. Snow Quartz aids you in developing self-discipline and a unity with the Forces of the Universe. This stone also serves to help one suppress or eliminate the illusions of the ego.

CYMOPHENE: "Cat's Eye"

Certain varieties of this stone can be a dull red with white markings which to some cultures in the Far East consider to be unlucky an a cause of domestic strife. But the Cat's Eye stone is a medium of inspiration and freedom. Being tied down in a domestic situation can be inhibiting of certain types of mental creativity and inspiration and the energies possessed by this stone demand release from limitations. However, if one is in a un-restrictive partnership or marriage relationship which encourages mental, emotional and spiritual exploration and independence, the red and white Cat's Eye Stone can be beneficial rather than detrimental.

Cymophane or Cat's Eye has soft feline lights and bars of color that shift and change as the stone is moved, giving it a unique kinship to the Uranian temperament of Aquarius. The other colors of Cat's Eye are more beneficial than the red and white stone, according to the ancient masters. The red and white Cat's Eye seems to encourage independence in women, a quality men of ancient times and even of today find difficult to deal with. It was used as a protection against witchcraft and was believed by the Arabs to make the wearer invisible. It corresponds to the 39th marriage year.

DIAMONDS

In ancient times, Diamonds were worn as battle talismans because of a reputation of power and strength. Diamonds attract and collect all forms of energy and amplifies it as much as a hundred fold. They are perfect for storage, but can be difficult to work with since the Diamond does not transform the energy it collects. There are many legends and stories surrounding the "curse" some Diamonds carry. Diamonds symbolize perfection, purity and innocence, if those qualities are corrupted by the selfishness and greed of man, the powerful energy inherent in the diamond reacts by enhancing the aura surrounding it, drawing more and more negative vibrations until disaster erupts. Diamonds can provide unique and wonderful insights, but they are dangerous to work with unless the motives of the individual are pure.

YELLOW DIAMOND

To the Atlanteans, the Yellow Diamond represented the power of the Sun, eternity of the spirit, and the forces of light. They believed the Yellow Diamond contained an eternal flame of Truth within its heart. Unlike its close relative, (the regular diamond), the Yellow Diamond symbolized incorruptibility to many of the ancient cultures. The Atlanteans considered this stone to possess the "essence" of life, its energy patters were innocent and constant.

This particular diamond has a more harmonious vibration than the regular diamond. It symbolizes durability and magnanimity. It corresponds to the 60th marriage year. The yellow diamond also symbolizes spiritual initiation and represents the higher self in humankind. The name diamond means "invincible".

EMERALD

This stone, as well as other green colored stones, are very relaxing and soothing to the emotions. Green is the color of the Heart Chakra symbolizing peace, balance and love. Its energies are neither feminine or masculine and can be used equally effectively by both sexes. Emeralds symbolize the growth of spiritual awareness and harmony with all life. The energy of this stone promotes a pleasant family life and provides protection on journeys.

The Atlanteans used the energy vibrations of the Emerald to draw out the innate intuitive and psychic talents each individual possesses. These stones are also associated with spiritual forecasting and the development of a good memory. In the Far East, Emeralds represent Immortality, youth and hope. It is used to ward off blindness and evil fascination. European culture believes the Emeralds are protection against witchcraft and snakes. The Emerald also corresponds to the 5th marriage year.

FELDSPAR

The energy of the green Feldspar stimulates the thought processes and emits the vibrations needed to eliminate ideas which create an imbalance between the mental, emotional, and spiritual bodies. This stone grants inspiration to artists, especially those who work with sculpting, jewelry making, and clay. The stone has been used in the Middle East as a talisman for sunstrokes. The Temple of Healing in Atlantis and Egypt used the energies of the Feldspar in treating problems of the "head", this could have been actual physical trauma or psychological problems.

FLUORITE

The unique properties of this stone activates the power of the third eye. The energy of Fluorite is ideally suited to enhance the function of the Brow Chakra. It promotes the advancement of the mind, develops the ability to comprehend and integrate non-physical and physical dimensions.

BLUE-inner peace, mental calmness and serenity.
PURPLE-devotional, committed to spirit.
YELLOW-wisdom and understanding.
WHITE-purity and oneness.

GARNET

This deep rich red stone symbolizes the profound love of Soul Mates. It is a stone of permanence and loyalty. Garnets represent distinction and determination which makes it an excellent stone to wear when beginning new projects or starting a new job or career. The energy of this stone infuses the personality of the wearer with charisma and charm, bringing out leadership qualities and enhancing self-esteem.

Almost all of the stones in the "red" spectrum of color are good for the circulatory system of the body. They stimulate the Kundalini of the body and invigorate the heart. Garnets were used by the Lemurians to clear the thought process in order to bring balance within the three states of consciousness. Because of Garnet's intimate connection with the deeper, purer side of love, they can be used to promote peace and calmness. Garnets were used as talismans by the Greeks and Romans as a means of protection against accidents and/or difficulties while traveling.

HAEMITE see Bloodstone

HYACINTH see Zircon

JADE

The Lemurians used the powerful vibrations of Jade to draw out negative energy from the physical, mental and emotional bodies. Because it can extract energy from its surroundings, Jade was widely used in the temples. Large statues, pillars, and mosaics were carved from different shades of Jade and placed in strategic locations. There are 9 shades of Jade, each vibrating to a specific Universal Truth. In Chinese, the name Jade means "precious" and is related to the virtues of Justice, Wisdom, Courage, Charity, and Modesty. Qualities which were and still are highly prized by the Chinese.

Jade is considered to be universally lucky. However, to activate the "lucky" aspect of Jade, one should not purchase Jade for themselves. Jade should be given or received as a gift in order for its qualities of prosperity, happiness and luck to be properly released. The energy of Jade can be used to prevent fatigue, and is beneficial for all internal disorders, especially the kidneys, (which eliminates negative waste).

PINK JADE

This shade of Jade represents the Divine Mother principle, the feminine aspects of the Creator. Pink Jade symbolizes enlightenment, generosity, and a special kind of wisdom that comes through dedication to Universal Truths and a willingness to accept Initiations and Testings. All shades of the Jade stone have their roots in the ancient Lemurian Civilization.

JET

Refugees from Atlantis who settled in the British Isles found the fumes of this mineral to have healing properties when burned like incense. The healers from Atlantis also discovered Jet to have unusual mystical properties. The Druid Priests and Priestesses, descended from the Atlanteans, wore necklaces and other jewelry made from Jet to insure their inner mystical journeys would be successful. The Celts believed Jet brought luck and protection, and highly prized its unique properties.

LAPIS LAZULI

Lapis Lazuli is an excellent stone for the Throat Chakra. Individuals who lecture, public speakers, and singers of all ranges would find the Lapis Lazuli to be a beneficial stone to wear. It greatly aids communication skills and promotes a balance between the mental thinking process and the need to communicate one's thoughts.

The energy pattern of Lapis Lazuli stimulates and enhances creative and artistic work. Lapis is a mental and spiritual cleanser, it draws the mind inward to seek its own source of power. This stone has the ability to release and heal charged emotional wounds from the present life and "psychic" wounds carried over from previous incarnations. Lapis Lazuli is considered a "good luck" charm both in ancient times and the modern era. It also represents universal love and luck.

Lapis Lazuli was called by magicians of ancient times the "Stone of Heaven". This stone symbolizes self-assurance and increases sensitivity to higher vibrations. It was reputed to grant the wearer the gift of strength and ensure prosperity. Lapis Lazuli was sacred to the ancient Egyptians and used extensively in their tombs for they believed that this stone would protect and guide the dead on their journey into the afterlife.

MALACHITE

The energies of this stone vibrate in tune with the Solar Plexus Chakra, allowing it to serve as a grounding force to channel higher energies onto the planet. Malachite absorbs and transmutes negative energy, dis-ease and helps surface the psychic-emotional reasons for illness. Malachite has the ability to harmonizes the duality within one's self or within a relationship. It also clears away static or repressed emotions. Malachite has also been used since ancient times as a talisman against the evil-eye, as a teething aid by medicine women, and was considered to ensure a safe and easy childbirth.

MOONSTONE

Because of the special vibrations of this stone, it has the ability to improve sleep and to clarify experiences while dreaming or astral traveling. Moonstone has the ability to soothe and balance emotions while allowing awareness to unfold which promotes the experience of calmness and peace of mind. This stone has the power to neutralize negative emotions. Moonstone is a balance for female energy.

To Atlanteans, the Moonstone was a gem of emotion and was said to arouse the tender passions of young lovers. In ancient mystical legends, the moonstone was revered for its ability to empower its wearer to perceive the future, but only if the stone was carefully placed under the tongue on the night of the full moon. In East Indian traditions, the moonstone is the gem which symbolizes the third eye. It is said to give clarity to spiritual understanding and to assist those in the astral realm.

OBSIDIAN

This stone vibrates to the First Chakra of the body or the Root Chakra. It is the "Warrior of Truth" and pertains to the physical plane, to survival and to fulfillment of the personal will. Obsidian acts like a magnet that draws spirit forces into the body to be governed by our conscious will under the guidance of the higher astral realms. To the ancient peoples of Lemuria, Obsidian taught them that the "Black Hole" within them was caused by fear.

This ego oriented fear or veil of illusion could easily be overcome by the Forces of Light in the Universe. Obsidian also teaches, on a subconscious level and during the dream-state or while in meditation, how to utilize the light forces properly in order to channel positive-healing energy into a dark world.

OLIVINE

In ancient times, this stone was carved into drinking vessels to improve the properties of medicine. Olivine works with the natural healing forces of the body to stimulate the efficiency of the Immune System. Medicinal herbs and roots were stored in jars or vessels made of Olivine to protect and improve their potency in healing. This stone was also worn as an amulet or a talisman by Healers in many ancient cultures, a custom dating back to the Atlantean Age.

ONYX

The legends around this stone are both positive and negative. It is lucky to some people, and unlucky for others. One of the most interesting aspects concerning Onyx lies in its ability to augment the energy pattern of its wearer. This can be a double edged sword, for if you are depressed, angry, bitter, or display a general negative personality, the Onyx will augment those energies, increase them until they reach an overwhelming stage.

On the other hand, if you are generally a positive person, an individual who strives to walk the enlightened path with forgiveness and unconditional love and acceptance as your goals, the Onyx will act as a powerful augmenting force to the energies you generate. Onyx, in its various color shades, has been carved into a vast variety of shapes to represent spirit guides or ancient gods and goddesses by many different cultures. Charms and talismans have also been carved from this stone to ensure good fortune and prosperity.

OPAL

Many cultures consider the Opal to be a stone of bad luck since this stone does react to the aura of the individual who wears it. If the individual is selfish, materialistic, or greedy, somehow the Opal amplifies and attracts negative or "like" energy which usually results in some calamity befalling the owner. The Healers of Atlantis considered Opals to have remarkable healing properties if used properly. Opals are non-crystalline silica, containing varying amounts of water or other liquids and gases. These characteristics clearly mark the Opal as the property of Neptune.

When carefully cut, cleaned and polished, the Opal glows with the varied color harmony of Neptune. Each Opal is unique, no two stones are ever exactly alike in color. Some Opals reflect the rich varied colors of the sea, others appear to have captured the heart of a flame within their opaque essence. I have even seen some specimens of Opals which were a deep dark blood red, shot with veins of golden yellow. They are beautiful stones, but easily cracked and chipped if not handled properly.

The Lemurians used the power of the Opal to stimulate creative ideas. Artists, writers, musicians, poets, or anyone involved in the creative arts benefit from the stimulation provide by Opals. To the Lemurians, Opals symbolized purification of the psychic nature, faithfulness and spiritual intensity. They used strings of Opal stones during meditation and while saying prayers because the intense power of this stone enhanced the purity of intuitional visions from the Universal Mind.

Some cultures believed Opals ensured happy marriages and promoted reliable friendships. Many modern-day occultists believe opals can bring legal success and protect the wearer from anger.

BLACK OPAL

People who wear these rare and beautiful stones must have high standards, warm hearts, and an unselfish generosity. No evil can linger in their hearts or minds for the Opal will bring the wearer only what they deserve. The Black Opal is a stone of Karma and very powerful. Opals are destined to be worn by those individuals who possess a passion for life and a deep seated desire to make a positive difference in the lives of those they touch. For the person whose vibrations are right for the Black Opal, when wearing this stone and meditating, they can be given important insights on the working of Karma.

PEARL

For thousands of years, the Pearl has been the emblem of chastity and purity. It corresponds to the 30th marriage year. To the healers of Atlantis, Pearls represented the feminine principle and the special inner beauty that emanates from a woman who meets the trials of life with faith, love and forgiveness in her heart. This stone represents the mystical energies of the moon which can be used positively or negatively. The Pearl also symbolizes triumph of the Spirit over adversity, strength against all opposition and the determination to succeed against all odds. The Pearl has the quality of Self-Transformation and the ability to use the power of Transmutation in a positive effective manner.

BLACK PEARL

This jewel of the sea symbolizes a Karmic Catalyst. When wearing it, the individual is activating their own karmic history, both of the present life and of previous lives. By activating this karma, the individual is able to free themselves from its binding ties. Karma is neither good nor bad, it is important to remember this. But it does keep us connected to the Earth Plane and the physical body.

PERIDOT

The energy field of the Peridot has the ability to cleanse the emotional body of hurt feelings, anger, and jealousy, it also soothes bruised egos by reminding the individual not to place so much importance on demands of the ego. The Atlanteans found this stone to be mentally stimulating with strong powers of rejuvenation. Healers from Lemuria and Atlantis used the power of the Peridot to balance the endocrine system thereby regenerating the physical body. This stone also has a beneficial effect on the adrenal glands and the liver.

Peridot was used in ancient times as a potent love amulet, and when worn on the left arm it attracted lovers who possessed sweet, considerate, and loving dispositions. In ancient cultures, the Peridot was believed to bestow eloquence and persuasiveness to the wearer. When set in gold, Peridot is supposed to exert great powers over negative people.

PUMICE STONE
This was used by ancient cultures as an amulet for ensuring safe childbirth. Pumice was also considered to be a purifying stone and could purge negative energy from a human or an animal. Ancient cultures used the Pumice Stone as a cleansing agent as well.

RHODOCHROSITE
Rhodochrosite was used in Lemuria as an aid to meditation. Good size thin slices of this stone were framed in copper, much like a picture, and held in the hand or set in a wall, while the individual focused their attention on the unique free-form patterns to be found in the stone. The Rhodochrosite assists in quieting the conscious mind so that the link between the individual's subconscious mind and the Universal Mind could be opened. This stone is similar in its function to Rose Quartz and its energies can also soothe difficulties in relationships.

RUBY
The cultures of the Far East have always considered the Ruby to possess magic powers. They have used this stone as an antidote for poison, evil thoughts and self-indulgence. In India, the Ruby is used to enhance love and friendship, they even make amulets from this stone to preserve the integrity of a loved one's affections. As with other red stones, the Ruby endows the wearer with courage and self-esteem. This stone has a very beneficial effect on the heart and circulatory system, contributing to longevity.

The Lemurians believed the Ruby symbolized mastery of spiritual laws. Its energies were used to develop the power of telepathic-empathy. When an initiate of the Temple had successfully passed their final "tests", they were presented a Ruby set within a copper or silver band to be worn around the head, allowing the Ruby to rest on the "third eye". This symbolized the elevated status of a High Priestess or Priest.

The energy patterns of the Ruby revitalizes the Kundalini, stirring the passions of the "desire" nature to a higher, less selfish level. The awakened passion is then channeled into service for others because the energy of the Ruby has created a "reservoir" of power to draw from. Kings and Queens throughout history have coveted rubies for their crowns because of the inherent "dignity" the Ruby outwardly projects. Along with Sapphires, the Ruby is next in hardness to the Diamond.

SAPPHIRE
The Lemurians believed Sapphires symbolized the virtues of devotion, spirituality, and Universal Truth. The vibrations of the Sapphire enhance meditation and contemplation. In Lemuria, those men and women who dedi-

cated their lives to spiritual pursuits valued the power of the Sapphire to preserve their vows of chastity because it has a cooling, tranquilizing effect on the "desire" nature. The ancient Egyptians believed that Sapphires and even dark blue glass beads gave protection from evil. Their mythology associated the color and stone with heavenly attributes.

The Atlanteans used the energy force of Sapphires in the healing temples to sooth excess energy. These healers discovered the power of this stone was very beneficial for any kind of inflammation of the body involving muscles, nerves, tendons, joints, etc. In esoteric lore, Sapphires are associated with the spiritual influences of the planet Venus. The vibrations of Sapphires have been used to even out the temper and as an antidote to poison.

In Atlantis, Egypt and Greece, the power of a Sapphire was used to increase the understanding of their "oracles" or prophets, and could cleanse poisonous attitudes from the mind. In Eastern countries this stone is considered a charm against blindness. It is also good for making medicine Cups.

SODALITE

Sodalite has the ability to clear away old mental patterns from the subconscious which block or limit growth and progress. This stone also increases one's ability to think rationally and intellectually, allowing for logical conclusions to be made. Sodalite has the energy patterns needed to stabilize mental power and assist the individual in gaining understanding of oneself in a situation. This stone corresponds to the third eye and its vibrations can open the "brow Chakra". When used properly, Sodalite will prepare the mind to receive inner sight and intuitive knowledge.

SPHENE

This is a rare stone which has the ability to overcome negative energy. It is very useful in stabilizing a "flighty" personality, or for an individual who constantly "flip-flops" from one side to the other unable to make up their mind. The Sphene generates an energy force which is very beneficial in dealing with "mood swings". This stone helps an individual to become "balanced" and therefore able to deal with personality or behavior patterns which they wish to transform. The word "Sphene" ln Greek means "a wedge", a description which aptly describes the power of this stone. The Sphene serves as a "wedge" between materialism and spirituality, opening the passageway for Divine Light to flow unobstructed.

SPINEL

This stone serves as a generating force to renew energy reserves. Spinel also gives one the confidence, determination, and drive to continue with difficult tasks. This stone effects the physical and mental state in a positive manner by creating a current of energy which stimulates and activates the adrenal system of the body.

STALAGMITES

In Lemuria, Stalagmites were considered to be artistic gifts of beauty from the Earth itself, whom the Lemurians considered to be a sentient being in its own right. In later cultures which followed the Lemurians and Atlanteans, these rock formations were used by the ancient peoples as amulets and talismans against witchcraft and evils. The Celts of Britain and Europe considered Stalagmites to be the work of Dwarfs or spirits of the Earth or even the work of Dragons who were seeking to protect their dwelling places.

STAR RUBY
This stone symbolizes penetrative wisdom. It corresponds to the 52nd marriage year. It is a stone of physical honor and action. It represents a self-knowing and the ability to communicate the essence of knowledge learned from the lessons an individual has met and mastered in previous lifetimes as well as from their present incarnation.

STAR SAPPHIRE
This stone symbolizes wisdom. It corresponds to the 26th marriage year. Star Sapphires represent a mental creativeness that is in union with the Life-Force of the Universe. This is an excellent stone for Spiritual Teachers to wear because it helps the teacher to focus their thoughts so they can channel Knowledge and Wisdom from the higher realms to those who need it.

SULFUR
This stone cleanses the aura and the Chakra Centers of unwanted energy. It is also considered a talisman against hypnotically induced sickness and the effects of "voodoo". Sulfur was used by the Lemurians to eliminate or neutralize negative emotions such as jealousy, greed, and anger. Medicinal cups were also made from Sulfur to serve as a stimulus to the herbs and medicines administered.

TEKTITE or Meteorite
The potent astral energy of this "stone" stimulates the mind to glean as much knowledge from the encounters and circumstances of life as is possible. The Lemurians considered these stones to be sacred and to have the power to release any residual from unpleasant experiences from an individual's psyche. Tektite also serves as a source of Inspiration and Illumination. It represents a gift from the Universe, and possesses powers which can only be unleashed by those individuals who are "Light Workers". Any attempts to use the stored energy of the Tektite for selfish or negative reasons is not allowed. Those individuals who try to use the powers contained by the Tektite in negative ways find the stone unresponsive.

TOPAZ
The Topaz has the power to bring forth true individuality and creativity for those who work with this stone. It encourages confidence in trusting one's decisions and supplies the energy needed to replace negativity with love and joy. Topaz represents spiritual inspiration which is often manifested in some form of creative or artistic expression. This stone corresponds to the 16th marriage year. To the ancient Atlantean Civilization, the Topaz symbolized Divine Goodness, wisdom and the unlimited awesome power of the sun. Gifts

of Topaz were often exchanged between "clans" to insure friendship, loyalty and fidelity when alliances were arranged. The Topaz was also used in the construction of "Light Wands" by temple artisans. Many Priests and Priestesses wore the Topaz on a copper, silver, or gold band around the head, resting on the 3rd eye because the Topaz served to enhance and amplify the visionary qualities of the 3rd eye.

TOURMALINE

This stone increases the Light Force within and creates a passageway for the Light Forces of the Universe to flow into and through an individual. Tourmaline has the ability to transform the denser vibrations of the material plane into positive currents of energy. Tourmaline has the power to weave strands of joy, strength, peace, and compassion through one's nature. It also has the ability to surround one with a strong protective shield.

Green: purifies and strengthens nervous system. Inspires creativity. Its energies have the ability to adjust to the specific needs of the individual.

Pink: corresponds to the Heart Chakra, removing blockages to that power center. It is a giver of love, creating joy and enthusiasm for life.

Black: deflects negative energy and turns it back to the source it emanated from.

There are some specimens of raw Tourmaline which have layers of rainbow colors, one layer on top of another. This particular type of Tourmaline was highly prized by the Lemurians and Atlanteans who learned how to harness the "pyro-electric" powers of the stone. Tourmaline has a strong magnetic influence which releases blocked creativity and clears away the veil of illusion caused by the ego.

TURQUOISE

This stone is strongly linked to Lemuria and Atlantis and to Native American Indians, who many psychic and metaphysical adepts considered to be direct descendants of the Atlanteans. The Turquoise symbolized the virtue of perfection, but like the stone itself which is easily marred, perfection is a state requiring constant care and vigilance. The Aztecs, also descendants of the Atlantean civilization, consider turquoise to be a sacred stone, more precious than any other stone or metal.

Temples in Lemuria, Atlantis and Egypt generally had one whole wall inlaid with turquoise. The vibrations of this stone was considered to ensure obedience to the will of the Creator and thus was very sacred. In secret mystical rituals, the High Priests or Priestesses of the temple would use the power of the turquoise to communicate with the Universal Forces. To the Lemurians and their descendants, turquoise was used to enhance telepathic communication.

Turquoise is considered to be endowed with the power to channel direct knowledge from the Universal Mind to the individual wearing the stone. When activated, the power of this stone acts like a cleansing fire, burning away blockages to the higher intuitional mind. It enables an individual to communicate clearly and precisely, sometimes this "communication" manifests in artistic creations which establishes a non-verbal unconscious mind-link between the artisan and the individual viewing the artwork. The sky-blue color of this stone, which is sometimes tinged with green and laced with iron or copper veins, represents the element of Air. This connection to the air element symbolizes the powerful link Turquoise has to the astral realms. Shamans wear turquoise amulets to assist them in "dream-walking" and on "vision quests". The dynamic vibrations of this stone can be used as an aid to "astral traveling" and will serve to protect the individual while on these out-of-body journeys.

As with Jade, Turquoise should always be given or received as a gift. To purchase this stone for personal use is considered to by unlucky. However, to receive it as a gift, ensures luck, prosperity and happiness.

ZIRCON or Hyacinth

This stone has the power to nullify enemy influences. It is considered to be generally lucky for health and happiness. It corresponds to the 19th marriage year. Zircon has the same positive qualities of the Diamond, but, unlike the Diamond, the Zircon does not store negative auras or energy patterns. Instead, the influence of the Zircon "short-circuits" negative vibrations, scattering them safely away from the individual.

This concludes the chapter on Geological Symbolism. There is still more knowledge pertaining to Gems, Minerals, and Crystals which I haven't covered here. Some of the knowledge will only be revealed to you through personal experiences and experimentation. More knowledge will come from other sources, Meditation, Scientific experiments, dreams, etc. At least you have a starting point, one of the "Keys" needed to unlock the door of ancient memories, of knowledge buried deep within you.

As with the Chapter on Color Symbolism, it is my hope that you will treat the chapters on Astrological and Geological Symbolism like a manual or workbook and add your thoughts, experiences, ideas, and intuitive insights to what is already given here. Collecting rocks, minerals, crystals, and gems in their unrefined state is an adventure in itself. These spiritual messengers of the mineral kingdom almost seem to talk to you as you work with them, and indeed, many people have reported "conversations" with stones on a non-verbal or mental level.

The more knowledge you accumulate, the more wondrous the Universe becomes, and the more attuned you will be to the energies which permeate this constantly evolving Cosmos. Therefore, the more you interact with knowledge the closer you come to your goal of Self-Realization, which is the purpose of this book.

SPECIAL NOTE

Connie Church has written a book titled: *Crystal Clear* which is an excellent manual on different techniques to use with Quartz Crystal. An added bonus that comes with Connie's book is a piece of Quartz Crystal. If you haven't already started collecting stones, this will give you a nice beginning. On the other hand, if you already have specimens of quartz or other stones, for the price of the book, you get one more crystal to work with free.

With a little imagination, intuition, and experimentation, all of the techniques Connie discusses in her book can be adapted for use with any of the other stones, minerals, or gems defined in this chapter. Programing your stone, cleansing it, personalizing its energies to you, all of these techniques and more will greatly assist you in enhancing your "spiritual gifts", developing your inner voice, empowering your visualizations and affirmations, and transforming negative behavior patterns. Using Crystals, Minerals, and Gems with Meditation techniques also creates an aura of positive energy around you and helps you to focus.

Part II:
PRACTICAL EXERCISES TOWARD SELF-REALIZATION

CHAPTER EIGHT
MEDITATIONS

Meditation is one of the many "Keys" or "Tools" that can be used toward the goal of "Self-Realization." There are many good books out with different approaches to the ancient practice of Meditation. These different techniques will give you a good background in Meditation plus give you material to work with. But the best type of Meditation is the kind you devise yourself. Sometimes taking two or even three or four different Meditations and combining various elements you are comfortable with from those Meditations to create your own unique version will get the best results for you.

One good method for Meditation is using a cassette recorder to record the meditation along with very soft music. Meditation is an intimate experience and we need to be able to totally relax when attempting this mental and emotional exercise. Believe it or not, we respond well, on a subconscious level, to the sound of our own voices. Perhaps it is because the element of fear has been totally removed and we can trust our own voice better than the voice of a stranger which brings in an element of the unknown and may trigger our mental defense mechanisms.

Setting up the recording of the Meditation with music may take a little practice at first, especially if you are not used to recording your own voice for playback. You will need to read the meditation aloud into the recorder in an unhurried manner, pacing yourself in a slow but rhythmic manner. You want your recorded voice to be soothing, relaxed and intimate, without distractions. This may take a little experimentation to achieve, but it can be easily done. The music you choose to record either with the meditation itself while you are speaking, or when played separately during the meditation exercise, should be the type of music which enhances your mental imagery.

Some of the best music I found for meditation is by Andreas Vollenweider, Kitaro, Vangelis, and Steven Halpern. I recommend the following titles by these musicians:

ANDREAS VOLLENWEIDER
1. *White Winds*
2. *Down to the Moon*
3. *Caverna Magica*

KITARO
1. *Silkroads Vol. 1 & 2*
2. *Silver Cloud*
3. *Oasis*
4. *Tunhuang*
5. *Ki*

VANGELIS
1. *Antartica*
2. *Heaven and Hell*

STEVE HALPERN
1. *Zodiac Suite*
2. *Rings of Saturn*

3.*Mask*   3.*Spectrum Suite*
4.*China*
5.*The Best of Vangelis*

There are other "new-age" musicians which have beautiful music for meditation besides the ones I have already mentioned. David Arkenstone's *Valley in the Clouds* is a wonderful tape to use for Meditation. One excellent group whose music is perfect for meditation is named *Mannheim Steamroller* and their records can be found under the title of *Fresh Aire*. I urge you to listen to a variety of different musicians and judge what is appropriate for you. I refer to these musicians as "new-age" because that is the section of a record store you will find these albums, cassettes and discs. You might find some of the classical masters such as Mozart, Bach and Beethoven to have music which will serve your meditation purposes just as well as the "new-age" musicians. You won't know until you experiment with an open mind.

Learning to flow with music, letting it transport you to other realms, other realities, away from the limitations of the physical earth plane, is also a Key for Self-Realization and can unleash creative potentials you may have been unaware you possessed on a conscious level. However, the music you choose should contain no singing or words because it would distract your attention from the Meditation exercise you have recorded. Pure instrumental music is suited best for Meditation purposes.

There are certain little "Rituals" you can follow before beginning your Meditation which help to focus your thoughts and deepen the meditative experience. It is not mandatory that you do these rituals before meditating, but they do have a relaxing mood-enhancing effect on your physical body and mental-emotional state. Most people tend to set aside time for meditating in the morning after they first get up, or in the evening just before sleeping. Some people prefer   to meditate both in the morning and evening out of sheer enjoyment of the exercise. Others will attempt to keep a   schedule which includes three meditations daily. However, it is not the amount of meditations you do, but the quality of your meditations which are important. Experiment....be flexible and open.....enjoy....these are key words to keep in mind.

MEDITATION RITUALS

Step 1: Don't try to meditate after you've eaten, especially if you've eaten a heavy meal. The digestive process of the body does not harmonize well with meditation since the purpose of the exercise is to lighten the body and mentally lift you from the physical plane. Wait at least 3 to 4 hours after a meal before meditating. The same goes for Caffeine beverages which tend to stimulate the nervous system. The purpose of the meditation exercise is to calm and relax not only the nervous system, but your entire body and mind as well.

Step 2: Don't try to meditate after strenuous exercising, the adrenaline rush in the body makes it very difficult to quiet the mind and focus. Wait at least a half hour to an hour after exercising to meditate. Since each individual responds differently to exercise, you will have to experiment to see what the optimal time for meditation is after you exercise.

Step 3: Try a warm soothing bath before meditation. The warm water will loosen your tense muscles and help you to relax those nerves which have been tightened by stress which will allow you to center your attention more quickly while meditating. A hot shower can also do the same thing as long as you take your time and don't rush. This step serves two purposes: one purpose is to aid you in relaxing; and the other has to do with the ritual of purification.

Step 4: Wear loose, comfortable clothing, something that feels good against your skin. Anything that binds, restricts or irritates you will end up distracting you from focusing inward and deepening your meditation. If you are the adventuresome type, try meditating in the nude, it is a unique experience.

Step 5: Drink a glass of water or juice made from lemons or other fruits before you meditate. The water or lemonade will cleanse your mouth and palate in preparation for your meditation. White grape juice is another excellent aid. Be sure to drink the water or juice slowly, swishing it around in your mouth before swallowing. This step is also part of the purification ritual.

Step 6: If you are a smoker, be sure to brush your teeth and use a mouthwash to rinse out your mouth thoroughly before you begin meditating. This step will complete the ritual of purification.

Step 7: Set the mood. Turn off or turned down the lights, or use candles. If you like the smell of incense now is the time to light it. Music is optional, but I can not stress enough the influence good music has on the Meditation experience, however, it is not mandatory.

The first Meditation exercise given here is basic and simple. With this Meditation you are learning how to focus and quiet your mind in preparation for more complex and detailed exercises. It is designed to be used in conjunction with Affirmations or Prayers, although it is not mandatory that you do so. In Chapter Nine, there are several examples of Affirmations you can adapt to your own personal needs.

Okay! Now you are ready for the first Meditation Exercise I call "Opening the Gate". This is the time to decided whether or not to record the mediation exercise together with your chosen music on one tape, or wait to play music separately while listening to your recorded instructions during the actual meditation. Now, the first thing you need to do is record all of the following steps on your cassette so when you use it for the meditation you will automatically go through the steps outlined here by your own voice.

For the most part, I have given the following Meditations to you in the "third person" rather than in the "first person". The choice is yours to make whether or not you wish to use "I" instead of "You". Experiment with both methods and see which one "feels" more comfortable for you. Finally, I want to bring your attention to "Chanting". In the East, chanting a mantra during meditation is an accepted practice. In this first meditation, I have given you a phonetic mantra to use. It is not always necessary to use a mantra while meditating, especially in the ones given here. However, since this first exercise is designed to "open the gate" to higher awareness, the chanting of a mantra greatly enhances this experience.

MEDITATION EXERCISE #1: "OPENING THE GATE"
(use with or without music)

BEGIN RECORDING

Sit comfortably in a chair or lie on your back in bed. Allow your hands to lay loose and relaxed at your sides or on your lap. Relax....Take a deep breath through your nose and exhale slowly through the mouth. Close your eyes and begin to softly chant: "AUMMM", allowing the vibrations to fill your head with a pleasant buzzing sensation. Repeat the chant again: "AUMMM".......One more time...."AUMMM".

Take a deep breath through your nose and exhale slowly through the mouth, feeling the tension and stress slip away from your body. Relax and let go of any anger you have been storing. Take a deep breath through your nose and exhale slowly through the mouth, letting go ... relaxing ... letting go. Begin repeating this longer chant:"AUMMM--VAY--DAH--AH" ... again ... "AUMMM--VAY-DAH-AH" ... once more ... "AUMMM--VAY--DAH--AH".

Let the hum of the mantra permeate every cell of your body....energizing you....removing blockages to your flow of energy. Feel the vibrations deep within you. Feel the rhythm of life pulsating in your veins. Take a deep breath and exhale slowly. Repeat the mantra: "AUMMM" ... again ... "AUMMM" ... once more, feeling the hum, feeling the vibrations ... "AUMMM".

Mentally visualize yourself standing on the shore of a beautiful crystal lake. Its boundaries are limitless. See how the sun's rays dance and sparkle on the surface of the lake. You are one with the crystal lake. Each thought that distracts you is reflected here as a ripple or wave on the surface of your lake. You are in control of the lake. You have the power to smooth the surface of the lake, to make its surface as calm as a mirror which reflects the beauty of the sky above.

Look at the crystal lake, the reflections you see there are reflections of yourself. If the surface of the lake is rough it is because of disquieted thoughts racing around in your mind which defy your control. Use the power of the crystal lake to subdue these thoughts. Use the power of the crystal lake to take charge of your mind. You possess the power... the crystal lake and you are one. Assert your Will, it is your right.

Once the surface of the crystal lake is completely smooth and reflective you will feel a sense of tranquility surge through your being. The crystal lake offers you peace and a true "one-ness" with the forces of the Universe. Feeling your attunement with nature you can begin your Affirmations, knowing that the power of the lake and the power within you are combined and will manifest these affirmations into reality on the physical earth plane.

THE AFFIRMATIONS

I am a Child of Light blessed by Divine Love.
I have the power to control my emotions....to erase old thought patterns which "limit" my expression.
I choose to express the positive and to transform the negative.

Through the Divine Light within me I am in control at all times.

I choose to let go of the past... to let go of old hurts... to let go of the power it had to cause me pain... I choose instead to forgive.

In letting go and trusting in Divine Love, I have chosen to accept the wonderful opportunities given to me.

I choose to channel the light of Divine Love to all I meet... I choose to project my inner harmony to those I work and interact with.

I am filled with Joy... with Peace... with Contentment. Today I have awakened .... Today I affirm my oneness with the Universe.

Take another deep breath through your nose and release it slowly through your mouth. Repeat: "THERE ARE NO PROBLEMS OR SITUATIONS IN MY LIFE WHICH I CANNOT HANDLE WITH THE GUIDANCE OF DIVINE LOVE AND LIGHT." Take another deep breath through your nose... hold it... then release it slowly through your mouth. Feel the exhilaration flooding your being. Feel the strength pouring into you from the Universe. Take another deep breath... hold it... and release.

Slowly open your eyes... gently returning to this plane of reality carrying with you the gift of empowerment from the crystal lake and the Universe.

END RECORDING

This next Meditation exercise is called "Creative Visualization" because of its potentials for unlocking your hidden creativity. This is an excellent meditation for Writers, Artists, Musicians, Teachers, or anyone who needs to explore and use their creative potentials to the fullest. Through this particular meditation, previously untapped sources of inspiration can be reached and explored.

MEDITATION EXERCISE #2:
"CREATIVE VISUALIZATION"
(use with or without music)

BEGIN RECORDING

The first step is to get comfortable, either by laying down or sitting relaxed in a chair, then close your eyes. We are about to begin our Seeker's Journey to a special place you will create for yourself. This special place will always be available to you. It is a place of tranquility, of peace and contentment. This special place is your refuge from the distractions of the world. This is where you will come to be renewed in mind, body and spirit. No one can touch you here, this is a place of safety.

Now, take a deep breath through your nose and let it out slowly through your mouth. Feel your muscles relaxing... letting go of tension. Take another deep breath through your nose, visualizing the air a brilliant white light and let it out slowly through your mouth. Each deep breath of White Light cleanses you of negativity... of anxiety and worry. Each deep breath of White Light revitalizes your being... fills you with serenity. Your muscles are getting looser... the tension is easing away from you... leaving you relaxed and comfortable... your mind is quiet and serene.

Now... I want you to visualize the color **RED**. A **RED** rose, a **RED** carnation, a **RED** apple, anything that helps you to visualize the color **RED**. Once you have seen the color **RED**, go **UP** to the next color which is **ORANGE**.

Visualize the color **ORANGE**. A freshly poured glass of **ORANGE** juice, a mound of fresh **ORANGES** in a bowl, a Buddhist monk in an **ORANGE** robe, the inside of a cantaloupe, anything that helps you to visualize the color **ORANGE**. Once you have seen the color **ORANGE** go **UP** to the next color which is **YELLOW**.

Visualize the color **YELLOW**. Picture with your mind's eye the **YELLOW** center of a daisy, the **YELLOW** sun burning brightly on a summer's day, a bowl of bright **YELLOW** lemons. Once you have seen the color **YELLOW**, go **UP** to the next color which is **GREEN**.

Visualize the color **GREEN**. The **GREEN** leaves of a tree, a freshly mowed **GREEN** lawn, a **GREEN** lime, a **GREEN** four-leafed clover. Once you have seen the color **GREEN**, go **UP** to the next color which is **BLUE**.

Visualize the color **BLUE**. The soft **BLUE** color of a cloudless sky, the **BLUE** of the ocean, the **BLUE** of a robin's egg. When you've seen the color **BLUE**, go **UP** to the next color which is **PURPLE-INDIGO**.

Visualize the deep rich purple color of **INDIGO**. The dark **INDIGO** of a ripe plum. Or the deep **INDIGO** of Elderberries. When you've seen the color **INDIGO**, go **UP** to the next color which is **VIOLET**.

Visualize the color **VIOLET**. The delicate blossoms of the **VIOLET** flower. The tiny **VIOLET** flowers called Pansy's. Allow your mind and senses to be bathed in the relaxing essence of **VIOLET**. Visualize your entire being flooded with the spiritual energy of the color **VIOLET**.

Now mentally see yourself standing in a corridor surrounded by a **VIOLET** colored mist. There is a soft golden white light at the end of this short corridor. Start walking down the corridor in the direction of the golden white light.

When you reach the golden white light, stop.

In front of you, at your feet, you'll see that you are standing at the foot of a staircase leading **UP**.

There are 13 steps on this staircase. As you go **UP** the steps, see yourself **ASCENDING** the stairs. Mentally **FEEL** yourself moving up these stairs when we begin counting them.

You are on the bottom step. The 13st step.

Step **UP** to the 12th step... **UP** to the 11th... the 10th... step **UP** to the 9th step.

You are going HIGHER and HIGHER.... step **UP** to the 8th step....the 7th step...the 6th... the 5th... HIGHER AND HIGHER....**UP** to the 4th step....the 3rd...the 2nd...the 1st.

You are at the **TOP** of the stairs. Take a deep breath, draw in the golden white light....feel the warmth and welcome.... and feel the special atmosphere of this new higher level.

There is an opaque curtain in front of you. Look at it. describe it to yourself. What kind of material is it made of? Silk? Satin? Cotton? Wool? Nylon? Glass beads? Does it have silver threads? Or gold threads? Does it have any designs on it? What color is it? Does it look light or heavy? This is **YOUR** curtain, the curtain which protects and conceals your secret world from the eyes of the earth plane. Look at it carefully, mentally reach out and touch the curtain. Feel the texture of the material. Is it soft? Scratchy? How does the curtain feel to the touch?

Before you draw the curtain aside....know there will be a path for you to walk. This path will take you to a beautiful crystal castle. This is your personal castle....it belongs to you. It is your personal place of **POWER**.

Now, mentally reach out and draw the curtain aside... Step through the gateway on to the path. Mentally visualize yourself walking down the path... up ahead you can see your beautiful crystal castle bathed in the rays of the sun....walk up to the door of your castle... reach out and touch the door with the palm of your hand. Feel the door turn warm under your touch... feel the essence of your spirit transform the door to a shimmering veil of light... walk through the veil into the heart of your castle.

Look around you.... see how the rays of the sun has turned the inside of your castle into a prism of light and color. Feel the energy of this special place... take a deep breath through your nose and hold it until the count of 8... slowly release your breath... through your mouth... Feel the tingling sensation run through your body awakening your potentials... feel the powerful vibrations of light and love surround you... cradling you with gentleness. This is the Dwelling place of Divine Light, a place from which you are constantly RENEWED and REVITALIZED.

Now that you have been renewed in spirit, you will walk through another doorway out into a beautiful scene from nature... a scene from nature you would like to see. Your journey to self-discovery is just beginning... Walk to the door... open and step out side. Look around you... What do you see?

Are there trees? Mountains? Birds? Flowers? A river? Clouds in the sky? Rocks? Green Grass? Animals? Cathedrals in the distance? An ocean lapping against a sandy beach? WHAT DO YOU SEE?

If there is something here that you don't like, CHANGE IT. This is your private world, so you can change it to suit yourself. If there are Mountains and you don't like mountains, just mentally close your eyes and erase them and they will disappear. Change anything in this scene that you don't like. Is it Spring or Summer? Or would you prefer Fall or even the beauty of a Winter Wonderland. It is your choice, you are in control and may create whatever takes your fancy.

Are there things missing from your world? Would you like a small waterfall? Or a babbling brook? A crystal clear lake? A tropical island with swaying palm-trees overlooking the vastness of the ocean? Or perhaps a small cottage nestled deep in a green primeval forest? If you do, just visualize them, they will appear. All it takes is a wish, and you can have what ever you dream of in your secret world. You can create as you choose to here.

Listen for sounds. Are there any? Birds? Music? The sound of the wind rustling the leaves of trees? Are there Voices whispering faintly in the background? LISTEN to the sounds of your secret world.

Take a deep breath. Bring in the air of this unique and wondrous place deep into your lungs. What do you smell? Flowers? Perfume? Incense? Take a deep breath and bring into your lungs the healing freshness and purity of this incredible air.

Continue walking around in your private world. Stroll around and set your seal of approval on what you see. Find a comfortable place and sit down, maybe under a tall oak tree, or a beautiful weeping willow by the side of a slow moving stream. Maybe you want to perch on a rock, or maybe you just want to stretch out on the soft grass and stare up at the beautiful blue sky.

Do you wish to see Unicorns? or Fairies? Do you like Dragons and Elves? If you do, just wish and they will appear. You can choose to remain alone here, or you can invite any mythical creature you want to share the special magic of this place with you. Nothing may harm you here in this sacred place for it is protected by the Forces of Light.

Go ahead. Do whatever you wish, letting the beauty and the purity and the peacefulness of this place saturate your very being. If you have questions that need answers, know that you can find them here. Know that here, in your secret world, there is an Oracle of Wisdom and Truth. This Oracle serves as a source of Divine Inspiration and Guidance to all who are willing to accept its gifts.

My voice will leave you for a short time so you may enjoy the beauty of your creation without any distractions. This is your secret world now and you were meant to explore and enjoy its beauties. My voice will return shortly to lead you back.

Do not record the following instructions. Let the tape continue to play either with or without music for APPROXIMATELY 5 to 15 MINUTES, (or for however long you want to stay in the trance). During this time you should be deep into your meditation, visualizing and creating wonderful things. Because of the deepness of this meditation you will have to record the following instructions to lead yourself back out in order to retain the full benefit of this exercise. This process completes the exercise without abruptness which would leave a restless aftertaste otherwise. When you begin recording again, make sure your voice is very soft and low so you don't startle yourself.

BEGIN RECORDING AGAIN

As you hear the sound of my voice continue to feel the calm peacefulness of your secret world. Let the sound of my voice lead you back to the crystal castle.

Mentally visualize yourself getting up from where you have been sitting or lying and stretch. Look around you... drink in the magnificent sight you have created... take a deep breath through your nose and release it slowly through your mouth. Slowly turn around and begin walking back to the crystal castle. Go through the door and enter the inner sanctum of your beautiful castle.

Allow yourself one last look at the spectacular prism of color within the • heart of your castle. Let yourself be bathed in its wondrous light once more. Continue walking through the castle until you walk out onto the path that brought you here. Mentally see yourself walking down the path back to the curtained gateway which gave you entrance to your secret world.

Reach out and pull the curtain aside as you walk through the gateway back to the top of the staircase. See yourself standing at the top of it, and as I count, see yourself stepping on each step and going **DOWN** the staircase to the bottom of the stairs.

You are on the 1st step. Now move **DOWN** to the 2nd step. Now **DOWN** to the 3rd step. **DOWN** to the 4th... the 5th... You are going back **DOWN** the stairs now... to the 6th... You are halfway to the bottom. Walk down to the 7th step... down to the 8th... the 9th... the 10th... **DOWN** to the 11th... the 12th... the 13th. You are on the bottom step.

Ahead of you is the corridor bathed in the **VIOLET** light. Starting walking towards that light. When you reach it stop.

Now you are bathed in that **VIOLET** color. See yourself surrounded by the **VIOLET** light.

Now that color changes **DOWN** into **INDIGO**.

It changes DOWN into BLUE.

It changes DOWN into GREEN.

It changes DOWN into YELLOW.

It changes DOWN into ORANGE.

It changes DOWN into RED.

Welcome back to the Earth Plane. Your Seeker's Journey is completed for today. Open your eyes and stretch. You have returned.

END RECORDING

Now that you have read through the Meditation, see how important background music can be? You will want to choose music which will enhance your creativity and add color to the visions you see in your mind's eye. I have led this particular Meditation Exercise as a group exercise in the past and have had excellent reports. Each person's vision was so different from the others, yet so filled with creativity it was amazing. As soon as you experience this meditation fully, you should keep a journal or a record of what occurred. Write a description of what you saw, what colors appeared, what creatures you met, etc.

This meditation should leave you refreshed and filled with creative vitality. Once you get used to this particular meditation you can modify it, add other elements to it, use it to research past-lives or create a fantasy you may want to write about or even express artistically. The uses for this meditation are as endless as your imagination. But primarily, this particular Meditation serves to assist you in discovering the source of power within your being, a power which links you to all Life in the Universe and stimulates your intuitive connection to the Universal Sub-Conscious.

The more you work with the different "Keys" or "Tools" for Self-Realization, the more important it becomes for you to keep a journal or personal record of what you experience. You are charting the steps of your own growth and learning the patterns of your life when you keep a record or personal journal of your experiences. Writing down your dreams, what you see or experience during meditation, or even what cards you unveil while working with a Tarot Card Lay-Out is a very useful method for Self-Counseling.

MEDITATION EXERCISE #3
(use with or without music)

BEGIN RECORDING

The first step is to relax and get comfortable either by sitting in a chair or by laying down. Now, close your eyes and feel your muscles slowly begin to let go of the tension. Breathe deeply through your nose and let the air expel from your lungs slowly through your mouth. Just concentrate on the deep breathe you are bringing into your body. Feel how it calms and soothes as you let it out slowly through your mouth. Keep breathing deeply and feeling the tenseness of your muscles relax and flow away from you as you exhale.

Feel your feet begin to relax, as you stretch your toes....feel the tension flowing away from you. Feel the calves of your legs begin to relax and let go of their tenseness. Keep breathing deeply through your nose and exhale slowly through your mouth. Feel the tightness of the muscles in your upper thighs relax and become loose. The tension of the day is slipping away from you. Feel your torso become relaxed as you breathe in deeply and slowly exhale through your mouth.

Slowly, rotate your shoulders and feel the tightness work loose and fall away from you. Gently shake your arms and hands a few times and feel the tension let go and fall away. Feel how relaxed your arms and hands are when you place them on your lap. Slowly rotate your neck and head a few times, loosening the knots and the kinks there. Breathe in deeply through your nose and exhale slowly through the mouth and feel the tension leave the muscles of your face and your forehead. Keep breathing in and out slowly and deeply. Each breath brings more relaxation. Each breath fills you with peace and calm.

Now, visualize with your mind's eye, a misty white cloud in front of you. Feel the softness of this misty white cloud as it envelops you. Breathe deeply through your nose, inhaling the energy of this cloud. Let your breath out slowly through your mouth and feel the tingling energy the cloud leaves within your body. Slowly, the misty white cloud begins to disappear. As the cloud disappears you will see yourself in a beautiful forest, richly green and gold in color. The magnificent trees tower high above you, reaching for the sky.

There is a path in front of you, leading deeper into the forest. Start walking down this path. Feel the cool serenity of this place as you walk down the path. The tall trees on either side of this path welcome your presence. Smell the freshness of the air here. Listen for the sounds of the gentle breeze as it whispers through the leaves. Further and further you go into the depths of the forest. The path you are taking is leading you to a cave deep in the heart of the forest.

The opening of the cave is large and has bushes of flowers near its entrance. What kind of flowers are these? What color are they? Step closer. Touch them. What do they feel like? Do they have a scent?

Pick one of the flowers and take it with you into the cave. As you step into the cave you will see that it is illuminated with a soft golden glow. It is not dark in this cave, but filled with a gentle golden light which allows you to see every detail of the interior. What does the cave look like inside? How are the walls shaped? What kind of rocks do you see inside this cave? What color are the walls of the cave?

Step deeper into the cave. As you walk deeper and deeper into the vastness of this cave you will see before you a small lake with a sandy shore. Walk closer to this small lake, feel the sand beneath your feet, feel how it cushions your steps. As you come up to this small lake, sit down on the sand close to the waterline. Take the flower in your hand, which you picked at the mouth of the cave, and gently toss it into the lake as a gift.

Now... watch closely as a small underwater spring bubbles to the surface underneath the flower. Higher and higher the spring rises from the lake, carrying your flower gift high into the air. Watch as the fountain of water continues to rise all the way to the ceiling of the cave with your flower nestled at the top. Once the fountain reaches the top of the cave and touches the ceiling with the flower, it is magically transformed into a beautiful gem stone.

Slowly the fountain sinks back into the still waters of the lake carrying the transformed flower back with it. Once the transformed gem stone touches the surface of the lake it is gently washed back to shore as a gift for you.

Reach out. Take the gem stone. This is a gift from the lake to you. The transformed flower, now a gem stone, is beautiful to behold and fits perfectly in the palm of your hand. What color is the gem stone? What kind of gem stone is it? Do you like it? It is yours to keep. Treasure it.

It is time to leave the cave. Mentally rise and turn back towards the mouth of the cave. The golden light will guide you as you walk back out into the forest and onto the path that led you here. Feel the gentle warmth of the sun as it filters through the trees to caress your face as you begin walking back on the path. There is a lightness to your steps as you walk along the path for you carry with you a gift of Love from the Lake.

Up ahead of you is a misty white cloud. Follow the path right into the misty cloud. Feel the mist surround you... bathing you in its softness. Breathe deeply through the nose one more time, inhaling the white mist of energy surrounding you. Release your breathe slowly through your mouth and open your eyes. You have returned from your Forest Quest.

END RECORDING

This particular meditation, in which you are given a gift by the Lake, represents a gift to you from the Universe. The gem stone you received has a special message for you. In Chapter Seven of this book you can look up the meanings of various gem stones, minerals and crystals. This will give you an idea or a starting place to understand the message the gift brings to you. Also, the color of the stone is important and should be interpreted as well. The type of flowers you saw at the mouth of the cave and the one you picked has a special meaning which needs to be explored. The color of the flowers is also important.

This meditation also teaches the lesson that: "the cost of giving is receiving."

MEDITATION EXERCISE #4
(can be done with or without music)

BEGIN RECORDING

Sit or lay comfortably with your limbs loose and relaxed. Close your eyes and breathe deeply through the nose to the count of 4. Hold your breath to the count of 4 and then release it through your mouth to the count of 4. Continue to repeat this breathing exercise as it releases the tension and tightness from your body.

Feel the cleansing action of your breathing. Breathe deep through your nose to the count of 4 and **FEEL** the vibrant energy filling you. Hold this breath to the count of 4, then release it slowly through your mouth... letting go of all that distracts you... unwinding and relaxing... letting go of the stress you've accumulated.....letting go... relaxing... unwinding... letting go.

Continue to breathe slowly and deeply through your nose and release the breath through your mouth. Effortlessly... without conscious thought... continue to breathe slowly and deeply... relaxing and letting go. With your mind's eye, see yourself walking along a golden stretch of sandy beach... feel its softness between your toes... on the bare soles of your feet. Feel the soft gentle caress of the wind on your face. Smell the clean fresh air from the ocean. The Sun's warmth gently enfolds you in its embrace.

Ahead of you is a well worn path leading away from the sandy beach. Take this path and follow its trail up a gradual incline. At the end of this path is a beautiful and ancient Temple. What kind of design does this magnificent Temple have? What is it made of? What color is it? What type of decorations does it have on the outside? Is it plain? Or does it have statues or carvings?

As you come closer to the Temple and walk through the open outer courtyard, you will see a door which leads to the Inner Sanctum of the Temple. This door will open for you with the slightest touch of your hand. Before you open the door, take a deep cleansing breath through your nose... and exhale slowly through your mouth.

Open the door and step inside of the Temple's Inner Sanctum. Close the door behind you and walk over to the altar centered in the middle of the Sanctum. On the altar is a beautiful... fragrant lotus flower. Visualize this Lotus Flower growing larger and larger... filling the room with its natural beauty. See with your mind's eye the Lotus Flower growing larger... so large that you can easily separate the soft petals and step inside of the Lotus.

As you step into the heart of the Lotus, feel the energy it is radiating to you.... surrounding you... enveloping you with warmth and love... feel the softness of its center on the bottoms of your feet. Mentally see yourself sitting down within the heart of the Lotus. Look up. Are the petals closed over your head? Or are they open to the beauty of the star-filled cosmos? What color are the petals of the Lotus? What color is the sky above you?

Feel the gentle pulse of the Universe surround you. Feel the echo of its rhythms in your veins. You are one with the Universe... with its power and majesty... You are one with all living things and stretch out... relax in the heart of the Lotus. Feel the cares and worries that weigh you down... drift away...

allow the loving energy of the Lotus enfold you and take your cares away.

Mentally lie back and take a deep breath through your nose... exhale slowly... look at the sky above you... see the diamond brilliance of the stars sparkling and glittering like gemstones in the velvet softness above. Watch as the stars begin a graceful dance through the heavens... spinning and turning... performing an intricate ballet for your delight. Look at the shapes the stars form. What kind of shapes do you see? Are they simple or complex? Do they form recognizable pictures? What do you see?

Through the dance of the stars the Universe is sending you a special message... communicating with you... offering you inspiration... guidance... and the opportunity to feel one with the vastness of the Universe. Listen carefully... open yourself up to the Divine Spirit contacting you... allow yourself to touch the heights of joy and contentment... accept the unconditional love being sent to you... know that you have been consecrated to the Forces of Light.

You have opened the Gateway to the loving presence of the Divine Mind. You have established a special link with the Forces of the Universe... a link which can never be broken. Mentally rise from the Heart of the Lotus and step back through the petals. Visualize the Lotus slowly begin to shrink in size... smaller and smaller... it gradually reduces to a small flower lying on the center of the Altar.

Mentally pick up the Lotus Flower in your hand... it is small enough to fit in your palm. Place it on top of your head and visualize the flower gradually turning into a violet mist that slowly penetrates into your skin. You are a sponge soaking up the violet mist... absorbing it into your being... inviting it to become a permanent part of you. See yourself standing in the Inner Sanctum of the Temple... feel the Lotus within your being... know that you and the Lotus are now one in spirit.

Take a deep breath through your nose... hold it to the count of four... then release it slowly through your mouth. Repeat the breathing one more time. Now... open your eyes... maintaining your deep feelings of tranquility and joy as you return once more to this plane of reality.

END RECORDING

FURTHER NOTES

If you are still unsure about Meditation and feel a need for more guidance, I suggest you try Workshops on Meditation or purchase a "Learn At Home Course" from the Association of Research and Enlightenment, (A.R.E.). These learn-at-home-courses from A.R.E. come with cassette tapes and step-by-step instructions on Meditation. One of these courses is titled "MEDITATION MADE EASY", and another is titled: "A.R.E. MEDITATION COURSE" The address for the Association is as follows:

ASSOCIATION FOR RESEARCH AND ENLIGHTENMENT, INC.
67TH STREET AND ATLANTIC AVENUE
P.O. BOX 595
VIRGINIA BEACH, VA 23451
PHONE NUMBER: (800)-368-2727

You can call them or write and request a catalogue from their Bookstore which contains books, tapes, and courses available for purchase. There are, of course, other sources for tapes and lectures on meditation and a bookstore near you might be able to help you in your search. Bernie S. Siegel, M.D., the author of "Love, Medicine and Miracles" has a meditation tape available titled: "Personal Reflections and Meditations" which has some excellent guided meditations on it. Even though these meditations are mainly geared toward bringing in healing energy to a "dis-eased" body, the techniques he uses are wonderful to experience.

Another possible source for guided meditation is Joy Messick who is well known for her guided inward journeys based on the Shaman lore of the American Indian. Shamanism is a practice of spirituality in intuitive form, and is as old as humankind. Shamans function as healers, psychologists, teachers, prophets, seers, and storytellers in society. The Shaman holds together the web of life, and acts as a mirror for the people reflecting back the Cosmos view of humanity.

Joy Messick is a practicing Shaman who has been a pioneer in the intuitive management field and is co-founder and partner in Hart Systems, a management consulting company. Joy teaches intuitive development, creativity and spiritual awareness for many diversified groups throughout North America and Western Europe. She frequently does lectures and workshops for various SFF Chapters as well as for the different National Retreats. SFF has local Chapters in each state so I don't have a phone number for SFF, but the address of the central headquarters is as follows:

SPIRITUAL FRONTIERS FELLOWSHIP
P.0. BOX 7868
PHILADELPHIA, PA 19101
The address and phone number for Joy Messick's firm is as follows:

HART SYSTEMS
P.O. BOX 12181
BIRMINGHAM, MI 48010   PHONE: (313) 644-2777
JOY MESSICK: Intuitive Management consultant

CHAPTER NINE

PRACTICAL EXERCISES

In this chapter, I will focus on Practical Exercises and Affirmations you can try which will enhance your experiences in self-awareness and greatly assist you in your goal of Self-Realization. Actually, this chapter serves as a guide in creating your own "Workbook" to go along with the Personal Journal I have encouraged you to keep.

In Chapter One, the basic background of numerology was provided so you could discover, for yourself, what numbers vibrate to your name and birth date. If you have nicknames, they too, should be broken down to their numerical components. Although nicknames do not have as strong an impact on you as your given name at birth, nicknames still exert subtle influences over you, especially if that nickname is used more often than your given name. This information should go into your journal for future reference.

The first step in your Workbook-Journal should be a Numerology Profile of yourself. Determining your Life Lesson Number, Path of Destiny Number, Soul Number, and Outer Personality Number will serve as the beginning for your Profile. The next step would be to determine your Numeric Karmic Challenges as outlined in Chapter One, and your Personal 9-year cycles discussed in this chapter. For the purpose of Creative Visualization, I have included Affirmations for each of the Personal 9-year cycles.

The Personal 9-year cycles are an important element in the ancient Science of Numerology. Knowing what number you are personally affected by for each year, allows you to use your energies in harmony with the Universal Flow. To discover what number cycle you are in for any given year, you take the month and day of your birth and add it to the current year you are interested in. For example:

Birth date; MONTH AND DAY: 12-24   CURRENT YEAR: 1987

$$1+2=3 \quad 2+4=6 \quad 1+9+8+7=25/7 \quad 3+6+7=16/7$$

On December 24th, 1987, the individual with this birth date enters under the influence of the number 7 until their next birthday in 1988. The 9-year Cycles go from birthday to birthday, not from January to January. All through that year, (12-24-87 to 12-24-88), the number 7 will have subtle influences over the individual's life. The characteristics of the number 7 will be experienced in a variety of ways, depending on the choices the individual makes. The cycles only predict "patterns" and "potentials" because we have FREE WILL and may choose to use the energies of the number 7 in anyway we wish. Ideally, we will utilize the positive energies of the number 7 in ways that will enrich our lives and the lives of others. But, we can choose to manifest the energy potential of the number 7 in negative ways as well. The choice, of course, is ours to make.

One of the best books on Numerology and its correlation to Tarot and Astrology is titled: *NUMEROLOGY AND THE DIVINE TRIANGLE*, by Faith Javane and Dusty Bunker. In this book, the authors nave given detailed information on the cycles based on a numerology interpretation of the Tarot. For example: The number I came up with when I added the birthday and month to the current year was 16/7. In Faith and Dusty's book, they have correlated the Tarot Card called "The Tower" with the number 16/7. They then present the definition in two ways, first as a permanent influence, such as a Life-Lesson Number, and then as a temporary influence such as found in the yearly cycles.

Therefore, one of the first entries into your journal should be a Numerology Profile you create pertaining to yourself and others who are important to you or who have a great deal of influence in your life. This is one of your "Keys" to self-awareness.

To assist you in creating your Numerology Profile I have included two appendixes on numerology worksheets at the back of this book. Appendix A is a completed worksheet using a friend's name and date of birth as an example. Appendix B contains blank worksheets for you to experiment with.

Another important entry into your Workbook-Journal should concern the Color Symbolism and Astrological---Geological Symbolism which pertains to you.

FIRST STEP: What is the predominate color of your wardrobe? Your lingerie or underclothing? What is the secondary color of these items?

SECOND STEP: What is the predominate color of your environment at home? The walls, furnishings, sheets and towels?

THIRD STEP: What is your favorite color? What color do you least like? What color makes you feel good? What color irritates you?

FOURTH STEP: This next step may seem a little strange, but it serves to make you aware of the state of your subconscious. First, choose a Mandala design and choose the colors for it based on how you feel. In other words, use the colors on the Mandala that represent how you feel or best describes your state of mind. This exercise stimulates "Right" brain activity, that part of your brain which governs intuition and creativity.

Next, choose another Mandala design, (it can be the same one if you choose), but this time pick out the colors that represent the qualities and energies you *"want"* to have in your life. You can use the color pattern of this Mandala to meditate on or as a focus when turning your mind's eye inward in order to relax and release tension.

FIFTH STEP: Using the information on Color Symbolism given in Chapter 4, chart the patterns of colors in your life and write down their meanings. If a pattern emerges which seems more negative than positive, this energy can be changed very simply by eliminating the colors with negative energy. If you can't repaint your walls or change your furniture, the addition of art work, (paintings, watercolors, posters, sculptures, etc.), which has harmonious color schemes will help as will the addition of throw pillows or rugs.

The same can be done with your wardrobe. If you can't replace your wardrobe, the addition of sweaters, shirts or blouses, scarves or ties, shawls, jewelry, etc., will balance out those colors which have a negative effect on you. Then, gradually, you can replace your wardrobe one piece at a time with others whose colors vibrate on a positive level with your personal energy pattern. Or, if you like the colors of your wardrobe, but want to incorporate additional energy vibrations, you can accomplish this through the use of Crystals, Minerals or Gems.

SIXTH STEP: In this step, it is important to know the Astrological Sign of your Sun, Moon and Ascendant. Taking the Color and Astro-Geological Symbolism for each of these signs and incorporating them into everyday use will create a harmonious balance of energy for you. Wearing the Crystal, Mineral, and Gems associated with your signs will help to focus patterns of energy you vibrate to or that you need to vibrate to.

SEVENTH STEP: This is an optional step you might consider trying, especially if you find coloring designs to be relaxing and rewarding. In order to try this step you will have to get copies of the following books: *THE TAROT DESIGN COLORING BOOK* and *THE ZODIAC DESIGN COLORING BOOK.* Both of these books are created by Caren Caraway and are published by Stemmer House Publishing, Inc. The designs in these two books are wonderful to use when you add your own color preferences.

In the Tarot Design book, you can choose to color any one of the 78 tarot cards in the colors which appeal to you or which you feel describe the hidden meaning of the card. I find this exercise very beneficial when creating a "Tarot Board". A Tarot Board is a unique way to make "affirmations" using the individual meaning of the Tarot Cards themselves. You can use just one card, 3 cards, 5 cards, or as many as you want to create the "board". For example:

Let's say you want to create the energy of success around you. Using a 3-card focus for this purpose, I would choose the tarot card called "The Magician" as my first card. Then, on a stiff board or heave piece of cardboard I would tape the card in the bottom left hand corner. That position represents me as I am now and what talents or abilities I have to work with. The second card I would choose is "The Wheel of Fortune". Then I would tape it in the center of my board to represent the energies at work in my life. The third card I would choose is "The Universe". This last card would go in the upper right hand corner and it represents the outcome I wish to manifest.

You can use this technique to manifest other "desires" or energies as well. If you desire love and romance in your life, you can choose the cards that best represent what you would like to attract into your life. All this exercise does is concentrate the focus of your thoughts on what you want in life. Thoughts that are backed with positive concentrated energy can materialize much faster than if you just "wished" it would happen. I firmly believe in the old adage: "Ask and ye shall receive." But you've gotta *ask first*!

The second book I mentioned concerning Zodiac Designs can be used as an alternative to Mandala designs or in addition to them. With this book you can pick out the design for your "Sun Sign", "Rising Sign (ascendant)" or "Moon Sign" and choose the colors which vibrate to you astrologically or the colors which represent the qualities you want to develop. These designs too, will work well as a focus when you wish to quiet your mind for meditation or for simple relaxation. It would also be a good exercise for your creative and artistic abilities if you tried designing your own tarot card and zodiac sign pictures.

The purpose of this suggestion has been to get you in touch with your own special creativity. The side benefit to coloring designs is the sense of relaxation and contentment you feel. This is a creative way to relieve stress and tension, for you will feel a genuine sense of accomplishment when you are done. Check with your local bookstore for these coloring books or other design coloring books and give it a try. If the bookstore doesn't carry these books in stock, I have included the address and phone number of the publisher in case you want to contact them directly or have your bookstore do it.

Dept. TDC Stemmer house Publishers, Inc. 2627 Caves Rd. Owings Mills, Maryland, 21117. Phone Number: (301) 363-3690.

Other Workbook-Journal Entries can center around your work with the Tarot and different Lay-Out Spreads. Choosing the appropriate Lay-Out Spread and recording the pattern of the cards in the Spread will give you a reference guide pertaining to your personal challenges. Using the Tarot as a tool in focusing help, you develop the discipline needed to open the Intuitive Channel you possess. Eventually, you may find you no longer need the Tarot to focus with and that you can immediately see the behavior patterns and challenges occurring in your life through simple Meditation Techniques which "tune in" the Voice of your Higher self.

The practical exercises outlined next, concerns building up your "psychic" energy, creating a reservoir of personal strength you can draw on. The first exercise for you to try is as follows:

1. Sit under a shady tree, your back up against the tree trunk and the palms of your hands face up in your lap. Close your eyes and take a deep breath through your nose to the count of 4. As you are breathing in, visualize the air as a brilliant *red* light. Hold your breath to the count of 12. Then, let it out slowly, through the mouth, to the count of 8, visualizing impurities leaving your body as you do so.

Repeat the breathing exercise again, only this time visualize breathing in a brilliant *orange* light. Take a deep breath through your nose to the count of 4... Hold it to the count of 12... Then let it out slowly, through the mouth, to the count of 8, again visualizing impurities leaving your body as you do so.

Repeat the breathing exercise again, only this time visualize breathing in a brilliant *yellow* light. Take a deep breath through your nose to the count of 4... Hold it to the count of 12... Then let it out slowly, through the mouth, to the count of 8, again visualizing impurities leaving your body as you do so.

Repeat the breathing exercise again, only this time visualize breathing in a brilliant *green* light. Take a deep breath through your nose to the count of 4... Hold it to the count of 12... Then let it out slowly, through the mouth, to the count of 8, again visualizing impurities leaving your body as you do so.

Again, repeat the breathing exercise, only this time visualize breathing in a brilliant *sky blue* light. Take a deep breath through your nose to the count of 4... Hold it to the count of 12... Then let it out slowly, through the mouth, to the count of 8, again visualizing impurities and tension leaving your body as you do so.

Again, repeat the breathing exercise, only this time visualize breathing in a brilliant *indigo* light. Take a deep breath through your nose to the count of 4... Hold it to the count of 12... Then let it out slowly, through the mouth, to the count of 8, again visualizing impurities and tension leaving your body as you do so.

Repeat the breathing exercise one more time, only this time visualize breathing in a brilliant *violet* light. Take a deep breath through your nose to the count of 4... Hold it to the count of 12... Then let it out slowly, through the mouth, to the count of 8, again visualizing impurities and tension leaving your body as you do so.

This is a Yoga Breathing exercise used to cleanse and open the 7 Chakra Centers of the Body. This allows "psychic" energy to pass in and out of the body without impediment. It also stores excess energy in the Chakra Centers for you to use when needed at a later time. I have tried this exercise when I have a bad headache and it works really well. A dear friend of mine, who has had asthma since she was a child, uses this exercise when she starts having an attack, it serves to relax her and lessens, considerably, the severity of the attack.

You can also do this exercise indoors, with soft meditation music playing in the background. It doesn't have to be done outside under a tree, but at least try that method once just to experience the sensations it creates. This is also an excellent exercise to do before working with the Tarot or before Meditating. This would be a wonderful "habit" to get into every morning or every evening.

2. Another exercise involves working with Evergreen Trees or Pine Trees. Try gently stroking the needles or branches of a pine tree with your fingertips. You will immediately feel a tingling in your hand that will travel up your arms. Try taking the branch and gently stroke your face with it. It gives a tickling feeling to the body and at the same time sharpens the senses. Without damaging or harming the tree, gently stroke your whole body with the pine needle branches. You will feel a surge of energy entering into your body, imparting a feeling of contentment, even joy.

As I have stated before, Evergreen Trees or Pine Trees are natural storehouses of "psychic energy". These trees enjoy, yes enjoy, sharing this stored energy with others. If you are willing to accept it, you can "feel/sense" the love emanating from these trees to you. Evergreens or Pines have the unique ability of absorbing all kinds of energy, even negative energy, and transforming it into healing, rejuvenating energy. There is nothing more invigorating than walking through a Pine Tree Forest, stroking the branches and hugging the trees as you go.

3. This exercise involves walking barefoot on a sandy beach or through earth that has recently been tilled, making it easy for you to wiggle your toes in the dirt. Even standing in the shallow part of a lake, river, stream or creek, wiggling your toes and feet into the sand or mud at the bottom is good for you. The

purpose of this exercise is for you to get a "feel" for the energy of the planet, to "feel" the strengthening vibration of the Earth itself. With your feet firmly planted in the earth itself, hold your hands, palm-side up, to the rays of the Sun. You will experience a channeling of energy between the Sun and the Earth. The feelings this exercise generates is greatly intensified if you hold a small crystal in each hand and allow the Sun to penetrate the crystal as well as the palms of your hands. Lift your face towards the sun, close your eyes and let the rays of solar energy flow through you into the earth itself.

4. This exercise deals with the vibrations and energy patterns of Crystals, Minerals and Gems. The first thing to do is choose one of the "Earth Treasures" outlined in Chapter 7. Perhaps the particular Earth Treasure you choose has properties you wish to absorb into your own consciousness and energy pattern, or you want to use the energy from a particular Crystal, Mineral, or Gem, to enhance your own abilities. What ever the case, after you have chosen the appropriate stone to work with, lie down in a quiet place, either in bed, or outside under a tree, or even on the sand. The location is immaterial as long as it is a place where you are undisturbed and can relax comfortably.

Place the "Earth Treasure" you have chosen on your "third eye", (located between your eyebrows, just above the bridge of the nose and on the forehead.) The "Third Eye" is the 6th Chakra Center which rules Intuition, inspiration, Visions, telepathy, and the "psychic senses". Now comes the hard part. LISTEN to the subtle murmurs of your Earth Treasure. If there is a problem or situation in which you need guidance, LISTEN for the awakening wisdom within. With your eyes closed, you can SEE pictures or "Visions" which can shed enlightenment and understanding.

Placing a Crystal, Mineral, or Gem on your "Third Eye" awakens the clairvoyant and clairaudient abilities your possess. It may take a few attempts on your part to fully open your Intuitive Channel. For some people, it helps if they do deep breathing exercises with the "*Earth Treasure*" placed on the "third eye" first before attempting to listen to the voice of the stone. Connie Church's book: *CRYSTAL CLEAR*, outlines several different techniques using crystals to activate the power of the "Third Eye".

AFFIRMATIONS AND PRAYERS

There are many people who are uncomfortable with the word "Prayer" because it seems to represent old dogmatic religious doctrine they have abandoned, symbolizing fearful pleas and entreaties to a stern judgmental God. Or, they are under the mistaken idea they need an intermediary between them and God, that they are not worthy to ask God anything because they are not purified enough, holy enough, or just aren't good enough because they are sinful.

All that Prayer really is, is a dialogue between you and your Creator. Prayer does not have to be poetic, unless you are poetically inclined and enjoy that particular creative and rhythmic method. Prayers do not have to be said with solemn ceremonial intonations either. Prayers can be humorous, lighthearted, filled with laughter and joy. Prayers can be requests for understanding and guidance, for help and assistance. Prayers are what *you* make them.

If it is hard for you to verbalize your inner most feelings, your fears, desires and needs, try writing a letter to God. If you are still uncomfortable with the idea of "prayer", try using "Affirmations". Affirmations are positive statements about yourself, about your situation, and about the environment and people around you.

In the following paragraphs I will give examples of both Prayers and Affirmations you can use. I hope they will inspire you to create your own, unique versions.

"Why worry, when you can pray?
Know that the power of Ego is limited.
The power of the Creative Forces is Unlimited."
Edgar Cayce

FIRST AFFIRMATION

Beloved Creator;
I choose to be a Channel for Thy Peace,
That where there is hatred, I may bring Pure Love.
That where there is fear, I may bring forth Your Miracles.
That where there is judgment, I may bring the Spirit of Forgiveness.
That where there is discord, I may bring forth Harmony.
That where there is error, I may bring forth Your Truth.
That where there is doubt, I may bring forth Faith.
That where there is despair, I may bring forth Hope.
That where there is illusions, I may bring forth Your Light. That where there is sadness, I may bring forth Joy.
For it is by Giving, That one Receives.
It is by forgiving, That one is forgiven.
It is through Perfect Love and Acceptance,
That one awakens from dreams of darkness and limitations.

SECOND AFFIRMATION

Wherever I am... wherever I go... the Presence of Divine Love is with me, for this Love stands with me... beside me... and behind me. Every hand that reaches for mine blesses me with the opportunity to share the Divine Love I have received. Through the power of Love my awareness has grown. I can feel the light of Universal Truth in all I see... in all I touch... in all I hear. Enveloped by Divine Love, the Earth plane no longer has the power to impose limitations on my creativity. No longer can a physical body contain the true fullness of my Spirit. I am free to express the entire range of my potentials... the Presence of Divine Love has taken away my fear.

THIRD AFFIRMATION

When I am faced with the many choices life challenges me with, the Divine Light within me will show me the right decision to make. I will quiet the shrill voice of the Ego and turn away from its fear induced voice. Instead I will turn inward and listen to the Voice of Divine Light whispering softly in my heart. The Truth it speaks will guide my unsteady footsteps down the right path to enlightenment.

When I listen to the voice of illusion I become confused and unsure. But the beloved Voice of Divine Light calmly lifts the veils which have blinded me to reality. When I get angry or make a mistake, the guilt I feel overwhelms and paralyzes me. But the all-encompassing Love of the Creator washes away the stain of my errors and reminds me that forgiveness is the key to unlock the chains that bind me.

I accept the gift of Divine Light into my life. I ask to be guided by its gentle presence, to be shown a better way. By surrendering the demands of my ego, I will grow in awareness and gain true spirituality.

FOURTH AFFIRMATION

Today I joyfully accept the wonderful spiritual gifts the loving Universal Life Force sends my way. Happiness, prosperity, peace, and contentment are my birth-right as a Child of Light. All of these treasures and more are waiting for me to claim them. The treasure house of the Creator is overflowing with an abundance that never diminishes. As I confidently claim these gifts for myself, I realize that I am claiming them for all my brothers and sisters on the earth plane. The fulfillment I receive will not take away from the joy that is available to all who are willing to accept their birth-right. None of the Creator's children profits at the expense of another. Content with my heritage, my happiness radiates outward to others, inspiring them to claim their heritage as well.

FIRST PRAYER

"Thank you God, for allowing me to be a window
through which Your Light shines
and a mirror to reflect
Your Love to all I meet."

SECOND PRAYER

"Dear Father/Mother God
Lend me the faith and courage
to accept change as a positive force.
Help me to put the past in perspective
and to see the new opportunities for the future.
Bless me with the wisdom to know

the difference between limitation and challenge.
Protect and guide me through the
stormy seas of life I have created.
Remind me that I am not alone
or unneeded in the world.
Show me the way to serve the needs of others
so I may grow in compassion and understanding.
Teach me of the joy there is
in accepting others as I accept myself.
Allow me to contribute to the never-ending
pattern of Love and Light.

NOTE

There is an excellent Astrological Prayerbook written by Alda Marian Jangl and published by Samuel Weiser Inc., P.O. Box 612, York Beach, Maine, 03910, which contains prayers for each of the 12 Zodiac Signs and for the planetary aspects of a natal horoscope chart as well as prayers for progressed planetary aspects and the Moon's Nodes. It is an extremely useful tool for it takes the art of Astrology a step beyond the simple search for self-knowledge. Alda Jangl shows you how to change the prayers into affirmations if you should so choose, making this book applicable to all Seekers. I strongly recommend this book as an addition to your library. The book grants you an insight to your spiritual lessons which serves your goal of Self-Realization.

In that spirit, I am including the Affirmations pertaining to the Numerological 9 year cycles of Progression. Also included are the master numbers 11, 22, 33 and 44, all of which occur once in awhile as the number vibration for a personalized year. I am concentrating on Affirmations rather than Prayers out of respect for your personal belief systems. However, please feel free to alter the Affirmations into Prayers if you so choose. Either way is extremely effective and beneficial. The Affirmations are as follows:

AFFIRMATION FOR PERSONAL YEAR NUMBER ONE

This year begins a new cycle of opportunity for me, it is time for me to start new projects, open new doors, cultivate new interests, and develop new attitudes. This is my year to demonstrate my creative talents and show the world what I am capable of. I will accept the opportunity to advance my original and innovative ideas to people who are in positions to implement them.

The vibration of leadership is strongly active in me this year. I have the energy, drive and ambition to succeed at whatever I put my mind to. Employers and people in positions of power and authority will be impressed with the inspired way I handle the challenges I am faced with. My family and friends will appreciate my willingness to assume responsibility and take charge of any difficulties that may arise.

During the influence of this cycle, new people will come into my life who can have an important impact on my success. I will take the time and effort to nurture each friendship or relationship I develop and give generously of myself and my time because these new people could well become a permanent fixture in my life. The opportunity to travel this year will provide me with a variety of experiences I can utilize creatively in the future.

The changes occurring in my life during this year represent opportunities for happiness and success as long as I keep an open mind and listen to my inner intuitive guidance. I will take the initiative and do things for myself which will help me to break out of old behavior patterns that have limited me in the past. What I do now, how I direct my energies during my personal One-year will set a pattern for my entire 9-year cycle. Courage, faith and a positive outlook are the qualities through which I channel my energies during this cycle.

AFFIRMATION FOR PERSONAL YEAR NUMBER TWO

The influence of this cycle brings a sense of relaxation, a slowing down after the hectic pace of the previous year. The efforts I expended last year will begin to bear fruit in my present cycle. I can joyfully accept the rewards this year produces because of the good impressions I made during my preceding cycle. Unexpected but welcome surprises occur this year bringing with them offers I will need to carefully examine for long-term benefits.

The energies a 2-cycle creates involves partnership, cooperation with others, and collaborative efforts. The independent aura I cultivated last year will be tempered with the spirit of "teamwork". I may have the opportunity to unite my talents and capabilities with another individual or with a group this year providing I demonstrate a willingness to share responsibility and to cooperate with out "taking over" or "taking charge" at every turn.

With the positive energies of the number 2 channeling through every facet of my life this year, my intimate Personal affairs will be enhanced. People will be attracted to me on a personal level during this cycle providing an opportunity to widen my circle of friends. With all the new people coming into my life now the chances are good I may meet a potential lover or mate. However, it is vitally important for me to use my inner intuitive guidance when evaluating these new acquaintances so I do not unwittingly attract unsavory characters into my life.

The intensity of emotions I experience this year may bring difficulties or problems for me to handle in a positive manner. It is important for me to remember that obstacles are really opportunities for growth when approached with courage and patience. Nothing is impossible if I believe strongly enough and set my talents and abilities toward solutions. Understanding, compassion, cooperation and tact are qualities which will assist me in overcoming many of the "challenges" and "opportunities" this year will bring my way.

AFFIRMATION FOR PERSONAL YEAR NUMBER THREE

The influence of my personal 3-year brings socializing, pleasure, and fun into my life. Happiness, joy and special successes are the highpoints of this cycle. My personality is more vivid and expressive under the influence of this vibration which is very attractive to other people. The energy of self-expression, symbolized by the number 3, provides me with the ability to present my ideas in unique ways which assists in my advancement in the world.

This is my year to develop my abilities as a writer, even if I have never tried it before. Keeping a Personal Journal, writing about personal experiences, fictional short stories or novels, how-to books on creative expression, any of these subjects and more would be good outlets for me and my chances of selling my ideas will be very good this year. The intense need to express my creativity is very strong, and even if writing doesn't appeal to me now, there are many artistic outlets I could also choose to pursue.

Words, written or spoken by me, can have positive beneficial effects on others. However, they can just as easily have a negative effect if I use them as weapons against others. Therefore, I will think things out carefully before speaking so I do not cause problems or hurt people's feelings in a thoughtless manner. Instead, I will focus this cycle's gift for words to uplift the spirits of others.

The energy vibration of number 3 affects human sexuality, and because of its influence on me this year my sensuality will be stimulated to new heights of expression. Because of this increased sexual awareness, it is important that I not fall into the trap of indulging in purely physical relationships. However, taking advantage of my increased sensual awareness by enjoying romance and sensuality with my mate can enhance our relationship in positive ways and bind us closer together.

Regardless of my job, career, or vocation, this is the year for me to improve my attitude, my environment, even my appearance. This is the year for me to indulge myself and enjoy the many opportunities that come my way. The 3-vibration brings opportunities for romance and excitement and its up to me to either take the opportunities or reject them. Whatever I do during this cycle, I should learn to enjoy it and appreciate the potentials given to me.

AFFIRMATION FOR PERSONAL YEAR NUMBER FOUR

The influence of my 4-cycle stimulates my need to lay foundations for future Financial rewards and recognition from my peers. During this year of steady determination I will gain experience and knowledge which will be invaluable to me in the future. My previous cycles have served as an initial period of planning and organizing, the time has arrived for me to implement those ideas I have been in the process of developing.

It is important for me to decided what it is I want to accomplish and then start the routine necessary to achieve my goals. Organizing my time and my thoughts to achieve maximum benefit and setting up a schedule where nothing will interfere or prevent me from reaching my goals requires determination on my part because I may find heavy burdens developing from time to time this year. I may have to work extra hard in compensation for lost time or unexpected delays.

However, everything I devote myself to wholeheartedly this year will bring rewards at a later date. This is a cycle of investment, of time, energy, money, and self so I do not expect to reap great financial rewards this year. My financial rewards will come later. I will have my material needs taken care of, but I must use common sense and be conservative in my spending this year. The "Greater" rewards I am entitled to through my hard work and dedication will develop after this year of "planting and sowing".

The 4 vibration is one of building, determination and strength, endowing me with these same qualities to stick with my efforts. Not only am I building financial and career stability, I am also building the firm and reliable foundations in my personal relationships. This is an excellent time to develop the groundwork for intimate relationships because they can be built on compatibility, understanding, mutual need and consideration rather than on pure "physical" attraction.

AFFIRMATION FOR PERSONAL YEAR NUMBER FIVE

The power of a 5-cycle acts as a catalyst in bringing about change in my life, allowing me to begin to reap some of the rewards of the hard work I have expended in the past. The number 5 is the symbol of change, communication, freedom, release and progress, therefore, I should ready myself for a year filled with the unexpected. Since "change" is the keyword for the number 5, this year will bring about a major turning point in my life which could happen under unusual, even surprising circumstances. However, this new direction will be very important to my spiritual development.

Because this is a year of dramatic changes, it is important for me to accept these changes rather than try to fight them. I will not allow myself to become fearful over the challenges and opportunities that come my way. Nor will I fall into the futile trap of worrying over every small detail that develops unexpectedly, or be apprehensive of the offers I receive which seem to promise attainment of some of the goals I have set for myself. I will instead, be grateful for the chance to explore new possibilities and to realize my dreams.

Like the number 3 vibration, the number 5 vibration has an affinity for words, for writing and communicating. During this personal 5 year, I will have the opportunity to develop and utilize any gifts I possess which have to do with communicating with others. Speaking, lecturing, advertising, writing, even performing are areas I can explore with success this year since the number 5 represents the energy force behind these endeavors. Opportunities for travel will arise during this cycle which will give me the opportunity to experience adventure and excitement.

Since the 5 vibration is one of change and fluctuation, things that I begin early in this cycle may have disappointing results at first, but if this occurs, it will be to my long-term benefit. The unstable influence of this cycle could affect my financial situation unless I pay attention and am ready to take appropriate action. Because of the energy affecting my life now I will be cautious about making commitments regarding business, partnerships, leases, contracts and personal relationships.

AFFIRMATION FOR PERSONAL YEAR NUMBER SIX

The energy generated by my 6-cycle involves harmony, responsibility, love, domesticity and balance. Therefore, these concerns will be my focus during this cycle. I am very sensitive to the aura or energy vibrations of my environment, both at home and in the work-place. Negative energy can create an imbalance in my system affecting my concentration and increasing levels of stress. Therefore, I will take time to meditate, relax and surround myself with harmonious vibrations.

During the influence of this cycle, my personal relationships will gain more prominence as I find myself subconsciously reacting to the "nesting" instinct. The home, a mate and children will become the, focus of my energies this year, and if I don't deny or fight these instincts, I could achieve the emotional fulfillment I have been seeking. I am more openly loving and affectionate with those I care about, friends, as well as family and lovers. Accepting the love offered by others will provide me with a great deal of happiness and satisfaction.

The number 6 also represents beauty, art and creativity. This powerful influence affects music, painting, sculpture, and other forms of artistic expression. My creative juices are stirring to life, demanding a productive outlet. New doors of opportunity will be available to me where I can gain the interest of those people who are in a position to promote my artistic work. This is a good time to receive recognition for my creative endeavors.

This cycle creates an aura of protection around me, blessing me with contentment and happiness.

AFFIRMATION FOR PERSONAL YEAR NUMBER SEVEN

The unique influence of my 7-cycle creates an environment ideally suited to mental and spiritual pursuits. I welcome the opportunity to indulge in mediation and contemplation, for it affords me, the solitude I need to explore my mental universe. These periods of quiet contemplation will allow me to immerse myself in esoteric wisdom which will help me to develop a positive pattern for achievement. By devoting time to studying metaphysical and spiritual teachings I will greatly contribute to my personal storehouse of knowledge, enabling me to grow in awareness.

Through meditation and practical spiritual exercises I will heighten my intuitive abilities and develop the self-discipline necessary to achieve the goals I have set for myself. One of the most important benefits I will gain by devoting my energies to mental pursuits is the attainment of self-awareness. In my pursuit of personal perfection it is important to remember that not everyone is focused in the same direction I am. Criticizing others, even when meant for the best reasons, can create misunderstandings with those I care about.

The pace of a 7-year cycle is a slow one and can seem twice as long as it really is. Cultivating a positive attitude and practicing mental discipline will provide me with the patience I need. The influence of this cycle will incline me toward solitude and I must take care not to become a hermit or neglect my family and friends. Very few social events will seem important enough for me to disturb the peacefulness of my mental routine, but I will make an effort not to completely cut myself off from the outside world.

Although my personal 7-year vibration is not good for taking risks in financial matters, it is excellent for creative expression, literary work or invention. Through my intuitive channeling of the Higher Vibrations of the Universe, I will receive unique inspiration which will give me the confidence to be unusually creative and could lead to recognition of my talent if I am willing to discipline myself. It is important for me to follow up on any opportunities that are offered to me now, because they could lead to something very important.

AFFIRMATION FOR PERSONAL YEAR NUMBER EIGHT

The Personal 8-year vibration is a time of reaping what I have sown before in previous cycles. Unusual opportunities for achievement are available to me this year if I am willing to work diligently and consistently. This is a year of action and reaction which is under the influence of a very powerful vibration. The goals I set for myself in the past and towards which I have continued to expend time and energy can be realized this year, for the number 8 is the symbol of fulfillment in material goals.

Under the influence of the number 8, business enterprises will prosper greatly. However, now is not the time to rest on my laurels and wait to reap the benefits. It is important that I continue to strive towards my goals and accept the opportunities that come to me during this period. Confidently, I will seek out those individuals who are in positions of authority and responsibility to assure the success of my endeavors.

The opportunity to utilize my leadership abilities will materialize during this cycle, inspiring my sense of independence and originality. The power of number 8 comes from its intimate association with the laws of Karma. I will personally experience the power of this force in operation during this cycle. What has been sown by me in the past will be ready for reaping this year. If I have worked diligently during the preceding cycles, I will reap the rewards.

The wonderful benefits I gain this year will give me the chance to express the generous side of my nature and allow me to give of myself as well as give materially. My personal talents and abilities will come in handy in charitable or non-profit organizations I have an interest in. My personality is enhanced now and can influence even conservative individuals to make contributions of either time or money to the organization I have chosen to represent.

All in all, this 8-cycle can be a wonderful, fulfilling experience for me and I am determined to make the most of it.

AFFIRMATION FOR PERSONAL YEAR NUMBER NINE

The powerful vibration of a 9-cycle combines the ending of old situations, environmental factors, and outlooks with the formation or beginning of new things. This is the perfect time for me to sort out what goals, ideas, and plans are really important to me, what will truly making me feel fulfilled and happy. The things I have been involved with for the past several years, whether they are personal relationships or business oriented, should be carefully examined to see what has value and has a positive effect on me.

The cleansing energy of the 9-cycle assists me in putting the past behind me, and helping me to prepare myself and my life for a new beginning starting next year in my 1-cycle. Obstinately refusing to let go of relationships, activities or affairs which have proven to be inviable will prevent spiritual progress and delay my own potential for achievement and happiness. With the dynamic power of number 9 behind me, I have the insight and wisdom to eliminate that which creates obstacles and pain.

The internal changes I am going through can cause me to be short tempered and easily irritated, reactions which need careful monitoring on my part for to cause others pain or to hurt them even unintentionally can be avoided if I pay attention to my own actions. At the same time, I need to be aware that the reactions I am having to certain people is a signal from my intuitive self forewarning me that the relationship has served its purpose and I must be prepared to sever my emotional ties and allow them to follow their own chosen road in life. If I ignore the subconscious message sent to me by the Universal Mind, I risk carrying excess emotional baggage with me into my new cycle that will eventually become a heavy burden to bear. There is a fine line between giving unselfishly of oneself and becoming a victim, a lesson the vibration of this year is attempting to teach me.

The energy created by the number nine takes discernment and judgment to utilize properly in determining where I should concentrate my efforts and attention. Because of the importance of this year to me, I will be firm in my opinions and I will not allow others to distract me or sway me from the course I must set for my life. Only my Higher Self and the Divine Beings who inspire and guide me know the true nature of my destiny and therefore know what obstacles must be cleared from my path. It is to this Source I defer my decisions and choices, resting assured of my ultimate victory.

AFFIRMATION FOR PERSONAL YEAR NUMBER 11

The number 11 is a Master Number, and as such the vibrations which affect me this year are very powerful. Therefore, it is important that I live up to the potentials this master number brings or it will simply revert back to a 2 vibration which will bog me down in details and compromises. The influence of the master number 11 vibration offers me creative inspiration and psychic clarity which could bring me fame or recognition if I follow the guidance of my intuition and am not afraid to act on my hunches.

This is a year filled with sudden unexpected events and circumstances, requiring me to keep on my toes, act decisively and to make decisions competently. With all the exhilarating situations occurring during this cycle, my impulsiveness needs careful monitoring. It is important that I keep my patience and tolerance close to the surface while coping with the state of flux my life takes on this year. This is the time for me to eliminate wrong ideas and discontinue actions which have created any negative vibrations or circumstances in my life. Having the "right" attitude will do more to help me achieve what I desire for the future than any influential person or organization could possibly do.

Under the powerful influence of this master number cycle, my mind is receptive to the further development of my psychic and intuitive abilities. Studying metaphysics, meditation, diverse spiritual disciplines, the occult, parapsychology, or ESP would be an excellent way to utilize my excess energy. This energy could also be channeled into physical manifestation through artistic or creative outlets such as art, music, writing or dance.

The master number 11 symbolizes active intuition which I may manifest during my dream-state, while meditating, or through other spiritual means, if I am willing to open myself up to the Universal Subconscious. The desire for further knowledge will become important to me during this year because of the intense psychic and spiritual impressions I receive which urge me to seek the deeper meaning of life and my place in the Universe. Perhaps taking classes will help me achieve the knowledge I am seeking, if so, then the opportunity will become available to me.

If I have done my work properly in the past cycles, my originality and innovative talents could come to the attention of people in positions of authority who will be impressed enough with my efforts to assist my career. There will be many chances to advance myself in my chosen profession during this cycle if I am willing to accept the opportunity. This is a special period in my life, full of challenges and initiations. These challenges occur to teach me how to channel my energies into something worthwhile and lasting. The vibrations of the Master Numbers offer Master Opportunities. How I choose to deal with these opportunities is my choice.

AFFIRMATION FOR PERSONAL YEAR NUMBER 22

The number 22 is a Master Number, and as such, the strong, compelling vibrations created by this number will teach me how to combine the inspirational and spiritual with the material and practical. The power of this cycle can create the right energy for me to reach an important goal or achieve the fulfillment of a deeply cherished desire. I will not be afraid to make big plans or dare to do the things I have only dreamed about before. As long as I keep my plans practical and well organized, there should be no problem in accomplishing what ever I set out to do. This is a year to help in creating practical and beneficial things for the entire world, not just for myself or my community circle because the possibilities are limitless under the vibration of the master number 22. If the master vibration of the number 22 is not utilized properly, its energies will simply revert to the vibrations of number 4, creating more limitations than opportunities.

AFFIRMATION FOR PERSONAL YEAR NUMBER 33

The number 33 is a Master Number and as such, the powerful vibrations of this number will effect my confidence in myself and my abilities, teaching me valuable lessons in "discernment" during this cycle. How I choose to perceive the energy of this vibration is my choice. I can "experience" it in a negative manner, lose confidence in my abilities, have doubts about everything, even feel victimized by an apparently uncaring world. Or, I can "experience" this vibration in a positive manner, using my talents to help others with their problems, offer compassion and understanding, and most importantly, be willing to put myself out for the benefit of others.

I will be blessed with the spiritual strength I need to help others. The more I give, the more energy I will receive from the Forces of Light who have given me this opportunity to serve as a Channel for Love. In spite of the Challenges which arise during this year, I will maintain my faith and trust in the Creator for I believe in the Law of Karma and know that what one gives out to others, one receives 10 fold in return. Unusual encounters and experiences will occur during this special time in my life which will activate my intuitive awareness. I will be able to see clearly, without illusions to distract me, and the purpose I have been given for this life will be revealed.

AFFIRMATION FOR PERSONAL YEAR NUMBER 44

The Number 44 is a Master Number and as such, it indicates a major turning point in my life. The vibrations created by this number grant me the opportunity and the time to assess and take measure of the direction my life is currently headed in. During this period in my life, it is important for me to decide which course of action will produce the most opportunities while allowing me to remain "in-tune" with the Universal Mind. This is a major assessment period for me, if the course I have set in the past has been productive and worthwhile, then this is the time when I will see the most results and rewards.

The diverse situations and occurrences during this cycle are not the result of chance nor are they random. They occur in order to demonstrate what I am lacking in my life, what I need to incorporate into my life so I can bring it into alignment with the Universal Flow. The material world is making its presence known in my life, but, how do I unite the material world with the spiritual world? How do I use the resources available to me in constructive ways that help others as well as myself? What can I do to make a difference in the world?

The questioning that constantly goes through my mind is my subconscious cry to the Universe for answers that can help me to put the world I have created into better perspective. The answers I seek are available to me if I will be still a moment and listen to the Voice of Love. This master number cycle brings me the opportunity to reach out to the Universal mind, to touch, to feel the Love the Creator has for me. The gentle wisdom which is offered to me is not for my use alone, it is to be freely given to others so they too may find spiritual liberation and freedom.

HOW TO DETERMINE THE "CYCLES" IN YOUR NAME

In Chapter Two, "Symbolism of the Alphabet", definitions were given concerning the active "cycle" or "phase" a letter has. One of the ways to discover when certain letters become "active" in your life has to do with your full given name. Each letter of your name vibrates to a number which, in turn, represents a span of years. I will use my name for an example:

MARILYN JEAN ENNERS
4 1 993 7 5 15 1 5 5 5 5 5 91

Next, we set up the following graph to depict the corresponding years and letters, beginning with my birth.

M=4	From Birth to age 4
A=1	From age 4 to age 5
R=9	From age 5 to age 14
I=9	From age 14 to age 23
L=3	From age 23 to age 26
Y=7	From age 26 to age 33
N=5	From age 33 to age 38
J=1	From age 38 to age 39
E=5	From age 39 to age 44
A=1	From age 44 to age 45
N=5	From age 45 to age 50
E=5	From age 50 to age 55
N=5	From age 55 to age 60
N=5	From age 60 to age 65
E=5	From age 65 to age 70
R=9	From age 70 to age 79
S=1	From age 79 to age 80

Once you've reached the end of your name after correlating the appropriate years of your life, you start the whole process over again beginning with the first letter of your first name. This is one of the methods for discovering which letter has been activated and what energy influences it is bringing into your life. The influence of the letter will "color" the energy around you for the amount of time the letter represents, subtly affecting your personal year cycles.

Sometimes during dreams or in meditation, letters will seem to randomly appear on a sheet of paper, on the page of a book, etc. Even if the letters you see during these experiences do not appear in your name, the vibrations of these letters have been activated by Universal Forces or by Karmic Law. In this case, it is important to pay attention to the subconscious message your intuitional mind is sending you. The energies that are being released into your life have a special purpose and it is wise to know how to constructively use its power.

20 KEYS FOR CONSTRUCTIVE SELF-COUNSELING

There have been many "Keys" or "Tools" defined and outlined in the preceding Chapters of this book, all of which are geared towards the ultimate goal of Self-Realization. These "Keys" are, by nature, both metaphysical and esoteric, structured to open the Gateway to your Higher Intuitive Self, that part of you which has constant access to the Universal Mind. Awakening your Intuitive abilities and creating an awareness of your intimate connection to the Universe has been the major focus of this book.

However, since this chapter is devoted to "Practical Exercises", I feel its important at this time to give you 20 "Keys" or common sense tips to work with and utilize which can be beneficial to you on a day-to-day basis. The "keys" or "tips" listed below are suggestions to try when you are feeling depressed, overwhelmed by the world, or anxious, or simply have the "blues". These tips are geared toward Self-Awareness and Self-Analysis of problems or situations which cause feelings of inadequacy.

FIRST KEY:

First and foremost you must realize that people who have problems are not weak or spineless. Nor do they have problems because they "deserve" them from a karmic standpoint. As a matter of fact, it isn't "normal" not to have problems occasionally. Problem solving is part of our growth experience on the Earth Plane. Problems or Challenges as I prefer to call them, are ways for us to discover our strengths and to correct the weaknesses we possess. We would not be incarnating in a physical body on the Earth Plane if we were perfect, and this bit of information is important to remember.

SECOND KEY:

Take the time to write out a list of all the things that are troubling or disturbing your peace of mind. This can include people, situations, relationships, environment, finances, job, the future, politics, world affairs, etc. By making a list such as this, you bring into *conscious* focus what is bothering you rather than allowing vague rumblings of disquiet to break up the peace of your sub-conscious mind. Knowing what problems or troubles are affecting you helps you to take control of them. And when you are in control, you feel less like a victim.

THIRD KEY

Study each of the items on your list individually and carefully. Be honest in your evaluation of the list. Once you thoroughly understand the nature of what's troubling you, it lessens the power and ability it has to cause fear and apprehension in you. Look for subtle patterns between your problems and see if there is not a common thread that runs between all of them. If you can isolate a common theme or cause, you can focus the power of your being towards eliminating the root problem, which, in turn, will provide solutions for the problems which have stemmed from a single root source.

FOURTH KEY:

Ask for the input and viewpoint of a close friend or confidant concerning your "list". Sometimes we are too close to a problem to see it clearly which can make it more overwhelming than it has to be. A fresh insight from someone who is not personally involved with your situation can provide you with a new perspective and thereby reveal previously unthought of solutions.

FIFTH KEY:

Another important point concerning your "list" should be determining whether or not a problem or difficulty is actually yours. If a mate or family member is the one who has the "problem" or difficulty, such as drugs, alcoholism, gambling, etc., you must realize it is their problem, not yours. You cannot shoulder the burdens of other people. This doesn't help them, it only prolongs their problems. They are responsible for their own choices. However, you can and should offer what support and understanding you can, but at the same time you must accept they are the ones who will have to find their own solutions, you can't do it for them.

SIXTH KEY:
Pray. This is one of the most comforting and emotionally satisfying actions you can take. Use Affirmations and believe in them. Know that you are loved by the Infinite Creator of the Universe and that whatever troubles you is not too insignificant for the Creator to be told of. We are never alone, no matter how impossible a situation seems to be, we are not abandoned here on the Earth Plane.

SEVENTH KEY:
The single most important thing you need to realize is that *You alone* are responsible for your happiness. Your state of happiness must come from within, not from another person or thing. Make a conscious decision to enjoy yourself, to accept your own uniqueness, and above all, to love yourself regardless of the external circumstances around you.

EIGHTH KEY:
Be willing to take risks. Have the faith and trust to try something new. Don't be afraid to take a new job or begin a new career after being a homemaker for many years. You have talent and value you haven't even begun to explore. Take adult education courses, go to seminars or workshops geared for the needs of women. If you are a man or woman in a high-stress career and you want out, don't be afraid to make the move. Even if the high-powered job you are in seems to be financially rewarding, is the promise of more material prosperity enslaving you instead of freeing you? Simplify your life and you may mind many of your problems disappearing.

NINTH KEY:
Learn how to say no. Don't take on more and more responsibilities until the sheer weight of them overwhelms you. Guilt is a wonderful weapon of the Ego, requiring you to suffer in self-righteous martyrdom. This is not necessary and it is potentially dangerous to your health and emotional mental well-being. Nor should you allow other people to prey on your feelings of guilt for their own purposes. *LEARN HOW TO SAY NO.*

TENTH KEY:
Laugh, it stimulates your immune system and generates a sense of well-being and contentment. More and more research is being done on the immense benefits of laughter on physical and mental illnesses. Several years ago, Norman Cousins wrote about the positive effects of laughter he experienced in his book "Anatomy of an Illness". Laughter is one of the best medicines available to us. Simple "slap-stick" comedy movies can be a good source of fun and laughter. The bigger the laugh, the better you'll feel.

ELEVENTH KEY:

Attune yourself to your body. Listen to the messages it is giving you. If you are troubled by insomnia, or have pains in the stomach, (or other areas of the body), which has no apparent medical reason for occurring, it may be your body telling you to cut down on the stress in your life. Physical aches and pains may be the only way your body has to let you know it needs more nurturing. Your emotional state also affects you physically. If you are emotionally drained, there can be uncomfortable physical symptoms to indicate this state. Treat yourself gently and lovingly, if you can't be good to yourself, how can you genuinely be good or caring towards someone else?

TWELFTH KEY:

One good idea to reduce stress and create a more harmonious atmosphere in your environment is by adopting a pet. A dog, cat, bird, tropical fish, etc., offer you unconditional acceptance and love, two qualities we search for in other people and rarely receive. Studies have been done recently demonstrating the positive effects of animals on the elderly, on the mentally impaired and on people who were suffering from a variety of illnesses. The simple act of holding a kitten or puppy in their laps, stroking the soft fur or being kissed by a warm eager tongue, lowered the blood pressure, and promoted feelings of contentment and well-being.

THIRTEENTH KEY:

Depression can become worse if you stay indoors all the time. Try taking a walk around your yard or the block and smell the freshness of nature. Drink in the vitality of the trees and flowers. In the winter, rejoice in the crystalline beauty of snowflakes or the sparkling clarity of ice. Find something positive about whatever season you are experiencing. Feel the rhythms of nature and realize you are a part of the never-ending cycle of renewal.

FOURTEENTH KEY:

On the spur of the moment and for no particular reason, get dressed up. Put on your nicest outfit and accessories just because it makes you look good, and when you look good, you also feel good about yourself. Try looking at yourself in the mirror and say: "I'm beautiful. (or I am handsome) There isn't another person like me in the universe. I am a unique being, filled with unlimited potentials." You might end up with a fit of the giggles when doing this, but that is good too. When you see yourself smiling or grinning in the mirror, you will realize just how beautiful your personal energy is. It makes your eyes light up, your face glows with an inner radiance, and you end up standing just a little bit taller, a little more proudly.

FIFTEENTH KEY:

Just for the hell of it, treat yourself to something special. It doesn't have to be expensive or excessive, just something you enjoy or that makes you happy. Give yourself some of the pampering and tender loving care you give to others. A little self-indulgence is not harmful, and when used wisely, indulging yourself can brighten your outlook on life. You're entitled to be happy and joyful.

SIXTEENTH KEY:

Instead of watching or listening to the Television, turn on your stereo or cassette player and listen to music. While working around the house, apartment, outside, or even at work if you can, sing along with the music. It's a great feeling and makes your tasks seem lighter and go quicker. Music, of all kinds, has the unique ability to lift our spirits, stir up sluggish auras, and energize the mind and body.

SEVENTEENTH KEY

Find the time to do some form of volunteer work. Visit the elderly, offer to help a disabled neighbor with yardwork, housekeeping or shopping, or get involved with a charity or a non-profit organization whose ideals you believe in. What's important is that you offer yourself, not your money, but yourself in service to others. The satisfaction you reap from giving of yourself unselfishly to others is immeasurable.

EIGHTEENTH KEY:

Enroll in an adult education class or a college course on some subject that has always fascinated you. Take up a craft, hobby, or some form of creative art. You will surprise yourself at the hidden talents you have. In exercising your own creativity you achieve a sense of fulfillment which uplifts your spirit.

NINETEENTH KEY:

Investigate various self-help groups or clubs. There are many, many organizations whose focus may be just what you are looking for. There are organizations dedicated to investigating and experimenting with metaphysical knowledge, or psychic phenomena, or meditation techniques, etc. There are writing clubs, ceramic clubs, foreign language clubs, and more which may fit your needs, all you have to do is check them out for yourself. Its a great way to meet other people whose needs are similar to your own.

TWENTIETH KEY:

If all else fails and your feelings of depression, loneliness, anxiety and/or general malaise is not lifted, don't be ashamed or afraid to seek out the services of a professional counselor, psychologist or psychiatrist. Perhaps talking to a Spiritual Counselor or Minister would serve your needs and help you find the answers you are seeking. Remember, you are not totally alone or unloved.

NOTE TO READERS

In keeping with the spirit of this chapter on practical exercises, Chapter Ten, titled : "Mandala Designs", is offered to you in a continuation of the experiential nature of Part Two of the book. In chapter 10, I have included a wide variety of unique an unusual Mandala's for you to work with. These Mandala's were created and designed especially for this book by John Tyksinski, who is a master craftsman in abstract art. John's Mandalas are specifically geared to stir an emotional reaction in the subconscious. I hope you enjoy the inner journey they lead you on, for the gift of self-awareness is offered to those who are willing to accept their challenge.

The chapters following the Mandala Designs are focused on the Spiritual Aspects of Tarot and how these aspects relate to "Self-Realization." Chapter 11 is an introduction to the Tarot and contains some historical background of the cards. A variety of Lay-Out Spreads is also included in this introduction for you to experiment with and use as a basis for creating your own unique spreads. The esoteric symbols and colors of each card are explored and defined so that you can see the abundant arcane wisdom captured in the pictures of the Tarot.

The information concerning Tarot can be used in different ways. Some people choose a particular Tarot card as a focus in meditation as in the creation of a "Tarot Board" discussed earlier in this chapter. Other people use the Tarot as a guide to the patterns at work in their life, and a few individuals see the rich symbolism of the Tarot as a pictorial reference for ancient wisdom. You can use the symbols of the Tarot to create Mandalas as well. Whether you use the information on Tarot in Lay-out spreads or study it for other purposes, the spiritual aspects of the Tarot can be applied in practical ways to one's everyday life.

Explore and then use the various "keys" given to you in this book. In simple terms, "self-realization" means knowing you have been blessed with many talents or "gift's", and that it is an important part of your personal growth to develop and use them in the most positive and constructive ways you can. You are such stuff as dreams are made of, so manifest your special beauty here on Earth.

"My creativity slumbers deep within me,
restlessly tossing and turning
waiting impatiently for me to awaken it.
Cautious and unsure, I gently touch its power,
only to watch in stunned amazement
as it uncurls its awesome beauty before me,
for in awakening my own creativity
I have tapped the secret essence of the Universe."

CHAPTER TEN

MANDALA DESIGNS

In my workshops on Keys for Self-Realization, one of the exercises I use to unlock the subconscious creative potentials of my students is coloring different Mandala Designs. The design they choose, the colors they choose, and how they color their designs gives them insights into their own emotional state of being. It is also one of the most relaxing and creative exercises you can do.

The following designs given in this chapter have been designed by John Tyksinski and Emilia Schelling. Another source of "Mandalas" can be found in a series of books by Ruth Heller titled: *Designs For Coloring*, published by Grosset & Dunlap. Many of these designs can be easily adapted into Mandala's. If you are not "challenged" creatively by any of the Mandala Designs I have here, check with your local bookseller for workbooks on Mandalas.

I would like to make a suggestion to you concerning the Mandala's in this chapter. Rather than coloring the different Mandala's in the book, use the designs as "Master Copies" and have the designs copied on a copy machine so that you can have more than one copy of a design. That way you can color a single design in many different ways, depending on your mood and creative impulse. Because they are reduced to fit in this book it might be helpful to find a copier with enlarging capabilities. I also suggest that you use felt tip pens for coloring, colored pencils are also okay, but the felt tipped pens give a more vivid picture.

While experimenting with the Mandalas, considering creating a special and unique Meditation Mandala based on the colors which vibrate to you on an Astrological level. This will activate, on a conscious level, the energies which surround you on a subconscious and universal level. Astrological Mandala's provide a powerful focus for meditation and contemplation, and work in harmony with your own vibrant energy fields.

For example You can have an Aries Sun Sign, a Libra Rising Sign, (Ascendant), and the Moon in Pisces. If you take the colors which vibrate around the 3 signs, (Aries, Libra and Pisces), you will create an Astrological Mandala based on your own birth data. If there are certain planets very strongly placed and aspected in your chart, and you wish to utilize that energy consciously, the colors ruled by that planet can also be incorporated into the Mandala.

The Astrological Mandala is just one of the color mandalas you can create to help you visualize and focus. Another color mandala you could create might be concerned with the Business or Corporate World. Using the Yellow and Gold hues, Brown, a touch of the Green and Blue spectrum, and others which strike your fancy, you could create a Mandala specifically geared to focus your powerful subconscious mind on achieving success in the business world.

The same principle can be applied in the creation of a "healing mandala", using the appropriate colors which represent physical, mental, emotional and spiritual healing. One friend of mine, who is very much involved in the preservation of nature, has created a beautiful "healing mandala" for the planet Earth which she focuses on daily during meditation. Working with color and mandalas trains your conscious mind to be "in-tune" with Universal Forces so you can attract those powerful energies to you.

This next exercise using Mandalas is to be done in conjunction with learning about the hidden spiritual meaning behind each of the 22 Major Arcana Cards. The chapters following this one are focused on the arcane wisdom of the 78 cards referred to as the Tarot. Numerology, Astrology, Color Symbolism, and Esoteric Symbolism are combined together to create a visual pictorial explanation of universal forces and the patterns of human destiny.

Once you read through the chapters on the symbolism of the 22 Major Arcana of the Tarot, you will have enough background information to begin creating a series of "tarot mandalas". What I would like you to do is choose one Mandala Design to represent one of the 22 Major Arcana Cards. Go through the different Mandala Designs and choose the one which seems to represent the "essence" or forces at work on a particular Major Arcana Card. Then, using color symbolism, "color" the Mandala Design to represent that particular Major Arcana design.

When you have completed this exercise, you will have 22 different Mandala Designs colored to represent the 22 Major Arcana Cards of the Tarot. If you don't see a Mandala Design to fit the card you have chosen to work with, try designing your own mandala. The "tarot mandala" series you create will make an excellent focus for meditation and contemplation because you have invested your creative energy into the design to capture the essence of the universal forces the card represents. This particular exercise is designed to "awaken" your intuitive creativity and to help you establish that vital link or "channel" to the Universal Subconscious. This will also give you the opportunity to put into practical use a great deal of the information you have been exploring in this book. Many of the Mandala's in this chapter have symbols incorporated in the design representing hidden esoteric meanings. Some Mandala's may even stimulate unconscious memories of the distant past. This should help to make this exercise a "challenge" to your intuition.

If you are feeling very inspired and creative, try creating your own geometric Mandala design. Perhaps you can combine different shapes from the designs given in this chapter, or you can create a design which is entirely free-style. If you happen to be a computer whiz, you can even program your computer to create different geometric designs to work with. However you choose to work with this suggestions in this chapter, it is important for you to remember that the purpose of working with color and Mandala Designs is to unlock your hidden creativity and to gain insight to the state of your subconscious. It is also meant to be a fun, relaxing way to release tension. As with all things, Mandalas are what *you* make them to be.

MANDALA DESIGN #1

Created by John Thomas Tyksinski

MANDALA DESIGN #2

Created by John Thomas Tyksinski

MANDALA DESIGN #3

Created by John Thomas Tyksinski

MANDALA DESIGN #4

Created by John Thomas Tyksinski

MANDALA DESIGN #5

Created by John Thomas Tyksinski

MANDALA DESIGN #6

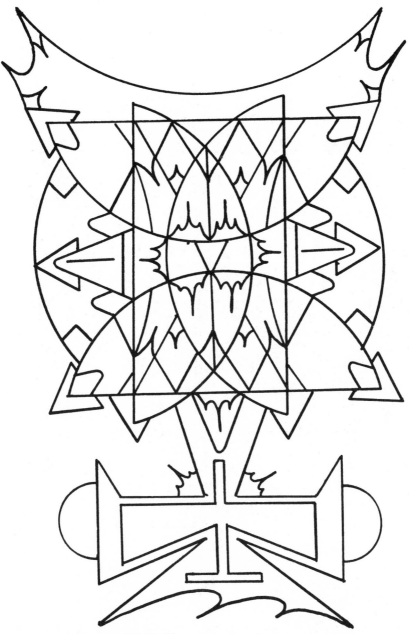

Created by John Thomas Tyksinski

MANDALA DESIGN #7

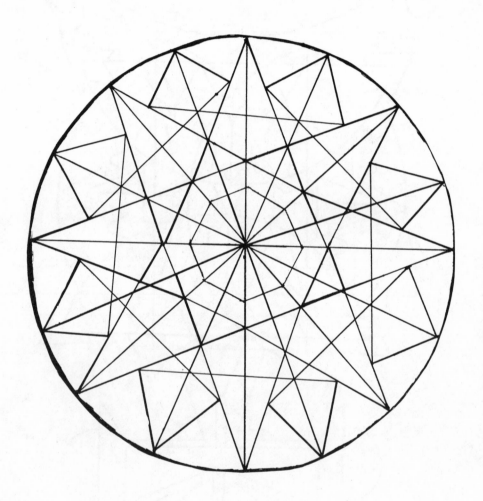

Created by John Thomas Tyksinski

MANDALA DESIGN #8

Created by John Thomas Tyksinski

MANDALA DESIGN #9

Created by John Thomas Tyksinski

MANDALA DESIGN #10

Created by John Thomas Tyksinski

MANDALA DESIGN #11

Created by John Thomas Tyksinski

MANDALA DESIGN #12

Created by John Thomas Tyksinski

MANDALA DESIGN #13

Created by John Thomas Tyksinski

MANDALA DESIGN #14

Created by John Thomas Tyksinski

MANDALA DESIGN #15

Created by John Thomas Tyksinski

MANDALA DESIGN #16

Created by John Thomas Tyksinski

MANDALA DESIGN #17

Created by John Thomas Tyksinski

MANDALA DESIGN #18

Created by John Thomas Tyksinski

MANDALA DESIGN #19

Created by John Thomas Tyksinski

MANDALA DESIGN #20

Created by John Thomas Tyksinski

MANDALA DESIGN #21

Created by John Thomas Tyksinski

MANDALA DESIGN #22

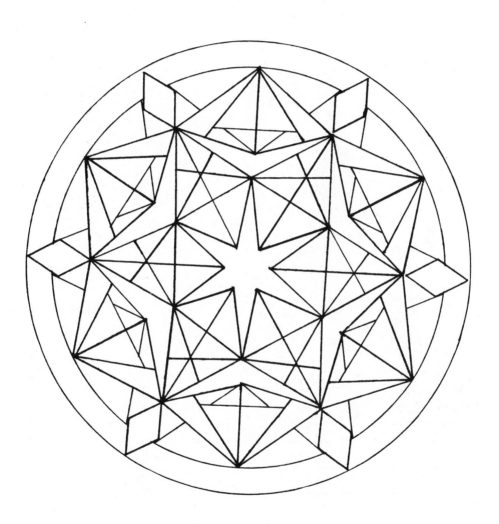

Created by John Thomas Tyksinski

MANDALA DESIGN #23

Created by John Thomas Tyksinski

MANDALA DESIGN #24

Created by John Thomas Tyksinski

Part III:
THE TAROT AND
SELF-REALIZATION

CHAPTER ELEVEN

INTRODUCTION TO THE TAROT

The Tarot is one of the "Keys" used to unlock the Gate of your subconscious, of allowing your Higher Self, which is in direct communion with the Creator, to guide you and to offer you a different way of looking at the situation you are facing. Through this new perception of your situation, it becomes much easier to resolve conflicts, to utilize the positive energies which surround you, and to take charge of your life rather than letting "life" take charge of you.

The Tarot is an excellent Tool for learning how to focus, for learning how to turn inward for your answers. Using the Tarot properly helps you in this learning process with practical applications on how to block out distractions from the outside and to quiet the restlessness within yourself so that you can "hear" the answers you seek. These "answers" are potentials or options you can initiate into your life, or you can choose to ignore them entirely. Color Meditation, as well as other types of Meditation are more "Tools" or "Keys" used for this purpose too. Many students of the Tarot use different cards from a deck to meditate with.

The colors and symbols on the Tarot call to deep racial memories of Egypt, Atlantis and Lemuria, as well as to other civilizations and dimensions which existed even before these legendary ones. Similar versions of the Tarot have been used in India and the Far East for thousands of years. Before the invention of the printing press in the mid 1400's, the Tarot Cards were all hand designed by artists, creating a "one-of-a-kind" deck for those who could afford the luxury and price.

Learning how to set aside your physically oriented consciousness or Ego allows the colors and symbols on the cards to communicate with you on a non-verbal level. Part of the goal of this book is to teach you the basic Spiritual Aspects of Tarot, and then allow you, the Seeker, to develop your own intuition, your own spiritual gifts so that you can contribute to the Upward Spiral of Spiritual Evolution occurring on this Earth Plane.

Personally and professionally, I believe that the greatest value in utilizing the spiritual symbolism of Tarot lies in the Self-Analysis or Self-Counseling which results from the practical application of the arcane wisdom inherent in the Tarot. The Tarot can't solve your problems for you, or give you "magic" solutions to Life's inequities. Studying the spiritual aspects of Tarot will go a long way toward giving you a greater understanding of the potentials available to you, as well as the vibrations which are affecting you, either positively or negatively and how to constructively resolve the inner and outer conflicts you have created, either knowingly or unknowingly in your life.

Each Tarot card reveals a Spiritual Lesson and/or Challenge which is operating in your life at that particular time as well as the potentials which surround you. Each Tarot card also conveys a Gift to you to help you with the Lesson, Challenge or potentials presented to you. Using Spiritual Truths as Guides to the Tarot enable us to meet our Challenges, Lessons, or potentials and turn them in to the positive growth experiences we need in order to grow rather than allowing the vibrations around you become obstacles. This is an important element of the self-realization process.

To show you the connection between the Higher Truths and the symbolism of the Tarot I will share the following with you

THE SUITS

There are 4 suits to the Minor Arcana of the Tarot and 4 Universal Elements associated with each one. These Elements are also associated with Astrology and the Grand Trines the Zodiac makes in regards to the elements. Each element has 3 astrological signs associated with it. As a result, these 4 groups of 3 signs each are associated with each of the 4 suits of the Minor Arcana. There are 4 Archangels associated with the 4 directions and the 4 elements, we also have 4 seasons to our year.

THE SUIT OF WANDS

This suit represents the element of Fire, energy, growth, and the constant renewal of life on all levels of the Earth plane, animal, plant, mineral, and human. Wands are associated with the world of ideas, with creation in all its forms, writing, art, music, painting, the sciences, etc. The Archangel Michael is associated with the element of Fire and therefore with the Suit of Wands in the Tarot.

This Suit also represents the Search for Spiritual Enlightenment, the growth and awareness of the Higher Self and all of its potentials. To the Priests and Priestesses serving and teaching in the ancient temples, the Suit of Wands was the spiritual symbol of the Basic Virtues in life, Faith and Hope. Wands indicate a willing subservience and joyful eagerness to serve the Will of God.

Wands vibrate to the Fire signs of the Zodiac: Aries, Leo and Sagittarius. The Fire Element is the primal force of creative expression. It is the desire for life, the will to be, and the act of Individualizing the self from the rest of Humankind. It is the Element of Fire which serves as the animating force behind an individual's self-awareness.

Wands symbolize Divine Fire, the element which cleanses, purifies and heals. But when used without awareness or wisdom, it becomes an instrument of self-destruction.

THE SUIT OF CUPS

This suit represents the Element of Water, emotions, receptiveness, beauty. Cups are associated with relationships, hopes, wishes, fertility, intuition and happiness. They also deal with our interaction with others. Cups represent the Gateway to Spiritual Awareness and psychic activity, the growth and development of the Intuitional Mind and all of its potentials. The Archangel Gabriel is associated with the element of Water and therefore with the Suit of Cups in the Tarot.

Cups are the spiritual and esoteric symbol of Universal Love or Perfect Love, (Agape). This is the Love which stretches upward to God and outward to embrace all life on the physical and astral Planes. This Love transcends all barriers of race, creeds, nationalities, sex, or religion. This Love requires gentleness, sympathy, kindness, acceptance, non-judgment, and a sincere willingness to serve others. Spiritually, the Suit of Cups symbolize the Virtues of Forgiveness and Acceptance.

Cups vibrate to the Water Signs of the Zodiac: Cancer, Scorpio and Pisces. The Water Element is feeling, sustaining and receptive. It is emotional, intuitive, responsive, sensitive and deep. It is the element which provides understanding and compassion for the feelings of others.

Cups symbolize the Divine Waters of Life, the "cosmic womb" of creation. Uncontrolled, the element of Water can "flood" over the rational mind, allowing the primitive emotional nature to react in violent or destructive ways.

THE SUIT OF SWORDS

This suit represents the Element of Air, the intellect, the development of thoughts and ideas. Swords represent communication, teaching and philosophy. This suit also represents the cutting away, or "releasing" of things and people in your life. Swords can also indicate aggression, strife, sternness, boldness and courage. Sometimes they indicate disaster, the destruction of ego-oriented thoughts, followed by a Rebirth and a New Awareness. The Archangel Raphael is associated with the element of Air and therefore with the Suit of Swords in the Tarot.

The Suit of Swords deals with the mental relationship of the individual to the infinite universe and to God. Swords demand Growth of the Spirit, they demand uncompromising honesty and rigid self-control. Spiritually, Swords symbolize the Virtue of Justice and Karma. They are primarily concerned with the communication of ideas and abstract reasoning.

Swords vibrate to the Air Signs of the Zodiac Gemini, Libra, and Aquarius. Air is the element of the MIND. It is necessary to convey words which one person uses to speak to another. Like Fire, Air is a very important Tool. It is a force which cools us on a hot day, propels our sailboats and windmills, and in the form of steam, heats our homes. But when Air is uncontrolled, it can cause tremendous destruction in the form of cyclones, hurricanes, and tornadoes.

Swords symbolize the Divine Mind, that powerful force which envisioned the complexities of the Universe and Life. Through the Divine Mind, all life on all levels are inexorably linked, for we are the result of "divine thought" or expression.

THE SUIT OF PENTACLES

This suit represents the element of Earth, the material, physical world. Pentacles deal with security, prosperity, centering, securing what exists and building on past foundations. Esoterically, Pentacles represent achievement, scholarship, lofty ideals and ambition. The Pentacle represents the realm of physical experience, the ideas which express the measurable, tangible concerns of the external world. The Archangel Uriel is associated with the element of Earth and therefore with the Suit of Pentacles in the Tarot.

The lessons of Pentacles teaches us how to establish worthwhile Goals. This is a Suit which represents constructive and creative forces at work on the Earth Plane. Spiritually, Pentacles symbolize the Virtue of Charity and Generosity. They are primarily concerned with the desire to create something out of matter and they do this through gathering material possessions, and the actual building of physical aspects.

Pentacles vibrate to the Earth Signs of the Zodiac---Taurus, Virgo, and Capricorn. Earth is the element of FORM and is the element through which the infinitely complex processes of creation and evolution manifest their various physical forms. The nature of life lessons which take place all around us, the goals set by our society, and the tools with which society supplies us with in order to achieve these goals come under the jurisdiction of the Element of Earth.

Pentacles symbolize "Mastery" of the physical material plane. Mastery is achieved through karmic experience on the earth plane and by learning to overcome the temptations to be absorbed or enthralled in materialism.

THE CARDS

There are also 4 Court Cards in each suit of the Minor Arcana, again echoing the connection to the 4 Universal Elements and the ties to Astrology. These 4 Court Cards have a special meaning as do the Aces.

KINGS: represent the Spirit
QUEENS: represent the Soul
KNIGHTS: represent the Ego
PAGES: represent the Physical Body
ACES: represent the Hand of God giving protection and guidance, offering a gift to the individual. They also represent new beginnings, new starts, the birth or creation of something.

The other nine cards in each suit of the Minor Arcana have a special meaning derived from the science of Numerology and adapted for use with the Tarot. Their meanings are as follows:

TWO'S: represent choices, commitments, union, or the balancing of two options. They deal with the confirmation of new directions, new paths.

THREE'S: represent Unity or the Holy Trinity, planing and preparation. They also represent trials and initiations, expression and creation, as well as the 3 states of consciousness. Three's also have to do with seeking a path.

FOUR'S: show the manifestation of plans that have been made into reality. They represent a Foundation upon which to build for the future.

FIVE'S: symbolize the need for freedom, to be released from the past and its restrictions or limitations. Fives also indicate change, which can be difficult but represents a testing or initiation for the individual which will result in growth and knowledge. It is a very challenging number to address.

SIX'S: represent Harmony and Balance. They also deal with communication, satisfaction, contentment, achievement, the calm after the storm. It is a domestic vibration as well, and Six is the number of Venus or Love.

SEVEN'S: represent the mystic, the seeker who searches to expand their base of knowledge, to uncover secrets and learn from them. Seven's indicate a search for new directions through the use of mental disciplines. It is the number of Potentials and Possibilities, qualities which first must be clarified, analyzed and synthesized in the Mind.

EIGHT'S: represent the presence of the Creative Force in the Universe for the sign of infinity is inherent in the figure 8. This number also represents structures and order which can be binding or releasing for an individual, it depends on how they use the energy. Eight's also teach us how to set up our priorities through proper choices.

NINE'S: represent the closing of a cycle, completion, reaching a goal. Nine's also can represent problems and compromises to be faced if the individual has waited until the end of the cycle to deal with them. Nine also symbolizes Universal Wisdom and situations which help an individual to learn so they, in turn, can teach others.

TEN'S: represent a door, a turning point in one's life where certain obligations have been fulfilled, goals have been reached, achievement has been attained and now a new path is to be chosen. It also represents a new beginning, new growth, and new goals are to be established.

To assist me in demonstrating the importance of color and other symbolism on the Tarot Card, I will be using 2 different Tarot Decks as examples for both the Major Arcana and the Minor Arcana. The differences between the two decks I use are subtle at times, but in other areas, especially in color, they can differ considerably. The actual Tarot Card itself is not what is important, it is the way that card opens up your own intuitive flow based on the symbolism it displays.

The Decks that I use are the Rider-Waite Tarot Deck and the Mary Hanson-Roberts Tarot Deck. There are many fine Tarot Decks on the market which are equally as useful to you, but for reasons of simplicity, I had to choose only two decks to work with in this book. I want to encourage you to experiment with different Tarot Decks until you find the one which "speaks" best to you.

One of the best ways I know to "pick" a Tarot Deck is to look at the colors, illustrations, and symbols on the cards themselves. If they appeal to you, then hold the deck in your hand and see if it "feels" warm or gives you a prickling feeling in your hand. Sometimes, all you will "feel" is a sense of rightness, of comfortableness with that deck. I like to look at the pictures on the card itself, and then see if the pictures tell me a story, if it does, then I know that my creative intuitive mind has found a "key" to unlock its Gate. However you decide to choose your deck, it is important for you to realize at the outset that the Tarot Cards are not a game or a source of amusement. If you can't take them seriously or at least with an open mind, then the Tarot will not be a good tool or "key" for you to use. As with all things, you get back what you give out. The Tarot, too, is influenced by the laws of Karma. With this in mind, if you approach the Tarot with seriousness and sincerity, they will not disappoint you in their revelations or in their ability to guide you in Self-Counseling. But you must be willing to make a commitment to Self-Discovery or Enlightenment, or the tarot will be useless to you.

The information given in this chapter serves to build a "foundation" of understanding which you can build on when exploring the intricate facets of knowledge contained within the 78 cards of the Tarot. For some people, a "hands-on" approach to knowledge serves them better than simply reading about the subject. To accommodate that need, I am going to give you different "Lay-Out Spreads" to work with now, before the actual definitions of the Tarot Cards. This way, if you would rather "do" a layout spread before reading further, you will have the necessary information to do so. You can choose a "lay-out spread" and then look up the meanings of the Tarot cards which appear in your spread. Or you can choose to read through the material on the Tarot first and then do a "lay-out spread". Either way is perfectly acceptable.

PREPARATION OF TAROT FOR LAYOUTS

To begin with, you will have to select a deck of Tarot Cards which feels comfortable to you or creates a sense of excitement. Its important that the Tarot Deck you choose has the right "feel" to you, otherwise it may be difficult to work with. There are many, many different and unusual Tarot Decks on the market, each distinctive and different in design, if not in concept as well. If your local bookseller doesn't have a wide enough selection, write to U.S. Games Systems in New York for one of their catalogs. Their address is as follows:

U.S. Games Systems, INC.
179 Ludlow Street
Stamford, CT 06902
Phone Number: (203) 353-8400

Once you have chosen your deck, I recommend that you keep them under your pillow for 3 nights so that the cards can soak up your aura. Each day shuffle the cards thoroughly and return them to underneath the pillow. Once you complete this little ritual, you will be ready to continue with your cards.

Another method to imprint your "aura" or "self" to your new deck of cards is to spread them all out, face down on a table, mix 'em up thoroughly, then place your hands over the pile. Then close your eyes and say, "I seek the Path of Truth and Enlightenment. I seek to understand the potentials and the patterns within my life. Grant me the gift of Knowledge and the Wisdom to use this gift properly."

This method allows you to use the cards immediately after purchasing them if that is your choice. This little prayer is also an excellent one to use all the time when consulting the cards for what ever purpose. The important thing to remember, is that the Tarot Cards are merely a tool to help *you* get in tune with your Source and serves as a focusing device for tapping the Universal Subconscious.

When you are through working with your Tarot Cards, you should store them in a special box wrapped in a silk scarf. The cards should be treated with respect and kindness for they are your "tools" for Self-Realization.

THE LAYOUT

I have several different layout methods for you to experiment with in this section. But, although I provided you with a few different layouts, I do encourage you to develop your own spread, to suit your needs.

Position #1: represents the aura around you, the conditions which are affecting you. The issue at hand.

Position #2: indicates what is there to help or hinder you in obtaining your goal.

Position #3 represents your destiny, the goal you will achieve if you so choose to.

Position #4 shows the immediate past.

Position #5 indicates the distant past which has set up the circumstances you are now facing.

Position #6 represents the immediate future.

Position #7 and #11 represents the individual having the reading.

Position #8 and #12 represents the individual's environment, or what's surrounding them.

Position #9 and #13 indicates the hidden influences at work in your life. Sometimes it can represent hidden fears as well.

Position #10 and #14 shows the final outcome, what the other cards have been leading to.

Position #15 this crowns you, gives you extra protection, a gift from God, so to speak, or it can represent a challenge or initiation this reading is leading to.
There are 6 additional cards you can use on this spread. Layout Diagram #1A shows the proper placement of these additional cards. They are as follows:

Position #16 and #17 these 2 cards are placed crowning card position #14. This addition will help to clarify the final outcome if needed.

Position #18 and #19 crown card position #10. These too, help to clarify the final outcome.

Position #20 and #21 are used to crown the card position #15. These 2 cards will help to clarify your Heavenly Gift or Challenge.

LAYOUT #1

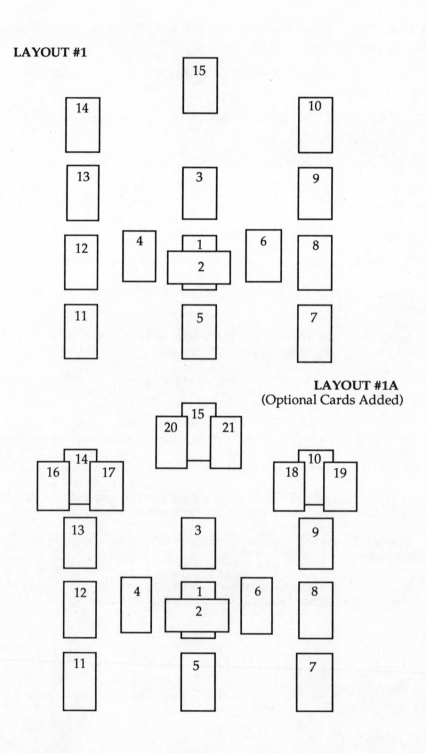

LAYOUT #1A
(Optional Cards Added)

LAYOUT # 2

SIX CARD FOCUS

1. The role you play in the current situation
2. The true nature of the current situation.
3. What led up to this situation.
4. How the situation is affecting you
5. Where this situation is likely to lead.
6. Key Factor.

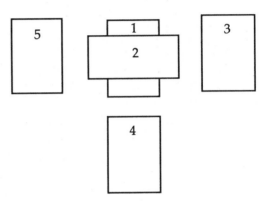

LAYOUT #3

THE THREE SEVEN'S SPREAD

*Key cards serve as focal points for that row.
The other cards revolve around them.*

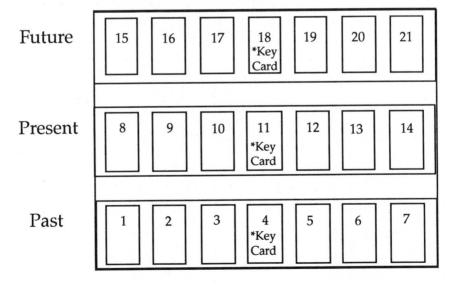

LAYOUT #4

GENERAL LIFE CONDITIONS

1. Your present circumstances.
2. How the people and environment around you affect you.
3. The hidden influences at work.
4. Something you believe in or hope for.
5. What concerns you on a subconscious level.
6. Your emotional state of being.
7. The situation you are in.
8. Immediate outcome or short-term result.
9. The long term outcome.
10. The Key Factor

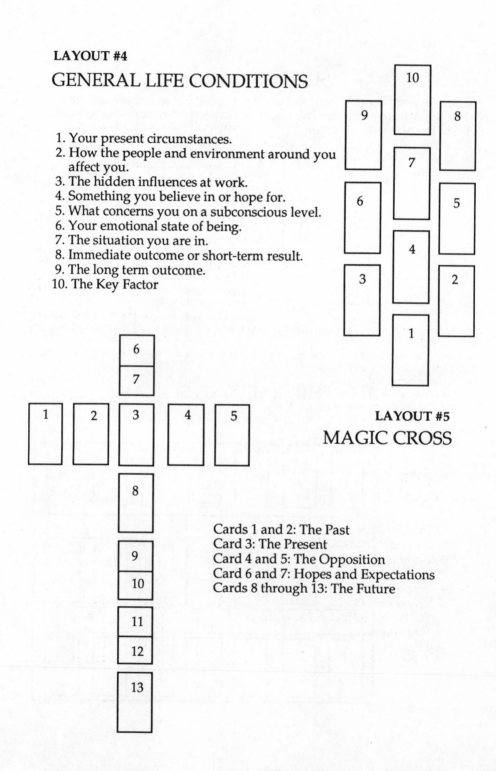

LAYOUT #5

MAGIC CROSS

Cards 1 and 2: The Past
Card 3: The Present
Card 4 and 5: The Opposition
Card 6 and 7: Hopes and Expectations
Cards 8 through 13: The Future

LAYOUT #6
THE HOROSCOPE

1. The Self you are projecting to others.
2. What you value right now. Your financial situation. Your atitude toward money.
3. What is stimulating your curiosity or your mind. What is happening in your community, neighborhood or to siblings.
4. What is making you feel emotionally "at home" or secure.
5. The ways in which you use your creativity and/or artistic abilities. Love affairs, casual sexual encounters, and children.
6. Your daily routines and your health. How you need to make adjustments in yourself and your life. Your job/career.
7. How your partners are affecting your life. What is happening in regard to your primary relationship.
8. What you are repressing. How you are interacting with other people's money. Taxes, loans, psychic or intense sexual encounters.
9. How you want to grow and expand. Educational or traveling opportunities. How traveling looks for you right now.
10. What is happening with your career. Your reputation and responsibilities. How the true work of your life is unfolding.
11. Goals, friends, group involvements. Societal pressures you want to break away from.
12. Your spiritual situation. Your secrets and connections with other lives that are affecting you right now.
13. Key Factor: Blessing or Challenge.

LAYOUT #7
MASTER NUMBER 11

1. The Question or Issue at hand.
2. God's gift to the seeker, could also be a challenge.
3. Present circumstances.
4. Immediate Future.
5. Future events.
6 - 9. Hidden influences at work.
10. Final outcome.
11. Destiny

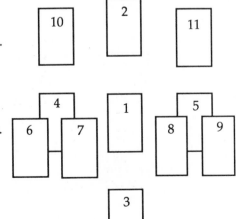

LAYOUT #8

PAST - PRESENT - FUTURE

1. The past, as you remember it.
2. The present, as it stands now.
3. The future, as it will probably unfold.

| 1 | 2 | 3 |

LAYOUT #9

WHAT'S HAPPENING NOW?

| 1 | 2 | 3 |

1. The nature of your situation.
2. Your attitude toward the situation.
3. The main thing for you to keep in mind.

LAYOUT #10
CLARIFYING ISSUES

1. The issue at hand.
2. What this issue represents to you.
3. The true nature of this issue.
4. The forces at work around this issue.
5. The obstacles or challenges that affect this issue.
6. The advantages of continuing on this path.
7. The disadvantages of continuing on this path.
8. The future outcome.
9. The key factor regarding this option.

CHAPTER TWELVE

NUMBER 0: THE FOOL

RIDER-WAITE DECK

In symbolism, the Fool represents Innocence. It represents a pure and unsullied force about to descend into the physical, material plane. The number 0, which designates this first Major Arcana card, represents the God Force, the Alpha and Omega. In numerology, the number 0 indicates infinity, eternity, that which has no beginning and no end.

The Fool symbolizes the essence from which *all things* emerge, and to which all things return. The figure depicted on the card, which could be a young male or female, stands on a ledge, high above a valley. The ledge represents one level of the Spiritual Heights found in the non-physical world; there are still more Higher levels of spiritual attainment to be reached.

The figure is about to take a step from the ledge which represents the Spirit or Soul descending into physical manifestation, full of faith, trust and confidence, but untried by the temptations of the earth plane. The figure carries with them a white rose which symbolizes purity and union with God, and a wand or staff to be used in measuring their earthly accomplishments. In the corner of the card there is a white dog which represents the benign forces of Nature willing to be tamed or willing to work in harmony with humankind.

Under the figure's tunic they are wearing a white shirt next to their body. The color white represents union with God and is a symbol for the Christ Consciousness. The tunic itself, has a busy design of flowers which symbolize growth. The colors are a bright orange, yellow, and green on a black or dark evergreen background. It is hard to tell for sure, what the back ground color is because of the dominant greens and yellows.

There are snow capped mountains in the distance, beyond the ledge, symbolizing just how far away total spiritual perfection is. Yet it is attainable, if one is willing to make the choice or make a commitment to travel the path of enlightenment. On the staff or wand that the figure carries over their right shoulder, is a satchel, purse, saddle-bag, or carry-all, (the name for it doesn't really matter). This bag represents Universal or Cosmic memories and instincts which are billions of years old. The bag also contains the experiences of previous lifetimes which the figure can draw upon in this lifetime.

The dominant color of this card is Yellow. Yellow indicates intelligence, the active mind, and clear thinking. Yellow is also the color of joy and the figure on the card does appear to be in a joyful mood, eager to experience what life on the earth plane has to offer, an eagerness that can lead to foolishness if the individual does not think things through clearly before making choices.

The ledge on which the figure is standing is basically brown, with touches of yellow and orange which represents the blending of the active mind with practicality and strength on the physical material plane. These three colors together also indicate a great deal of energy which needs to be channeled in ways which will benefit others. The white sun rising in the corner symbolizes the power and force of God which can never decline.

MARY HANSON-ROBERTS DECK:

Because I am using this deck as the second example, I plan to focus mainly on the color symbolism. For the most part, the symbolism, other than color, used on the Mary Hanson-Roberts deck is the same as the Rider-Waite deck. There are, however, some cards in the Hanson-Roberts deck which uses different symbols than the Rider-Waite, and when this occurs, I will discuss the difference between the symbols used as well as the color difference.

One of the dominating colors of the Hanson-Roberts Fool is the reddish Orange tunic the figure is wearing. Orange is the color of physical healing. It is the balance between the physical and mental aspects of an individual. Orange shows a combination of intelligence and energy, resulting in good judgment. Orange, as the 2nd Chakra Center, rules the emotions and the appetite. Red, as the 1st Chakra Center, is the base of the Kundalini. It is the color of passion, sexual energy, the urge to create something on the physical plane. It is also the color of new paths or beginnings. Sometimes this urge translates into pro-creation, sometimes it translates into artistic creation. The two colors combined together represent an "appetite" for life, for creativity, a need to experience what the Earth Plane has to offer.

The figure on the card is also wearing a sky-blue scarf around the neck. Sky-blue represents divine assurance and hope. It also indicates the preparation for a new existence or new things in an individual's life. Sky-blue is the color of the 5th Chakra Center which rules the throat, communications, creativity, and emotional healing. This color also symbolizes the healing of possessive tendencies and a passionless love. The figure is also wearing golden-brown pants or trousers, and a golden-brown hat. This color symbolizes the use of or blending of enlightenment with practicality and strength on the Earth Plane. It indicates one who is spiritual, but with their feet planted firmly on the ground. The hat the figure is wearing is also golden-brown with bands of sky-blue, violet, green, and a hint of red. These multi-colored bands combined with the color golden-brown symbolize the quest for Self-Realization on the physical plane and on the spiritual plane.

The cliff the figure is walking on is a lush carpet of green, symbolizing new growth and abundance. The mountains in the background are white with shades of violet. White symbolizes perfection and purity. The violet indicates self-realization, intuition, and spiritual growth. Because the mountains are in the distance, the individual has much experiencing to do on the Earth Plane before they achieve the pinnacle of perfection and attainment.

The figure is also holding a white rose which symbolizes a mental and spiritual union with the Holy Spirit and an unshakable Faith. The figure carries over their shoulder a dove-gray satchel symbolizing the ever changing consciousness of each individual as they ascend the spiral of spiritual evolution.

SUMMARY DEFINITION OF THE FOOL

Taking all of the symbols and color symbolism into account, the following information brings together or synthesizes all of these elements so that you can utilize it more efficiently when doing a Lay-Out Spread.

In Tarot Symbolism, the Fool represents the unexpected. There is an important choice to be made by the individual of the reading. Inherent in the card itself is the promise of fulfillment, completion, the reaching of a goal, attainment of the impossible dream if the individual's faith is strong enough. The Fool also represents ideas and thoughts, but this card also indicates inexperience and a need to temper ones enthusiasm with common sense. The Fool also indicates the rise of Spiritual Power, unknown possibilities of self-expression. In numerology, the number 0 indicates the God-Force in action on the Physical Earth Plane.

What is the Spiritual Lesson or Challenge that Number O---The Fool would teach us? The lesson concerns the development of unconditional Faith, and to realize that nothing we experience is by chance or at random. The Fool also teaches us not to be afraid of setting goals out of fear. It is important that we not be afraid to make choices or to face new experiences for as long as we have Faith, we can move mountains. No matter what path we choose to walk in life, we do not walk it alone.

CHAPTER THIRTEEN

THE MAGICIAN: NUMBER ONE

RIDER-WAITE DECK

In the Tarot, the Magician symbolizes the conscious mind manifesting the forces from the Higher Planes into reality on the Earth Plane. This card also represents concentration, dedication to a goal, and single-mindedness to achieve. By the way the Magician stands indicates that he realizes he is merely a channel or catalyst through which the Cosmic Life-Force flows onto the material, physical plane. The way his arms are positioned symbolize the ancient axiom, "As above, so below", or in other words, that before something can be manifested on the Earth Plane, it first must be manifested on the Higher Planes. The Horizontal figure 8 above his head is the symbol of Infinity, the Alpha and Omega, which has no beginning and no end

for it is eternal. This symbol also represents the Holy Spirit.

The Magician wears a loose, unfastened red robe which signify desires that are controlled by the Conscious Will. This red robe is loose, and can be shrugged off very easily since it is not tied or fastened to him. This subtle symbolism shows he has control over his lower desire nature and that he knows how to channel this Kundalini energy in constructive ways. His white tunic symbolizes union with the God-Force of the Universe. As a belt around his waist, there is a blue serpent biting its own tail which represents perfect wisdom and is also another symbol for eternity or infinity. The Magician is standing in a lush, flowering garden indicating growth, prosperity, fulfillment and unlimited potentials. The Red Roses symbolize passionate desires and selfless sacrifice. The White lilies represent purified desires and the resurrection of the immortal spirit of humankind, they also represent the blessings of the Divine Mother.

Before him, on an altar table, are the 4 elements of the Earth Plane at his disposal to be utilized in manifesting his will. The 4 elements are represented by the symbols of the 4 Minor Arcana suits: the Cup symbolizes the element of Water, the sword symbolizes the element of Air, the Pentacle symbolizes the element of Earth, and the Wand symbolizes the element of Fire. The Magician has been given these tools by the Creator for the betterment of humankind. How he will use them is his choice, part of the lesson he is here on the earth plane to learn. The Element of Water symbolizes the emotions, relationships, hopes and wishes, it is also the symbol of spiritual awareness and psychic activity. This element is also concerned with the growth and development of the Intuitional Mind and all of its possible potentials. The element of Water is also an esoteric symbol of Love or Agape. Spiritually, the element of Water represents the virtues of Forgiveness and Acceptance.

The Element of Air symbolizes the intellect, the development of thoughts and ideas. This element is also concerned with communication, teaching and philosophy, the growth of the spirit. Air is the element of the Mind and represents the communication of ideas and abstract reasoning. Spiritually, the element of Air symbolizes the virtues of Justice and Karma.

The Element of Earth symbolizes the material physical world and deals with security, prosperity, achievement, foundations and ambition. This element is also concerned with the establishment of worthwhile goals, of creating something tangible on the earth plane that will benefit others on a long term basis. Spiritually, the element of Earth symbolizes the virtues of Charity and Generosity.

The Element of Fire symbolizes energy, growth, and the constant renewal of life on all levels of the physical plane. This element is also concerned with artistic creation, the search for spiritual enlightenment and self-realization. Spiritually, the element of Fire symbolizes the virtues of Faith and Hope.

The dominant color in the background is Yellow, symbolizing the active mind, the joy one finds in exercising their intellect in a positive manner. In the Magician's hand is held a "Light Wand", a symbol from the ancient days of Atlantis. Light Wands were used by the elite or ruling class in Atlantis as a channel for the Life Force or Universal Force which permeates all of creation. Some used this powerful energy for healing, others used it for more selfish or materialistic purposes.

MARY HANSON-ROBERTS DECK

The first color that leaps out at you from this card is the soft Pastel Yellow of the background. Pale Yellow symbolizes the active mind which has achieved union with the Christ Consciousness. It is a mystical color tinged with innocence and purity. The Magician's tunic is a pale violet indigo which represents intuition, Higher Consciousness, tenderness, the Christ Mind working through the individual. It is the color of releasing, of letting go and letting God.

Different shades of green, emerald, evergreen, and soft green are also prominent on this card. Green indicates healing, peace, abundance, and material ease. These shades of green also indicate balance between the Mind, Body, and Spirit. The color Evergreen is especially prominent in the background symbolizing creative energy, a power to be utilized constructively. Evergreen is the color of endurance, of strength and generosity. It is also the color of triumph and attainment.

The altar table where the 4 elements are placed is golden brown in color, representing the blend of enlightenment with practicality and strength on the Earth Plane. The Cup and Pentacle are golden in color as is the wrist band, head band, and amulet the Magician is wearing. Gold is a color which symbolizes Soul-Gift or Soul-Grace. It is the color of spiritual blessings and prosperity, a "gift" to individuals who are willing to share their knowledge and abilities with others so they too may enjoy achievement.

The amulet or medallion the Magician wears around his neck is a symbol of the yin and yang, the polarities, positive and negative, male and female energies which are in balance. The "Light Wand" the Magician holds upraised to the heavens symbolizes his willingness to be a channel for the Creative Forces of the Universe and that through the conscious decision to direct his mind and his kundalini energy under the guidance of the Creator, the Magician chooses to serve the needs of humankind unselfishly.

SUMMARY DEFINITION OF THE MAGICIAN

Taking all of the symbols and color symbolism into account, the following information brings together or synthesizes all of these elements so that you can utilize it more efficiently when doing a Lay-Out Spread.

In Tarot Symbolism, the Magician represents a Channel for the Life-Force of the Universe. It indicates new beginnings, decisions to be made, an initiation on the path. The Magician symbolizes creative talents, skill and wisdom obtained from the Higher Realms of Consciousness. There is a great deal of impulsiveness in the Magician which must be channeled properly or it will create limitations or challenges that will have to be addressed at a later date. Concentration and attention to detail are also synonymous with this card. The Magician possesses the gifts of the Spirit and is in the process of learning how to use these gifts in constructive, positive ways.

In numerology, the number 1 indicates originality in thought and action. It represents the ability to take command and make decisions. Number 1 personifies the pioneer spirit in humankind.

What is the Spiritual Lesson or Challenge that Number 1: The Magician would teach us?

The lesson concerns the acceptance of our own creativity, our own ability to serve the Creator in unique and special ways. Don't be afraid of change, of beginning new things, or choosing to make changes in your life. The challenge is to strive for Unity with all life and with the Creator of all life. You have the ability to draw upon the forces from above and bring about a union between worlds of possibility and the visible realms of the physical earth plane.

CHAPTER FOURTEEN

THE HIGH PRIESTESS: NUMBER 2

RIDER-WAITE DECK

The High Priestess represents the Subconscious Mind and the Intuitional Mind. She is seated between two pillars, one Black and the other White, (on most Rider-Waite decks the pillar is gray, but it is supposed to be white.) The curtain, which stretches between the two pillars, is the balance between the Alpha and Omega represented by the White and Black pillars. The two pillars also symbolize the positive and negative energy forces in the Universe which are brought into balance and harmony by the actions of the subconscious Mind. These two pillars are also called Boaz, (the black pillar), representing the feminine Life-Force, and Joachim, (the white pillar), representing the male Life-Force. These two pillars are the keys to the esoteric wisdom of the Bible and to Nature.

The High Priestess wears a crown of moons, two crescent moons and one full moon symbolizing the receptivity of the subconscious mind or intuitional mind and her unity with the ebb and flow of nature and its forces. The crown of moons also represents the power of the Dream State and how we receive guidance, warnings, prophecies, etc., through dreams and their symbols.

The scroll she holds on her lap symbolizes knowledge which the Creator has yet to reveal. In other words, there are hidden forces at work which will be revealed at a later date. The scroll contains memories, both universal and personal, of all sentient life forms on the Earth Plane. In fact, the scroll could be said to represent the Akashic Records kept on the Astral Planes.

She sits on a cubic stone, which is 4 sided, indicating the foundation of knowledge, the building blocks for self-realization and for attainment. The white cross on her breast, or heart chakra, symbolizes the 4 elements, Air, Water, Fire, and Earth, elements, represented by the 4 Minor Arcana Suits, which the Magician also had at his command. The cubic stone also represents discipline, one the basic tenets of knowledge. Without discipline, knowledge contributes to chaos rather than provides the tools to dispels it.

The High Priestess is seated in an open-air temple on the shore of a lake or sea. Water, as symbolized by the Minor Arcana suit of Cups, represents intuition and emotional vibrations. Although she wears a crown of triple moons, her foot rests on another Moon at her feet. This represents her control over the emotional body. Although she is guided by emotions and intuitive energies, she is not ruled by them. She has learned how to utilize her own "psychic" or spiritual nature through meditation and disciplined will.

The High Priestess is the virgin daughter of the Moon. She represents the eternal Female principle. She also symbolizes spiritual enlightenment through meditation, inner illumination and an attunement to the forces of the universe which flow through her. The Fool and the Magician represent the potential to create, the High Priestess has the latent power to manifest this creativity into reality. She is a teacher to those who are undergoing an initiation of the Moon.

The main color that strikes you in this card is the Blue of the High Priestess's clothing, accentuated with white, and the blue background behind the pillars. The water and the sky are both the same Blue with only black lines showing the demarcation between the sky and the water. This shade of blue can be called Sky Blue or Robin's Egg Blue. This particular shade of blue indicates a preparation for a new existence or new things in one's life. It is also the color which symbolizes hope and Divine Assurance. Many of the ancient Priestesses who tended the temples of the Mother Goddess wore sky blue.

MARY HANSON-ROBERTS DECK

With this deck, the card depicting the High Priestess is richer in its color variations although you cannot tell that the temple she is seated in is an open-aired temple or that it resides on the shores of a body of water. Nor can you tell she is seated on a cubic stone. However, the color variations on this card serves the same purpose as actual symbols shown on the Rider-Waite card.

The clothing of this High Priestess is very different from the other High Priestess. The Hanson-Roberts Priestess looks as though she has a firm control over or understanding of the fluctuations which occur in the Universe. The knowledge she represents and the initiations required to achieve it, are not for everyone. Dedication and discipline are the twin pillars of her temple. She too, has one black pillar and one white pillar. But these pillars each carry shades of the other in a marble-like design. The tapestry that hangs between the pillars is a fertile green with ripe pomegranates at the top, and healthy, fruitful, palm trees on the side of the tapestry, depicting the lushness of the imagination and the latent power it has to create. Ideas are like seeds in the mind which needs a fertile plot to grow in. The ideas, which served the High Priestess, have germinated into their potential and born fruit. The ability to manifest ideas into reality takes discipline and knowledge, keys which the High Priestess possesses and knows how to use properly. It is important to remember that the fruit, which sprang from the seeds of ideas, also carries within its womb the seeds of change or transformation. Life is in a constant state of flux or change, and the attunement to the forces which brings about this transformation is the "key" of the High Priestess.

The High Priestess wears on her head a red turban with the symbols of the changing state of the moon. Her dress is red as are the pomegranate fruit on the Tapestry. Red symbolizes new beginnings and the Kundalini. Red is the color of desire and energy, both sexually and non-sexually. It is the color of the Root Chakra, the area of the body where the Kundalini lies coiled at the base of the spine. The Red Turban on the head symbolizes the mind's mastery over the powerful influence of the Kundalini, over one's sexual nature and drive. Red is also the color of a healthy life force and strength.

The power of the color Red is tempered with the presence of the sky blue robe and the gold collar and shoulder badge as well as the pale gold color of the moons on the turban. The Moons on the turban are more of a golden yellow symbolizing the active mind achieving union with the creative mind of the Universe. The collar and badge on the shoulder are more of a Peach Gold representing enlightenment and soul advancement. The badge, peach gold in color, symbolizes attainment.

There is a pale yellow quarter moon in the left corner of the card depicting the High Priestess's attunement to nature and the fluctuations of the Universe. The pale yellow color symbolizes a mystical union with the Christ Consciousness. The active mind is in the process of transmutation, of passing an important initiation on the Path of Spiritual Evolution.

This Priestess too, holds a partially opened white scroll. White symbolizes Universal Truth, purity, and union with the Supreme Being. It also represents the transition of the spirit from one level of being or knowing to a higher level. Having passed many of her initiations, the High Priestess now holds in her hands one of the "keys" to knowledge which others seek her for. But this knowledge is held in trust and is to be given only when the time is right.

SUMMARY DEFINITION OF THE HIGH PRIESTESS

Taking all of the symbols and color symbolism into account, the following information brings together or synthesizes all of these elements so that you can utilize it more efficiently when doing a Lay-Out Spread.

In Tarot Symbolism, the High Priestess represents hidden influences at work. There is a door opening for the individual creating changes that can be unexpected. The High Priestess symbolizes a gestation period, a time of waiting for seeds of change to take root and begin their process of germination. This is usually a slow process, and the changes occurring may go unnoticed at first. During this period, there is also a heightened "awareness" of the unseen world, a sensitivity to emotional and mental energies. Dreams may be more frequent and vivid.

Inspiration and guidance from the higher astral realms will be felt on a subconscious level, resulting in an increase of Self-knowledge if the individual is willing to cooperate and not impose their will on the Universe. Creative and artistic talents are manifested in unique and sometimes mystical ways. The High Priestess serves as a channel through which the pure light of creative ideas enter the realm of the conscious mind; often through dreams or meditation. This is an excellent card for people who are involved in the artistic or creative realms such as musicians, writers, poets, artists, composers, and inventors. Their patience and openness to the unknown will bring unexpected inspiration. Psychic ability is also indicated by this card.

In numerology, the number 2 represents duality, balance, cooperation, and unity.

What is the Spiritual Lesson or Challenge that Number 2---The High Priestess would teach us?

The lesson concerns patience with the mysteries that permeate our lives and the importance of a disciplined Will. Learning how to quiet the logical mind and how to open up the channel to our Intuitional Mind takes patience and discipline. Trusting in the Creator's Time Table rather than our own is not an easy initiation to pass. Our own impatience with waiting, with our inability to see clearly into the nebulous future at times, can be frustrating.

Using this time of waiting or gestation in a creative or artistic way, will result in a more fruitful harvest later. It takes time for our plans or the seeds of our ideas to sprout and it is hard to surrender our earthly time table to the Time Table of the Universe.

CHAPTER FIFTEEN

THE EMPRESS: NUMBER 3

RIDER-WAITE DECK

In symbolism, the Empress represents the Feminine aspect of God. In ancient times the feminine aspect of the Creator was worshipped as the Mother Goddess. In more recent times, the feminine aspect of God has been de-emphasized to the point that most people do not know that "God" or the "Creator" is a perfect blending of both the Male and Female Energies. In the Tarot, both aspects of the Creator are represented. The Empress represents the Female Energy of the Creator, and the Emperor represents the Male Energy of the Creator.

The figure of the Empress on the Rider-Waite neck is pregnant with life, with imagination and with ideas. Even the landscape around her is fertile and abundant. Her white dress is decorated with ripe pomegranates which symbolize feminine fertility. She is the symbol of the Great Mother who manifests love, growth, new beginnings, and beauty of the material physical Earth Plane. Like the High Priestess, the Empress represents the subconscious mind and highly developed intuition.

The lushness of the trees in the background and the ripened wheat in the foreground all represent the fertility of the subconscious mind and of Universal Memory. The stream in the background, weaving through the trees, indicates the presence of the active Life-Force which permeates the Universe. Having the stream cascade down a waterfall to collect into a pool shows the Unity between Mind, Body, and Spirit; Unity of the six senses of humankind.

The dominant color on this card is yellow, representing the active mind, the joy to be found in creativity. The Empress's hair is a golden yellow, the color of spiritual blessings and riches, both material and spiritual. It is the color of fulfillment. She wears a crown of green leaves studded with 12 stars symbolizing that the Empress is a channel for healing love and her unity with the 12 Zodiac Arch-types. The stars also represent time itself, which means that it takes time to bring our desires or wishes into manifestation on the Earth Plane, but our desires or wishes are already manifested on the astral planes.

The scepter she holds symbolizes her control over creation on the Earth Plane, a control that receives its power only through Love, symbolized by the Venus glyph on the heart shaped stone at her side. The Empress has been impregnated with Love by the seeds of the Subconscious Mind, ready to bear the fruits on the material, physical plane. In symbolic terms, the High Priestess has been transformed into the Empress, for she has successfully mastered all of her initiations and found total union with the Life-Force of the Universe.

The Empress is seated on a gray throne decorated with orange cushions. Her feet are on the gray base of the throne. The color orange symbolizes the balance of the physical and mental aspects of human nature. Orange is the combination of intelligence, energy, and good judgment. It is a color which rules the emotions through the intellect rather than through instinct or base desire.

The dove-gray of her throne and platform, as well as the heart-shaped stone bearing the Venus glyph represents harmony within the midst of change or subtle changes which do not upset the balance of harmony already achieved. The changes represented by dove-gray are progressive ones, symbolizing the evolution of the spirit. This color also represents the peaceful acceptance of growth on a personal level, that the changes which are occurring represent "opportunities" for enrichment and fulfillment. One of the main things it is important to understand about the Empress is that she represents growth, and growth necessitates change.

Her white dress has designs outlined in violet pink, a color which symbolizes self-realization. Violet pink also represents artistic expression, creativity and attainment. This color symbolizes intuitive understanding of the way the Universe is structured and the laws which govern it. It is a highly spiritual color symbolizing unlimited potentials for attainment, for wish fulfillment, and for achieving the impossible dream.

When used in ancient Egypt, the tarot cards representing the High Priestess and the Empress symbolized the goddess Isis. The High Priestess was Isis veiled, virginal and waiting for completion, whereas the Empress was Isis unveiled, pregnant with life and possibilities for she had achieved fulfillment and union with the Life-Force of the Universe.

MARY HANSON-ROBERTS DECK

In this deck, the Empress is wearing a white dress with an orange tunic or robe over it. The color white symbolizes union with the Supreme Being, purity and perfection. The orange represents the balance of physical and spiritual elements, and healing of the physical body. She has a cloak, or outer-robe of Turquoise Blue which matches the back of her throne and represents protection and good fortune. It is a color which symbolizes the power of the Creator manifesting on the physical Earth Plane and represents Spiritual Blessings. Turquoise acts as a catalyst to re-awaken memories of past-lives and karmic ties, and of abilities an individual once possessed in another life.

The Empress's hair is golden brown and crowned with green laurel leaves and golden stars. These colors represent the use of or the blending of enlightenment with practicality and strength on the Earth Plane. They symbolize one who is spiritual, but who has their feet firmly planted on the ground and knows how to use spiritual blessings in constructive practical ways on the Earth Plane. Laurel Leaves have many meanings. To the ancient Greeks, they were sacred to the sun god Apollo. To the ancient Romans, they were used to crown the heads of the victorious. Laurel leaves are a symbol of success, of fame, and of faithfulness.

The back of the throne the Empress is seated on is Peach-gold in color representing enlightenment, soul advancement and restoration. It is the color of attainment. It is a color which indicates healing energies obtained from the Life-Force of the Universe. The 12 Stars, representing the 12 Zodiac signs, symbolize the union the Empress has with all humankind and that she has perfected and mastered the lessons or challenges of each of the 12 signs. The Empress knows, intimately, what challenges we face and is there to offer the nurturing and blessings we need to face life and triumph.

The Empress is surrounded by ripe wheat and ripe fruit symbolizing her fertility, both from a physical standpoint and a creative or artistic standpoint. On her left shoulder, she is wearing a rose colored heart-shaped broach with the symbol of Venus on it. Rose is the color of mystical Love, of empathy and sympathy. It is also the color of blessings from the Creator. The Empress has a genuine love and concern for all life. This is Pure Love or Agape, without taint of self or ego.

The color of the sky in the background represents the Dawn of a new age, a new beginning, the initiation has been passed, the darkness has been weathered. The image of dawn has many varied meanings, but the most significant one is that Dawn symbolizes hope, rejuvenation, and restoration. The Empress is also holding a brown scepter inlaid with turquoise and rose colors. The color of the scepter shows her control of the physical-material plane and the wise use of this power.

SUMMARY DEFINITION OF THE EMPRESS

Taking all of the symbols and color symbolism into account, the following information brings together or synthesizes all of these elements so that you can utilize it more efficiently when doing a Lay-Out Spread or when using this card to Meditate with.

In Tarot symbolism, the Empress represents love, beauty, happiness, pleasure, and success. It also indicates fruitfulness, good fortune, Attainment, and growth. In a Lay-Out Spread, the Empress can symbolize marriage or union, fertility for would-be parents, farmers, and for those involved in the many creative art fields. Material wealth accompanied with spiritual wealth is also indicated by this card.

The presence of the Empress assures you of progress and activity in your affairs. Important messages and writing, news to be heard and instructions to be received. Publication and/or recognition of one's talents is also indicated by the Empress. But one of the most important factors concerning the presence of the Empress in a Lay-Out spread is that this card warns you to beware of your wishes, for you will surely get them.

The Empress promises abundance and love, gifts which we all are entitled to. When real success or attainment comes our way, it is never at the expense of someone else's happiness or well-being. To wish it otherwise will only create negativity in your own life that will eventually have to be corrected. This is the meaning of the warning "beware your wishes".

In numerology, the number 3 represents creative expression and enjoyment of life.

What is the Spiritual Lesson or Challenge that number 3: The Empress would teach us?

The lesson concerns the unlimited power of Love, and how it manifests miracles in your life. Our hopes, wishes and desires, when they come true, seem like miracles, but the real miracle is the Love which manifests the abundance in our lives in ways we can only begin to dream about. Sometimes what we wish for is not in our best interests, but the Love which surrounds guarantees that what is best for us will come to pass, even though we may sub-consciously or consciously work against it. Part of our Spiritual Challenge is to be aware of the needs of others and nurture them as our needs are nurtured by the Empress. Sharing, through love, is one of the greatest miracles we can give to each other.

CHAPTER SIXTEEN

THE EMPEROR: NUMBER 4

RIDER-WAITE DECK

In the Tarot, the Emperor symbolizes the Male aspects of God on the physical Earth Plane. The Emperor represents the will of the Creator made manifest on the material plane.

In many different symbolic ways, the Emperor is the Magician who has grown older, wiser, and learned the lessons of the physical Earth Plane. He has learned to control conscious existence through the reasoning ability of his Holy Spirit, which is the function of the conscious mind. The Conscious Mind is the vehicle or Channel through which the Holy Spirit communicates the Will of the Creator.

The Emperor rules the Earth Plane because of his ability to discern the Truth in any situation and his ability to see through Illusions.

The Empress and the Emperor, who are halves of the same whole or Twin Souls, are the keys which show that what you sow with your conscious mind, (represented by the Magician), you expand through the High Priestess and the Empress, and finally reap in the manifestations of the Emperor. It is symbolic of what you can and do make of yourself through your own choices, your own will. No situation, circumstance, challenge, or obstacle appears in your life without your expressed permission on some level. Sometimes this permission is given long before you even enter your physical body in this lifetime. But it is you, as an individual, who is in control of your destiny, your path in life, no one else. Therefore you cannot blame others for what befalls you. Blame is a weapon of attack, and you do not attack unless you feel threatened or feel like a victim. Attack is a product of Fear, and Fear is both the servant and master of the Ego.

In his right hand, the Emperor holds the Egyptian Ankh, which represents the power and manifestation of the Creator, before whom the Illusion of Darkness gives way. The Ankh symbolizes the Truth and Way, Divine Will and the Light of the Father. In his left hand, the Emperor holds a yellow globe representing the power of Pure Love, which is the only way to balance the physical and spiritual planes. He is wearing blue-white armor under his robes symbolizing his function as a Spiritual Warrior for the Forces of Light.

The Emperor is seated on a gray stone throne with carved ram's heads. His facial features are serious and somewhat stern. The head of a Ram or the entire body of a Ram symbolizes a leader who has won that position through strength and determination. Rams are also symbols of the zodiacal sign Aries and the beginning of Spring. Spring represents new growth and new life, the urge to unfold the inner being from the cocoon of winter when it lay dormant. The gray throne symbolizes stability in the midst of change. Each time the seasons renew themselves they bring with them change. A true Spiritual Warrior welcomes this chance for renewal and rebirth.

The sheer face of the rugged mountains behind the Emperor are indicative of the untamed power of Nature and the need humankind has to respect it. He has a white beard and white hair which represents perfection and unity with the Christ Consciousness. The brown robe draped loosely around his shoulders and front represents the mantel of power and manifestation. Brown is the color of practicality and strength on the Earth Plane.

The Emperor also represents the number 4. Four indicates foundations, stability, the building blocks for the structure and form of the Universe. The number 4 also indicates the four elements, Air, Earth, Fire and Water. To the priests and priestesses in the ancient temples, the Emperor taught them that the physical body was not the enemy of the Holy Spirit, but was Its Channel. Therefore, the Holy Spirit was not the enemy of the physical body, but was the driving Force that gave its manifestation meaning and purpose.

The Emperor wears a yellow crown on his head. The front of the crown is divided into five panels. These five panels represent the five physical senses. The background is a brilliant fiery orange symbolizing the combination of intelligence, energy, and good judgment. It represents the balance of the physical and mental aspects of human nature, and physical healing. This shade of fiery orange is symbolic of the raw elemental power that has been harnessed to the Will of the Creator.

MARY HANSON-ROBERTS DECK

With this card the colors which strike you first are the red robe of the Emperor and the gold accents of the throne and of his clothes. The color Gold symbolizes enlightenment, the power of physical and material manifestation through the Will of the Creator. The Ram's heads on the back and front of the throne are Gold as is the symbol of the Ankh the Emperor is holding in his right hand. His suit of armor is accented with the color gold as is his robe.

In his left hand, the Emperor is holding an opalescent globe representing the world, the world of possibilities. This is one of the rare times you will see the color I call "Opal" on the Tarot Cards. This is a color of gestation, where "seeds" are forming, taking shape, altering their molecular structure, getting ready to be transformed into something wondrous to behold. The "seeds" can be ideas, artistic or creative forms, or the "seeds of change", but a change that is transforming and elevating. I call this particular shade of "Opal", the "Sea-Shade" because of the blues, greens, and hints of purple and violet. The Sea represents the "Womb of Life" on our planet and is rich with the potentials for life and beginnings.

The suit of armor the Emperor is wearing under his red robe is of a medium blue trimmed in gold. The color medium blue represents serenity, spiritual blessings and peace which is gained by bringing the mental, emotional, physical and spiritual bodies into balance with the Will of the Creator. The Emperor is in harmony with the rhythmic flow of life. His red robe has a large purple and gold design on the left side of his body. The left side of our body is ruled by the right side of the brain. The right side of the brain is where our intuition, creativity, and sensitivity is located in scientific terms. The left side of our bodies is where our heart is located, that part of us which represents the giving and loving side of our nature. This represents mastery over the "Root Chakra" energies or the "Kundalini" force in the physical body.

The Emperor wears a crown of green laurel leaves wrapped around his head and encompassing his "Brow Chakra Center". This symbolizes the balance between the Mind, Body and Spirit, a balance which gives the Emperor the strength and wisdom needed as a Spiritual Warrior and Leader. The mountains behind him symbolize spiritual heights and achievements. The fact that the mountains are behind him show that he has attained the spiritual heights he desired for this lifetime. He has achieved what he came to this Earth Plane to do.

SUMMARY DEFINITION OF THE EMPEROR

Taking all of the symbols and color symbolism into account, the following information brings together or synthesizes all of these element so that you can utilize it more efficiently when doing a Lay-Out Spread or when using this card in Meditation.

In Tarot Symbolism, the Emperor represents the presence of the Creator in our lives. It means protection, victory, authorship, achievement, and the Love the Creator has for His Children, as well as His Compassion for us. There are powerful forces available for the individual to use under the direction and guidance of the Creator or the Holy Spirit. This raw elemental power must be harnessed for the benefit of humankind and not for selfish ambition for if the individual attempts to use the power in a negative manner, it can turn on them and destroy what they have labored to build. If one's energies are spiritually centered, new psychic and spiritual realms can be reached.

In Numerology, the number 4 means stability, practical creativity, and responsibility. It also indicates a foundation, a broad base from which to build.

What is the Spiritual Lesson or Challenge that Number 4: The Emperor would teach us?

The Lesson involves the recognition that we are not alone on our journey through the Physical Earth Plane. Our Will, when united with the Will of the Creator can accomplish and achieve goals that appear to be impossible. Our Challenge is to accept the fact each one of us has been gifted With originality and the energy and resources to manifest that gift on the material plane. Courage, leadership and stability are qualities symbolized by the Emperor and therefore are qualities we too possess, if we choose to accept them.

I think that one of the most important lessons you can learn about this Tarot Card is that the Creator desires us to be happy and content, and is more than willing to help us achieve this state as long as the happiness and contentment we seek does not deprive someone else of their happiness. The Creator does not take from one to give to another. That would limit the power of His gifts, and His gifts have no limits, they are endless and abundant for all who seek them.

CHAPTER SEVENTEEN

THE HIEROPHANT: NUMBER 5

RIDER-WAITE DECK:

In the Tarot, the Hierophant symbolizes our Inner Teacher, our intuition or Higher Self, that part of us which is in perfect attunement with the Holy Spirit. The Hierophant is seated between two gray pillars. One pillar represents the Laws of the Universe or Karma and the other pillar represents our right to choose whether or not to accept these laws. We do have the choice to accept the laws of the universe or we can fight against them, entangling ourselves deeper in a illusion-filled quagmire. Eventually however, in order to free ourselves from the self-made prison we created, we will have to recognize the "Logos" or Truth. The choice really lies in *when* we will accept the Light, not *if* we will accept it.

The gray color of these pillars means testing and initiation, followed by analysis of the changing circumstances in our lives. In the Rider-Waite Deck especially, you will find the color gray is used a great deal. Since gray represents change, it does reflect the circumstances of our lives. Whether you realize it or not, your life is in a constant state of change or "flux", simply because you are faced with choices everyday of your life. Its the awareness of these changes that you need to develop, because without awareness you will not be able to understand or realize what patterns you have formed in this life and in previous lifetimes.

At the feet of the Hierophant are two crossed keys which symbolize the "Keys" to self-realization. There are two kneeling priests or postulants at the throne of the Hierophant, one has red roses on his robe representing matter, and one with white lilies representing spirit. These three figures form a trinity and shows that the Hierophant is the bridge or channel through which the world of matter and the world of spirit is united or bridged, blessing both in the process.

The Hierophant wears a triple yellow crown. The first crown represents the 5 senses of humankind. The second crown represents the 7 Chakra Centers of the body, and the final crown symbolizes the 3 states of consciousness: The Super-Conscious, (also referred to as the Christ Consciousness), the Conscious, and the Sub-Conscious. The color Yellow symbolizes enlightenment and integrity. It is the color of the active mind and indicates intelligence at work. The staff the Hierophant holds is also yellow and symbolizes the Tree of Life, an ancient Kabbalistic sign, it is also a symbol that has been seen in Peru and Mexico, and many believe this staff has direct ties to Atlantis and Lemuria.

The Hierophant is wearing a loose-fitting red robe over a white and blue underdress, similar to the Magician. On the outside of the red robe is a white vestment with the sign of the cross embroidered on it three times. The color white symbolizes purity, perfection, and union with God. The crosses represent surrender to the Will of God and the sacrifice of the Ego. The figure is also wearing white shoes, each with a cross on it. The color blue, seen around the Hierophant's neck and on the hem of the underdress represents serenity and balance. The blue around the neck also represents the 5th Chakra Center, which deals with communication, self-expression and creativity. Blue is the color which symbolizes the 5th Chakra. The red color of the robe, with the white vestments symbolize control of the Kundalini by the Christ Mind or Super-Consciousness.

The Hierophant on the Rider-Waite Tarot appears androgynous. The figure is neither male nor female, yet both. This is deliberate, for it represents the uniting or marriage of the two polarities, or two energies forces in a harmonic balance.

MARY HANSON-ROBERTS DECK

The dominating color of the Hierophant with this particular Tarot Deck is golden brown and brown. Blue-gray is used prominently as well. The color golden brown represents the blending of enlightenment with practicality on the Earth Plane. It symbolizes one who offers themselves in selfless service to others. The twin blue-gray pillars are laced with a color I call "amber". The color Amber absorbs negative energy and transforms it. It has the ability to stabilize energy fields. Amber is considered to be a color of good-luck and prosperity. It is also the color of the "Life-Force" or "prana" energy.

The color Blue-gray represents the ability to analyze a situation even while experiencing great changes. It is the ability to detach yourself from an experience and to use your logical analytical mind to assimilate the new information being received because of the changes occurring. The Twin Pillars are blue-gray as is the robes worn by the two postulants at the feet of the Hierophant. The triple crown worn by the Hierophant is a golden yellow in color symbolizing Soul Grace or Soul Gift. The active mind has achieved union with the Creative Mind of the Universe and "True Wisdom" is now possible. Golden yellow is the color of spiritual blessings.

The two keys which the postulants desire for their use, are also a golden yellow in color. These two keys represent blessings which are granted to those individuals who know how to use and share their prosperity in positive constructive ways to help others attain achievement. They are the keys to vast spiritual treasures, the keys to hidden wisdom and knowledge, keys to unlock the secrets concealed by the twin pillars behind the Hierophant.

The brown color of the staff the Hierophant holds in his left hand and the brown color of his balcony railing symbolize the physical earth plane and the material world. The lesson taught by the color brown is one of practicality. If spiritual wisdom cannot be applied to one's everyday life, to the mundane or the materialistic world, then the spiritual wisdom has little or no value. Spirituality must be incorporated into one's physical world. There cannot be one set of rules governing one's spirituality and another set of rules when you deal with people or situations on a day to day basis. There must be a marriage or union between spirituality and practicality.

SUMMARY DEFINITION OF THE HIEROPHANT

Taking all of the symbols and color symbolism into account, the following information brings together or synthesizes all of these elements so that you can utilize it more efficiently when doing a Lay-Out Spread or when Meditating on this card.

In Tarot Symbolism, the Hierophant represents a turning point in your life, a change about to take place. It indicates Divine Wisdom, inspiration, endurance, and persistence. The Hierophant also represents a teaching experience, communication, possible marriage or union sanctified by Divine Law, and sexual encounters that become binding. The Hierophant serves as a bridge or a channel that links the realms of matter and spirit, blessing them both in the process.

This card can also indicate the presence of your Inner Teacher, intuition or inner hearing. It represents help from superiors, or from a philosophy which can change your life dramatically. The Hierophant represents patience, teaching and goodness of the heart as well. In numerology, the number 5 means change which brings about freedom and liberation from limitations imposed on us by Illusions.

What is the Spiritual Lesson or Challenge that Number 5: The Hierophant would teach us?

One of the most important lessons revealed by this card is that wisdom and truth are the keys to freedom. Another important lesson concerning this card is that we are all teachers, and what we teach others we are learning for ourselves. The Hierophant symbolizes union, this union is with our own three states of consciousness. There are other unions or alliances we form in life as well, and these unions offer us opportunities for change and growth while providing us with unique learning experiences.

CHAPTER EIGHTEEN

THE LOVERS: NUMBER 6

RIDER-WAITE DECK

In Tarot, the Lovers symbolize the union of opposite but complementary energies; male and female; positive and negative; yin and yang. The symbolism is shown by the two naked figures on the card, often referred to as Adam and Eve. These two human figures represent the two energy manifestations of the Creator, (male and female). These two opposite forces must become equal to each other in order to obtain the goal of Unity. It is part of the physical laws of the universe that within the heart of a female is a male energy force, it is also true that within the heart of a male is a female energy force. Not only must a male or female find equality and unity with their opposite but also find unity within themselves. Females must learn how to express their male energies in a positive balanced manner as Males must learn how to express their female energies in a positive balanced manner. This is very hard to do because our culture, our societies are not based on Unity but rather on the Supremacy of a small portion of humankind over a larger portion. Sexual and racial prejudice are the weapons of the Ego to prevent Unity.

With the yellow rising sun behind him, the Archangel Raphael offers blessings on the Union of the man and woman. The archangel knows that only through this union will the two humans find completion, for they are two half's of the same whole. The archangel wears a purple-indigo robe which symbolizes High Consciousness or the "Christ Mind". It is the color of the 6th Chakra Center referred to as the "Brow Chakra". Purple-Indigo is a raw electric color, indicating karmic voltage, (the sowing of karma), tenderness and selfless love. It is the color of the spiritual life, the color of releasing, of letting Go and letting God.

The Archangel's wings are purple and highlighted with Violet Pink. Violet Pink is the color of self-realization. It represents artistic expression, creativity, and attainment. Violet Pink also symbolizes intuitive understanding of the way the Universe is structured and the laws which govern it. The colors of the Archangel's head are a mixture of green and orange. Green representing love and growth; orange representing physical healing and emotional balance. The Yellow color of the rising sun symbolizes the active mind and joy.

The background color is sky-blue which represents hope and Divine Assurance. The presence of the color sky-blue indicates the preparation for a new existence or new things in one's life. It also represents the healing of possessive tendencies and a passionless love. Sky Blue is the color of the 5th Chakra Center, referred to as the "Throat Chakra". This Chakra rules communication, creativity, and mental healing. The mountain in the background is purple with touches of violet-pink. The mountain represents the goal of self-realization.

The man and woman in the picture are standing on a carpet of green grass. The color green represents love, growth, and abundance. Green is a color which channels the force of healing love. It is also the color of the 4th Chakra Center referred to as the "Heart Chakra". This Chakra brings balance between the Mind, Body, and Spirit. The Tree of Knowledge behind the figure of the woman is also green in color as is the serpent coiled around it.

The tree behind the male figure, or "Adam", represents the 12 Astrological signs of the Zodiac, and their link to human affairs. The tree behind the female figure, or "Eve", represents the Tree of Knowledge. Coiled around the trunk of the tree is a serpent, representing wisdom and the Kundalini Force. Humankind has the potential to create if they use the Kundalini Force properly. When the Kundalini Force is trapped at the base of the spine, (the Root Chakra), only the physical senses or appetites are given stimulation, resulting in an excessive sexual drive, aggression, and rage. It is our Spiritual Challenge to raise the Kundalini Force up the spine, and activating the Higher Chakra Centers as it passes through them, opening them up.

Through Eros-love or human sexuality, we have the ability to direct the Kundalini Force onto a higher plane, transforming it to Agape-love or Pure Love. By using the sexual act of intercourse as a way to worship one another's bodies and to ultimately worship the Universal Life Force that flows through you both, you achieve unity with all life. The act of sexual intercourse is sacred for this exchange of physical essences also results in the exchange of karma as well. Students of the occult and metaphysics have known for centuries of the importance of purity. Casual sex can become a trap for the unwary. The more people you have intercourse with, the more karma is exchanged, and the more of your essence is given away to someone whose exchange with you may not be beneficial. Its hard enough to deal with your own emotional garbage without taking on the emotional garbage of others.

Naturally then, The Lovers represent a choice to the Seeker. You can live only for the satisfaction of your physical senses or sexual appetite, or you can raise your consciousness to a higher level and reach Union with the Creator and with all life, a goal we are all seeking to achieve on some level or another. This is one of the most difficult tests or initiations an individual will face on their Spiritual Path. Some individuals will try to completely deny their sexuality which is not good for them either. Balance is the key, learning the difference between Eros-love and Agape-love is the Challenge.

MARY HANSON-ROBERTS DECK

One of dominant colors on this card is the golden yellow hair of the female and the golden yellow cloud from which the Archangel emerges. Golden yellow symbolizes the potential for Soul Advancement through the proper use of the Kundalini Force. This is the color of spiritual blessings and is given to those who know how to use and share their gifts with others. Golden yellow is the color of Soul-Grace. Her hair is studded with delicate white flowers symbolizing her purity and unity with the forces of nature.

The male is dressed in a white under-tunic with a loosely fitted red robe over the white tunic. Again, the white of his tunic symbolizes his purity and union with the Creator. The Terra-Cotta red robe with touches of orange represents desires and physical passion which can be purified by the conscious will of the male. This particular shade of red also represents past-life Karma which is affecting the individual in the present. This is the color of directed jealousy or envy. By his karmic actions of the past, the male figure has the choice to continue on the behavior pattern he has established in the past or choosing to unite with his Higher Consciousness and eliminate that negativity. This is done through the conscious raising of the Kundalini. Around his waist, the male is wearing a golden belt symbolizing his potential for soul advancement.

Surrounding them both is a lush, green, fruitful garden. There are 12 orange fruits in the tree behind the male which represents the twelve signs of the zodiac. The green color of the garden represents love, peace, and abundance. The Archangel above them is dressed in white with touches of violet and has a sash that is a dusky rose color. The color violet-white represents spiritual growth, wisdom, and universal truth. The dusky rose color symbolizes empathy, mystical love, and sympathy. It is also the color that represents Soul Mates or Twin Souls who have a bond that is far deeper than any physical bond could possibly be.

The color of the woman's dress is a golden brown which indicates the blending of enlightenment with practicality on the Earth Plane. This color also represents security and steadfastness. Some of the ribbons in her hair on her dress are an almandine garnet color which represents loyalty, determination, and permanence. There are also orange ribbons in her hair and on her dress which represents a balance between the physical and the mental bodies. Her eyes are sky-blue in color and his are a shade between topaz and amber. The expressions on their faces depict the great love they have found together, but also the conflicts that still face them and need to be solved.

SUMMARY DEFINITION OF THE LOVERS

Taking all of the symbols and color symbolism into account, the following information brings together or synthesizes all of these elements so that you can utilize it more efficiently when doing a Lay-Out Spread or when using this particular card in Meditation.

In Tarot Symbolism, the Lovers represent Union, both on a physical and a spiritual level. The Lovers symbolize a Choice that is now presented to the Seeker. Openness to inspiration, intuition, attraction, beauty, partnership and love are other elements which define this card. Creative potential is indicated by this card as well. The presence of this card in a lay-out spread indicates a time of testing and even trial, concerning physical attraction and union with another person. The Lovers represent thoughts of physical love and a possible change in one's love life leading to true fulfillment.

On a different level, The Lovers represent the union between the male and female energies within ourselves that must be accomplished in order for us to feel whole and complete. Learning how to express all the aspects of our creativity, physically, mentally, emotionally, and spiritually, is part of the evolutionary process we are all going through.

In numerology, the number 6 means harmony and willingness to accept responsibility for one's actions and for the results of those actions. The number 6 also symbolizes the two roads we have a choice between taking.

What is the Spiritual Lesson or Challenge that Number 6: The Lovers would teach us?

This lesson involves the potential for Self-Realization through the union of our own twin energies and through union with another person, ultimately leading to Union with the Creator. Developing the wisdom to deal with the power of the Kundalini and the influence it has over our physical desires is a major spiritual challenge we all face at one point or another during our evolutionary process. Agape or Eros, which form of "love" will take precedence in our lives? Which of these energies will we choose to invite into our lives? Will we learn how to develop our sexuality in positive constructive ways, or will we allow our base appetites to rule our actions? Do you know the answers to these questions? When you do, you will have passed an important initiation on the Spiritual Path.

CHAPTER NINETEEN

THE CHARIOT: NUMBER 7

RIDER-WAITE DECK

In the Tarot, the Chariot symbolizes our receptiveness to the Will of the Creator. The figure of the Charioteer represents our Soul and the chariot itself, represents the Body. In the picture, the Charioteer has no reins to hold on to. This is because you must use your mind in union with the Will of the Creator to direct the Sphinx which draws the chariot forward or puts it in motion. There are two sphinx, one white representing positive, yang energies, one black representing negative or yin energies, both of which are necessary for balance and is needed to power or draw the chariot forward into motion. The sky-blue canopy overhead studded with stars represents the influence of the heavens in our lives. It also symbolizes the vibrational forces of the planets as they relate to one's horoscope. The color Sky-Blue symbolizes hope and Divine Assurance. This color indicates the preparation for a new existence or new things in one's life. Sky-Blue is associated with the 5th Chakra Center which rules communication, creativity, and healing. The Charioteer's armor and dress is mainly Sky-Blue in color as well, showing the latent artistic and creative talents at his command. The Charioteer is also holding a "Light Wand" in his right hand. "Light Wands" are symbols from Atlantis, and represent the power of Channeled Energy or Channeled Will.

There are two moons located on the shoulder of the Charioteer, one on each side. One moon is waxing, the other waning which symbolizes time and the flow of the Universal Life Force. On the front of the chariot itself, there is a yellow disk with sky-blue wings symbolizing how the consciousness of humankind can be lifted towards the heavens through Faith. The red round wheel with the upright shaft through its center indicates the positive and negative energies which are united in a practical working relationship. The color red represents the desire and the strength to achieve this goal. The body of the Chariot itself is gray in color which indicates change and transition. Gray also represents analysis and mystical powers which affect the lower, psychic nature of a sentient creature. Gray is in the process of balancing, re-forming and expressing its newly combined energies. This is the color of testing and initiation. The background on this card is Yellow as are the wheels of the Chariot. Yellow symbolizes the active mind, intelligence, integrity and joy. The yellow color of the wheels indicate that the Charioteer can bring these gifts of the soul with him as he travels down the path to his destiny. Without the wheels, (the active mind), the chariot could not move, even with the harnessing of the power expressed by the two Sphinx.

Behind him, is a river which symbolizes the Sub-conscious mind. This symbol shows how the ideas and the creativity that germinate and form in the sub-conscious mind must be developed by the active mind or be lost. The red-tiled roofs of the buildings and castle behind the Charioteer represent wishes and desires that are already fulfilled or granted to the Charioteer on the higher astral realms. All that needs to be done now is to manifest these wishes or desires on the Earth Plane.

HANSON-ROBERTS DECK

The colors that strike you first with this picture of the Chariot is the White and Black Sphinx. Only the black color of the one Sphinx is more of an indigo purple or blue black. These Sphinx represent the two Universal Energy Forces. The White one symbolizes purity and perfection, the Christ Consciousness, and union with the Supreme Being. White is the color of self-mastery and wholeness. Although the second Sphinx is technically black in color, the color of the shading is very important. Therefore, this shade of Black represents an important Crossroads. It indicates a need to accept your Karma, both good and bad, and learn to move forward with it. Through this particular shade of Black, you will learn the art of transformation, guided by a Spiritual Master or Teacher. Black represents the Womb from which Life and Light are born, and in essence, the consciousness of the Charioteer is in the process of being reborn through its union with the Will of the Creator.

The symbol of male-female energies, is in the form of the yin and yang in white and black on a Terra Cotta Red shield. The hat and cloak of the Charioteer is also this shade of red. The color Terra Cotta Red is a color of Karma. The Charioteer is bringing this past-life Karma with him into his present life. At times this Karma may seem to impose limitations or restrictions to him, but he rises above that challenge by choosing to correct the errors made in the past and by accepting his need to forgive others who have built negative karma towards him through past-life violence. Only when the Charioteer is willing to let go of old hurts and resentments can he move forward, freed from limitations.

His Chariot is a dark silver gray in color which symbolizes self-discipline and mastery over the subconscious mind even in the midst of changing circumstances. Through this color, the Charioteer has links to mystical past, to the ages of heroes and heroines, legends, gods and goddesses. The "Light Wand" he carries is "Crystal Gray" in color as is part of his armor. Crystal Gray is a color which absorbs and collects negative energy and transforms it into pure energy, ready to be utilized at the Charioteer's discretion. Its potential for good is limitless, but the potential for misuse is also just as great.

The color Gold is also prominent on this card which symbolizes soul advancement and restoration. It is the color of attainment. Gold also indicates the power of physical and material manifestation. The rich blue shades of the canopy with the white stars indicate that the emotions are in a process of maturing, deepening, and coming to know the true meaning of Love. The Sapphire Blue in the canopy symbolizes mastery of the Ten Commandments, a goal the Charioteer is striving for, a goal that is attainable for him.

In the background there is a lush green field and a town with many buildings, some of which are a light shade of purple, almost violet in color. This represents the goal of self-realization, a goal the Charioteer is pursuing on a subconscious level. Whether or not he achieves this goal depends on the choices he makes on the path of destiny he is traveling.

SUMMARY DEFINITION OF THE CHARIOT

Taking all of the symbols and color symbolism into account, the following information brings together or synthesizes all of these elements so that you can utilize it more efficiently when doing a Lay-Out Spread or when using this card to Meditate with.

In Tarot Symbolism, the Chariot represents success for those engaged in artistic or creative pursuits. It indicates triumph over difficulties, victory over obstacles and a challenge to dare to be all you can be. The Chariot is a symbol for those who do achieve greatness if they are willing to master their desires and harness them to the Will of the Creator. The presence of the Chariot in a Lay-Out Spread also indicates unexpected news and contracts, the attainment of a desired goal or outcome. This is a card of hope and a sign to the individual that they possess the potential to do, to accomplish great things. It is also important for the individual to develop the habit of setting aside a certain amount of time each day for solitude and meditation in order to receive the inspiration necessary for creativity.

In Numerology, the number 7 represents spiritual, mystical, and intuitional influences. It is the number of the mystic.

What is the Spiritual Lesson or Challenge that Number 7: The Chariot would teach us?

This lesson involves the willingness to listen to the guidance of our Higher Self or to our Spiritual Teacher. It is important to ignore the attitude of "I can't" do this or "I can't" do that. These are limitations imposed by the Ego which does not want you to unite with the Will of the Creator. For when you unite with that Will, there is nothing that can prevent you from achieving the goals or function you came here to accomplish. You are challenged by this card to harness and use the gifts you were given in ways that uplift not only yourself but others as well. The opportunities for advancement will be provided once you accept your part in the adventure.

CHAPTER TWENTY

STRENGTH: NUMBER 8

RIDER-WAITE DECK

In the Tarot, the card titled Strength represents the triumph of our Higher Self over the physical desires and appetites generated by inhabiting a physical body on the Earth Plane. The woman in the picture is dressed in a long white gown with roses wrapped around her waist and attached to the roses around the lion's neck. The white gown represents the Christ Consciousness, purity and perfection. White symbolizes truth and the transition of the spirit from one level of "being" or "knowing" to a higher level. White is the color of self-mastery and wholeness. The lion in the picture represents the physical body and the Kundalini Force. The creature has been tamed by the "strength" of the woman clothed in white. It has not been tamed through force or subjugation, but rather through the strength of Love, Agape Love or Pure Love. The lion has physical strength, but the woman has the strength of Love which stems from the union she has with the Creator. The sign of Infinity is over her head, symbolizing the presence and protective Love of God.

The link between the woman and lion made with roses symbolize desires. These are desires that have been transformed and purified by the Higher Mind. The woman shows no fear in handling the wild creature because she knows there is nothing on the Earth Plane to fear. Her faith and trust is in the Creator who gives her the strength to be fearless. The woman has established a harmonic balance between the physical body and the spiritual body. The wreath of flowers in her hair shows her unity with and love for Nature.

The woman represents spiritual courage and power that we all have, but don't always realize because of our preoccupation with the physical body. Almost the whole background of the card is yellow in color. The color yellow symbolizes the active mind, enlightenment and joy. The ground she and the lion stand on is green. The color green represents balanced emotions, healing and growth. It is the color of the 4th Chakra Center referred to as the Heart Chakra and symbolizes love.

MARY HANSON-ROBERTS DECK

On this particular card there is a lot of golden brown and peach gold colors. Golden brown symbolizes the use of or the blending of enlightenment with practicality on the Earth Plane. It represents an individual who is spiritual, yet has their feet planted firmly on the ground. This is a color which symbolizes someone who offers themselves in selfless service to others. The peach-gold of the sky overhead represents soul advancement and blessings from the Creator. Since this is also a healing color, it indicates that the woman, through her selfless love for others, offers healing to those who are willing to accept it.

The woman wears a medium blue colored dress signifying serenity, balance and spiritual peace. Medium Blue is the color of Infinity and indicates the rhythmic subconscious flow of life. She also wears, loosely fastened to her shoulders, a red cape. Red is symbolic of the Root Chakra, the Kundalini Force which she has mastered. The color red represents desires, appetites, sexual energy, physical passion and sensuality. Because the cape is not bound to her, but can be easily taken off, it illustrates her ability to use these raw energies in constructive and creative ways.

Her eyes are closed, as if she were in a meditative state or in communion with the Holy Spirit or the higher spiritual realms. A look of peaceful joy and contentment is mirrored on her face. She has found union with the Creator and seeks to give this experience to others by example, but not through the force of her will. She has the "strength" to force others to obey her Will, but she would not mis-direct her abilities in this manner for she knows that perfect love and acceptance does not force, it waits patiently for others to choose the path of enlightenment.

The red roses in this picture, if you look closely at them, are tipped with white. The red rose of desire is in the process of being transformed into the white rose purity. The mountains behind her are a silvery gray in color which represents self-discipline and mastery over the subconscious mind, even in the midst of changing circumstances. The fact that the mountains are behind her shows that she has already passed through great changes in her life that have altered her perception of the physical earth plane.

SUMMARY DEFINITION OF STRENGTH

Taking all of the symbols and color symbolism into account, the following information brings together or synthesizes all of these elements so that you can utilize it more efficiently and effectively when doing a Lay-Out Spread or when using this Card in Meditation.

In Tarot Symbolism, Strength indicates control of the Life Force or Kundalini. It symbolizes the triumph of Love over hate or fear, spiritual power shall overcome material power. This card also indicates courage, confidence, and assurance. This particular tarot card also symbolizes Karmic Merit earned from past actions. This Karmic Merit represents seeds you have sown in the past which are now bearing their fruits for you. The tarot card titled Strength also indicates help is available from loved ones and friends. In other words, there are people in your life who have a purpose. They serve as catalysts which assist you in obtaining goals and objectives you need in order to advance along your Path in this life.

This card also deals with the power of the subconscious mind and how the thoughts, desires, and ideas we have greatly influence the world around us. Although mental thoughts do not have form or substance, they have energy; and this energy can have a positive or negative effect on us. Before something can exist on the physical earth plane, it must have its beginning as a thought, idea or desire. Therefore, it is not only important to be responsible for the actions and choices we make, but also for the thoughts, ideas, and desires we have because their influence is more far-reaching than we realize.

In Numerology, the number 8 indicates leadership, power, success, Karma, and material freedom. It is also a number which vibrates to God.

What is the Spiritual Lesson or Challenge that Number 8 Strength would teach us?

The lesson of this Tarot Card involves the realization that mastering the subconscious mind and harnessing it to our Will which is in a state of Union with the Creator is the true meaning of "Strength". It is important for us to trust in the Love and Strength that comes to us from our Creator. Any challenge, be it good or bad that we face, should be approached with confidence and assurance, *knowing* that it is not *our* strength alone which surges through us, it is the *combined* strength of ourselves united with the Creator. Recognizing that we always have this strength available to us in any circumstance we face removes the fear the challenge may generate. One of the most important lessons this tarot card teaches us is that what we sow, we reap, for this card symbolizes Karma.

CHAPTER TWENTY-ONE

THE HERMIT: NUMBER 9

RIDER-WAITE DECK

In Tarot, the Hermit represents the "Keeper of Divine Wisdom and Knowl-edge", he is the "Guardian of Time". The Hermit is the teacher who awaits all seekers on the Path, ready to guide and counsel them. He holds aloft a lantern filled with the Light of Creation and Divine Protection, symbolized by the six pointed star inside referred to as the "Seal of Solomon". The Hermit has achieved perfect wisdom. He stands on the summit of the mountains of Spiritual Perfec-tion. He stands ready to guide others to the same spiritual plateau he has attained. The dominant color is the Sky-Blue of the background. This color symbolizes Divine Assurance and hope. It is a color which indicates the preparation for a new existence or new things in one's life. Sky-Blue is the color of the 5th Chakra Center referred to as the "Throat Chakra" which rules communication and creativity. He stands on a mountain summit covered with white snow. Snow symbolizes purity and a spiritual master offering to reveal secret wisdom to those who have passed certain tests on the Earth Plane.

The Hermit is a symbol of an opportunity to pass spiritual initiations. It shows mastery over the illusions of the Earth Plane. The staff that the Hermit holds is the Magician's Wand which he has learned to control and use for the benefit of himself and others. It is a symbol of his authority and self-mastery. The staff is yellow in color representing enlightenment and the active mind working with integrity on the Earth Plane. In many ways, the Hermit symbolizes the Holy Spirit, ready to go to the aid of every human who cries out for the Light. He stands ever ready to instruct those who would dedicate themselves to the spiritual path in the art of transformation.

He is dressed in gray robes which indicates the many changes and transfor-mations he has experienced in order to reach the spiritual level from which he can turn and guide others. The star in the lamp is yellow as are the rays emanating from it. This symbolizes the Light of Enlightenment the Hermit offers to those who follow in his footsteps. The gray of his robes also indicate his ability to remain detached and aloof from the constant changes the Earth Plane goes through as the mists of Illusion form and then reshape the physical plane.

I am sure many of you have read the works of J.R.R. Tolkien; *The Hobbit* and the follow up trilogy; *The Lord of the Rings*. There is a character in those four books who is called Gandalf, the wise wizard. The first time I saw the tarot card titled "The Hermit", I immediately "saw" this hermit as Gandalf. Gandalf was wise, compassionate, self-disciplined, and had developed self-mastery, all qualities which reflect the meaning behind "The Hermit".

I wanted to share this with you to demonstrate how easy it is to make associations between the Tarot Cards Symbols and real or fictional characters.

When you can do that, I feel you gain more insight into the card itself because it is your Higher Intuitional Mind which is making those associations and is sending you a subtle message. Try this technique with each of the cards and see if you can "instinctively" relate them to real or fictional characters. By doing this, you will awaken the creativity and intuition in your mind and find it an enlightening experience.

MARY HANSON-ROBERTS DECK

On this card, the figure of the Hermit is dressed in robes of blue-gray. This color represents serenity amid change and transition. His Hood is a blend of purple and maroon in color which represents mastery of the Ten Commandments and emotions that have matured into pure love. There is a gold belt or sash around his waist which represents advancement of the soul through the successful passing of initiations. Gold also symbolizes spiritual blessings.

The background is a blend of Turquoise Blue and Indigo at the top. Turquoise Blue is the color symbol of protection and good fortune. It is the color of power manifesting on the Earth Plane. Because of the ties Turquoise has to Atlantis, this color acts as a catalyst to re-awaken those memories and re-awaken the abilities an individual once possessed. Indigo is the color of the "Brow Chakra" which represents intuition, higher consciousness and the Christ Mind. It is a raw electric color, indicating Karmic Voltage, (the sowing of karma). Indigo is the color of the spiritual life, the color of releasing, of letting go and letting God. This is the color of a Seeker. There are dark green or evergreen bands on the Hermit's robe. Evergreen symbolizes creative energy, a power to be used in constructive ways. It is the color of endurance, of generosity, of faith and strength against all opposition. It is the color of triumph and attainment. The staff he leans upon is golden brown in color showing his reliance on the use of enlightenment and practicality has brought him to the heights he has now achieved.

The heights of his achievements are symbolized by the snow capped mountain summit he stands on. All around him are other snow-capped mountain summits which symbolize the different paths that are available to a Seeker. Not all spiritual paths are the same, but they ultimately lead to the same goal, the same pinnacle. The snow on the mountain summits are violet-white in color which symbolizes self-realization. The Hermit stands serene on his mountain summit, shining his lamp so that others may follow the path to enlightenment. Symbolically, this card, taken as a whole, represents the Teacher or Master who would be our guardian who would lead us back to God. The Hermit also symbolizes the Holy Spirit within us, offering direction and guidance, but not demanding our compliance.

SUMMARY DEFINITION OF THE HERMIT

Taking all of the symbols and color symbolism into account, the following information brings together or synthesizes all of these elements so that you can utilize it more efficiently when doing a Lay-Out Spread or when using this card in a Meditation.

In Tarot Symbolism, the Hermit represents illumination from within, Divine Inspiration, wisdom, a teacher of teachers. He represents the ending of a cycle in your life, a change of job or residence, a turn for the better. The Hermit is a card of attainment. It represents wisdom sought for and obtained from above, divine guidance. Spiritually, this card symbolizes the union of personal will with Cosmic Will, a union that is necessary before further growth and enlightenment is possible.

This is a card of change and realization of goals. It represents understanding and compassion. The Hermit shows us through his illumination that the knowledge and experience we have gained up to this point will become worthless unless we learn how to share it with others. This is what he has done, and in the process made his knowledge a shining light from which we can see to continue our Seeker's Path. In numerology, the number 9 is the symbol of pure intellect and also a symbol of initiation because it is the trinity of trinities, (3 threes--the Father, the Son and the Holy Spirit). Nine is also the number of those who heal through unconditional love and acceptance, and the number of those who give unselfishly to others.

What is the Spiritual Lesson or Challenge the Number 9: The Hermit would teach us?

The Hermit teaches us that we are Channels for the Creator and that we manifest His Will on the physical earth plane. The Hermit also teaches us to let go of the past and the mistakes that we have made, or the hurts and pains given us by others. Useless emotional baggage is a limitation imposed on us by our Egos which is seeking to keep us trapped in illusions. Letting go is one of the most difficult, yet one of the most important choices we face. By doing so, we can achieve the self-mastery the Hermit has attained.

CHAPTER TWENTY-TWO

THE WHEEL OF FORTUNE: NUMBER 10

RIDER-WAITE DECK

In the Tarot, the Wheel of Fortune has four symbols, the Bull, the Lion, the Eagle, and the human, one in each corner, that represents the 4 fixed signs of the Zodiac. These fixed signs are Taurus, (the bull); Leo, (the lion); Scorpio, (the eagle); and Aquarius, (the human). They are all reading books which represent wisdom and the Akashic Records of the ages of life on the Earth Plane. This knowledge also indicates the Karmic Laws which govern the Earth Plane where humankind and other sentient life-forces reside. The wings on each of the figures symbolize their higher self, or spiritual self, striving all the time and in many different ways to achieve Union with the Supreme Creator.

The Wheel itself, is a circle without beginning or end. It symbolizes the ending of karmic debts from the past and that new beginnings are now possible. It refers to the biblical passage of, "As ye sow, so shall ye reap." If we sow Love, we shall reap Love tenfold. If we sow fear, anger, or hatred, we shall reap them tenfold. Karma, the Law governing the physical Universe and The Cycles of Life and new beginnings are characteristics of this card. It shows that change is a natural event on the Earth Plane, change is what makes it possible for growth to occur.

This card also teaches us that we are the ones who make the choices of what we want to see, what changes we want in our lives. We choose the seeds we want to reap, no one else. The presence of the Egyptian god Thoth, (the figure at the bottom of the Wheel, back pressed against it), shows how humankind is still evolving, still mutating into other shapes as the genesis of humankind continues its upward spiral to the Light and to self-realization.

The Serpent undulating downward, towards the Earth Plane, represents Divine Knowledge and Wisdom coming into manifestation on the physical plane. It's color is yellow symbolizing enlightenment. The Serpent also represents the Kundalini Force that has been transmutated from its raw energy state to a state of Grace. The Hebrew letters on the Wheel itself, spell the name God or Jehovah.

The Sphinx seated on top of the wheel is Sky-Blue in color and shows that humankind has risen above its animal instincts and is now working on its intuitional senses and mental abilities. The Sphinx holds the sword of discernment, indicating the importance of this quality in our lives.

MARY HANSON-ROBERTS DECK

The colors on this card are rich and varied, just as life is rich in varied in its experiences. The Wheel itself, is gold and orange with a rim of purple on the outside. The gold star burst in the center represents the presence of spiritual enlightenment to be found in each of life's experiences. The orange represents the balance of the physical and mental aspects of humankind. Orange is the combination of intelligence and good judgment. It deals with the emotions and the proper use of energy. The Purple color indicates karmic voltage, the sowing of karma, higher consciousness, intuition, and the Christ Mind.

The Jackal's head, symbolic of the Egyptian god Thoth, is a deep Sapphire blue, so dark it almost appears black. Sapphire Blue is a color which promises substance and expansion. It shows that the emotional nature has matured, become more purified. On an even higher, more spiritual level, the color Sapphire represents mastery of the Ten Commandments. The two-headed serpent, representing both Infinity and the Kundalini, is a light pastel green which indicates growth and awareness.

The head-dress of the Sphinx is gray with orange stripes signifying balance amid change and transition. The head-dress also has the symbol of the serpent around the brow chakra which represents Divine Wisdom. The sky is a mixture of different shades of soft pink and peach gold, which symbolizes nurturing love and tenderness along with spiritual blessings and soul advancement. These two colors together represent a sensitivity to the needs of other life-forms, as well as compassion for them.

SUMMARY DEFINITION FOR THE WHEEL OF FORTUNE

Taking all of the symbols and color symbolism into account, the following information brings together or synthesizes all of these elements so that you can utilize it more efficiently when doing a Lay-Out Spread or when using this card in Meditation.

In Tarot Symbolism, the Wheel of Fortune represents a change of fortune for the better. This card also indicates that some of the past karma you have been working to balance out has been accomplished. The Wheel of Fortune symbolizes destiny, intuition and new conditions. There is a door of opportunity opening for you, a chance to make a new beginning without the limitations of the past to pull you back. This is a card of unexpected good luck and signifies success.

In Numerology, the number 10, which is the number 1 with the God-Force of 0 after it, represents a new beginning, a new cycle about to start. The number 10 has many of the same meanings as the number 1, but with the added influence of the number 0 as well. Zero represents Divine Inspiration and limitless possibilities.

What is the Spiritual Lesson or Challenge that Number 10: The Wheel of Fortune would teach us?

The Wheel of Fortune teaches us, in very practical useful ways, that what we sow, we reap. Part of the Challenge lies in accepting this fact and learning how to move forward with it, using it as a measuring stick for future choices and actions. Forgiving ourselves and others for real or imagined transgressions is the key to understanding what this card is trying to teach us through its symbolism.

CHAPTER TWENTY-THREE

JUSTICE: NUMBER 11

RIDER-WAITE DECK

In the Tarot, the card Justice represents the Law of Cause and Effect, and the need for balance. The seated figure, dressed in flowing orange robes with a green mantle, holds an upraised sword in one hand and the scales of justice in the other. The Sword symbolizes discernment and the ability to use discrimination when dealing with the Illusions of the Earth Plane. The Sword, Sky-Blue in color with a yellow hilt, represents the need to eliminate wrong thinking and judgmental ideas. The upright position of the Sword symbolizes victory on the side of Truth and Justice.

The Scales are yellow in color, which represents the active mind which has been enlightened. The Scales also represent the ability to weigh choices, to weigh past and present beliefs or circumstances and judge whether or not they have meaning any longer in your life, which will allow you to achieve balance and correct past mistakes. This is a card which signifies the elimination of excess baggage, both emotional, material, and mental. The symbol of the scales represents the ability to make a choice between what is right and what is wrong, for you, not anyone else.

The figure is seated between two pillars representing the Conscious and Subconscious Mind, the positive and negative energy forces of the universe. The purple curtain between the two pillars also links or serves a bridge between these two states of consciousness or energy forces. The color purple symbolizes spiritual power, mastery, and the Christ Mind. It is from this Source that the figure seated between the pillars draws their strength to see through the veils of illusion to the Truth.

MARY HANSON-ROBERTS DECK

There are 4 dominant colors on this card; Orange, Crystal Gray, Muddy Olive Green, and purple or indigo. The Orange represents balance of the physical and mental. It is a combination of intelligence and good judgment. The Crystal Gray of the pillars, the upraised sword, and the crown the figure wears on top of the head symbolizes a very special spiritual challenge. Crystal Gray is a color that absorbs and collects negative energy and transforms it into pure energy, ready to be utilized at our discretion.

Before I explain the significance of the color olive green, I need to point out that the Tarot Card Justice symbolizes the law of Karma and the need to eliminate negative karmic emotions and actions. The color olive green represents self-deception, deception on the astral levels, envy, jealousy, malice, selfishness, betrayal, and even treachery. These are all emotions that must be recognized and eliminated.

Even though the figure's under-dress is this color, it is decorated with steel-blue diamonds. Diamonds are considered to represent the Light, constancy, eternity, durability, incorruptibility, and eternity of spirit by the Atlanteans. It is believed that the Diamond contains an eternal flame within its heart. The name diamond means "invincible." This means that despite the negative karma of past choices and actions, the human spirit will triumph in the end, through balancing, correcting, and eliminating past errors.

The purple color of the curtain means releasing, letting go and letting God. It is also the color of the Christ Mind or Super-Consciousness. It is raw electric color signifying karmic voltage, (the sowing of karma). Purple is the color of intuition, union and discernment. The Scales are a golden brown in color representing the perfect blend of enlightenment and practicality on the physical Earth Plane.

SUMMARY DEFINITION OF JUSTICE

Taking all of the symbols and color symbolism into account, the following information brings together or synthesizes all of these elements so that you can utilize it more efficiently when doing a Lay-Out Spread or when using this card in meditation.

In Tarot Symbolism, Justice indicates sudden events, quick decisions, and legal dealings. It also indicates tests or challenges to be faced, from which Spiritual Growth is the outcome. The Tarot card Justice also means the elimination of excess baggage, of wrong ideas, and useless forms of education or learning. Its presence in a Lay-Out Spread may also point to a marriage or marriage agreements, a union which is karmic in nature, a necessary learning experience. In Numerology, the number 11 is a master number meaning intuition, vision, inspiration and creativity.

What is the Spiritual Lesson or Challenge that Number 11 Justice would teach us?

The tarot card Justice teaches us, in practical ways, about the Law of Cause and Effect. This card reminds us of the importance of accepting responsibility for choices and actions we have made in the past, and to correct them. As long as we try to correct them, the Spirit of Love will see that they are corrected and eliminated from our Karmic Record, all we have to do is be willing to try.

CHAPTER TWENTY-FOUR

THE HANGED MAN: NUMBER 12

RIDER-WAITE DECK

The Hanged Man symbolizes an individual, (male or female), who looks beyond the projections of the Ego and sees the True Reality of other people. The Hanged Man sees other people as part of themselves, and together United with the Holy Spirit and God. This card represents an individual who can see through the distortions of Illusion, who can find the spark of Light even in the midst of darkness. The way the figure on the card is hanging and the colors it wears demonstrates this principle.

The Hanged Man is wearing a sky-blue tunic with a purple sash which symbolizes Divine Assurance and hope. The purple represents intuition and the super consciousness. The Head as well as the halo around the head is yellow in color which symbolizes enlightenment and the active mind. Yellow is also the color of spiritual awareness, of joy and gifts of the Spirit. His tights or pants are red in color symbolizing the raw energy or Kundalini force that feeds the fire of his creativity. The Hanged Man knows how to take the raw energy of the Kundalini and transmute it.

The way his legs are positioned form a number 4. Number 4 to the ancients represented the God-Force descending from the Higher Planes to manifest His Presence on the Earth Plane. The Hebrew name for God has 4 letters in it, showing the connection between the descent of Spirit into Matter, joining it to the God Force of the Universe. His arms are clasped behind him, symbolizing his openness to the Will of the Creator.

The philosophy of the Hanged Man sets him apart from the mundane and from others, but his philosophy is what brings him fulfillment and joy, qualities he would willingly share with others. He has transformed his physical, material desires into spiritual and compassionate concern for others. He has reversed his thinking and his way of life from what is considered to be normal by other people who are trapped in the web of Illusions. He has been initiated through tests and challenges to become a co-creator with God. He has surrendered himself to God in perfect trust. Others may see this surrender as sacrifice, but he knows differently, he knows that he has been freed while the others are still slaves to the maniacal whims of the Ego who uses Illusions to keep its prey entangled. The Hanged Man knows that what he gives to others, he is really giving to himself. For the only way to keep something for yourself is to give it away.

The Tree from which the Hanged Man is suspended is a living, growing tree. It represents the Tree of Life, from which wisdom is found. The Tree is brown in color with Emerald Green Leaves. Brown represents the physical earth plane. It is the color of security, steadfastness and material or physical power. The emerald green color of the leaves represents the Channeling of a unique and very special healing love which can center the mental, emotional, and physical bodies of other people. The heart is aligned to the "Logos" or Spiritual Truths and can, without being judgmental, offer acceptance and forgiveness to others. Emerald green has a way of cleansing the unwanted and the useless waste and distractions from our lives without pain.

MARY HANSON-ROBERTS DECK

With this Deck, the Hanged Man wears a Crystal Gray tunic which represents a very special spiritual challenge. Crystal Gray is a color that absorbs and collects negative energy and transforms it into pure energy, ready to be utilized at our discretion. Its potential for good is limitless, but the potential for misuse is also just as great, therein lies the spiritual challenge. Gray, in itself, represents change. Crystal Gray, in this instance, represents a change in Consciousness.

The color of his pants or tights is a cross between copper and brown. This is a difficult color to classify, but there are times when you will run across a color that is really a combination of several colors. When this happens it is necessary to take into account all of the qualities of each of the colors and synthesize them into an acceptable definition. Copper is a color which serves as a channel or conductor for energy, an energy that is limitless in its potential for expression. Brown is the color of the Earth Plane of security and steadfastness. Combined together, these colors represent Channeled energy on the Earth Plane which promotes security and serves the needs of others in a selfless way.

The ropes which have tied him to the Tree of Life are a golden color as is the halo around his head. Gold represents soul advancement, the power of physical and material manifestation, the Spirit descending to the Earth Plane. Gold is also the color of spiritual blessings and gifts of the Spirit. The Tree of Life is alive and rich with fruit and leaves. The red fruit symbolize the fertility of his enlightened mind. They also represent the gifts he has to share with others. Red is the color of new beginnings, new opportunities. The green leaves indicate healing, growth, and an unlimited source of abundance from the Creator. Green is the color of healing love. The background is a pale blue representing serenity and peace. The Hanged Man is at peace with himself and the world around him.

SUMMARY DEFINITION OF THE HANGED MAN

Taking all of the symbols and color symbolism into account, the following information brings together or synthesizes all of these elements so that you can utilize this knowledge more efficiently when doing a Lay-Out Spread or when using this card in Meditation.

In Tarot Symbolism, the Hanged Man represents wisdom, discernment, intuition, and prophecy. It indicates a change of view, a reversal in one's life, a quiet pause by which inner peace through meditation of the Christ Mind is possible. The Hanged Man means being centered within oneself, surrender to a higher being or to one's higher self which brings about a reversal in one's situation in life. The Hanged Man has attained an inner peace that no human Illusion can disturb.

On another level, the Hanged Man indicates that you must look beneath the surface of a situation or a person to find true understanding. The presence of the

Hanged Man indicates that all is not what it appears to be, the Ego or World of Illusion is trying to deceive you. This card represents a waiting period during which communication with the higher realms is necessary. The Hanged Man indicates prophetic powers and an opportunity to completely change one's life or situation.

In Numerology, the number 12 represents the 12 disciples, the 12 zodiac signs, the 12 tribes of ancient Israel, and the 12 months of the year. It is a combination of 1 and 2 equaling 3. One means the originator, the beginning. Two being the partner, the unifier. Coming to 3 which is the expression of the unified creator.

What is the Spiritual Lesson or Challenge that Number 12: The Hanged Man would teach us?

The Hanged Man teaches us that what we really sacrifice is the limitations and fears of the Ego when we surrender ourselves to the guidance, love and unlimited gifts of the Creator. Who would want to retain the "gifts" of the Ego, which must be bought at a high price, when we could have the "gifts of the Spirit" which are ours by right and cost us nothing accept relinquishment of the Ego?

CHAPTER TWENTY-FIVE

DEATH: NUMBER 13

RIDER-WAITE DECK

Unfortunately, the first time someone sees this card it frightens them, or makes them very uneasy. They automatically assume the literal meaning of this card and think someone they know or themselves are about to die soon. This is not true. In the Tarot, the Death card symbolizes Change and Transformation, a rebirth to a new level of awareness. It represents the ending of an old condition or situation and the beginning of new era or phase in one's life.

The number 13, which signifies this card, is sacred as is every multiple of the number 13. It represents one who is an Initiate, one who is reborn through transformation or transmutation of the Christ Consciousness. There were 12 disciples, Jesus was the 13th; there are 12 Zodiac Signs with the Sun as the focal point. The number 13 is even preserved in the measurements of the Great Pyramid in Egypt. Thirteen is a very spiritual number, and as such, frightens many people who are not yet awakened from the dreams of Illusion. They see it instead as an unlucky number, one to be feared, with many superstitions attached to it.

The skeleton figure representing Death wears black armor and rides a white horse. The White Horse is symbolic of the Christ Consciousness. The Black armor indicates a cross-roads, a turning point and an opportunity to seek a Master or Teacher who will instruct a Seeker on the path in the Laws of Transmutation and Transformation. On the banner which the skeleton carries there is a five-pointed white rose on a field of black. The five points of the white rose represents our five senses. The color white represents the mastery of these senses as well as purity and perfection.

The rising sun in the background between two towers symbolizes the Life-Force which never "dies", but merely changes its form. The Life-Force is eternal and can never be destroyed. The two towers symbolize the duality in nature, the yin and yang energies. This card represents the law of Karma. It shows that none, king or peasant, priest or layman, may escape the results of their actions, be those actions for good or bad.

MARY HANSON-ROBERTS DECK

The colors on this card are a rich and varied mosaic. The colors themselves show the variety and diversity of life itself. The figures look as though they were sleeping, waiting to be awakened from the dreams manifested by the plane of illusion. Color-wise, there are shades of purple and indigo threaded throughout the card. Rose, soft pink, and peach gold dominate the sky. Green and turquoise, golden brown and silver complete the color mosaic of this card.

The purple-indigo color represents karmic voltage, intuition and higher consciousness. It is the color of releasing, of letting go and letting God. The rose, soft pink and peach gold colors of the sky represent spiritual growth, attainment, creativity and self-realization. These colors also represent a warm, compassionate, empathic love. There is even a violet pink plume on the helmet of the skeleton representing faith, wisdom and understanding. There is a healing taking place, self-deception is being eliminated, true security is now possible, a security which all may share, not just a privileged few.

In one lifetime alone, we go through many small "deaths". For example: When you are single, you are experiencing life from a certain perspective. Once you are united or marry someone else, you are no longer a single entity, but part of a duo or pair. That part of you which was single, "dies" and is reborn as part of a unit with another. Each time you go through a major change in your life, the old you or old existence you experienced, "dies", but you continue on, transformed and changed. All that "Death" really means is change; sometimes drastic, sometimes subtle.

SUMMARY DEFINITION OF DEATH

Taking all of the symbols and color symbolism into account, the following information brings together or synthesizes all of these elements so that you can utilize this knowledge more efficiently when doing a Lay-Out Spread or when using this card in Meditation.

In Tarot Symbolism, the card "Death" represents Change which is voluntary or involuntary, depending solely on the choice of the individual. This change can happen very suddenly and unexpectedly. This is a card of Transformation, destruction of illusions which results in freedom. Fresh ideas, new concepts, a reconstructive period is indicated. This card does not represent physical death, instead this card offers you the opportunity for release from limitations of the past.

This is really a card of liberation, both a spiritual and a mental liberation. Sometimes this card can indicate the end of a restrictive marriage, union or partnership; not through death, but through the releasing power of Karma. In other words, the union has served its purpose as a teaching device and there is no longer any need to stay in the union if it has become restrictive or oppressive to your spirit.

In Numerology, the number 13 is considered to be a sacred number. It denotes an initiate or one who is reborn through the spiritual process of Transmutation. There were 12 disciples, Jesus was the 13th.

What is the Spiritual Lesson or Challenge that Number 13: Death would teach us?

The tarot card Death offers us liberation from the past, a renewal which promotes new growth and new opportunities to express our creativity. What the caterpillar calls death, the Butterfly calls Birth. Change is only painful when we try to fight it, growth is a natural process of Evolution, and we need to learn to accept the changes that come to us as opportunities for growth.

CHAPTER TWENTY-SIX

TEMPERANCE: NUMBER 14

RIDER-WAITE DECK

The androgynous angel symbolizes the perfect blending of opposites, male and female, positive and negative. The angel represents us, our higher selves in perfect harmony with the Life-Force, with the Universe as indicated by the yellow solar disc on the forehead. The violet and purple color of the wings symbolize self-realization, creativity, intuition, the development of the higher mind, and the super-consciousness. The triangle, (representing the Spirit), within a Square, (representing Reality or the Earth Plane), on the angel's breast has a total of 7 sides. Seven is the number of the initiated, the mystic, the seeker of enlightenment.

The two cups the angel is holding, with water, (representing the essence of life), flowing between them, symbolizes balance and harmony. This natural flowing from one polarity to another, represents the merging of Spirit into Matter, the flowing of the past through the present and into the future. The cups are yellow in color symbolizing the active mind, and intelligence. Yellow is the color of clear thinking, of joy and enlightenment. It is the color of integrity.

The angel stands with one foot on the water and one foot on the ground. The pond of water symbolizes the Subconscious, and the ground represents the Conscious. By standing with one foot on each element, the angel again symbolizes balance on the Earth Plane, and the blending of the intuition of the subconscious with the logic of the conscious. The water is sky-blue in color representing Divine Assurance and hope. It is the color of communication, creativity and healing. Sky-Blue represents the healing of possessive tendencies.

The ground around the angel is a rich emerald green color representing the opening of the Heart Chakra to allow the "Logos" or Universal Truth to flow in a loving stream outward to others. The Mountain Peaks in the distance are sky-blue in color and represent attainment of wisdom and understanding. The glowing yellow crown placed over the mountain peaks represents the culmination of spiritual achievement.

MARY HANSON-ROBERTS DECK

The angel on this card appears more dreamy, tranquil, and contemplative than the Rider-Waite angel. The colors are softer and have a delicate pastel shading. There is a touch, here and there, of the color Aqua or Blue-Green which represents the womb of life, rich, nurturing and filled with unseen wonders. It is a color which symbolizes the limitless bounty of Nature and of the Creator. Aqua is a color of joy and happiness, a color of love and security.

Rather than a pond of water, this card depicts the vastness of the ocean spreading its influence to land. This symbolizes the influence the subconscious mind has on the physical plane. The violet and gold colors on the card represent the creativity of the subconscious mind manifesting and influencing Reality on the physical plane. Violet and gold are also colors which symbolize self-realization, enlightenment and attainment.

The Angel has achieved a special attunement with the unseen forces of Life and knows how to direct these forces onto the physical plane, maintaining the delicate balance which exists between the two worlds of possibility. This is symbolized by the blinding white light of the open Crown Chakra showing direct communion with the Creator. The rich green foliage of the land represents abundance and growth. The golden brown of the angel's hair and in the landscape represent spiritual enlightenment blended with practicality on the Earth Plane.

SUMMARY DEFINITION OF TEMPERANCE

Taking all of the symbols and color symbolism into account, the following information brings together or synthesizes all of these elements so that you can utilize the knowledge more efficiently when doing a Lay-Out Spread or when using this card in Meditation.

In Tarot Symbolism, the card Temperance represents that which tempers, combines and harmonizes the spiritual with the material. It is the tempering of two elements resulting in success and the realization of a goal. This card indicates the use of the creativity within ourselves to create something unique, a book, a painting, music, etc. What we have imagined will come to pass.

Inherent in the presence of this Tarot Card is the theme of union or partnership. This union can be within ourselves, blending and combining the male and female energies we possess or achieving union with another person on a spiritual level. This union allows us to receive and express inspired ideas for there are no longer any barriers to prevent communion between our higher selves and the physical self we use on the Earth Plane.

In Numerology, the number 14 is a combination of the number 1 which is originality or beginning, and the number 4 which is the builder or foundation. The two together create the number 5 which expresses freedom and liberation. One must have a firm beginning or foundation in order to be truly free.

What is the Spiritual Lesson or Challenge that Number 14: Temperance would teach us?

The card Temperance teaches us about adaptability and self-control. In order to experience attainment and have success it is important that we learn self-discipline and have the ability to harmonize with others. When we combine forces with others and with our higher selves, we will achieve much more than if we tried on our own alone. But, whenever two personalities come together, inevitably there will be some conflicts, sometimes minor, sometimes major. Learning how to adapt to the energies or needs of others and teaching them, in turn, how to adapt to you and your needs is a lesson in Temperance, of blending and harmonizing what may seem to be opposites.

CHAPTER TWENTY-SEVEN

THE DEVIL: NUMBER 15

RIDER-WAITE DECK

In Tarot, the Devil represents the ego and obsession. The two human figures on the card have chained themselves to materialism, neglecting their spirituality. This card symbolizes the lack of discernment. It represents clinging to illusions rather than Truth. The black background of this card indicates ignorance, a closed mind, lack of light, depression, guilt, and fear. The color represents bondage to the material plane. A bondage that is self-imposed, as represented by the loose chains around the necks of the two humans. The Devil also represents religious dogma that has nothing to do with True Spirituality. In one way, this card symbolizes the Lovers, (number 6), who have indulged in their physical appetites and neglected their spiritual appetites. The devil has on his head an inverted pentagram, which means perversion of the five physical senses. He also holds an inverted torch indicating self-destruction through the misuse of the creative aspect of human nature. The torch, by burning upside down, is wasting its energy and does not give off any real Light. The devil is seated or perched on a square, which represents the physical earth plane, showing his ability to use illusions on the material plane which traps the unawakened in its net.

Because of the looseness of the chains binding the two humans, they could at any time, through the use of their Spiritual Will, remove the chains that bind them to material slavery. But it must be their choice, no one else can choose for them or free them. They must choose to seek the Light and leave the Darkness of Illusions behind. The suffering they experience is through their own making. Even though they have corrupted their Kundalini Force through satiating their physical appetites at the expense of their spirituality, the two humans can still lift the Kundalini through the Higher Chakra centers and reach union with God, leaving all suffering behind.

MARY HANSON-ROBERTS DECK

With this deck, the tarot card depicting the Devil shows how color symbolism can be used to represent characteristics. The devil himself is a muddy, putrid green. This ugly green color represents self-deception and illusions, betrayal and selfishness. It is the color of jealousy, envy, malice and treachery. His wings are a brownish-orange, the color of repression, both of the self and of others. His eyes are a bright red, symbolizing the corruption of the Kundalini Force.

This particular shade of green is a corruption of the power of Love. It has been abased by the physical appetites and is no longer a pure channel for the Love given us. The strong presence of the color brown with overtones of red indicate karmic conditions and difficult lessons to learn. There are temptations to be faced, chiefly the temptation to feel as though the whole world were against you, that you are being unfairly treated or victimized.

Even the light from the torch has been put to selfish use, turned upside down and emitting only enough light for the devil's use. If the torch were upright, it would burn with a brighter flame and cast a greater light for others to use as well. But the devil is selfish and concerned only for his own comfort and needs. The brown color of the square which secures the bonds of the two humans, represents the immersion of the Ego in materialism and the distractions of the physical plane.

The background, however, is a rich evergreen color which symbolizes faith and strength against all opposition. It is the color of endurance. Even though the two humans are responsible for the choices and actions they have made, the evergreen promises them release from guilt, fear, and "sin", (which merely means errors that need correction). Evergreen is a color which cleanses and purifies and gives the two humans the hope they need to break loose from the shackles that bind them to materialism and obsession.

SUMMARY DEFINITION OF THE DEVIL

Taking all of the symbols and color symbolism into account, the following information brings together or synthesizes all of these elements so that you can utilize the knowledge more efficiently when doing a Lay-Out Spread or when using this card in Meditation.

In Tarot Symbolism, the Devil represents bondage to the material and the need for discernment. This card indicates an attachment to mundane things and to the physical plane which creates self-made suffering. There is an indication with this card of judgmental attitudes, of dogmatic narrow views of life. The presence of this card in a spread indicates the acceptance of limitations and a self-defeating attitude.

The Devil also represents an uncontrolled or unfocused ambition. This arises out of ignorance and wrong-thinking. The influence of the Devil causes one to deal with fate and karma, the results of our past or present actions. This sometimes results in feelings of repression or victimization.

In Numerology, the number 15 is a combination of 1 which is creativity or originality, and 5 which is the expression of freedom. Combined together, they result in 6, the number of service. If we allow ourselves to forget to be of service to others or ignore the needs of others when we can assist them, we experience limitations on our own freedom and creativity.

What is the Spiritual Lesson or Challenge that Number 15: The Devil would teach us?

The Devil teaches us about the chains we form around ourselves when we become immersed in materialism to the exclusion of everything else. Judgmental attitudes and obsession take their toll on our strength, leaving us vulnerable to the deceptions of Illusions. Ignorance is not bliss, wisdom is the key to freedom from limitation.

CHAPTER TWENTY-EIGHT

THE TOWER: NUMBER 16

RIDER-WAITE DECK

The Tower symbolizes human ambition and the wrong use of personal will, the wrong use of the gifts of the Spirit. The flash of lightning symbolizes an awakening, an awakening which comes from God and the Holy Spirit. This card can also represent the Kundalini Force blasting through the Crown Chakra, illuminating the spiritual or God-Force of the Universe. Notice too, that the lightning strikes on the yellow "Crown", or "Crown Chakra", this is the seat of higher wisdom, of intuition and oneness with God.

The background of this card is a stark black with gray clouds. The color black stands for materialism, obsession, a closed mind which needs a powerful force to awaken it, to blast away its judgmental attitudes. This color represents Illusions, limitations, and earthly bondage to the material world. Black is the color of Karma and the need we have to accept the consequences of our actions and choices and learn to move forward with it.

The Gray of the tower and the clouds represents change and transition. The yellow color of the lightning symbolizes the active mind in union with the Creator. It is the shaft of clear thinking which pierces the illusions of the Ego and frees an individual from the grips of blind ambition. The tower is constructed on a high cliff, or mountain peak which symbolizes the isolation created by ambition and misuse of personal will. The attitude of the builder of the tower separated them from others, creating a loneliness that can eat away at the soul.

The two figures, a male and female, represent the twin energies that reside in each of us. These two figures also represent wrong thoughts, racial prejudice, and arrogance toward others being knocked out of the Seeker's Consciousness. The tongues of flame falling from the sky are called "yods" in Hebrew and represent blessings from God. Now that the arrogance and prejudice is being blasted out of the consciousness, the blessings of God can lead to true security, abundance, and prosperity. Blessings which all can share and benefit from, not just a privileged few.

MARY HANSON-ROBERTS DECK

The tri-colored sky or background of this card represents the three states of consciousness. The Conscious, (indigo); Sub-conscious, (purple); and Super-conscious, (violet). It is the Consciousness that is receiving the bolt of lightning from the Creator, shaking loose the grip of the Ego. The clouds of the tri-colored sky are violet with rims of gold. This represents self-realization and spiritual awakening, two "gifts" that permeate all three states of consciousness. Even the "yods" are a violet-gold color. The full moon represents our dream state and how we are guided and enlightened through our dreams.

The tower, at first glance, may appear white, but if you look beneath the surface you will see many different shades of color reflecting the various aspects of life. This is the color I call Opal and represents "seeds" of creative thought in the process of gestation, of forming and changing shape, altering their structure in order to be transformed into something wondrous to behold. But the tower, rather than providing simple protection for these "seeds" to germinate, has turned into a prison created by the Ego.

The opal-colored tower rests on a green cliff, isolated and not easily accessible. The green shows that even though the individual has strayed from the Path, the foundation or love which has guided them in the past, is still there, ready to guide them again. Green stands for healing, for peace, and for unconditional Love. It is this color which will help the seeker to re-examine their life and make the changes that are necessary to bring them back to the Path of Enlightenment.

SUMMARY DEFINITION OF THE TOWER

Taking all of the symbols and color symbolism into account, the following information brings together or synthesizes all of these elements so that you can utilize this knowledge more efficiently when doing a Lay-Out Spread or when using this card in Meditation.

In Tarot Symbolism, the Tower represents an awakening, baptism by fire, high magic and miracles. It symbolizes the Divine Fire that destroys evil and illusions while purifying the good within ourselves. It signifies the liberation from bondage, a flash of enlightenment from the Godhead. The appearance of the Tower in a spread indicates unforeseen and sudden events that will liberate you from self-imposed burdens. Sometimes this card will indicates a quarrel with another person or within yourself about the direction you want to take your life in.

The presence of this card in a spread is a sign for you to seek God within, for oftentimes you find yourself Filled with confusion, inner turmoil, and even depression. The seeking of God will end this confusion and doubt, and pour the oil of love on the troubled waters of your life. This card also indicates change, and a dramatic turn of events, leading to freedom from illusions.

In Numerology, the number 16 is a combination of 1, which is the creator or originator; and 6, which is the number of service and love. Together these numbers create 7, the number of the seeker, the mystic, one who follows the Path of Enlightenment in order to find the Logos.

What is the Spiritual Lesson or Challenge that Number 16: The Tower would teach us?

The Tower teaches us the danger of blind ambition, of letting the material world become our god. That path leads to imprisonment and isolation. Prejudice, in any form, denies us the Love we seek and need in order to survive the Illusions of the ego and the earth plane. The Tower shows us that sometimes it is necessary for us to get the "rug pulled out from under us" in order to gain our attention. When under the control of the ego, we don't realize how far we stray from the Path of Enlightenment until there is an intervention from Someone who loves us.

CHAPTER TWENTY-NINE

THE STAR: NUMBER 17

RIDER-WAITE DECK

The card represents the unlimited creative and intuitional powers of the Universal Sub-conscious mind which knows that all secrets can be revealed if one gains union with the Creator. The figure of the woman is kneeling, resting one foot on water and one foot on the ground showing balance. Water is the symbol of the Universal Life-Force. All life on this planet originated in the primeval oceans. Water is also the Universal Solvent, and can be temporarily changed to many forms then return to its original state. Water is truly a life-sustaining miraculous substance. The woman is pouring water, her gift of miracles, on the land and in the pond, showing her willingness to be of service to others. The water from the pitcher used on the land divides itself into 5 streams. These 5 streams symbolize the 5 senses of the physical body. The leg she is kneeling on forms a right angle which represents the number 4. Four is the number of foundation, order, and reason. The other foot, resting on the water, shows her reliance on the intuitive mind and its link with the Universal Sub-conscious.

The water being poured from the pitchers represent Universal Wisdom, knowledge which must be shared with the rest of humankind. It is what nurtures and sustains the human spirit, imparting strength and creativity. Her pitchers will never become empty, for her Source is the Divine Life-Force which is limitless and Infinite. The more she gives, the more there is to give. She knows that the cost of giving is receiving and when you give to others, you are really giving to yourself.

There are 7 white stars surrounding a larger 8-pointed yellow star. The 7 stars represent the 7 Chakra Centers. The larger yellow star represents the awakening of the 7 chakra centers. It is the channel for enlightenment and integrity, for joy and love, for gifts of the spirit offered to all who are willing to accept them. The purple mountains of attainment are in the distance, waiting for the shift in consciousness, which is taking place, to be completed. There is an Ibis bird in a tree behind the woman. Legend calls the Ibis bird the "Bird of Love". It serves as a bridge between heaven and earth, between dreams and reality. The rich green lushness of the land echoes the symbol of love, for green is the color of abundance and growth and represents the Heart Chakra.

MARY HANSON-ROBERTS DECK

This is one of my favorite cards in the Hanson-Roberts Deck. I love the use of color on this card and when I see it in a spread it makes me feel *good*. This is one of the best cards to use in Meditation too. It reminds me of an Enchanted Forest filled with wondrous things, a theme I have found very useful in

Meditation. In another chapter I will go into more detail on that particular form of Meditation, but for now, back to Symbolism...

The colors on this card from the Hanson-Roberts Deck are very soft and pastel. There is an aura of gentleness about this card that is soothing and relaxing. It is meant to be this way for The Star represents very special gifts. The different shadings of Blue represents hope, the preparation for a new existence or new things in one's life. The Blue shades also represent Divine Assurance, serenity, a gentle nurturing love and peace. The Violet pink and violet white of the mountains of attainment represent self-realization, creativity, intuition, and spiritual growth. The hair of the woman is a pale blond color symbolizing fertility, abundance, and ripeness. The color Blond represents the harvest, the reaping of what you have sown previously. The brilliant white of the stars represent perfection, purity, and union with the Creator. The green of the lush and fruitful plants indicates renewal, love, wisdom, and faith. The golden tones of the woman's skin symbolizes one who offers herself in selfless service to others, and offers love and understanding without judgment or conditions.

SUMMARY DEFINITION OF THE STAR

Taking all of the symbols and color symbolism into account, the following information brings together or synthesizes all of these elements so that you can utilize this knowledge more efficiently when doing a Lay-Out Spread or when using this card in Meditation.

In Tarot Symbolism, The Star represents hope, good fortune, rewards, unexpected help, and inspiration. Great Love will be given and received. Unselfish aid will be given, spiritual love will be offered. The Star also indicates potential fulfillment, bright promise and expectation, gifts of the Spirit. It is the Light of Truth unveiled and without Illusion, granting clarity of vision and spiritual insight.

On another level, the Star signifies a channel for the Higher Forces to work through. A flow of energy streaming through the opened Chakra Centers enables one to accomplish miracles. This card represents harmony and balance, attunement with the Forces of the Universe.

In Numerology, the number 17 is a combination of 1, which is the creator or originator and 7, the seeker or mystic. Combined together they create the number 8 which represents success on a material and spiritual level because the 8 vibrates to the influence of God, (as symbolized in the upright sign of Infinity).

What is the Spiritual Lesson or Challenge that Number 17---The Star would teach us?

The Star teaches us about true fulfillment and the importance of hope and encouragement. Our creativity, whether it is artistic, musical, material, etc., has its Source in the Universal Subconsciousness. Through Meditation we can easily reach the deep well of inspiration and creativity available to all who seek it. We all share the need to create, a need that will not be denied. How we channel and manifest that need is a Challenge whose roots are deep in our own subconscious, calling out to us in subtle ways.

CHAPTER THIRTY

THE MOON: NUMBER 18

RIDER-WAITE DECK

The twin towers on this card symbolize the gateway to the unknown, the boundaries of the physical body. There is a dog and a wolf, symbolizing two aspects of human nature. The dog is the controlled physical desires and the wolf represents the wild and instinctive nature of humankind. The dog is brown in color, representing practicality on the Earth Plane. The wolf is yellow with red eyes, representing the intelligence that has been activated by the fires of the Kundalini.

There is a purple sea-creature with a shell emerging from the water indicating the creative force of the Universe leaving the collective subconscious of all life, manifesting as a newly formed creature on the Earth Plane. Purple is the color of an electric raw karmic energy. It is the color of intuition and heightened awareness. The shell is a protective device for the sea creature, protection it feels it needs on the physical plane. The shell can also serve as a barrier or limitation for the creature as well.

There is a path ahead of the shellfish, a path which leads to the mountains of attainment in the distance. This is a narrow, winding path indicating that dedication and perseverance is needed when dealing with the challenges and opportunities that arise in life. The path itself is yellow demonstrating that the path is also an evolutionary one. Through the process of spiritual evolution, the shellfish will achieve the awakening it seeks as it follows the path to the mountains of attainment.

The Moon has three phases, pictured all in one on the Moon. These three intuitional phases correspond to the physical body, the mind, and the Spirit. The woman's face on the moon indicates she is asleep. This shows that through the sleep state, through our dream-walking, we come into contact with all the different aspects of "life" on all the astral planes. During our sleep state we are also vulnerable to the influences of the lower astral planes. These lower planes can be the source of nightmares, fears, and illusions.

The lower astral planes contain negative thoughts, obsessions, unevolved souls who refuse to go into the Light, and the newly dead who are on their way to the higher planes. It is this lower astral plane that the early church referred to as "purgatory". This is why it is so important that you understand the power of thoughts. If you think negative thoughts, but do not act on them, they settle in the lower astral planes. Since "like attracts like", other similar negative thoughts gather together and combine their energies and grow in strength. Thoughts are energy, and that energy continues to exist and exert influence on us.

To the unenlightened and un-awakened souls, the Moon represents the dark night of the soul. To them, the Moon offers only Illusions and causes self-deception. To the enlightened and awakened souls, the Moon represents the passageway through the abyss of the lower astral planes, and with its gentle light offers protection on the path to the higher astral realms.

MARY HANSON-ROBERTS DECK

One of the outstanding colors on this card is the greenness of the land. Green represents growth, love, abundance, and healing. It is the color of the Heart Chakra which represents balanced emotions. Through dreams and meditations we often find tremendous growth experiences. We may not always understand the lessons we learn through our dreams, but eventually the message filters down to our conscious mind where we can try to rationalize it to our heart's content.

Another outstanding color on this card is the deep indigo-purple of the sky. This color represents intuition and the higher consciousness. Indigo is the color which symbolizes the need to let go and let God. The pathway for the shellfish in this picture is golden representing soul advancement. Gold is the color of physical and material manifestation as well as the color of rejuvenation. The pool of water from which the shell-fish emerges is an Aqua Blue representing the Universal Sub-Conscious and the Womb of life.

The golden yellow rays on the Moon itself represent gifts of the Spirit and enlightenment through dreams. The violet pink horizon and gold tipped mountains of attainment symbolize the goal of self-realization can be achieved through Dream Initiation as well as through other initiations. The tears in the sky represent a cleansing, a releasing of deeply buried hurts and disappointments which have hindered progress in the past. Clutching old resentments and anger to you can lead to self-deception and disillusionment. The tears encourage the release of these self-defeating and self-limiting emotions.

SUMMARY DEFINITION OF THE MOON

Taking all of the symbols and color symbolism into account, the following information brings together or synthesizes all of these elements so that you can utilize this knowledge more efficiently when doing a Lay-Out Spread or when using this card in Meditation.

In Tarot Symbolism, The Moon represents dreams, both prophetic and initiatory in nature. It also indicates the brink of an important change, a voluntary change, an initiation which will result in an important step in spiritual evolution for the individual. The Moon also warns that Truth is being veiled by subtle Illusions, that you must look beneath the surface of situations and people in order to understand their True meaning. New doors will be opened to you, and those which have served their purpose will be closed.

This card indicates a state of bewilderment and possible deception for the individual. The imagination has been activated and is receiving mixed signals from the subconscious. There is an unfoldment of latent psychic powers which have yet to be brought up to a pure spiritual level. This causes the confusion because lower psychic powers are subject to the influence of the lower astral planes. Some people may even experience surges of fear and anxiety as they struggle to bring their intuitive emotions under the direction of the Higher Forces.

In Numerology, the number 18 is 1+8 equaling 9. 18 is a multiple of 9, and it represents the second initiation on the path of Spiritual Enlightenment.

What is the Spiritual Lesson or Challenge that Number 18: The Moon would teach us?

The Moon teaches us insights into the Soul. When we begin to develop the gifts of the Spirit, there are many temptations we face and many initiations we must confront. Some people, when faced with these "gifts", retreat from them, afraid of the changes these "gifts" will bring in their lives. Others, accepting the Challenge, begin the development, then get distracted by the phenomena and go no further. But, there are those people who embrace the changes, study the phenomena of "psychic" gifts briefly, then take these gifts to a higher level where their true power is revealed. This becomes the critical stage, for at this higher level, the temptations are even stronger and the potential for misuse is greater. How we respond to these temptations is one of the greatest challenges of the Soul we will ever face.

CHAPTER THIRTY-ONE

THE SUN: NUMBER 19

RIDER-WAITE DECK

The major symbol of this card is the face of the Sun. The Sun represents our face or head. It indicates that this card brings to a head the myriad potentials of life. The Sun also brings light and life, which is a symbol of the great Divine Power of the Universe. Truly, everything on the planet Earth is a manifestation of the Sun. It is the Sun which regenerates and activates the currents of Life, from humankind to single celled entities swimming in the rich nutrient soup of the oceans.

There are 21 rays coming from the face of the Sun. These 21 rays symbolize the 21 Major Arcana Cards, or "steps" in Tarot. There are 22 Major Arcana Cards in the Tarot, the rays represent 21 one of those cards and the Sun itself represents the 22nd card. The Sun is yellow in color representing integrity, enlightenment, the active mind and joy. Yellow is the color of the 3rd Chakra Center which deals with clear thinking, studying and all learning. The 3rd Chakra Center is called the "Solar Plexus" Chakra.

There are 4 Sunflowers, another arcane symbol of Divine Power. The number 4 alludes to the four elements of the physical plane: Air, Fire, Water and Earth. Sunflowers always turn their "Faces" to the Sun as it travels across the sky, drawing to them the "fire" or energy of the Creator and storing it in their seeds. The faces of the sunflowers are orange in color, the perfect blending of red and yellow, the merging of intelligence with the Kundalini.

The nude child riding the gray horse indicates the naked truth and innocence. The innocent never fear the truth for they have no reason to hide, (hence the nakedness of the child). The horse symbolizes solar energy with which the child has established an affinity. This affinity or attunement is demonstrated by the lack of a saddle or bridle which would physically control the horse. The fact that the horse is gray in color represents the changes we all undergo as Enlightenment dawns in our hearts and minds.

The naked child has another old connotation as well. It tells us that we should become as little children; innocent, trusting, and unconditionally loving, for we have a Father/Mother God who loves us and would take care of our needs if we would only allowed it. But many of us fear this because the Ego whispers of sacrifice and giving up control. Many of us believe that surrendering ourselves to the Will of the Creator means surrendering who we are. But the truth is only through surrendering will we really be free to discover our reality. The child is happy and carefree because the child has perfect faith and trust.

The orange banner the child carries indicates action and vibration, aspects of the Sun. This energy permeates all living things and fills them with contentment and peace, with a sense of fulfillment. This is a card of achievement, of joy and love which has been given and received.

MARY HANSON-ROBERTS DECK

With this deck, the sun is a golden yellow with three radiating rays of peach gold, pink gold, and pink. These three rays represent the 3 states of consciousness: the Sub-Conscious, Conscious, and Super-Conscious. The various shades of gold symbolize soul advancement and attainment. Peach gold represents enlightenment, restoration and the power of physical and material manifestation in one's life. The pink-gold color represents healing energies obtained from the Life-Force itself. It is a color of rejuvenation and spiritual blessings. The petals of the sunflowers are golden yellow, and the centers are brown with highlights of yellow. This color combination represents a blending of spirituality with practicality on the Earth Plane. It also represents prosperity and selfless service to others. Even the green leaves of the sunflowers are tinged with golden yellow, showing the connection between growth, love, and spiritual blessings.

The child rides a white horse in this picture. The color white symbolizes purity and perfection, unity with God and the Christ Consciousness. The two ride joyfully across an abundant green field. The child carries a sky-blue banner representing Divine Assurance and hope. It also shows the beginning of new things in one's life. There is yellow gold highlights on the banner as well representing creative and artistic expression, attainment and understanding.

SUMMARY DEFINITION OF THE SUN

Taking all of the symbols and the color symbolism into account, the following information brings together or synthesizes all of these elements so that you can utilize this knowledge more efficiently when doing a Lay-Out Spread or when using this card in Mediation.

In Tarot Symbolism, The Sun represents success, triumph, victory, gain, glory, and recovery from sickness. It indicates obstacles have been overcome and new beginnings are possible. Happiness and contentment of the spirit is enhanced by good fortune and prosperity in material affairs. The Sun represents achievement in the creative arts, in science, and in agriculture. This card symbolizes rewards for the good you have done in the past. Sometimes the presence of this card in a spread indicates a good marriage.

Growth and creativity abounds now in your life. You have developed sensitivity and re-discovered the joys of innocence. You have learned from the lessons and challenges of the past and are now ready to go on to new experiences, new opportunities. The period of doubt and deception has passed, you have come into the Sun-light after the darkness and trials of the night.

In Numerology, the number 19 is a combination of 1, which represents the originator or beginning, and the number 9 which represents the end of a cycle or learning experience. Together these two numbers add up to 10 which symbolizes a new door opening in your life.

What is the Spiritual Lesson or Challenge that Number 19: The Sun would teach us?

The Sun teaches us joy and contentment, which is the result of a light heart, a heart filled with trust and faith. The Sun teaches us about the rewards we receive when we surrender the temptations and distractions created by the Ego to the Higher Will of the Creator. Thus, unlimited and without self-deceptions, our boundless creativity results in fulfillment and accomplishment. The Sun shows us that our goal of self-realization is easier to attain than we suspected. This joyful card symbolizes the perfect union between ourselves and the Life-Force of the Universe.

CHAPTER THIRTY—TWO

JUDGEMENT: NUMBER 20

RIDER-WAITE DECK

The Key-Word for this card is "Awakening". The Arch-Angel Gabriel is calling to all humankind to awaken to their own spirituality, their own connectedness to the Universal Life-Force. The coffins represent the limitations we impose on ourselves, limitations we really do not possess. The coffins also represent the physical body and how our bodies can distract us from our true nature. This card symbolizes the concept of "Atonement", through which our past errors or "sins" are completely erased. In this aspect, the tarot card Judgement means "Renewal" or "Realization". It is a card of true immortality, for we are, in truth, deathless. We merely go through one change after another as a means of finding our way back to God.

The coffins are on water, the element which symbolizes the Universal Sub-Conscious. They are gray representing the change in consciousness required to experience a spiritual awakening. The interior of the coffins is black, symbolizing the lack of light the humans once endured. The three people in the foreground represent the three states of consciousness: Subconscious, Conscious, and Super-Conscious. The three figures are repeated again further back in the picture. The significance of the double set of three figures alludes to the Holy Trinity.

The yellow trumpet used by the Archangel is a channel through which the Word of God is made manifest on the Earth Plane. The yellow color symbolize enlightenment. There are seven lines streaming from the trumpet. These lines represent "words" designed to open the 7 Chakra Centers found on the human body. The flag hanging from the trumpet symbolizes balance and harmony of Universal energies. The mountains in the background represent the heights of mental, emotional, and spiritual attainment.

MARY HANSON-ROBERTS DECK

The Hanson-Roberts deck depicts this card without the coffins. Instead the 3 figures are seen standing in Aqua-Blue waters, welcoming the appearance of the Archangel. The color Aqua-Blue represents womb of all life. It symbolizes the limitless bounty of Nature, of the Creator. It is rich, nurturing and filled with unseen wonders. Aqua is the color of joy and happiness, a color of love and security.

Because the figures have turned their consciousness upward, they are filled with the song of joy coming from the golden trumpet. They are being blessed with hope, Divine Assurance, love, healing, growth, and a new existence. The peach gold of the sky represents soul advancement and rejuvenation. The Archangel, dressed in white robes, is emerging from violet-pink and gold clouds which symbolize restoration and self-realization. The white robes represent Union with God, purity and self-mastery.

The Archangel serves as a channel for the Creator, offering all who will listen the gift of liberation, freedom from Illusions and the deceptions of the Ego.

SUMMARY DEFINITION OF JUDGEMENT

Taking all of the symbols and color symbolism into account, the following information brings together or synthesizes all of these elements so that you can utilize this knowledge more efficiently when doing a Lay-Out Spread or when using this card in Meditation.

In Tarot Symbolism, Judgement symbolizes a major turning point, the end or conclusion of something important. It is a card of completion, of liberation from limitations. A new current for the future has appeared, promising renewal and rebirth. Fame of an intellectual nature is now possible if you should so choose it. This card also shows an ability to adapt to new circumstances or situations as they occur.

To the ancients, Judgement represented an individual who had passed very special tests of Initiation and was then called the "Twice Born". They believed the Power of the Spirit belonged to the individual who had achieved this status, granting them special knowledge and wisdom and thus required them to act responsibly with this new knowledge.

In Numerology, the number 20 is a combination of 2, which is Unity, with the number 0, which represents the God-Force in action. Together, these two numbers signify Infinity, that which has no end, a true union of Spirit with Matter.

What is the Spiritual Lesson or Challenge that Number 20: Judgement would teach us?

The Tarot Card Judgement teaches us of the gentle love and caring which the Creator has for each and every one of us, regardless of our choices or actions. Continually, throughout our lives, we are offered repeated opportunities to awaken our consciousness to the Truth, and accept the blessings offered to us. God never gives up on us, no matter how stupidly or insanely we may seem to act at times. Although God is determined we shall regain our unity with Him, He will never use force to bend us to His Will. Granting us the gift of free will, the Creator has granted us Immortality.

CHAPTER THIRTY-THREE

THE WORLD: NUMBER 21

RIDER-WAITE DECK

The Tarot Card titled "The World" represents perfection and triumph on the physical material plane. It is the final step in the Major Arcana, and culminates all of the lessons the previous cards have sought to teach. The 4 astrological symbols in the corner appeared before on #1O---The Wheel of Fortune. But now, these symbols are represented by their heads, rather than their complete bodies. This shows the Kundalini Force has been raised through the Chakra Centers and now has opened the "Crown Chakra", that center which represents Self-Realization and Unity with the Life-Force.

The Astrological symbols which appeared on the Wheel of Fortune earlier, now appear on the World, having completed their karmic tests, and now are free of karma. The signs represented are the fixed signs of Aquarius, (the man) Taurus, (the bull) Leo, (the lion) and Scorpio, (the eagle). These 4 symbols also represent the four elements: Air, Earth, Fire, and Water. These symbols also represent the 4 suits of the Minor Arcana which follows the Major Arcana. The Suit of Swords relates to the element of Air. The Suit of Pentacles relates to the element of Earth. The Suit of Wands relates to the element of Fire. And the Suit of Cups relates to the element of Water.

The woman in the center of the card, has dominion over these elements because of her elevated consciousness, her Unity with God. In both hands, she holds wands of power or "Light Wands", Channels for power to manifest on the Earth Plane. She possesses two wands to show the balance of power, the harmony necessary for attunement to the vibrations of the Universe. The woman has a purple scarf draped casually around her figure. This purple scarf represents the raw karmic voltage she has learned to use properly. Purple is the color of intuition, of letting go and letting God.

The raw electric power indicated by the color purple represents the sowing of karma, Karmic seeds the woman deliberately plants knowing what the results will be. There is a green egg-shaped wreath framing the figure of the woman, which makes reference to the seed of Life from which all things come forth. It is a symbol of Divine Power. The green color of the wreath represents growth, abundance, prosperity, and love. The wreath also represents the "crown" given to those who achieve the initiation of Spirit which gives them access to Divine Wisdom. The background is sky-blue in color representing hope and Divine Assurance. It is also the color of compassionate love.

MARY HANSON-ROBERTS DECK

The astrological symbols of the 4 fixed signs and the 4 elements are pronounced on this card. They are also a golden brown color symbolizing enlightenment blended with practicality. These signs and elements have come through many tests and initiations, and in the process now understand their function on the earth plane. They have learned the importance of practical selfless service to others, offered out of love and empathy.

The background of this card is a rich sapphire blue showing the emotions have matured. Sapphire Blue represents the promise of substance and expansion. On a high spiritual level, sapphire blue symbolizes mastery of the Ten Commandments. The color Sky-blue radiates from around the green wreath indicating hope and Divine Assurance. The center of the wreath is white representing self-mastery and union with the Creator. The woman in the center is also fully clothed in white with an Aqua blue scarf draped over her arms. The Aqua Blue color alludes to the Cosmic Womb, the source from which all life emanates. The green color of the wreath symbolizes growth, prosperity, love, and healing. It is the color of the 4th Chakra Center called the "Heart Chakra", the center of balanced love in the body. There is bands of orange wrapped in 4 different spots on the wreath. This represents energy and strength used in a positive and creative manner.

SUMMARY DEFINITION OF THE WORLD

Taking all of the symbols and color symbolism into account, the following information brings together or synthesizes all of these elements so that you can utilize this knowledge more efficiently when doing a Lay-Out Spread or when using this card in Meditation.

In Tarot Symbolism, the World represents attainment, achieving self-awareness. It is completion in the highest terms, success in one's undertaking. The World represents the path of liberation, freedom obtained through self-mastery. A longed for goal is reached, triumph of one's hopes and dreams. The presence of this card in a spread can indicate a change of residence as well.

The World also indicates love and happiness arising out of the union of soulmates. There will be movement in your affairs, movement in the direction you wish for. You are in control of your life. The World is a sign of karmic law: "As you sow...so shall you reap." You are in the process of reaping the seeds you have sown before. On a higher level, this card represents the longed for union between ourselves and our Source, (God).

In Numerology, the number 21 is a combination of number 2+1, resulting in the number 3 which represents creative expression, happiness, and enthusiasm for life.

What is the Spiritual Lesson or Challenge that Number 21: The World would teach us?

The World teaches us the meaning of Synthesis or the Union of what seems to be diverse elements coming together to form a whole, to experience completion. This is a card of perfection and self-realization. The tarot card titled "the World" also represents the seeds of Karma, creativity, and the intuitional mind. This is the final step of the Major Arcana, what all the other cards have been leading to. If the lessons learned previously have been implemented properly and in a positive manner, those "seeds" will bring great rewards. The World symbolizes the Cycle of Life and the opportunities we are offered for advancement. It is our choice whether we act on these opportunities or not.

CHAPTER THIRTY-FOUR

SUIT OF WANDS

The basic nature of Wands is progressive, future-oriented, energetic, and creative. Wands represent growth and awareness, progress and advancement. Their element is Fire, which can warm and sustain life, or consume and destroy it. The use of this power is always the decision or choice of the individual who activates a Wand Tarot Card. Wands are associated with the Astrological Fire signs of Aries, Leo and Sagittarius.

The Wands pictured on the Tarot Cards are always in flower, or are bearing leaves, symbolizing growth, new life, new beginnings, and the cycle of renewal. Wands are also associated with creative ideas, with writing, art, science, and agriculture. Because of the basic nature of Wands, they are associated with the search for spiritual enlightenment. Wands are connected with the desire for wisdom and knowledge. The Wand stand for spiritual power inherent in all humankind and in all sentient creatures. The Mary Hanson-Roberts Deck refers to the Suit of Wands as the Suit of Rods. These terms mean exactly the same thing, so for the sake of simplicity, I will continue to use the term "Wands" even when referring to the Hanson-Roberts Deck.

KING OF WANDS

RIDER-WAITE DECK

The major focus of this card is the King seated on a throne, looking into the distance or into the future, contemplating what actions to take next. The back of his throne is decorated with Lions and Salamanders, creatures which are associated with the element of Fire and with the Fire Signs in Astrology. Leo, (the lion), is a fixed sign in astrology, denoting the fixed laws of the Universe, laws the King is aware of and uses properly.

The Salamander sitting near the king's throne and the salamander designs which appear on his robes of state, symbolize his ability to control and direct the lower nature, the fiery physical side of our natures, the Kundalini Force. The Salamanders on his robe are biting their tails, creating a circle which represents the cycles of life, and the potential of the God-Force to manifest desires on the earth plane.

The King is holding a live, leaf bearing Wand. This Wand represents the Spiritual Power that all enlightened creatures possess. The Wand serves as a channel for the Will of the Creator when the will of the individual using the wand is in attunement with that Creative Force. This wand can be traced back through the Major Arcana to the wand of spiritual arcane knowledge which both the Magician and the Hermit possessed.

The King wears a yellow crown symbolizing clear thinking and the active mind. Yellow is the color of integrity and enlightenment, qualities the King of Wands possesses. There is a great deal of orange in the picture. Orange is the color of energy and good judgment. It also rules the emotions and appetite. The King also wears green boots and has a long green collar around his neck. Green is the color of growth, abundance, prosperity, love, and most importantly, of balance. The King has learned how to balance his fiery nature with intelligence and good judgment.

MARY HANSON-ROBERTS DECK

The Wand held by the King in this picture is ready to burst into flower. The bud is a violet pink color, representing spiritual growth and attainment. Violet Pink also indicates the harnessing of creative forces for the benefit of others. There are red strings tied to the base of the flower on the wand representing new beginnings, new opportunities for self-fulfillment. The wand itself is brown, representing the Earth Plane and stability. Brown is the color of security.

The salamanders on the King's robes are an evergreen color. Evergreen symbolizes creative energy and generosity. This color also represents endurance, faith and strength against all opposition. It is the color of triumph and attainment. The sky is a rich peach gold showing the advancement of the soul through self-control and the proper use of The Kundalini. The dark brown pyramids in the background represent eternal wisdom, and the struggle to obtain it.

SUMMARY DEFINITION OF THE KING OF WANDS

In Tarot Symbolism, this card indicates an honest, loyal, ardent man of action who controls the Wand of Power for spiritual and physical gain. He generally represents a man whose Sun or Ascendant is in Aries, Leo or Sagittarius. However, it can also represent a man whose astrological chart has a heavy fire sign dominance, though not necessarily as a Sun sign or Ascendant.

The King of Wands has qualities of generosity, impetuosity, pride, and swiftness. He is handsome, passionate, and agile in mind in body, though sometimes he is too hasty. But he is a romantic at heart. The King of Wands is a future-oriented individual and has the ability to foresee the results of present choices.

This card also indicates a good marriage or a proposal. There is a possibility of an unexpected heritage. It can also indicate passion and physical desires.

What is the Spiritual Lesson or Challenge that the King of Wands would teach us?

The King of Wands teaches us the importance of learning how to properly use the gifts of the Spirit and to control the Kundalini force we all possess. We need to learn to harness our desires and our will in a direction that brings us unity with the Creative Life-Force of the Universe.

QUEEN OF WANDS

RIDER-WAITE DECK:

The Queen sits on the throne of Fire, possessing the power to manifest on the Earth Plane. She sits with her legs spread apart, symbolizing her openness and receptiveness to Divine Influence. She wears a yellow gown and has a yellow crown. The color yellow represents the active mind in tune with the intuitive and Creative Forces of the Universe. Clear thinking and enlightenment are also attributes of the color yellow.

In one hand the Queen is holding a sunflower representing her attunement and affinity for Nature, as well as her obedience to the Will of God. Sunflowers are the symbol of Divine Fire, the power of manifestation on the Earth Plane. The Queen and Nature work in cooperation with each other, benefiting all involved. The Queen intimately knows the rhythms of nature and intuitively understands the delicate balance that must be maintained.

Like the King, the Queen also holds the living wand of Spiritual Power, symbolizing her unity with the Creator. A black cat sits at her feet, alert and watchful. Cats are very psychic and intuitive animals, sensing energy patterns and a "presence" before we do. The Queen has at her feet the intuition and guidance from the astral realms which she needs to govern or counsel others wisely.

MARY HANSON-ROBERTS DECK

All of the colors on this particular card are warm fiery shades, hinting at the element of Fire which the Queen of Wands has learned to control. At her throat is a large Star-Ruby. The Star-Ruby symbolizes penetrative wisdom. It represents a self-knowing and the ability to communicate the essence of knowledge learned from the lessons an individual has met and mastered. This gem-stone, because of its symbolism, expresses perfectly the qualities of the Queen of Wands.

There are a lot of golds and golden-brown colors on this card representing the proper use of the gifts of the Spirit. The Queen has attained her position of leadership through her own soul-advancement and self-mastery. The mountains in the distance represent lessons she has mastered and now can pass on the knowledge she gleaned from those various experiences. The subtle yellow hues permeating the card represent clear thinking and an active mind in concert with the creative forces of the Universe

The back of her throne has a large solar disk with tongues of red flame radiating outward. This represents Divine Fire and the Kundalini Force. The Queen has gained mastery over her own Kundalini nature, and has raised up through the Chakra Centers of the body to ignite the fires of the Crown Chakra, opening her up to the collective Intuitive Sub-Conscious of the Universe. The Queen is attuned to Nature, at one with the physical body, and at one with the Creator of all life. The Queen has the power to attract what she wants out of life to her.

SUMMARY DEFINITION OF THE QUEEN OF WANDS

This card indicates a woman of adaptability, persistent energy, calm authority who has the power to attract. She is generous, but impatient at times of opposition. Generally this card indicates clairvoyant abilities. It also indicates success in undertakings and a loving personality. She exercises control over the natural forces and is successful in business matters. This card generally indicates a woman who has a astrological chart dominated by fire signs or has the Sun, Moon, or Ascendant in Aries, Leo or Sagittarius.

What is the Spiritual Lesson or Challenge the Queen of Wands would teach us?

The Queen of Wands would teach us the importance of patience. Learning to control the impulsive, aggressive side of our nature, and gracefully accepting the "time-table" of the Creator rather than our own "time-table" is a necessary step in our spiritual advancement. The Queen of Wands was not always patient and accepting, it took many lessons, many "mountains to cross" before she learned how to control that aspect of her nature. It is the same for us.

KNIGHT OF WANDS

RIDER-WAITE DECK

The Knight of Wands is dressed in full armor, ready to do battle with the Illusions of the Earth Plane. His tunic, which is yellow, shows the active mind, intelligence and enlightenment which guides him on his quest. Yellow is also the color of clear thinking showing that even though he has a fiery temperament, he has learned how to channel it constructively. The symbol of the salamander biting its tail on his tunic indicates an initiation which has been passed, a test or challenge to the Spirit which has been met with success and honor.

There are pyramids in the distance which represent the vast storehouse of arcane knowledge contained in the Akashic Records. This knowledge is available to all who seek it, providing they are willing to attune themselves to the Universal Sub-Conscious. Pyramids are also symbols of the mysteries of life, mysteries still unsolved even after all these centuries. Some scholars believe the pyramids are energy collectors and use the energy collected in unique ways. They believe pyramids regenerate living tissue and activate the intuitional mind.

The Knight rides a powerful horse representing the Kundalini which has been balanced under the guidance of the active mind. He carries a wand as a symbol of his Divine Power, power which must be used correctly and therefore represents a choice of actions to the Knight; for he is on a quest for Divine Truth and Wisdom. He has the potential to choose to join the Forces of Light or the Forces of Darkness.

MARY HANSON-ROBERTS DECK:

With this deck, the Knight is dressed in rich deep golden armor which represents soul advancement. The active mind has achieved union with the Universal Sub-Conscious and true wisdom is now possible. Gold is the color of attainment and also indicates the power of physical and material manifestation on the Earth Plane.

The Knight is a dedicated and determined Warrior for the Forces of Light. He knows how to direct his energies toward the cause of the righteous and no task is to difficult for this Knight to attempt for he carries the flowering wand of Divine power on his quest.

The other dominant colors on this card are orange and red indicating healing energy, a combination of intelligence and energy. Red represents desires, sexual energy and physical passion. It also indicates a healthy life force, along with a temper. Since the Knight wears a red mantle loosely clasped to his shoulders over the golden armor, it indicates he has gained mastery over his own "Kundalini" force, or the "Root Chakra".

In the background, the pyramids and the land around them, is dark violet in color. This color indicates that the pyramids contain the "keys" to self-realization. Violet is the color of intuition, creativity and the higher consciousness. There is a golden dragon on the top of the Knight's helmet which indicates his allegiance with the Divine Forces. The position of the golden dragon is related to the opening of the Crown Chakra.

SUMMARY DEFINITION OF THE KNIGHT OF WANDS

This card symbolizes a swift, strong, and impulsive young man or woman who has strong astrological ties to the fire signs of the Zodiac. The Knight is generous, noble, just and has a strong sense of humor. However, since Knights deal with the Ego, this card indicates the individual in question has a dual nature. On one hand they are kind and generous as a lover, but they could also be cruel and, in extreme cases, brutal. The Knight is hasty in all he/she does.

The Knight of Wands represents success after difficulties or challenges. Sudden decisions, change of residence, a trip of some kind is possible. Knights, in all the 4 suits, symbolize the coming or going of an important matter in your life. Someone who brings something new or disturbing into the home environment.

What is the Spiritual Lesson or Challenge the Knight of Wands would teach us?

The Knight of Wands teaches us of the consistent attempts made by the Ego to surround us with Illusions. All of us are potential Warriors for the Forces of Light, but the Ego is always trying to subtly bring us into the ranks of the Forces of Darkness. We can rid ourselves of the temptations created by the Ego through Union with the Divine Mind and through gaining our goal of "self-realization"

PAGE OF WANDS

RIDER-WAITE DECK

The figure of the Page is in a classic pose of a messenger. The Page can be either a very young male or female. He or She stands fearlessly, wearing the salamander robe of Divine Protection. Again, there are pyramids in the distance representing the store-house of all Universal Knowledge or the Akashic Records. The wand the Page holds, symbolizes beginnings, and the Page is announcing the beginning of a new enterprise or endeavor.

MARY HANSON-ROBERTS DECK

This time, the Page is right next to the Pyramids as he/she delivers the messages from the Universal Sub-Conscious. Around the neck, the Page is wearing a symbol of Divine Fire and Creativity, indicating that he/she is under the protection of the Divine Life-Force and is a willing and eager servant to this powerful Force. The Page has developed a special attunement with the Creative aspect of the Divine Fire.

One of the major colors on this card is golden brown representing the blending of enlightenment with practicality and strength on the Earth Plane. The sky is a golden yellow signifying the active mind or intelligence at work combined with integrity. The Page wears a cloak of orange-red showing the development of discipline over the Kundalini Nature, though the Page has yet to attain complete mastery of this force. The green belt around the waist and on the hat indicates love, growth, and healing.

SUMMARY DEFINITION OF THE PAGE OF WANDS

This Page is a bearer of tidings, messages, letters, or hasty news of importance to the individual. The information brought can be about announcements such as the announcement of a birth, a new beginning or an offer. The Page brings good news, promising pleasure and satisfaction to the individual.

The Page is a messenger who has a nature that is sudden in love or anger. They are enthusiastic, courageous, individualistic, brilliant, daring and have a great deal of energy. In emotional situations, the Page's simple eagerness implies a faithful lover eager to tell of their love. Wands indicate beginnings, and the Page especially indicates the start of projects or love affairs. The Page can represent either a male or female. The individual represented by the Page is youthful, either in chronological age or in personality. Being a Wand, the person represented by this card has a strong Fire Element in their astrological chart or has the Sun, Moon, or Ascendant in a Fire Sign.

What is the Spiritual Lesson or Challenge the Page of Wands would teach us?

The Page of Wands teaches us the importance of enthusiasm and courage when approaching any aspect of our lives. These two qualities are not only a gift to yourself, but a gift to those around you who may need that spark of energy in order to shake off feelings of inadequacy. If we approach the varied circumstances in our lives with a spirit of adventure and the expectation of miracles rather than with a "Why me?" or "Not again!" attitude, we will reap far more benefits while demonstrating to others the miracles awaiting them.

ACE OF WANDS

RIDER-WAITE DECK

The picture on this card shows the Hand of God emerging from a cloud offering a living wand, the wand of Divine Power. This Wand represents creativity, beginnings, and enterprise. Some of the leaves are floating to the ground denoting sparks of Divine Inspiration, the descent of Spirit to the physical Earth Plane. In the distance, there is a fortress or castle high on a hill top. This indicates the goal of a journey or enterprise, the attainment of one's desires. The Ace of Wands symbolizes a gift from God to the individual.

MARY HANSON-ROBERTS DECK
The Wand in this picture is almost in full flower, suggesting the abundance of creativity and inspiration that is being offered to you. The deep purple clouds in the sky, edged with gold represents the Super-Consciousness and intuition working together toward enlightenment and soul advancement. These two colors together also indicate the power of physical and material manifestation on the earth plane. The clouds appear to be giving way to the power and majesty of the Sun, symbol of Divine Fire and the Creator. This symbolism represents the limitless Source from which all miracles or gifts are manifested.

SUMMARY DEFINITION OF THE ACE OF WANDS
The Ace of Wands represents the Hand of God offering something of a creative nature to the individual. It could be the beginning of an enterprise, an artistic creation, or perhaps even the beginning of a family, a birth. The Ace symbolizes bursts of elemental energy, a charging up, so to speak, from God.

The spark of inspiration and creation is represented by the Ace. It indicates a letter, a book, an important piece of writing, perhaps an important contract. There is activity stirring in one's life, wisdom from above, energy, strength and force. For beginnings and the start of enterprises, no other card could indicate the potential fulfillment better. Important news, a revelation is also indicated. The Ace shows something wonderful which can not be taken away from the individual.

What is the Spiritual Lesson or Challenge the Ace of Wands would teach us?
Since the Ace of Wands represents the Hand of God offering us opportunities for attainment and fulfillment, it is important that we learn to ask for these gifts. "What so ever ye ask of your Father, ye shall receive." God will not interfere in our lives. If we want something, we must ask for it, through prayer, meditation, affirmations, or any method which feels comfortable and "right".

TWO OF WANDS

RIDER-WAITE DECK
The man who is standing with the world in his hands represents unlimited opportunity for achievement in any endeavor he chooses to pursue on the material plane. He is standing on the battlements of the castle which appeared in the Ace of Wands, indicating he has the material success he desires. He has two wands of power at his disposal, one he holds, the other he keeps in reserve. In the background, there are well tended gardens and part of the mountain range where the castle itself has been built. The garden symbolizes the hard work the man has done in previous lifetimes which he is reaping in this lifetime.

The man is gazing outwardly. He has reached a point in his life where he is facing a crossroads, an important choice. He has asked for and received the opportunities needed to achieve material success. Now, he is wondering if there isn't more to life than he first envisioned. "What profit a man if he gain the whole world and lose his soul?"

The battlements are gray in color, indicating a change or transition about to take place. The man is wearing a long outer robe of purple. Purple is the color of electric, raw karmic voltage. This karmic voltage pertains to the seeds he is now planting or sowing. His actions and choices are at a critical phase in his development. Is material success alone worthwhile? Is it fulfilling? Why am I empty? Why do I feel so alone? These are questions the man is asking himself as he contemplates the world in his hand.

MARY HANSON-ROBERTS DECK

The domination of reds and golds on this card shows how the man has been seduced by the material world even though spiritual enlightenment had been obtained before. The color combination shows one who has strayed from the spiritual path to become entangled with the illusions of the material world. Although the man has achieved success and power on the physical plane, there is a feeling of emptiness within, a feeling of separateness which leaves the man in a melancholy frame of mind.

The red roses symbolize desires and the white lily represents the power of thought and how ideas, stimulated by desires, become manifested. The dark gray of the castle walls reflect the inner turmoil and struggle for change taking place within the man. The reddish-orange of the sky shows the power and energy that has been unleashed. This energy is very strong and can overwhelm an individual very quickly, leading one from the spiritual path before you are even aware of it. Gray is also the color of initiation, and this too, is merely an initiation on the spiritual path.

SUMMARY DEFINITION OF THE TWO OF WANDS

This card indicates unlimited opportunities for material achievement, success, and fulfillment of a purpose or goal. But, this card also shows that riches carry with them a heavy responsibility. This is a card of success, yet the individual may feel cut off or out of touch with the "real" world because of the preoccupation with the material world. The individual possesses kindness and generosity but may have a proud and/or unforgiving nature. The Two of Wands also indicates creative and artistic ability which may not be utilized by the individual. Inherent in this card is a caution against pride or arrogance. This is a card of strong ambition, strong desire and the will to succeed.

What is the Spiritual Lesson or Challenge the Two of Wands would teach us?

The Two of Wands teaches us the heavy responsibility we have when we achieve material success. Keeping an even balance between spirituality and materialism is not easy, it takes a great deal of strength and determination. It takes very little to tip the scales toward materialism for the temptations to do so are enormous. But, this card is also a testing for the individual, for even if we have "strayed" from the path, we are always given opportunities to change our minds and direction. Eventually, all paths lead back to the Creator. Some are just more meandering than others.

THREE OF WANDS

RIDER-WAITE DECK
The man standing on the bluff overlooking the sea is waiting for his ships to come into port. These ships will be bringing him material prosperity and the realization of his deep faith and trust in God. The ships are the ideas, thoughts, and beginnings the man has made toward his goal. It takes time for the seeds of ideas to germinate and it takes time for an enterprise or endeavor to get past the planning stages and into actual implementation.

Wands stand for spiritual power and the number 3 stands for the Holy Trinity. The man standing with the 3 wands represents maturity, an inner strength that comes from his union with God. He has at his disposal the three wands of Divine Power or Energy. The sea on which the ships are sailing is golden symbolizing spiritual blessings and advancement. Again, the number 3 symbolizing the power of the Holy Trinity is found in the 3 ships.

MARY HANSON-ROBERTS DECK
The merchant has sent his ships, (or wishes) out to sea, trusting that God will see to his needs. The Sea represents the Collective or Universal Sub-Conscious. And behold, as the ships return to the harbor, they are anointed with the Golden Rays of the Sun, the blessings of God, symbolizing the realization of hopes. The golds, rich shades of blue, greens, blue-white, and indigo are all colors promising abundance, divine assurance, hope, and fulfillment. This is a card which represents the rewards of those who are patient, and have absolute trust in the Creator. The figure on the card has learned to ask for or express his needs to God and now waits patiently for the answers.

SUMMARY DEFINITION OF THE THREE OF WANDS
This card represents success and fulfillment after struggles. It is the realization of hopes. The three emphasizes the successful beginning of a project or creative endeavor. Business and commercial opportunities will be presented to the individual. Possible partnership or contract may be offered, assistance may come from someone already established or in power or control.

The Three of Wands indicates communications, instructions, messages, writing, postage, and letters. It signifies the end of troubles and the suspension of or ending of adversity. There will be cooperation in business, trade or commercial activities.

What is the Spiritual Lesson or Challenge the Three of Wands would teach us?

The Three of Wands teaches us the virtue of patience and faith. We cannot succeed if we are not willing to turn obstacles into stepping stones, or if we are afraid to try because it may be too difficult. We must be willing to make that first step toward a goal, and acknowledge the fact we do not walk alone as we journey to that goal. The dreams we have to achieve can be realized if we do not allow ourselves to be defeated before we even start. Fear of failure and the subconscious fear of success are powerful influences, but can affect us only if we allow it to.

FOUR OF WANDS

RIDER-WAITE DECK
In numerology, the number 4 represents foundation, the beginning of stability and form. The number 4 symbolizes a base from which to build and expand. Without foundations or a solid base, you cannot build anything that will have lasting value. On this card, there are four wands planted in the ground serving as a foundation for a canopy of flowers, representing a celebration. Things have come to completion or fruition. There are people in the background coming toward the canopy bearing more flowers and more fruits of their labor.

There is a joyful feeling in the air. The dark night of the soul has passed and the clear light of day has arrived to dispel the darkness. This card also represents the harvest or reaping of seeds or deeds initiated earlier. The patience the people have exhibited is being rewarded. The red roofed towers in the walled city symbolize that desires and hopes have been realized. This card represents a time of great happiness and fulfillment.

MARY HANSON-ROBERTS DECK
The entire picture on this card is one of absolute joy and happiness. The colors alone show the abundance, prosperity, joy, and love that is promised by this card. The main body of the wands is brown in color indicating security, power and steadfastness on the Earth Plane. Brown is the color of physical and mental satisfaction, and receiving recognition from one's peers for creative endeavors or for services rendered.

However, mixed with this material security indicated by the brown colors, is the abundant soft pink flowers and buds on the wands themselves. Soft pink is the color of devotion, tenderness, reverence and sensitivity to the needs of other Life-forms. Soft Pink represents a nurturing compassionate love, an empathy that extends itself deeply. The sky is a soft golden yellow representing enlightenment and soul advancement.

The white castle in the background, with the red capped towers, indicates purified desires and the attainment of those desire for there is a bridge which spans the golden waters of the moat leading to the other side. The golden waters of the moat represents spiritual blessings. The hard work and persistence of the people have resulted in such wonderful rewards they feel a need to celebrate and give thanks for the blessings they have received.

SUMMARY DEFINITION OF THE FOUR OF WANDS
This card symbolizes celebration, previous actions which have led to fulfillment. This is a card of completion, of fruition. Desires are realized, prosperity and the longed for hope or wish has come to pass. It indicates love and romance, the union of two minds, a possible coming marriage. Dreams which are fulfilled, satisfaction in love or partnership. The four of wands indicates an increase and unexpected good fortune.

This is a card of reaping, reaping the good seeds of Karma. The presence of this card in a Lay-Out Spread indicates satisfaction and joy. Something the individual has been working towards is now possible and will bring great happiness. Hard work and persistence is being rewarded. There are or will be settlements in the individual's favor. Struggles and difficulties are finally over.

What is the Spiritual Lesson or Challenge the Four of Wands would teach us?

The Four of Wands teach us the rewards of patience, trust, and persistence. We can achieve our hopes, wishes and desires if we are willing to make a commitment to their realization. Naturally, it is important that we clarify what goals we want to achieve in life before we set out to plant the seeds. But this card shows us the promise of a bountiful harvest, the realization of our hopes and dreams if we lay the proper foundation for them. The more your goals or dreams affect the lives of others in positive, helpful ways, the more bountiful the harvest or realization of the dream will be.

FIVE OF WANDS

RIDER-WAITE DECK

There are five rowdy youths brandishing their wands of power as if in combat or competition. In the Tarot, fives generally represent drastic or dramatic change, an upheaval in one's life. Sometimes this upheaval causes a loss of some kind or forces closed a door or chapter in your life which has served its purpose and no longer has any relevancy. Since the suit of Wands represents the fire signs of the Zodiac and the element of Fire which, if unchecked or not controlled properly can cause a disaster through its consuming flames, the five of wands represents a dramatic change influenced by the unchanneled energy.

In a way, this picture can be called the battle of life. If these youths would stop attacking one another and join together in cooperation, they could accomplish so much more. Instead, they are wasting their energy resources in nonproductive, even destructive ways. This card can refer to the internal battle we wage with the different aspects of our own personality as one aspect tries to gain dominance over the whole. This card can also refer to the external battle we wage with others in the business world, in our environment, within our family or in our relationships with others.

Wands represent energy and desire, but the number five indicates that this power can be used negatively by the individual, or those around the individual. The nature of this card is restless, lacking serenity. The real symbolism of this card, or the lesson if you will, is that in attacking others, you are only attacking yourself. If others attack you, they are really attacking themselves and do not realize it. You are one with all creation and to attack any part of that creation is to attack your own invulnerability. This is an important lesson to learn.

MARY HANSON-ROBERTS DECK

The colors on this card have dark tones to them as if the Light is being obscured by Illusions. There are a lot of reddish brown colors which indicate past-life violence, envy and jealousy. Reddish brown is a "karmic" color in that it indicates situations in one's life that are a direct result of actions taken in the past, either in this lifetime or in a previous one. This karmic backlash could have been initiated by the individual, or committed to the individual who now has to deal with releasing and letting go of that energy.

There is also the color bronze present on this card. Bronze is kind of a dirty gold color and represents unresolved karma. The color Bronze indicates the need to adapt the laws of moderation on the Earth Plane into one's life. The red overtones represent the unleashing of the Kundalini in undisciplined ways. It is a true axiom that if humankind cannot make love, it will make war, the result of misdirected kundalini energy.

SUMMARY DEFINITION OF THE FIVE OF WANDS
The Five of Wands portrays the battle of life, the struggles generated by the illusions of the Earth Plane. This card represents mental restlessness, competition, and lack of serenity. It is a card of quarreling and strife, indicating there are obstacles to be overcome and challenges to be faced. The Five of Wands can also indicate divorce, legal proceedings or discussions along that line. However, the five of wands shows a change for the better in one's business circumstances and success in financial speculation, usually won through vigorous competition.

What is the Spiritual Lesson or Challenge the Five of Wands would teach us?
The Five of Wands teaches us the price we pay when we concentrate all our energies in competing with others, determined to vanquish our adversaries. We lose our serenity, our balance when all we focus on is winning at any cost. Certainly you will win, but at what price? And how long will you maintain your position as "king of the mountain"? There will always be someone who comes along to challenge your right to be at the top, to be the leader.

SIX OF WANDS

RIDER-WAITE DECK
The horseman in this picture is crowned with a laurel wreath, the ancient symbol of heroes. He also carries another laurel wreath on his wand of power. He is on his way to claim his lady, and crown her with laurel, binding them together. The hero has completed his quest, he is triumphant and victorious and now he can claim the woman he made a pledge to. The people surrounding him are cheering him on, happy that he has achieved his goals.

The others marching at his side share his victory, his triumph. They are the witnesses to his spiritual attainment, and he serves as an example for them. The hero leads them to their path of enlightenment with confidence, knowing that because he succeeded, so can they. His purple robe symbolizes the Super-Consciousness, union with the Creator. It is a color of Intuition and raw karmic power. This raw karmic power represents the sowing of karmic seeds. The hero is making choices and initiating opportunities which will benefit him in the future as well as in the present.

MARY HANSON-ROBERTS DECK

The golden glory of the Sun, symbol of Divine Fire, highlights the triumphant procession of the hero. The golden colors symbolize integrity, enlightenment, and advancement of the soul. This radiant Light bathes the horseman as he comes closer to his goal. He rides a brown horse which represents his mastery over the physical and material desires of the Earth Plane and his own lower nature. He also wears a golden helmet crowned with a green laurel wreath. The green indicates growth on the Earth Plane, abundance and love.

He wears a red robe over his armor, symbolizing the Kundalini. Red is the color of desires, sexual energies and physical passion. This cloak or robe rests lightly on his shoulders for he has learned to use the Kundalini force in a creative and constructive manner. In this picture, the hero himself carries 3 wands, one in his hand and two strapped to his back in reserve. The number three is a symbol for the Holy Trinity, the number of completion and unity with the Source of all Life.

SUMMARY DEFINITION OF THE SIX OF WANDS

This card represents victory after strife, good news, advancement in the arts and sciences. Sixes in the Minor Arcana deal with communication and gifts and the six of wands deals with rewards, and/or settlements in one's favor. The Six of Wand symbolizes hope, wish, desire, and expectations are fulfilled. This is a card of great news, a crown of hopes fulfilled. Another connotation of the six of wands has to do with a good marriage, an alliance or partnership with someone that brings great happiness and satisfaction to you. This is a card of love, gain and success.

What is the Spiritual Lesson or Challenge the Six of Wands would teach us?

The six of Wands teaches us that we are all potential heroes and heroines. The way we use the gifts of Divine Fire within us, how we creatively express the Life-Force flowing through us, is what makes heroes and heroines. Each of us has a unique talent or ability that must be developed and used with faith and confidence. The sense of fulfillment and achievement that results when we are willing to try and express our creativity serves as an inspiration to others who may not have tried their "creative wings". In this way, we serve not only our own needs, but the needs of others, giving them "proof" they can succeed if they will only have the faith to try.

SEVEN OF WANDS

RIDER-WAITE DECK

This is a card of fierce determination. The figure has a position of advantage where they are standing. The one wand the figure holds is the symbol of his union with God, with the blessings he has received to use on the Earth Plane. The six wands facing him represent the 6 senses that humankind has to develop, (taste, touch, sound, sight, smell, and psychic or intuitive sense). However, these 6 senses have only been developed to the lowest common denominator. The man or the Seeker is not about to be seduced into accepting only these senses. He knows there is something more, he knows that the spiritual realm is what he truly wishes to achieve. Seven is the number of the Mystic, the master of arcane wisdom.

The Seven of Wands symbolizes the determination to SEE, to see beyond the illusions of the Earth Plane to the True Reality which is the Seeker's right, his inheritance from the Creator. He stands above the temptation to settle for just the physical and mental promises of the lower psychic realms. The 7th wand he holds, which represents the Spiritual Ideal, is all he needs as protection from the temptations of the Earth Plane, the plane of Illusions. He uses the 7th wand as a shield, not as a weapon against someone else. He is not afraid of the tricks or illusions the other wands manifest, because he stands above them and his Faith serves as a mirror to reflect back what is sent to him.

MARY HANSON-ROBERTS DECK

The look on this youth's face is one of eager anticipation. The youth knows that with the power of God behind them, there is nothing they cannot overcome or achieve. Nothing can stand before the forces of Light, all illusions must give way before the Light of Truth. The violet pink and gold color of the sky signify spiritual growth and self-realization. Enlightenment and integrity are the gifts which protect and guide the youth on his or her path in life.

The youth wears a brown cloak which indicates steadfastness and practicality on the Earth Plane. The golden brown colors of this card symbolize the blending of enlightenment with practicality and strength. This color indicates one who is spiritual, but who has their feet firmly planted on the ground. The youth is a spiritual Warrior for the Forces of Light. The high ground the youth stands on is a crystal gray color, the color of transition, change, and initiation.

SUMMARY DEFINITION OF THE SEVEN OF WANDS

This card indicates certain victory against all opposition. Victory obtained through courage and determination. This card shows a position of advantage for the individual. The presence of this card in a spread often indicates negotiations and/or contracts. The Seven of Wands also represents an individual who is determined and who can be stubborn as well.

What is the Spiritual Lesson or Challenge the Seven of Wands would teach us?

The Seven of Wands teaches us how steadfastness in the face of opposition or illusions will result in ultimate victory for us. Keeping our eyes on the Light, and ignoring the distractions that arise on the Path, is a sure way to reach our ultimate goal. It is not necessary to stop and fight against illusions, simply ignoring them takes away their strength and their power. Fighting the illusions empowers them with energy.

EIGHT OF WANDS

RIDER-WAITE DECK

This picture shows 8 wands moving swiftly through the air. Their direction is East, towards the source of Light, aiming to bring enlightenment to the conscious and subconscious mind of the Seeker. The green earth represents the Conscious Mind and the winding blue river of water represents the Subconscious Mind. The wands themselves, symbolize growth and Divine Fire. The lowest wand is almost touching the earth which represents the adage, "As above, so below."

This card also represents the approach to a goal, the conclusion of a matter which is in the favor of the Seeker. The wands themselves, imply swiftness and movement in the affairs of the individual, but under the direction and guidance of the Creator. The sky-blue background of the card represents Divine hope and assurance. And the wands, representing the Divine Fire of the Creator symbolizes action being taken concerning the hopes and wishes of the individual.

MARY HANSON-ROBERTS DECK

The direction of the approaching wands is more steeply depicted on this card. This represents the decent of Spirit into the Earth Plane. It is the flowering of spiritual potentials, of growth and love. Soft pink, the color of the flower tipped wands indicates a nurturing love, tenderness, reverence and compassion. These qualities are being offered to the individual. The rich golds and greens on this card echo the offers of love, peace and harmony the individual has been searching for.

SUMMARY DEFINITION OF THE EIGHT OF WANDS

This card represents Great Hope and rapid movement toward the individual's goals or hopes. This is a card of swiftness, and great haste. The eight of wands also represents messages and opportunities. It can also indicate the arrows of love, or action taken in a love affair as in a declaration of intent. Proposals made and accepted. A journey reaching its end. This is a card of freedom and joy.

What is the Spiritual Lesson or Challenge the Eight of Wands would teach us?

The Eight of Wands reminds us of how quickly our prayers can be answered if we seek for goals that benefit others as well as ourselves. All that is necessary to receive answers to our prayers or requests is the belief that they will be answered.

NINE OF WANDS

RIDER-WAITE NECK

The number 9 represents how we deal with problems and with the compromises that problems sometimes demand of us. The figure in this picture has obviously been in a struggle of some kind. There is a shield of 8 wands behind him, and he holds the 9th wand in his hand. The shield of wands serves as a barrier the individual has struggled to plant between himself and the illusions of the earth plane. It has not been easy for the figure on the card to accomplish this, his weariness is evident in the way he leans on the wand in his hand.

MARY HANSON-ROBERTS DECK

The colors of the sky in the background indicate the dawn of a new day, the forces of Light overcoming the darkness of Illusions. The power of the Light has come to deliver the figure depicted on the card from difficulties and problems caused by the physical earth plane. The evergreen color behind the wands promises release and freedom to the individual, hinting at the renewal of spirit the individual will undergo.

SUMMARY DEFINITION OF THE NINE OF WANDS

This card depicts strength and persistence, success after opposition and strife, the passing of an initiation. The nine of wands can also represent recovery from illness. It implies latent power both physical and spiritual. The nine of wands shows preparedness, responsibility, and recognition for achievements. In numerology, nines represent the ending of a cycle, the completion of a goal. It is also a time of transition, a time of subtle transformation.

What is the Spiritual Lesson or Challenge the Nine of Wands would teach us?

The Nine of Wands shows us that many experiences on the Earth Plane require strength and persistence. Not all lessons are pleasant ones mainly because of our perception of them. If we can find the Seed of Light, even in the darkest of situations, we have found the way to banish the darkness from us. But to do this takes strength and persistence, fear only makes it harder to accomplish our goal.

TEN OF WANDS

RIDER-WAITE DECK

The figure on this card has bound his forces together to preserve them not realizing that by binding the Wands of Power he has created a burden for himself rather than using the inherent power in the wands to free him. He is headed for the city in the distance where, at last, he can surrender the burden of limitations he has gathered for himself. When the Wands are bound in this way, their gifts cannot be shared, and it is only by giving what we receive, a hard lesson the individual depicted on the card is learning.

MARY HANSON-ROBERTS DECK

In contrast to the Rider-Waite Deck, this card seems to suggest the old man has willingly gathered together gifts of the spirit which he has chosen to deliver to the castle in order to distribute them among the people there. The wands are over his shoulder, not obstructing his view or creating limitations for him. The selfishness depicted by the Rider Waite Ten of Wands does not seem to be present here in this deck.

Even though the man has chosen this mission, it has not always been an easy one. The dark gray undertunic underscores this interpretation. The terra-cotta red of the man's outer tunic indicates past karmic actions needing correction, which is why he has willingly assumed these burdens. However, the rich violet pink, golds, rose tones, and violet-white colors surrounding the castle he is headed towards show spiritual advancement, integrity, self-mastery and realization.

SUMMARY DEFINITION OF THE TEN OF WANDS

This card represents the binding of one's forces. A burden that has been willingly assumed. A problem soon to be solved. Sometimes this card represents the end of a love affair, marriage or union that has become a heavy burden or difficult experience. The ten of wands indicates separations and endings leading to the individual's freedom from self-bondage and self-limitation.

What is the Spiritual Lesson or Challenge the Ten of Wands would teach us?

The Ten of Wands teaches us that we are never given a problem or burden without also being given the solution at the same time. The "sins" we commit are merely errors that need correction. And we are given many opportunities in life to correct the errors we have made in the past. The correction of errors does not have to be a painful burden, but rather a joyful release from that which limits your potential.

CHAPTER THIRTY-FIVE
SUIT OF CUPS

The basic nature of Cups is emotional, intuitional, and receptive. Cups represent the present based on the foundation of the past or past actions. This is an emotional suit, dealing with Peace, love, beauty, happiness, and fertility. Its element is Water, the universal solvent, the symbol of the Sub-conscious Mind. It is through the Sub-conscious Mind that we receive intuitional impressions, a feeling of being centered within the Universe and at peace with the flow of life. Cups are also associated with the Waters signs of the Zodiac; Cancer, Scorpio, and Pisces.

The Cups depicted on the Tarot Card, for the most part, are pictured as full or even overflowing, suggesting attainment and fulfillment. They represent the gateway to spiritual awareness and psychic activity. Another aspect of Cups deals with the interaction one has with others in relationships based on emotions such as love, passion, sexual desire, deep feelings, and physical satisfaction.

The Water element of Cups also suggests fertility in its most basic and primal form. All life on this planet owes its existence to the ocean, the liquid cradle of life. Fertility not only refers to procreation of species but also to creativity, for when we create something such as an art form, music, writing, poetry, a cathedral, etc., we are putting a part of ourselves into it in order to make the creation whole.

The Suit of Cups represent the Gifts of the Spirit, love, happiness and joy. The water or liquid contained in the cups is a symbol of the "Milk of human kindness". It represents pleasure and contentment. Cups are also associated with the "Dream State" all sentient creatures experience to some degree or other. The Dream State has a strong relationship with the astral realms and often serves as a bridge between the earth plane and the astral planes.

KING OF CUPS

RIDER-WAITE DECK
This King is the epitome of emotional responsibility and controlled emotions. His seat of power, (the gray throne), is floating on the waters of Life from which he receives his inspiration and intuitional guidance. The King of Cups also represents an individual who has an astrological chart strongly dominated by water signs or has the Sun, moon, or ascendant in Cancer, Scorpio or Pisces.

The yellow fish the King wears around his neck is an ancient symbol for the followers of the "Nazarene", (Jewish Christians). Since he wears it as a personal emblem, it shows he is deeply involved with the spiritual side of his nature.

Yellow is the color of clear thinking, integrity, and enlightenment. The first followers of the Nazarene believed in the power of Love and the blessings of Peace, qualities the King of cups possesses.

There is a live fish jumping from the waves of the ocean behind the King. Fish not only serve as an ancient symbol for the Nazarene but also serve as the link between the Subconscious and Conscious Mind and the link that exists between all life and nature herself. The King wears a fish symbol around his neck to show his understanding of that link and his attunement with it.

Seated on the turbulent waves of the ocean, the King maintains his balance, his stability in the physical world of Illusions. The ship in the distance, headed for shore, indicates the coming prosperity or fulfillment he will enjoy. It symbolizes the achievement of his goals and dreams. The rich blues and greens of his clothing also symbolize prosperity, abundance, Divine Blessings and Love. The touches of red here and there on his robes show his mastery of the Kundalini and his ability to channel this energy force up through the Chakra Centers.

MARY HANSON-ROBERTS DECK

This King is dressed in royal purple robes symbolizing his use of the higher intuitional mind. Purple is also the color of karmic voltage, or "the sowing of Karma". It is a color which represents tenderness and selfless love. Purple is the color of releasing, of letting go and letting God. His undertunic is a rich green with red trim, representing love, growth, and healing. Green indicates abundance, peace, material and monetary ease. The red trim of his robes show the proper use of the Kundalini.

The King wears a golden crown, holds a golden scepter with a violet pink tip and holds a golden cup with violet at the base of the cup and at the bottom of the cup. Gold is the color of enlightenment and soul advancement. It is the color of spiritual blessings and honor. The golden cup the King holds, with its violet pink and violet white trim, represents self-realization, creativity, and artistic expression.

He sits on a brown colored throne symbolizing the Earth Plane. This symbolism shows the King uses his gifts of the spirit in practical and meaningful ways. Brown is also the color of security, steadfastness and power on the physical plane. It indicates physical and mental satisfaction as well as receiving recognition from others for one's achievements.

SUMMARY DEFINITION OF THE KING OF CUPS

This card indicates a man of wisdom and commerce. He makes wise use of emotions and is quick to respond to attraction as well as being easily enthusiastic and exceedingly sensitive. He represents balance and peace, art and science. The King of Cups has learned to control his emotions and has learned that responsibility comes before self-expression. He uses his creativity for his work.

Friendships, love, and partnerships are a part of the lifestyle represented by the King of Cups. The card in a lay-out spread indicates success, achievement, and mastery. Usually the presence of this card in a spread indicates a bachelor with a poet-like imagination in the individual's life. This man is inclined toward helping the individual. Also, the King of cups represents a man who is good marriage material.

What is the Spiritual Lesson or challenge the King of Cups would teach us?

The King of cups teaches us responsibility in developing our emotions towards positive expression. He reminds us that we are in charge of what we perceive and how we perceive it. We gain balance and peace in our lives by learning how to channel our emotions in creative outlets.

QUEEN OF CUPS

RIDER-WAITE DECK
The Queen sits on a throne decorated with cherubs and angels, symbolizing Divine Protection and Guidance. She holds in her hand a very ornate cup in which clairvoyant visions come to her. The Cup itself is covered, indicating the visions which come to her are not for all to see. She has had to develop discernment regarding what she reveals to others. Many are not ready to receive the gifts she has to offer. Some of her visions for the future come to her in dreams.

She is surrounded on one side with the water of the ocean. Water is feminine in nature and receptive, it indicates the gift of intuition and prophecy. Since her throne rests on land, it signifies her ability to give others revelations of the future that is practical and useful in nature. The Queen has the ability to take the creative imagination and manifest it into action on the Earth Plane.

The Queen of Cups represents an individual who has strong water sign dominance in their astrological chart or has the Sun, Moon, or Ascendant in Cancer, Scorpio, or Pisces.

MARY HANSON-ROBERTS DECK
In this picture, the Queen is wearing a golden crown on her "brow" and is holding a large golden cup. Gold symbolizes soul advancement, enlightenment and Gifts of the Spirit. This color also indicates the power of physical and material manifestation. Her dress is a Rose-red color, representing empathy, mystical love and sympathy. The outer-robe she wears is an evergreen shade indicating creative energy, a power to be used in constructive ways. Evergreen is the color of endurance, of generosity, of faith and strength against all opposition. It is the color of triumph and attainment. The scarf on her shoulder is various shades of green and the design resembles the scales of a fish symbolizing her attunement with the Universal Sub-conscious.

Her throne is shaped like a sea-shell and has a violet-pink backing. Violet is the color of intuition, creativity, self-realization and Universal Wisdom. It is the color of a visionary, one who is clairvoyant and has the gift of prophecy. The Queen of Cups is the epitome of feminine intuition. She is at-one with the forces of Nature, at-one with the "Mother-Goddess" aspect of the Creator. The Queen serves as a channel for the Higher Forces.

SUMMARY DEFINITION OF THE QUEEN OF CUPS

This card represents a woman who possesses the gifts of clairvoyance, the ability to "see" images in a reflective surface. Divine beings guide and protect her. She is dreamy, tranquil, poetic, imaginative and kind. This Queen is a mature, visionary woman, honestly devoted to her family, loved ones, and friends. She has the special gift of being able to bring success and happiness to others. She is the Beloved.

The Queen of Cups also indicates a promotion in the world and fame. The card represents love, happy marriage, success and pleasure. Many times, the presence of this card in a lay-out spread indicates someone in the individual's life who possesses these qualities and is affecting the individual's environment in some way on a positive level.

What is the Spiritual Lesson or Challenge then Queen of Cups would teach us?

The Queen of Cups shows us that we can choose to serve as channels for the Higher Forces. We all possess the potential for direct and controlled Intuitional Guidance. All that is necessary to utilize this ability is to attune ourselves to the Universal Sub-Conscious. The "gifts" the Queen has are "gifts" we have as well. There is nothing "supernatural" about these abilities for they are "tools" waiting to be used by us. They are a part of our heritage, our birth-right.

KNIGHT OF CUPS

RIDER-WAITE DECK

The Knight is a messenger, bearing a yellow cup filled with blessings and gifts of the spirit. The cup could also hold a proposal, an offer, an advance, or a message of acceptance which will bring intense joy to the individual. It is the cup of happiness being offered. The yellow color of the cup represents joy and integrity. The gray color of the Knight's horse represents changes for the better in one's life. The horse also stands on yellow sand representing the active mind in a state of receptiveness to the Universal Sub-Conscious.

In a poetical sense, the Knight is leaving the realm of the Mind or Subconscious and is ready to cross over the waters of Universal Consciousness to enter the physical earth plane, bearing the gift of inspiration and love. The touches of violet on the Knight's clothing represent the opportunity for self-realization being offered to the individual. The 4 Knights of the Minor Arcana Suits represent the coming or going of an important matter.

MARY HANSON-ROBERTS DECK

The Knight's cloak is a perfect blending of blue and green representing peace, love, growth, ease and abundance. He sits on a brown saddle indicating that even though he is a dreamer, he has balanced that side of his nature with practicality and steadfastness. This Knight too, holds a large golden cup filled with dreams and inspiration. The opportunities he comes to offer are very special and represent emotional fulfillment.

The horse he rides is white, representing union with the Creator and purity of heart. The mountains in the distance are violet white, symbolizing the 7th Chakra Center or "Crown Chakra". These are the mountains of spiritual attainment and represent the perfect blending of ourselves with the Universal Life-Force. His sky-blue over-tunic indicates the Divine Hope and Assurance he carries with him.

SUMMARY DEFINITION OF THE KNIGHT OF CUPS

This card indicates a romantic, dreamy gentle man who may be bringing love to the individual. The Knight may also be the bearer of messages, of opportunities for fulfillment. This man is a dreamer of sensual delights, graceful and poetic. As with the King and Queen of Cups, the Knight represents an individual with strong water signs in their astrological chart or has the Sun, Moon, or Ascendant in Cancer, Scorpio or Pisces.

This card shows a time of peace and contentment. There is an aura of love around this card. It can also indicate advances, a promotion or proposition, or an invitation, something that will bring you emotional fulfillment. The Knight of cups can indicate an unexpected arrival, advance or approach. This card in a Lay-Out Spread may also indicate unexpected money coming to the individual.

What is the Spiritual Lesson or Challenge the Knight of Cups would teach us?

The Knight of Cups teaches us of the unexpected joys that come into our lives when we are open to the influence of love. Because the Knight is an open channel for Pure Love, he has no need for defenses and although the Knight wears armor, it is the armor of Love.

PAGE OF CUPS

RIDER-WAITE DECK

The figure of the Page is dressed in Pink and Blue, showing a balance between the male and female energies within. Pink is considered a feminine color because it represents compassion, nurturing, and emphatic love, elements which are emotional in nature. Blue is considered masculine because of the emphasis on mental qualities rather than emotional qualities. The Page can be either a man or woman.

Gazing into the Cup, the Page has received the message he/she has asked for. The Page's diligence and studiousness has paid off. The Page is a student, just beginning to walk the path of enlightenment. Behind the figure of the Page is the rolling sea, representing the Universal Sub-Conscious. The Page is just beginning to form a link with the Universal Sub-Conscious, a link which fills him/her with a sense of wonder and joy.

MARY HANSON-ROBERTS DECK

There is a look of absolute awe and amazement on this Page's Face, while gazing at the golden cup in hand. The Page's cape has designs of kelp or seaweed on it representing the influence of the sea, cradle of life. The fish in the Page's cup, a creature of the deep sea regions, indicates an initiation concerning the deeper emotions and the ability to master astral conditions. The fish is presented in various shades of blue with a white underside representing union with the creator, purity, and self-mastery.

The dominant colors on this card are gold and various shades of green and blue, colors representing the advancement of the soul, abundance, growth, love, and fulfillment. The Page is in the process of honing the gifts of the Spirit, readying himself or herself to give service to others. The Page is learning how to harness the powers of the Kundalini to the Will of Creator, transforming and perfecting this energy to a pure state.

SUMMARY DEFINITION OF THE PAGE OF CUPS

The Page represents creative ideas the individual receives when opening the channels to the Higher Consciousness or the Universal Sub-Conscious. These ideas are important for they are a key to enlightenment and advancement of the soul. The Page represents a young man or woman who is willing to render a service to the individual. The Page is studious, but given to bouts of melancholia at times since he/she is only in the process of learning how to control their emotions. The Page is dreamy, romantic, gentle and kind.

The card itself depicts messages of all kinds forthcoming. These messages can come through meditations, dreams, or other people. They may concern the birth of a child, the beginning of a creative enterprise, or a new lifestyle. The Page of cups indicates good news, a proposal of marriage or a love affair. Love and passion is being transformed into love and compassion for all humanity. The Page of Cups also symbolizes psychic talents and sensitivity.

What is the Spiritual Lesson or Challenge the Page of Cups would teach us?

The Page of Cups teaches us the importance of mastering the Kundalini energy within us which helps us to open channels of communication between ourselves and the Universal Sub-Conscious. Guidance and wisdom from the Masters becomes available to us when we have disciplined the constant chattering of our minds to allow messages from the Higher Planes of Consciousness to reach us.

ACE OF CUPS

RIDER-WAITE DECK

From a cloud, the Hand of God offers us a cup overflowing with love and miracles. The five streams coming from the cup represent the five senses of humankind which has been uplifted by enlightenment. The White Dove represents the descent of the Holy Spirit into matter, illuminating it and releasing it from limitations. The little drops which are falling from the over-flowing cups are called Yods. Yods are miracles or blessings from God which are manifesting on the physical earth plane for the individual.

The lily pads and the lilies themselves represent our desires and wishes which can come true through the Love the Creator has for us. The lily pads are green which symbolizes abundance, peace, love, and ease. The lily flowers are red, representing new beginnings or opportunities for fulfillment. The lilies are plants which thrive on water the element of the Universal Sub-Conscious. This represents the inspiration which comes from the Sub-Conscious and the nurturing of ideas which takes place on the Higher Conscious Levels.

MARY HANSON-ROBERTS DECK

The sky on this card is a beautiful peach gold representing attainment. This color symbolizes the power of physical and material manifestation. It is the color of rejuvenation, restoration, and soul advancement. There are 4 streams of life-sustaining water on this card. Three of which serve to replenish the waters of the Universal Sub-Conscious and represents the power of the Holy Trinity. The fourth stream goes into the Golden Cup of Life itself.

The white dove flying over head symbolizes the union between the individual and God. The clouds in the sky are a mixture of Pink, Violet, and White representing self-realization, creativity, and the power force of Love. The soft blue-green color of the water symbolizes blessings and serenity, Divine Hope and Assurance from the Creator. This is a card rich in the symbolism of love and abundance, attainment and fulfillment.

SUMMARY DEFINITION OF THE ACE OF CUPS

In the Tarot, the Ace of Cups represents the Hand of God offering Divine Inspiration and Perfect Love. It indicates spiritual protection and guidance. The Cup is overflowing with the gifts of the spirit, giving a sense of completeness, of union with the Creator and all life. It is a card that promises fulfillment on an emotional and creative level.

The Ace also indicates abundance in all things, fertility, joy, and contentment. The beginning of a love affair. This is a card of pleasure, happiness, and love. It also represents intuitive knowledge or "knowing" that will be realized, a prophetic or clairvoyant gift. The Ace of Cups can also mean the beginning of a great love affair either with a person or a creative endeavor.

What is the Spiritual Lesson or Challenge the Ace of Cups would teach us?
The Ace of Cups is really a reminder of the Love the Creator has for us and how this love is manifested in abundant and fulfilling ways in our lives. Joining one's will with the Will of God should be a joyful happy experience. It is not meant to be a burden or to give one a sense of negative servitude. True Love is unconditional and is more interested in giving than receiving, this is the Love which we all are entitled to and the Ace of Cups serves to remind us of this.

TWO OF CUPS

RIDER-WAITE DECK

This card is the symbol of commitment, of union, and of love given and received. Both the man and the woman are offering each other yellow cups. The yellow cups represent the exchange of joy and minds which have achieved union on a universal level with the Creator and with themselves. The woman wears a wreath of green leaves in her hair which represents love, vitality, abundance, and peace. Green is the color of the "Heart Chakra". The Heart Chakra is concerned with the balance of emotions, the balance of passion and compassion, of physical and spiritual love. The fact the woman wears the symbol of the Heart Chakra around her "Brow Chakra" shows she has elevated her personal emotions, her "love" nature or nurturing instincts to their highest level.

The man wears a wreath of red flowers which shows he has the physical passion, the sexual energy, the physical love the woman needs. He has learned to control his physical appetites and the Kundalini Force with his Higher Mind since the wreath circles his "Brow Chakra". This division between the male and female is very traditionalist. It shows the male as physical and the female as emotional.

The red winged lion above them indicates Divine Power and Creation. It also represents the power to teach others the wisdom which is available to all from the Holy Spirit. The winged lion too, represents human sexuality raised to its highest level with the wings of Divine Inspiration. There are also two intertwined serpents, representing the raising of the Kundalini Force in both the male and female. The serpent also represents spiritual knowledge. The couple stand on yellow ground representing clear thinking, integrity and enlightenment.

MARY HANSON-ROBERTS DECK

The white cross is formed by Light when the two golden cups are touching, represent the union of man and woman on 3 levels. The first level is the Conscious or physical level representing sexual intercourse, sexual union. The third is the Super-Consciousness representing spiritual union, the merging of two into one. This symbolism represents a Holy Relationship which encompasses all aspects of life, the physical, mental, emotional, and spiritual, a true union all relationships strive to attain.

The background of this card is a rich peach gold representing advancement of the Soul, the power of physical and material manifestation. Peach gold is the color of restoration and rejuvenation, a renewal that is both spiritually elevating and physically satisfying. The winged lion overhead is various shades of brown, representing steadfastness on the earth plane. The wings are white representing Union with the Creator and Self-mastery.

The Hanson-Roberts design of the Two of Cups demonstrates more clearly that the man and woman are Soul-Mates or Soul-Twins. In the Rider-Waite deck, the woman wears the traditional feminine green and the male, the traditional masculine red. On this card, the roles are reversed, showing that the union between these two individuals brings out the hidden facets of their natures, giving them completion. Every woman has a hidden male side to her nature as every man has a hidden female side to his nature. True union between man and woman brings these facets into balance. Hence, the male is wearing the feminine green and the female is wearing the masculine red demonstrating the perfect union which exists between them, the potential all unions have.

The golden cups they are offering to each other represent the unconditional love and acceptance they have to give. They are making a gift of themselves to the other, surrendering their egos in order to achieve "wholeness".

SUMMARY DEFINITION OF THE TWO OF CUPS
This card represents commitment. It indicates love, harmony, intense joy, and ecstasy. When it appears in a lay-out spread, it may signal the beginning of a love affair with one's soul-mate. The card itself represents spiritual and physical union, marriage, pleasure, passion, attraction, and lovemaking (intercourse). This card also symbolizes luck beyond imagining.

The two of Cups can also indicate unions, partnerships or contracts concerning artistic creations. It is a favorable sign for business as well as pleasure, indicating wealth, honor and love. It also symbolizes the resurrection of the Spirit, and active intuition.

What is the Spiritual Lesson or Challenge the Two of Cups would teach us?
The Two of Cups reminds us of the power of physical unions. Sexual energy is Divine and should be treated as such. Each time we have a physical intercourse with another person, we are exchanging our life essence with that person. In the ancient temples it was taught to initiates that each time they sexually joined with another person, they took on some of that person's karma. In today's society, we have reduced the sexual act to a brief physical pleasure. The two of Cups reminds us of the inherent power behind sexual intercourse and how this power, used properly, serves to unite, to strengthen, and to enlighten the couple involved. Sexual energy is the raw, unchanneled force of the Kundalini, misused it can have disastrous consequences, used properly it can lead to Spiritual Rejuvenation and Enlightenment.

THREE OF CUPS

RIDER-WAITE DECK
This card represents the harvest of the good seeds of Karma, a celebration of achievement, of accomplishment. What we have imagined will come to pass, dreams will be realized. The three yellow cups held aloft by the three women, present boundless joy and happiness. The cups are filled with blessings and miracles each has received and shared with the others. This sharing of blessings or miracles is very important to the three women, for they have learned that only through giving do they receive.

The power and presence of the Holy Trinity is shown in the 3 women sharing joy, and in the 3 Cups they hold. The three women are crowned with flowers, the symbol of attainment. At their feet is the fruit of their planted wishes which have sprung forth or manifested on the Earth Plane for them. In many ways, this card symbolizes the granting of 3 wishes; love, happiness and prosperity. The time of waiting has finished, the reaping has begun.

MARY HANSON-ROBERTS DECK
One of the major colors on this card are different shades of green. Green is the color of the "Heart Chakra", the channel of healing love, of balance between Mind, Body and Spirit. It is a color which symbolizes growth, love, abundance, and vitality. One of the women is wearing an Emerald Green dress. Emerald Green symbolizes the cleansing away of unwanted and useless distractions

which cloud our lives with pain. It is the color of trustworthiness and compassion.

The background is yellow representing the active mind and clear thinking. It is the color of enlightenment and integrity. Shades of gold and peach gold are found all over this card representing gifts of the Spirit and fulfillment. Gold is a color representing a blessing that is granted to those individuals who know how to help others realize richness in their lives. Peach Gold is the color of attainment, the power of physical and material manifestation in one's life.

There are shades of brown representing practicality and steadfastness. Shades of white representing union with the Creator and purity of heart. Shades of Blue representing Hope and Divine Assurance and shades of Pink, representing the realization of a personal, physical and spiritual love. All of the colors on this card speak of great happiness and joy.

SUMMARY DEFINITION OF THE THREE OF CUPS

This card represents abundance, plenty, celebration, rejoicing and fulfillment. Congratulations are in order, a longed for goal has been reached. The rewards of past actions are now evident. There is a happy result from an undertaking. Success, good fortune, and victory. Either a crisis has finished, leaving the individual in better circumstances or some creative work has produced good, successful results. This card can also represent the realization of love, a love that is mutual. The three of cups indicates sharing the wonders of life with others. A pledging or a uniting together with others.

What is the Spiritual Lesson or Challenge the Three of Cups would teach us?

The three of Cups shows us how, through sharing our joys, we increase their benefits in our lives. When we share a burden with others, that burden becomes lighter, and the problem can be solved much easier. The key word here is "sharing", for it is by sharing our gifts with others that our "Cups of Joy" are continually replenished.

FOUR OF CUPS

RIDER-WAITE DECK

The figure in this picture is leaning against a yellow tree trunk. This tree represents the Tree of Knowledge. Its yellow trunk represents clear thinking and the active mind. The figure appears to be in a state of meditation or contemplation, instinctively relying, (leaning against the tree trunk), on the Universal Wisdom available to us when we are contemplating actions or reactions to life's situations and opportunities.

There are three full cups before the figure, representing the accomplishments he/she has already experienced. The individual is contemplating new directions to take in life, considering the options or choices available to them. The accomplishments of the past has brought satisfaction to the individual and has led the individual to the situation they now find themselves in. It is important to remember that cups represent wishes, hopes, dreams, and the fulfillment of the emotions.

In the picture, a hand, emerging from a cloud, offers the figure in the picture another yellow cup. In the Tarot, whenever a hand appears from a cloud, it represents the "Hand of God" offering a gift, blessing or miracle. The Hand of God offering the individual in the picture a cup is offering them new opportunities, new fulfillment, joys and happiness. In the four of cups, this offering may represent a dream or hope the individual has always wanted to come true, or may represent a miracle the individual never even dreamed of.

MARY HANSON-ROBERTS DECK

At this point, I want to explain the symbolism of the Evergreen Tree. Evergreens are considered the most highly evolved trees of the plant kingdom. They can be likened to Avatars in the human kingdom. These trees maintain their "greenness" throughout the year and do not undergo the seasonal changes other plants do. If you stroke the needles of a pine tree softly, you will feel a tingling charge of energy in your fingers which will continue to move up your arms. Evergreen Trees are natural storehouses for spiritual and psychical Energy.

Many tribes of Native American Indians considered the evergreen Tree to be sacred and filled with the power of the "Great Spirit". To sit under a pine tree is to seek the stored energy, the wisdom and knowledge of the Universe. There is no better place to meditate than in a forest of pine trees. It is even better to be able to sit under a pine tree. It is even better to be able to sit under a pine tree, lean up against its trunk, and meditate. The figure on this card is sitting under and against a pine tree. The face of the individual shows deep contemplation, even meditation.

The Hand of God, bearing the golden cup of opportunity, emerges from a soft pink cloud which symbolizes the nurturing and compassionate love the Creator has for the individual. The cloak the individual wears, is sapphire blue with green trim. This color represents substance and expansion, it is the color symbol of the Higher Mind showing that the emotional nature has matured, become more purified. The Green represents growth, abundance, and love.

SUMMARY DEFINITION OF THE FOUR OF CUPS

The number Four in the Tarot signify the manifestation of plans an individual has into reality. Longed for goals and dreams are attainable now because of the foundation built in the past. The Four of Cups symbolizes the Hand of God offering a new path or opportunity to the individual. This offered cup also represents hidden wisdom. This card also indicates quiet contemplation, meditation and contemplation of a goal. In a lay-out spread, the four of cups indicates results of "seeds" or actions and choices made in the past.

New relationships are now possible, new goals and ambitions. There will be kindness and assistance from others. A possible love affair or relationship with someone known to the individual but, as yet, has not started. There is a hint of anxiety or worry which could limit the individual's response to opportunities being offered to them. The individual could be afraid to take what is offered, fearing they may not be worthy of the gift or may be afraid they are deceiving themselves on the outcome.

What is the spiritual Lesson or Challenge the Four of Cups would teach us?

The Four of Cups teaches us how foolish we are when we allow fear thoughts to limit us in any way. There are no strings attached to the gifts the Creator offers us, no conditions we have to meet. These gifts or opportunities for fulfillment are given unconditionally and with Perfect Love.

THE FIVE OF CUPS

RIDER-WAITE DECK

The symbolism of this card represents regret concerning wrong choices which have brought about sorrow to the individual. The three spilled cups symbolize the wasting of God's gifts either through recklessness or by taking them for granted. What the figure in the picture seems to have forgotten is that there are still 2 full cups behind them which have not been lost or wasted. This card represents a lesson which needed to be learned by the individual. Even though this lesson has brought some pain to the individual, because it is hard for them to admit to mistakes, their feelings of abandonment are not real. There are still blessings available to them.

Self-pity is a vicious non-productive trap to fall into. It makes you feel like a victim in the world you see, powerless and alone. This is not true. To eliminate this wrong thinking is not easy, for the ego does cling to illusions, but all that is needed is a change in perception; to see the painful events as a cleansing of unwanted emotional baggage. The bridge in the background of the picture leads from the losses of the past to the new beginnings of the future. The whole picture on the card symbolizes the idea of not wasting energy regretting past mistakes, to learn from them, and then go ahead with the future which is bright with promise.

MARY HANSON-ROBERTS DECK

The color of the spilled wine from the golden cups is a reddish purple representing Karmic Testing or Suffering in this life due to physical offenses committed to others in previous lifetimes or the past. However, once the individual stops fighting against their Karma and learns how to forgive themselves as well as others, the suffering ceases and the heavy burdens they carried are lifted away.

The figure in the picture is wrapped in an evergreen cloak signifying they are going through an emotional purification. A beautiful Turquoise Blue river runs by the individual promising hope and Divine Assurance. It also indicates the preparation for a new existence or life for the individual promising hope and Divine Assurance. It also indicates the preparation for a new existence or life for the individual as well as new opportunities. The new opportunities can be of a creative nature dealing with communications of some kind. Number five represents change and freedom. The Five of Cups represents freedom from the past and a change for the future, for the better.

SUMMARY DEFINITION OF THE FIVE OF CUPS

In the Tarot, Fives in a Suit represent difficulties which will necessitate in an adjustment on the part of the individual. They also symbolize change or challenges to address, a testing of sorts. The Five of Cups indicate disappointment. Possibly a loss of friendship, or disappointment in a love affair. It indicates a karmic learning experience. The Five of Cups can also signify bitterness in a marriage and separation.

This card also represents an obstacle facing the individual that needs to be turned into a stepping stone towards new opportunities. Obstacles are not meant to stop us, they are given us to teach us to be more creative in the way we look at things and the way we do things. Obstacles are only initiations along the Spiritual Path, a way for us to test our strengths and grow from experience. Obstacles are not meant to be seen as negative events, merely as opportunities for spiritual growth and understanding.

What is the Spiritual Lesson or Challenge the Five of Cups would teach us?

The Five of Cups teaches us that the past cannot be changed, therefore regretting the actions, choices or decisions made in the past serves no useful purpose. It is important to realize the only time that is important is the "Now". How we proceed from here is what counts, the past does not exist anymore. The Challenges we face in life teach us about ourselves and our place in the Universe.

SIX OF CUPS

RIDER-WAITE DECK

The symbolism on this card represents opportunities for a fruitful, prosperous life. The 6 cups filled with blooming flowers symbolize abundance and fulfillment of hopes, wishes and dreams. The white, five pointed star-flower signifies the transmutation of our five physical senses onto a higher level of consciousness. These flowers can also represent a love which began on a more physical and sexual level has now deepened into something even more precious.

The two children represent the biblical passage; "become as little children", indicating we should accept that as children of God our needs will be satisfied in a loving manner by our Father/Mother God. The town square pictured in the card represents our security and foundation on the material plane. The bright yellows on the card show the active mind, integrity, enlightenment as well as Gifts of the Spirit.

There is an aura of gentleness and love to this card. One of the children is offering the other a gift of joy, a gift of love. He chooses to share his good fortune, to share himself with someone else. This act will guarantee his own continued prosperity, for the more you give, the more there is to give. The cross etched on the stonework is called the St. Andrew's Cross which is called the cross of humility and Faith. Many of these crosses appear on heraldic shields with the biblical inscription, in latin, of "Not my will Father, but Yours be done."

MARY HANSON-ROBERTS DECK

The overall view of this card is one of contentment and happiness. Various shades of Gold, which indicate the power of physical and material manifestation, are very prominent. Rich shades of green are also present indicate abundance, love, and healing. Sky blue is the color of the little girl's pinafore which represents Divine Assurance and Hope. There are gold roses in some of the flower filled cups symbolizing the attainment of the impossible dream if one is willing to accept the responsibility.

SUMMARY DEFINITION OF THE SIX OF CUPS

This card represents success, pleasure, happiness, and well being. It indicates satisfaction, ease, and fulfillment. It is the beginning of a steady increase, of new opportunities. The six of cups also represents emotions that have been purified. This card symbolizes the results, the benefits of good karma, of seeds sown previously which were sown in honor and faith. Unique and unexpected experiences may occur, bringing forth opportunities the individual has only dreamed about.

The Six of Cups can indicate love coming to the individual which has its roots in the past. New beginnings in relationships with the opposite sex are now possible. Love and romance blossoms into something unique and special.

What is the Spiritual Lesson or Challenge the Six of Cups would teach us?

The Six of Cups shows us we need not loose our innocence and faith when dealing with the experiences life has to offer. A heart filled with generosity and love has a shield no darkness can penetrate. Trust would solve every problem now and in the future. Trust in the goodness inherent in all beings, trust in the Light that dwells in every creature, trust in the Pure Love which permeates the Universe and you will be filled with the Joy and Happiness you are entitled to.

SEVEN OF CUPS

RIDER-WAITE DECK

The number 7 is considered a sacred number and represents initiations for the Spiritual Seeker. The Seven of Cups symbolizes the tests and challenges of the spirit which the spiritual warrior faces on their path to enlightenment. Six of the seven cups are filled with distractions to the Seeker. Distractions the ego plants on the path hoping to draw the Seeker from their spiritual quest. One cup, containing a laurel wreath represents worldly honor and fame. Another cup, in which a demon sits, represents envy, jealousy, and spite, negative emotions each of us must face, emotions each of us experience in some form or another, either when directed at us, or when we direct these emotions at others.

There is a cup which contains bright jewels representing the temptations of wealth without charity. Still another cup contains a serpent which represents the corruption of wisdom. Serpents are symbols of the Kundalini and of ancient wisdom. There is a beautiful head in one of the cups, representing personal vanity and preoccupation with physical beauty. The castle pictured in one of the cups represents the temptations of power. These cups are temptations created by the Earth plane and the ego to limit our true potentials. Once caught up in the illusions of the earth plane it can be difficult to extricate oneself from them and continue on the spiritual path.

Ironically, the very ideal we are seeking in life, self-realization, self-mastery and union with the Creator, is represented on this card by a figure in a cup hidden from view by a cloak with violet-pink rays. The covered figure represents our Ideal, the goal we are seeking. This card represents the need to learn Discernment, the need to discover Truth despite the tempting illusions of the earth plane.

MARY HANSOM-ROBERTS DECK

With the Hanson-Roberts Deck, this card depicts a wise wizard dressed in sapphire blue, standing beyond the illusions and temptations. Sapphire Blue is a color which symbolizes emotions that have matured and become purified. It is the symbolic color of the Higher Intuitional Mind. Sapphire Blue is a color which promises substance and expansion. It represents mastery of the principles of the Ten Commandments.

Although these cups are filled with temptations and challenges, they rest on a soft violet pink cloud which represents spiritual growth and attainment. Violet Pink also represents self-realization and artistic expression. The wise wizard knows that through the tests or initiations the seeker experiences, self-mastery will be learned and great spiritual wisdom will be gained.

SUMMARY DEFINITION OF THE SEVEN OF CUPS

The Sevens in the Minor Arcana Suits indicate choices or a seeking of new directions, variety, potentials, and possibilities. Yet, inherent in the seven is an unsureness of how to proceed. The card represents Illusions, temptations, the testing of an initiate on the Spiritual Path. This card can also indicate a preoccupation with the ego and all of the illusions it tempts us with in the material world.

However, our imagined desires can become realities if they are based on right-thinking and serve the needs of others. The Seven of Cups also symbolizes mystical and/or psychic experiences. Inherent in this card is a warning against scattering one's forces in too many directions.

What is the Spiritual Lesson or Challenge the Seven of Cups would teach us? The Seven of Cups teaches us that we must be willing to make choices based on spiritual precepts. This card also teaches us the importance of Discernment as well as the importance of being willing to see past the veils of illusion to the Truth that may lie hidden.

EIGHT OF CUPS

RIDER-WAITE DECK

In this picture there are five full cups in a row representing the fulfillment of the five senses and 3 full cups resting on top of this row representing the 3 states of Consciousness. The background color just behind the cups is an ugly mustard green representing jealousy, envy, and spite. The figure in the picture has turned his back on these negative emotions created by his own actions in the past. The jealousy and envy directed at him because of his success in the past has caused him to abandon material success.

The 8 full cups represent the fulfillment of desires on the physical earth plane which has served to distract the individual from spiritual fulfillment. The darkness of the mountains ahead show the attainment of spiritual heights will not be easy, especially if the individual is overly concerned with material matters. He is wearing a red robe and red boots symbolizing his desire for a new beginning, a desire to attain more spiritual wisdom.

The Sun and Moon together in the night sky is showing a state of eclipse which indicates inner urges that motivate us. The figure has walked across the river of water which represents the subconscious mind and shows the individual is now obeying the direction of his higher intuitional mind.

MARY HANSON-ROBERTS DECK

Both the sky and the river of life depicted on this card are varying shades of blue. The horizon is violet pink, meeting the night sky of sapphire blue just past the mountains of spiritual attainment. It is from the mountains of spiritual wisdom and attainment that the river of life receives its infusion of Divine Inspiration in the form of a waterfall. The blue of the sky represents Divine Assurance and purification. It indicates balance, serenity and spiritual blessings.

The gold color of the cups represent the power of physical and material manifestation. The individual in the picture is dressed in brown robes representing practicality on the earth plane. The individual is no longer content to be immersed in the material world, but the steadfastness and practicality he learned there will help him on his quest for spiritual enlightenment. There is an indigo-purple scarf the individual wears representing Intuition and the Higher Consciousness which is guiding the footsteps of the individual.

SUMMARY DEFINITION OF THE EIGHT OF CUPS

This card represents dissatisfaction, even a sense of disillusion with the material plane. There has been material success, but is proving to be unsatisfying to the individual. The Eight of Cups indicates a desire for further knowledge, a need to experience something more meaningful. Even though material goals have been realized, a feeling of emptiness persists.

This card in a lay-out spread can indicate travel, a need for a spiritual quest. The individual may feel a calling to serve humanity in some way.

What is the Spiritual Lesson or Challenge the Eight of Cups would teach us?
The Eight of Cups teaches us the futility of material success without spiritual fulfillment. Great success or achievement can make one feel isolated, cut off from others, creating feelings of abandonment even in the midst of material ease. When material success is used to assist others, the feeling of being a part of something greater than yourself removes the sense of isolation.

NINE OF CUPS

RIDER-WAITE DECK

This card is the symbol of total and complete material and emotional satisfaction. It indicates that the wishes of the individual have been or will be granted. Hopes and dreams are now realities. The dominant color on this card is yellow, the color of joy. The 9 cups are arranged on a blue cloth covered table behind the seated man representing Blessings from the Creator and the rhythmic flow of the life-force.

The expression on the man's face is a very satisfied one. He has received the miracles promised by the presence of the cups. In most tarot books, the nine of cups is referred to as the "Wish Card", meaning the granting of one's wishes and desires. It is also considered to be a lucky card, promising abundance and fulfillment.

MARY HANSON-ROBERTS DECK

All of the rich colors on this card symbolize the attainment of one's hopes, wishes and desires. The golden color of the cups represent soul advancement, restoration and enlightenment. Turquoise blue and shades of green represent abundance, spiritual blessings, hope, and Divine Assurance. The peacock feather in the man's cap represents the illumination of the intuitive senses. The orange colors on his robes represent the balance of physical and mental aspects of human nature. Orange is a combination of intelligence, energy and good judgment. It also rules the emotions, energy and appetite.

SUMMARY DEFINITION OF THE NINE OF CUPS

This card represents physical and emotional well-being. It indicates abundant material success and satisfaction. It indicates the fulfillment of hopes and dreams. The Nine of Cups represents complete success, happiness, assured future, triumph, all difficulties will be surmounted. Also, success in matters of the heart is indicated by the presence of this card. There could be a possible wealthy marriage for the individual in the not too distant future. By wealthy, the card is referring not only to the material but to the spiritual. Stability and attainment are the key words for this card.

What is the Spiritual Lesson or Challenge the Nine of Cups would teach us?

The Nine of Cups teaches us to be aware that any gift we receive cannot deprive someone else and still remain a gift which will bring us happiness. Our wishes and hopes and dreams are important to the Creator, but He/She will not take from one to give to another. Both are equal in the eyes of God and both are entitled to the joy of Miracles.

TEN OF CUPS

RIDER-WAITE DECK

There is a rainbow in a blue sky which has as its center, ten full yellow cups. Rainbows are the symbols of miracles, of promises of joy from the Creator. Miracles happen to those who believe in them and the figures depicted on this card believe in miracles. The man and woman, arms around each other, show the union of male and female on the physical plane and on a spiritual plane as well for they have elevated their passions to a higher vibration. The children dance happily beside them in innocence and joy.

There is a home in the background, surrounded by lush green growth. Abundance is now present in their lives. They are being nourished by the love and commitment they have for each other. This is a card of lasting happiness for the river and the home in the distance represent the permanence of their achievements. They have attained their heart's desire and rejoice at their good fortune.

MARY HANSON-ROBERTS DECK

The colors on this card are even more rich and abundant signifying the fulfillment the man and woman have achieved. The man is wearing an ever-green coat and his pants are a deep sapphire blue, colors which symbolize purified emotions and self-mastery. The green of the landscape around them represents the deep love and abundance in their lives. Green is also the color of healing and vitality. All the colors of the Chakra centers are present on this card, showing mastery of the physical material plane.

The red roof on the white castle in the distance represents the rising of the Kundalini to its highest expression under the guidance of the Super-Consciousness. There are even white lilies in the foreground to emphasize this spiritual attainment. The rainbow contains shades of violet pink representing self-realization and artistic creation. The peach gold color of the cups symbolize the power of physical and material manifestation on the Earth Plane. The other golden yellow tones represent soul advancement, enlightenment and integrity.

SUMMARY DEFINITION OF THE TEN OF CUPS

The key word for this card is contentment. It represents lasting happiness and fulfillment because the inspiration comes from above, from the Universal Life-Force rather than from mere physical or material satisfaction. This card indicates love, happy changes and family ties which are not limiting but which serve to give the individual security.

The Ten of Cups signifies the permanence of achievement. This card can also indicate that a special person may enter the life of the individual. A love relationship which will bring lasting happiness and contentment. The Ten of Cups symbolizes the attainment of the heart's desire.

What is the Spiritual Lesson or Challenge the Ten of Cups would teach us?

The Ten of Cups teaches us to look for the rainbows of life rather than looking for the storms that bring them. In other words, our expectations have a lot to do with what happens in our lives. The power of thought should never be underestimated, and the Ten of Cups serves as a reminder of this powerful force. Expect love and miracles in your life, and do not allow the ego to distract you from the joy that is available to you.

CHAPTER THIRTY-SIX

SUIT OF SWORDS

The basic nature of the Suit of Swords is intellectual and mental, concerned with the development of ideas and thoughts. Swords represent a progressive, future-oriented suit that sometimes indicates strife and misfortune, the suit almost always represents change. Swords also symbolize the growth and development of the Conscious Mind. They indicate communication, teaching and philosophy. This suit also deals with the relationship of the individual to the Infinite Universe and the Creator. The element for Swords is Air, that which lifts up and is purified. Swords are also associated with the Astrological Air signs of Gemini, Libra, and Aquarius.

Swords also symbolize a cutting away, or "releasing" of things and people in an individual's life. Swords eliminate outmoded ideas, possessions and relationships. Sometimes, they can indicate disaster followed by a rebirth and a new awareness. Swords can also represent aggression, activity, force, boldness, strength, and courage. This suit often reflects an awareness of the "ties" between ideas and philosophies, the place one holds in the universal scheme of things and one's connection to others in that scheme.

The Swords pictured on the Tarot Cards seem to express a functional simplicity. There are very few frills, just the basic necessities as though "comfort and ease" cause distractions or create burdens when developing the intellect or mind. It is a no-nonsense suit, with little humor, and no extravagance or luxury is depicted on them. Swords is a suit which represents tests, challenges of the Spirit and karmic learning experiences. The aura of this suit is one of seriousness, as though life were a battle to be fought and won. The Suit of Swords symbolize the Warrior; dedicated, deadly and very serious.

KING OF SWORDS

RIDER-WAITE DECK

A stern faced man sits on a gray throne with the symbols of butterflies on the back. Butterflies represent the principle of reincarnation and freedom. The King is dressed in a robe of Sky-Blue representing Divine Assurance and balance between the mental and physical. The sword he holds upright symbolizes the preparation for a new existence or new things in one's life. He wears a yellow crown representing the active mind, integrity and enlightenment, qualities he puts to good use.

There are two moon symbols on his throne which represents the cyclicality or "cycles" of life, the connection between all life forms and rhythm of nature. These symbols also show that all life goes through different stages of development, different periods of growth, nothing remains in a permanent state. The clouds gathering behind him indicate the coming changes and tests he will have to face using his intelligence and integrity as his guidelines.

MARY HANSON-ROBERTS DECK

The figure depicted as King on this card is a Warrior, prepared to fight for the forces of Light. His sword is silver and has a brilliant white cross emanating from it. This symbolism represents the essence of the Super-Consciousness or Christ Consciousness ready to penetrate the earth plane with Truth, cutting away the illusions of the physical material plane. Even the hilt of the sword and the design on the blade itself is violet, the color of the Crown Chakra. This represents self-realization, spiritual growth and attainment.

The dominant colors on this card are silver and gray. The background scenery is being swept by the winds of change and transition. The King wears a blue robe with Sapphire Blue designs signifying self-mastery and control of his emotions. The brown color of his cloak and helmet strap represents the steadfastness and practicality of his Faith. Brown is a color which symbolizes security and the ability to bring logical reasoning to bear on emotional issues.

SUMMARY DEFINITION OF THE KING OF SWORDS

This card symbolizes a wise counselor, a skillful, clever and courageous individual who seems to have the power of life and death over intellectual ideas and pursuits. He has authority which he uses with perception and judgment. He is not afraid to take action when the situation warrants it. The King of Swords represents a man who has a strong domination of Air Elements in his astrological chart, or he could have the Sun, Moon or Ascendant in one of the Air signs such as Gemini, Libra or Aquarius.

The King of Swords in a lay-out spread can indicate legal dealings and swift justice. Swords divide the false ideas from the true. The King depicts challenging ideas, power and strength. It represents a professional man who could be involved in the individual's life, either as a critic, a boss, or someone from whom the individual is seeking advice or guidance.

What is the Spiritual Lesson or Challenge the King of Swords would teach us?

The King of Swords teaches us the importance of stripping away illusions. Truth is a sharp edged sword which can cut through the mists of deception and delusion.

QUEEN OF SWORDS

RIDER-WAITE DECK

This Queen sits on a gray throne decorated with butterflies, which symbolize reincarnation and the continuation of the life cycle, and with Cherubs which symbolize Divine Protection. The sword she holds upright is the Sword of Truth and Discernment, a Sword used to separate the Truth from Illusions on the Earth Plane. Her left arm is extended outward. This represents her willingness to face the unknown future, unknown situations, and her willingness to accept what is offered for she has the faith to meet any challenge. Her sword has been used to free her from confusion, doubt and fear, limitations of the Ego.

Her face seems stern and unapproachable, but this is not the case. Her apparent "sternness" is really her strength of character. She has faced most of life's challenges and tests alone, with only her link with the Divine Life-Force to guide her. The Queen is willing to share her hard won knowledge with others, but she will not pander to the vanity of an individual's ego. She has learned to subdue the Ego, and as a result this has set her apart from the masses. The single bird soaring in the clear air represents the solitude of her life. Her wisdom and experiences in life have made her a solitary person at heart. She is not afraid to be alone physically, for she knows the secret of true faith; none walk the path alone or unprotected, the shield of Love surrounds all who make the journey to awareness.

MARY HANSON-ROBERTS DECK

As with the King, the Queen has a Cross of Light emanating from her upraised sword. This Cross is more of a Blue-White color which represents purity, perfection and union with the Supreme Being or God. It is this union with the Creator which guides her life and sets her apart from the main-stream consciousness of the masses. She wears the silver color of mystical powers for she has underwent the initiation of the Soul.

Her robes are green and brown. The color green represents a channel for the healing energy of the Universe. It is the color of growth, peace and love. Green represents balance of the mind and body. Brown represents steadfastness of faith, strength and endurance. The mountains in the background are a violet white, the color of the 7th Chakra or "Crown Chakra". It represents self-realization, disciplined will and the intuitional mind.

The Queen of Swords is a Spiritual Warrior, fearlessly leading the way through the mists of darkness and illusions. The Sun is obscured by gray clouds indicating there is more to be revealed in the future. Change, tests, and challenges are part of that future. Many choices will arise, each leading to the development of spirituality.

SUMMARY DEFINITION OF THE QUEEN OF SWORDS

The Queen is a subtle, keen, quick-witted woman of authority. She is confident, gracious and just, but also is an intense individualist. This card also indicates a woman who has known sorrow or pain, and having faced it with courage and acceptance, has gained a wisdom which sets her apart from others. She represents kindness and firm discipline which would be of benefit to the individual. The Queen represents an individual who has strong dominance of Air Signs in their Astrological chart or has the Sun, Moon or Ascendant in an Air sign such as Gemini, Libra or Aquarius.

This card symbolizes changing conditions for the individual under divine protection. There may be separations, solitude, isolation, and even loneliness, or perhaps circumstances surrounding the individual makes them feel as though they were alone. This condition or circumstance is occurring for a reason. It is a Spiritual Challenge for the individual. It serves to teach them to seek within for their link to the Divine Love that is there for them. This card also indicates the ability to free oneself from confusion, doubt and fear.

What is the Spiritual Lesson or Challenge the Queen of Swords would teach us?

The Queen of Swords teaches us to have confidence in the Divine Guidance that is always with us when we face the unknown. Fear, doubt and confusion are energy forms the ego uses to form the Illusions which rise to plague us, to challenge us. Acceptance of Divine Love robs these negative emotions of the energy need to perpetuate themselves.

KNIGHT OF SWORDS

RIDER-WAITE DECK
The Knight depicted on this card is in a hurry to accomplish his purpose. He is riding against the wind, not allowing any obstacle to stand in the way of his function or mission. The Knight's sword is raised higher to cut through the illusions of the Earth Plane, illusions which distort the Truth he is so eagerly seeking to defend. There are five birds flying high over head, representing the five physical senses of humankind. The symbols of butterflies decorate his horse's tack. Butterflies represent the never-ending cycles of life lifting ever higher on the Spiritual Spiral.

MARY HANSON-ROBERTS DECK
Again, the dominant color on this card is silver and gray. The sword is the pivotal point for the pure white cross of Light. The hilt of his sword and gloves are brown, symbolizing his steadfastness, his dedication to the Truth, the Light and the Way. The Knight's cloak is various shades of green represent balance between the mind and the body. Green is the color of growth, of purified energy and vitality. The Evergreen shades represents energy to be used in constructive ways. Evergreen is the color of generosity, faith and endurance. It is the color of triumph and attainment.

SUMMARY DEFINITION OF THE KNIGHT OF SWORDS
This card symbolizes that no obstacle is too severe, no effort is too difficult for this knight to overcome. He is determined to prevail. The card indicates sudden events, someone or something about to catapult into or out of the individual's life. This is an intense situation. It also indicates challenging situations which arise suddenly and may be unexpectedly.

Since the Knight usually represents a person, male or female, the individual represented by the Knight of Swords would have strong Air Sign dominance in their astrological chart or have the Sun, Moon or Ascendant in an Air Sign such as Gemini, Libra or Aquarius.

Knights in the 4 suits represent the arrival or departure, the coming or going of a situation or individual in one's life. The Knight indicates an elusive and elastic mind, full of ideas and designs, and somewhat domineering. This card can indicate the start or end of misfortune. The Knight of Swords also represents good news received by the individual.

What is the Spiritual Lesson or Challenge the Knight of Swords would teach us?

The Knight of Swords teaches us the importance of perseverance. If we allow a small setback to defeat our ultimate goal, we are surrendering our right for attainment. Obstacles or setbacks occur in life to give us the opportunity to test our strength, to develop new methods and jog our minds into a creative mode. If there were no obstructions in life, we could not develop our full potentials for we would not know how to develop them and test their effectiveness.

PAGE OF SWORDS

RIDER-WAITE DECK

The Page depicted on this card wears a pair of red boots, representing new beginnings and the Kundalini Force. The yellow color of the Page's leggings and undershirt represent the active mind, clear thinking, and integrity. The Page has no frills or ornamentation, signifying an intellectual person, devoted to gaining wisdom, experience and Truth. The Page does not have time or the inclination to be swayed from his/her path. Theirs is the impatience of youth. The Page is very earnest in all he/she does. The Page can represent either a youthful male or female.

MARY HANSON-ROBERTS DECK

The Page has an outer tunic of emerald green, representing the cleansing away of the unwanted and the useless waste in our lives which causes distractions. Emerald Green is the color of trustworthiness and a pure heart. The Page is wearing a brown cloak representing his/her steadfastness of Faith. The white undershirt represents union with the Creator and purity. The Page is young and inexperienced, but his/her heart is strong and filled with purpose.

The gray clouds of the sky represent change and transition the Page faces.

SUMMARY DEFINITION OF THE PAGE OF SWORDS

This card represents messages, the attaining of a goal through diligence and hard work. The Page indicates disturbing and exciting news, messages which require thought and the examination of goals. However, self-control must be maintained in the midst of change. This card indicates vigilance and control must be exercised. There is a need for mental application and investigation.

What is the Spiritual Lesson or Challenge the Page of Swords would teach us?

The Page of Swords teaches us the importance of eliminating from our lives that which is counter-productive and wasteful. It is important that we develop our mental capabilities and harness them for the good of all. We can't accomplish this if we are weighed down with useless baggage, whether it be emotional, material, or mental.

ACE OF SWORDS

RIDER-WAITE DECK

The Hand of God emerges from a gray cloud offering a crowned double edged sword. This double-edged sword represents the sword of Truth and Discernment. The tip of the sword pierces through the crown of the material world. This symbolizes how Truth pierces the veils of Illusion on the Earth Plane and can be used to cut the limitations created there. Draped on the crown is a holly branch and a palm branch. The Holly Branch represents the Christmas Season and Birth. The Palm branch represents Easter and Resurrection.

There are six yellow Yods floating down to the Earth Plane which indicates the Descent of the Spirit into the physical and material world. Yods represent the Blessings of God on all of Creation. This card is a symbol of power. The Sword of Truth must be used with discernment and discrimination, tempered with compassion and forgiveness or this sword can become a weapon of destruction rather than an instrument of release.

MARY HANSON-ROBERTS DECK

The brilliant rays of white light emerging from gray clouds laced with violet, purple and indigo symbolize Divine Power. White is the color of purity, perfection and self-mastery. The One who welds the Sword of Truth must have self-mastery. The clouds are slowly dispersing before the power of the White Light, revealing the beautiful clear blue sky. The color of the sky represents Divine Assurance and Hope, and indicates the preparation for a new existence or new opportunities.

In the hilt of the Sword itself, there are amethysts. In ancient traditions, the Amethyst is symbolic of wisdom, benevolence, fearlessness, Truth, protection from evil and protection from self-indulgence. Amethyst is also credited with the qualities of humility, sobriety, and peace of mind. It is considered to be a stone of healing and a bringer of dreams and visions. Amethysts relate to the setting of ideals and achieving them.

There is also brown, green and blue on the Sword. The brown represents steadfastness of faith, practicality on the Earth Plane. Knowledge is only an idea unless it can have practical purposes in our lives. The Green represents growth and vitality. It is a color of peace and love, of balance. The Violet and Indigo colors in the clouds represent intuition and self-realization. Violet is the color of creativity and expression. Indigo represents the link between the intuitive mind and the Universal sub-conscious.

SUMMARY DEFINITION OF THE ACE OF SWORDS

Since Aces indicate beginnings, and the Hand of God represents the offering of protection and guidance, and the Sword indicates Truth; this card symbolizes the beginning of True Wisdom and Discernment offered by God to the individual. The opportunity to pierce the veils of Illusion is being offered to the individual by the Creator.

Honor, reward, and a change in environment are also indicated by the presence of this card. An affair may end, or people may leave the family circle. The Ace of Swords can also indicate Great Love or Great Hate, the choice being up to the individual. The Sword symbolizes victory over the distractions of the flesh, over the material plane. The Winds of Change are beginning to stir in the individual's life, changes which can herald a new era.

What is the Spiritual Lesson or Challenge the Ace of Swords would teach us?

The Ace of Swords teaches us the power of Truth, not personal truths, but Universal Truth. There is a difference. Universal Truth is a constant and cannot be changed by whims or illusions of the Earth Plane. Personal truths, on the other hand, can change many times, depending on the circumstances and the attitude of the individual. Let me give you an example of the difference between universal Truth and Personal Truth.

During World War II, the Japanese and the Germans were enemies of the United States. True? Yes. Now, in the 1980's, the Japanese and the Germans are our allies. True? Yes. This is an example of Personal Truth.

Universal Truth says that you and every one else on this planet are loved by God. Always have been and always will be, regardless of the errors or "sins" you commit. This cannot be changed. It is a Universal Truth which stands for all eternity.

Personal Truth is often clouded by the illusions of the earth plane. Universal Truth is beyond any limitations created on the earth plane. It is eternal and unalterable. Universal Truth is one of the foundations of creation, it cuts away the false and frees us from faulty perception.

TWO OF SWORDS

RIDER-WAITE DECK

The blindfolded woman is seated on a cubic stone which shows the firm foundation of her beliefs or faith. Her head is bound with a strip of white cloth which denotes wisdom. Behind her is the ocean, cradle of all life. The ocean also represents the Universal Sub-Conscious. A quarter moon shines low in the evening sky which represents the link between the subconscious mind and intuition. She holds two upright swords in her hands, her arms form a cross on her breast. This shows she is allowing her choices or decisions to be guided by Universal Truth and her subconscious link to the Divine Mind. She is dressed in gray which shows change and transition. She is passive to these changes, preferring acceptance to discord.

MARY HANSON ROBERTS DECK

The blindfolded woman seated here, on a violet pink cushion, is clothed in an orangish red dress indicating the balance of the physical and mental aspects. The sapphire blue and green bands on her robe represent choices which are based on the principles of the Ten Commandments. The violet pink cushion shows her reliance on her higher intuitional link with the Universal Sub-Conscious. This color also represents spiritual growth and attainment through the proper choices and decisions. The ocean behind her is green and white symbolizing growth, abundance and peace through union with the Supreme Being.

SUMMARY DEFINITION OF THE TWO OF SWORDS

In the Tarot, Two's represent choices or the balancing of two options to the individual. They also deal with the confirmation of new directions which were begun at a previous level. The Two of Swords deals with spiritual purity, with a firm foundations for convictions. It indicates victory without conflict or battle, a passive success. There are latent forces at work. The individual shows self-control and an attunement to others.

This card also suggests quarrels that have been resolved, although this could only be a temporary thing. There is some indecision indicated which results in a temporary balance. The individual is faced with choices and must make those choices regardless of how difficult they may seem to be at the time. Cooperation is the keyword.

What is the Spiritual Lesson or Challenge the Two of Swords would teach us?

The Two of Swords teaches us about self-control and the need for cooperation in our lives. Cooperation does not mean surrender, it means attuning yourself to the needs of others and choosing to work with those needs in concert with your own. "My way or the highway", is a self-defeating attitude and limits one in ways that may not always be apparent on the surface.

THREE OF SWORDS

RIDER-WAITE DECK

The first impression of this card is one of sorrow. If you look at the swords, they each form a cross as they pierce the heart. The heart represents the emotions. Taking these two symbols together, it means emotional pain or sorrow. The number 3 represents a spiritual initiation and the three swords represent truth. It is painful to let go of emotional illusions, to have to face reality concerning a relationship or an individual.

The background on the card is totally gray, representing change and transition. Change can be painful, even frightening at times, especially when you are not prepared for it and it comes unexpectedly. The swords piercing the heart on this card symbolize the need for spiritual discernment. If we persist in having expectations of others we are bound to experience pain. Learning to accept others as they truly are, without illusions and without judgment can spare us considerable sorrow.

MARY HANSON ROBERTS DECK

On this card, there are two black swords and one silver sword piercing the red heart. The color black represents a cross-roads, an opportunity to transcend the limitations of illusions under the guidance of a spiritual teacher. Silver represents an initiation which, at first, may seem painful, but will enable the individual to totally release the past. The serpents coiled around the hilts of the swords represent the Kundalini and Wisdom.

The color red represents the desire nature and is the color of the base root chakra, site of the Kundalini Force. If we allow our passions and desires to rule our actions and choices, rather than using this powerful energy in creative ways, we can experience many painful situations until we learn to raise the Kundalini Force from the mere physical to the Spiritual.

SUMMARY DEFINITION OF THE THREE OF SWORDS

This card symbolizes wisdom and growth gained through testing or challenges to the spirit. It indicates a need for tolerance and sympathy towards others. A need to develop spiritual discernment. This is a card of initiation, and is a symbol of clarity. Acceptance and Love can transform pain and sorrow into spiritual growth and wisdom.

On a mundane level, this card can represent separation, delay, sorrow and tears. The sowing of discord and strife. Stormy weather for the affections and possible flight of a lover. Quarrels resulting in separation, a feeling of being burdened. The greatest test will be of self-pity. This card denotes absence. Happiness depends on the integrity of the individual. More broadly, this card can indicate political strife and discord, even civil war.

What is the Spiritual Lesson or Challenge the Three of Swords would teach us?

The Three of Swords teaches us the importance of forgiveness and the release of Fear. If we forgive those who have seemed to cause us sorrow or pain, we will experience a release within our heart. Let go and let God take the pain and you will heal quickly and surely. Miracles are your right, but purification is necessary first in order to rid yourself of the burden of fear and limitation. All of us face this spiritual initiation at one point or another on the path, what we learn about ourselves, our strengths and abilities, makes this initiation an important one.

FOUR OF SWORDS

RIDER-WAITE DECK

This card represents the Spiritual Warrior who has surrendered his or her swords, or weapons of attack. One who has chosen instead to rest in the security of faith, and has given their future into the Hands of God in perfect trust. The three swords on the wall are all pointing down in an attitude of surrender or rest rather than upraised in preparation for fighting or struggle. The fourth sword rests under the Knight. The hands of the Knight are positioned for prayer, showing the importance of meditation, solitude and prayer.

MARY HANSON-ROBERTS DECK

The dominant color on this card is white. White is the color of purity, of perfection and is a symbol of the Super Conscious or Christ Conscious. White also indicates union with the Supreme Being. Through meditation and prayer this union is achieved. Golden brown is also present on this card as one of the foundations or supports of the church. This color represents the blending of enlightenment with practicality and strength on the earth plane. It indicates one who is spiritual but has their feet firmly planted on the ground. The hilts of the 4 swords are green, showing growth, peace, and ease.

SUMMARY DEFINITION OF THE FOUR OF SWORDS

This card shows the "calm after the storm"; the rest, relief and peace which follows all upheavals in our lives. Fours deal with the manifestations of plans or actions of the past into reality now. With this card present, it indicates that all conflicts have ended, worries are finally over. There will soon be a change for the better. The foundation for the future has been established.

This card indicates that now the individual is drawn towards mysticism, towards a growing understanding of the Spiritual Ideal. It denotes a time of meditation, of deep thoughts granting one the opportunity to gain peace and quiet. This is a card of *chosen* solitude, not of forced solitude. The individual is choosing to step back from the intense battle of life and contemplating their future direction.

What is the Spiritual Lesson or Challenge the Four of Swords would teach us?

The Four of Swords teaches us the importance of taking time out from the distractions of life and re-evaluating one's goals. Meditation and prayer are ways to get in touch with your higher self, that part of you which is in constant communication with the Creator. Solitude is not to be feared, but to be eagerly anticipated. Solitude gives one the opportunity for quiet reflection and inner guidance.

FIVE OF SWORDS

RIDER-WAITE DECK

Arrogance is the key-word for this card. The figure in the foreground has defeated two opponents in combat and is intensely satisfied at having humiliated them. He is taking joy in their pain and discomfort. In this conflict, rather than using kindness, acceptance and forgiveness, this individual has tried to force others to his way of thinking. What he does not realize is that one of his opponents is not truly defeated and will return to fight the individual another day.

The 3 figures on this card also represent the 3 states of Consciousness: the Subconscious, the Conscious, and the Super-Conscious or Christ Conscious. The aftermath of the battle shows an internal war going on within the individual between these three states of consciousness. Clearly, the ego, servant of Illusions, appears to have won the battle. But the figures walking away, dressed in yellow and gold, the colors of enlightenment, integrity and clear thinking, will be back to face the ego at some other time and place.

MARY HANSON-ROBERTS DECK

Reddish brown is the color of the first figures surcoat. This color indicates past-life violence, a blood-guilt karma. It can also represent jealousy toward the individual or that the individual is jealous or envious of the gains of others. This color represents a difficult lesson to be learned an experience which may cause disruption in one's life. However, there is green present on this card, promising eventual peace and ease of mind. Green is the color of growth and healing.

The swords in this picture are more gray than silver, indicating that they are not being used to discern the Truth, to cut away Illusions. The lowest vibration of the swords are being used, rather than their higher vibration. The touches of sky-blue on the hilts of the swords indicate there is hope for the individual and despite the negative use of their energy, the individual is still under the protection of Divine Love.

SUMMARY DEFINITION OF THE FIVE OF SWORDS

In the Tarot the Five's in a suit indicate difficulties, changes and challenges the individual will have to adjust to or make themselves. The Five of Swords represents conquest over others through physical or mental strength. Also indicated is a variety of new opportunities, travel and change. However, these opportunities will be an initiation for the individual. If the individual continues to operate under the guidance of the Ego, they will eventually experience defeat. However, if they learn from the mistakes of the past and turn inward for Divine Guidance, the new opportunities will result in spiritual growth and understanding.

This card also represents three attitudes of mind, showing that discrimination and discernment in all matters is very important. Blind impulsiveness at this time can bring about loss. Gloating over one's triumph will bring about a downfall or defeat at a later time. It also indicates the finish of a job or challenge in which the individual was successful.

What is the Spiritual Lesson or Challenge the Five of Swords would teach us?

The Five of Swords teaches us that we are responsible for the choices and actions we make in life. Acceptance of one's responsibilities is an important lesson to learn. We have to learn not to blame others for our seeming "misfortune" or difficulties. The longer we deny acceptance, the harder and more difficult it will become later.

SIX OF SWORDS

RIDER-WAITE DECK

With six Swords as a shield at the front of the boat, a man with a woman and child leaves the troubled waters behind them as he steers their boat to calmer waters. They are on a passage away from difficulties. Their faith is the beacon that guides them. The water is a sky-blue and dominates most of the card. This color represents hope and Divine Assurance. It also indicates the preparation for a new existence and new opportunities for growth and prosperity.

MARY HANSON-ROBERTS DECK

With this card, we have a man delivering the Swords of Truth to the Earth Plane. His boat, the foundation, is golden brown representing the blending of enlightenment with practicality and strength on the earth plane. He goes to offer himself in selfless service to others. The rim of the boat and the hilts of the swords are sky-blue, the color of spiritual blessings and Divine Assurance. The water before him and the sky above him is in shades of violet pink and white, the color of spiritual growth and attainment.

SUMMARY DEFINITION OF THE SIX OF SWORDS

This card symbolizes the calm after the storm. It also indicates success after anxiety, a heart tried by fire. The Six of Swords represents the realization of a goal, the passage from difficulty. An invitation to join a new endeavor leading to fulfillment is also indicated by this card.

Companionship, love, and a meeting of minds is indicated by the Six of Swords. Harmony, earned success, work, publicity, and a revelation are keywords to describe this card's message. A messenger, surprise or travel is also indicated by the presence of this card in a lay-out spread.

What is the Spiritual Lesson or Challenge the six of Swords would teach us?

The Six of Swords teaches us not to let the difficulties or pain we have experienced in the past sour the potentials we have in the present and future. Attainment of one's goals requires some struggle on our part to achieve. But these struggles serve to show us what our strengths and abilities are.

SEVEN OF SWORDS

RIDER-WAITE DECK

What a sneaky looking character! It seems as though greed is what motivates his actions. He is dressed in a muddy green tunic and walks on ground of the same color. This putrid shade of green represents malice, envy, jealousy, and greed. The individual seeks, by stealth, to take what doesn't belong to him, but what he thinks he deserves. Because of the tents in the background, which represent a temporary situation, his good luck will not last long. He will only temporarily have the advantage he seeks.

The individual has not learned to share with others. He desires, (the red hat on his head), to claim as much as he can for himself. He is a traitor and is under the mistaken idea that by the use of deception he can get away with his actions. He does not yet know or accepted the Truth that as ye sow, so shall ye reap. Ironically, the swords he has stolen were put point side down in the ground which represents a non-threatening gesture on the behalf of those he has stolen from. His "enemy" meant him no harm.

MARY HANSON-ROBERTS DECK

Motivated by the need for material power and possessions, this individual, by using deception and stealth, is making away with what does not belong to him. This is symbolized by the dominant color brown. Gray storm clouds gather in the sky, the sign of turbulent change. The figure wears a black undertunic showing he has chosen to walk on the dark path of life. His mind is temporarily closed to the influence of the Light, instead he is under the thrall of the ego and of illusions.

SUMMARY DEFINITION OF THE SEVEN OF SWORDS

This card represents hesitation, uncertainty, partial or temporary success. The health of the individual may need attention. There could be arguments or an unwise attempt to make off with something not belonging to the individual. This card can also indicate the individual is using wrong thinking in business or other enterprises. It may show that in some project or situation, the individual is acting alone, not listening or accepting any inner guidance.

What is the Spiritual Lesson or Challenge the Seven of Swords would teach us?

The Seven of Swords teaches us of the temporary nature that gifts from the ego have. Choosing to satisfy only our physical desires, whether it be through sexual situations, business, material possessions, etc., we end up with nothing of lasting value. Acting out of spite or envy towards others only ends up hurting us in the long term. Learning how to deal with jealousy and other similar emotions is a necessary process in cleansing ourselves from unwanted emotional and mental baggage.

EIGHT OF SWORDS

RIDER-WAITE DECK

The figure of a woman, bound and blindfolded, is the center point of this card. Behind her is a wall of swords which prevent her from going backwards. This card symbolizes self-imposed limitations and worry for no reason. If she choose to, the woman could leave her limitations behind and merely walk way from this prison, (her hands and feet are not bound). It would be easy for her to remove the bonds that restrict her. Nothing is preventing her from leaving this sorry situation expect her own fear.

She is standing with one foot on ground and one foot in water. Water represents the Universal Sub-Conscious and land represents the earth plane. She is torn between listening to the limitations of the ego whispering in her mind and the gentle intuitive guidance of the Universal Mind. The castle in the background, high atop a cliff, represents the achievements she has made in the past, achievements which have brought about heavy responsibilities and burdens she is now worrying about.

MARY HANSON-ROBERTS DECK

Choices. Decisions. Which way should she turn? What action should she take? These are questions which plague this woman bound by her own fears and worries. It would be easy for her to slip a hand free of the ropes which bind her and remove the blindfold and get rid of the rope. She could then take one of the swords which stands before her or behind her and use it to her advantage. But *she* must **CHOOSE** to do this. No one can free her from her fears but herself.

The gown she wears, the hilts of the swords and the castle in the background are various shades of purple and violet. These colors symbolize self-realization, spiritual growth, intuition and the Higher Consciousness. The sky, water and swords are gray showing change, a transition taking place. The woman is facing a spiritual initiation in her life. The touches of green and sky-blue indicate that peace will be found and growth will be experienced.

SUMMARY DEFINITION OF THE EIGHT OF SWORDS

The individual may feel restricted or limited in someway. There can be worry or anxiety over a situation that has not happened and may never happen.

There could be difficulties with relatives or interference. Criticism, possible conflicts are also indicated. Narrow or restricted surroundings, bondage or limitations are self-imposed because the individual is hesitating or fearful of the outcome. But all will work out to the satisfaction of the individual once they correct their lack of persistence and have more faith.

What is the Spiritual Lesson or Challenge the Eight of Swords would teach us?

The Eight of Swords teaches us about the true nature of limitations. We have no real limitations except those we choose to accept. We accept limitations when we allow ourselves to become fearful and filled with anxiety.

NINE OF SWORDS

RIDER-WAITE DECK
A woman has awakened from her sleep, haunted by the dreams she has received concerning her loved ones. Her blanket or comforter has the signs of the Zodiac on it and red roses. Beside her, on the wall, hang 9 swords whose tips are pointed to the east, to the rising sun. This symbolizes new beginnings which will come at the dawn of a new day. Doubts and fears are powerless before the Light. The 9 swords pointing in the direction of the Source of Light are there to remind her of this.

MARY HANSON ROBERTS DECK
The reflective white Light of the 9 swords immediately catch your eye on this card. Despite the woman's fears, she has the protection of Divine Light. She is covered with a reddish-purple blanket which represents karmic suffering and testing in this life due to wrong choices in past-life situations. This karmic testing is not happening to the woman directly, but to those she loves and feels helpless to assist.

The black background of this card represents a mind besieged with doubts, depression and fears. Black also represents a cross-roads. The woman can look up, see the Light the swords are pointing to and find the comfort she needs to face the difficulties ahead. These difficulties pertain to others in her live she feels responsible for in some way. The Sapphire Blue and Navy Blue colors represent her selfless concern but also her sense of isolation.

SUMMARY DEFINITION OF THE NINE OF SWORDS
This card symbolizes worry and anxiety over a loved one. There is fear of loss for a loved one and a feeling of helplessness over a difficult situation. Struggles, unselfishness and doubts are represented by the Nine of Swords. There can be an inability to make a choice in an important matter due to confusion and doubt. The Nine of Swords may indicate a possible miscarriage for someone the individual loves. The delays experienced will bring about self-control over the emotions.

What is the Spiritual Lesson or challenge the Nine of Swords would teach us?

The Nine of Swords teaches us that worry is like a rocking chair. It gives you something to do, but doesn't get you anywhere. From time to time, those in our lives we love and care for must face difficulties and even painful situations. We cannot shield them from these events, but we can be there for them giving the faith and hope, understanding and compassion they need. We encourage them to pray, as well as pray for them ourselves. But we must accept that difficulties are a part of life on the earth plane, and that difficulties can be turned into opportunities for tremendous growth if we will only choose to perceive it so.

TEN OF SWORDS

RIDER-WAITE DECK
This card symbolizes the need for complete and utter surrender of the Ego and its illusions. This means giving up thoughts of revenge, envy, jealousy, malice and spite. The ten swords piercing the figure on the card symbolizes the defeat of the Ego, a defeat which will bring about a great spiritual awakening. This is not a card of death, violent or otherwise. The surrender to the guidance of the Higher Consciousness is represented by the crosses formed by the ten swords. This card indicates the defeat of the false personality through traumatic and dramatic circumstances.

MARY HANSON-ROBERTS DECK
The greed and lust for material possessions and preoccupation with mate-
rial security, (symbolized by the color brown), has been halted by the placement of the ten swords. The various shades of gray represent the ending of an old way of life, an old way of believing which was grounded in the material world of illusions. A new, spiritual oriented individual is being reborn through the challenges faced. This card represents the defeat of that part of ourselves which limit us and burdens us with wrong thinking.

SUMMARY DEFINITION OF THE TEN OF SWORDS
This card symbolizes a spiritual awakening, a new awareness, the end of delusion in spiritual matters. This is a card of trials and testing brought on by karma of the past. It shows that burdens or disappointments are challenges for the spirit to be faced with determination and strength. It is an opportunity to turn to the God within for help and guidance. These trials the individual faces will lead to the discovery of their destiny and will lead to balance of the Mind, body and spirit.

What is the Spiritual Lesson or Challenge the Ten of Swords would teach us?
The Ten of Swords teaches us that the Ego will fight with all the strength it possesses and all the illusions it can muster to prevent spiritual awakening within ourselves. Clinging to Dogma is not true spirituality, though the ego masquerades spirituality thus. Learning to use discernment and truth to get through the illusions surrounding rigid dogma is painful for we must let go of many preconceived notions we once may have cherished. True enlightenment is a difficult ideal to achieve, but it is worth the attempt.

CHAPTER THIRTY-SEVEN

SUIT OF PENTACLES

The basic nature of the Suit of Pentacles involves securing what exists on the material plane. Pentacles represent the development of the material, physical world and the place an individual holds there. This Suit indicates security, (or the lack of), in one's life. The physical body and physical appetites as well as desires are also represented by the Suit of Pentacles. Pentacles indicate growth as well as security in jobs, careers, and other material resources. The element which corresponds to Pentacles is Earth. Astrologically, the Earth Signs of Taurus, Virgo, and Capricorn are represented by Pentacles.

This Suit is concerned with the realm of physical experience and the ideas which express measurable and tangible results in the external world. They also deal with worldly fortune and prosperity. Pentacles also stress the importance of balance between the physical material world and the world of Spirit. The past foundations of the individual is stressed by the Pentacles. Foundations are what we build upon, are what we base our future on, and even what motivates us in many cases. Underneath the material aspect of this suit, the Pentacles also symbolize a deep commitment and involvement with the uplifting of human-kind through the proper use of the material side of the Earth Plane.

The symbols on this suit are what the ancients referred to as Pentagrams, which were used in Alchemy and Magic in the distant past. The Five-pointed Star was, (and still is), a symbol used by occultists to represent the five senses of humankind. In the Tarot, this suit represents money, acquisitions of worldly fame, authority, business dealings and trade. The Suit of Pentacles reflect the outward manifestation of security, of sexual desires, and of the individual's health.

KING OF PENTACLES

RIDER-WAITE DECK
This King has subdued his warrior nature, (his suit of armor is hidden under his rich robes). He has taken that energy and directed it into constructive projects, creative endeavors, working with nature so that the earth itself will bear fruit to feed the multitudes. This king is a working king. He does not idly sit on his throne and expect others to do his work for him. Because of his attention to details and his industriousness, he is prosperous in all he under-takes.

This prosperity is symbolized by the rich robes he wears which bears the symbols of grapes and grape-leaves. This indicates his desires have been fulfilled on the material plane. The scepter he holds in one hand represents his authority over the material plane. The yellow pentacle in the other hand shows his ability to handle material possessions and money wisely and for the benefit of all. His throne is carved with the heads of bulls, symbolizing his steadfastness in pursuing his goals.

MARY HANSON-ROBERTS DECK

On this card there is a lot of rich purples and golds. The King's robes and throne are purple with gold symbols. Gold is the color of spiritual blessings, enlightenment, and attainment. Purple is the color of spiritual intuition, higher consciousness and the sowing of karmic seeds. It is the color of releasing, of letting go and letting God. The throne and the trim on the King's robes is a blend of gold and brown, representing the blending of enlightenment with practicality and strength on the Earth Plane.

Golden brown is a color representing one who is spiritual but with their feet firmly planted on the ground. This color also indicates one who offers themselves in selfless service to others. Violet Pink is the color of his castle and the color of the sky. This color represents spiritual growth and self-realization. It is the color of attainment and creative expression on the Earth Plane. Green is also present here, again representing growth and abundance.

SUMMARY DEFINITION OF THE KING OF PENTACLES

This card represents a man who is of a steady temperament, slow to anger, and who has success where business matters are concerned. He has the ability to handle money wisely, and possesses authority and power in the physical world. The King represents a reliable man who is noted for his intelligence and character. Since Pentacles represent the element of Earth, this card corresponds to a person who has strong earth elements in their astrological chart or who has the Sun, Moon or Ascendant in Taurus, Virgo or Capricorn.

The King of Pentacles indicates a promotion and rewards for a job well done. It also shows assistance to the individual working with this card in a layout spread. Influential people, especially those of the opposite sex, will advance the individual's position in life, job, or career. This card represents reliable success, victory and courage.

What is the Spiritual Lesson or Challenge the King of Pentacles would teach us?

The King of Pentacles teaches us the wise use of material prosperity. The more "gifts" you give to others, the more you will receive in return. All that we give, is really given to ourselves and this is the lesson the King of Pentacles teaches.

QUEEN OF PENTACLES

RIDER-WAITE DECK

The Queen sits on a throne decorated with the symbols of cherubs and the fruits of nature's bounty. The cherubs symbolize Divine Guidance and Protection. This woman is the epitome of the Earth Mother, the loving, generous, nurturing force which pervades all corners of the Earth Plane. Flowers are growing in abundant profusion all around her bower. She is the Queen of Fertility and of earthly love. The rabbit running through her lush garden is also a symbol of fertility.

This intuitive and gifted Queen is very aware of the magic or miracles of nature and the strength she receives from her union with it. She has a deep love for and a sense of one-ness with all of creation. This Queen is intelligent and in tune with the productive forces of nature around her. She is a creator on the physical plane. Holding the yellow pentacle, the symbol of material prosperity and abundance, she generously gives of her gifts to all who have need.

MARY HANSON-ROBERTS DECK
There is an abundance of fruits and flowers surrounding the Queen. She holds a tame rabbit in her hand, showing her dominion over the animal kingdom, a dominion earned through love and understanding, not through force or subjugation. The Queen has the power to grant fertility to those who ask. She blesses the sowing of seeds in the spring and the harvest in the fall. The Queen of Pentacles is the channel for the forces of nature.

The major colors which stand out on this card are the golds and browns. Gold represents the power of physical and material manifestation, enlightenment and advancement of the soul. The red roses have white borders on their petals showing that earthly desires are in the process of being transformed to a higher level, are being purified and cleansed of negativity. The mountains in the background are violet in color indicating spiritual growth and attainment, self-realization and artistic or creative expression.

The sky overhead is a blend of soft pink and rose, the colors of mystical love, empathy, and self-mastery. Pink and rose also represent nurturing love, devotion, tenderness, and a sensitivity to other life-forms. The brown of her throne indicates she gives gifts to others which are both practical in nature and are spiritually nourishing. The color green is found throughout the picture representing growth, abundance, healing and love. These are some of the gifts the Queen shares with others.

SUMMARY DEFINITION OF THE QUEEN OF PENTACLES
This card represents an affectionate, steady, fruitful, charming, kind and practical woman who establishes the home or foundation for growth and nurturing. She has the protection of Divine Beings who radiate love, peace, happiness, and contentment. This same protection she offers to the individual working with this card in a layout spread. The Queen is a creator on the physical material plane, she is the quintessential Earth Mother, generous with her gifts and filled with love.

She uses her talents and abilities well and for the benefit of all. This card in a layout represents financial security, travel, and educational pursuits. Help, assistance, material benefits, and security are also keywords representing this card. The Queen symbolizes a love for and a unity with the World. She is willing to render a service to the individual. Since Pentacles represent the earth element this card indicates an individual who has strong earth signs in their astrological chart or who has the Sun, Moon or Ascendant in Taurus, Virgo or Capricorn.

What is the Spiritual Lesson or Challenge the Queen of Pentacles would teach us?

The Queen of Pentacles teaches us our connection to and unity with Nature. This realization is important for our own growth for we are the Caretakers of the gifts Nature bestows. We have a responsibility to the Animal and Plant Kingdoms to nurture and sustain their rights to the planet. Oftentimes, mankind has abused and tortured the creatures of Nature, not realizing these actions reverberate back to the human kingdom, causing chaos and war.

KNIGHT OF PENTACLES

RIDER-WAITE DECK

The Knight in this picture is sitting on a large brown horse which looks like it could be part Clydesdale, (the long hair on the bottom of the legs). This is a working horse, strong, powerful, steady, and reliable. Beside the Knight is the freshly tilled earth. Purple is the color of the Higher Consciousness and intuition, the color of the plowed field symbolizing the sowing of karmic seeds and ideas based on intuition and guidance from the higher consciousness.

Both the Knight and the horse have fresh green sprigs decorating the helmet and bridle. This symbolizes their industriousness and willingness to work for results. The Knight holds a yellow pentacle indicating the reaping of material prosperity and security. But he does not relax his vigilance, knowing that continued growth depends on his continued efforts. He is hardworking, responsible and uncomplaining. He feels his ties to the Mother Earth strongly and is grateful for her nurturing love.

MARY HANSON-ROBERTS DECK

Dressed in white and silver, holding a golden pentacle, this Knight represents prosperity and security on the Earth Plane which has been inspired by Spiritual Principles. The brown color of the freshly tilled earth behind him indicates that the work he has done in the past will reap the financial and spiritual rewards he is seeking. The green of the fields and the fruit bearing trees behind him also indicate abundance, growth, and monetary ease.

SUMMARY DEFINITION OF THE KNIGHT OF PENTACLES

This card symbolizes the corning or going of an important matter concerning money or material possessions. It indicates a messenger bringing news of an increase in monetary security. This card also shows that attainment and success do not come from a lazy attitude. The Knight of Pentacles shows that success is very possible now, if one is willing to put for the effort and work towards this goal.

What is the Spiritual Lesson or Challenge the Knight of Pentacles would teach us?

The Knight of Pentacles teaches us the rewards of patience and hard work. Spiritual and material success is attainable if one is willing to develop the self-discipline necessary to achieve these goals.

PAGE OF PENTACLES

RIDER-WAITE DECK

This card represents choices for the future. The yellow pentacle of prosperity is held high and studied intently by the young Page. Dressed in green and standing on lush green fields, the Page is concerned with continued growth and learning. The mountain of spiritual attainment is in the distance, indicating the young Page still has a lot to learn on the Earth Plane concerning the material aspect of this plane before he is truly secure on a spiritual level as well as a physical-material level.

The yellow color of the sky dominates this card symbolizing the active mind, clear thinking, and integrity. The red hat the Page is wearing indicates he is learning how to use the Kundalini Force with integrity and enlightenment. because of his brown boots and hose, he already has material possessions that most people seek for. But he knows that material things are not enough, that there is more to life than monetary ease, and he wants to develop his spiritual gifts on a more elevated plane.

MARY HANSON-ROBERTS DECK

On this card, the Page appears to be more of a young girl than boy. The Pages in the Minor Arcana can represent a young person or either sex. Pages generally symbolize messengers, therefore, this young girl is bringing a message concerning money and prosperity. She seems to know, by the thoughtful and compassionate expression on her face, that this good news has been eagerly anticipated by the recipient.

The Page wears a white tunic with white embroidered flowers on it, a color indicating her purity and innocence. It also shows she is the instrument of the Creator in delivering the longed for message. The soft rose and pink color of the sky shows this message is a loving gift from God to the individual designed to assist them on their path in life.

SUMMARY DEFINITION OF THE PAGE OF PENTACLES

This card indicates opportunities for attainment. Social invitations may bring new opportunities. It could represent a scholar or student, or the bringer of good news about money. This card can also represent a message or letter of importance dealing with money or a job. It may be a message from an editor, director, book-keeper or assistant. Sometimes this card will indicate a meeting with a committee or a board of directors concerning something the individual has created or is proposing.

What is the Spiritual Lesson or Challenge the Page of Pentacles would teach us?

The Page of Pentacles teaches us not to allow the world of illusions to rob us of our innocence, our joy in life or our faith in the Creator's Love for us. Material needs can weight heavily on us at times, cloaking us in despair. When this occurs, it is not always easy to see that when one door closes, another opens, leading us to a better life and new opportunities.

ACE OF PENTACLES

RIDER-WAITE DECK

The Hand of God is offering material security and abundance. The yellow Pentacle the Hand is holding symbolizes prosperity and the beginning of a new life, new opportunities. There is a lush green garden in the foreground filled with a variety of different flowers. A yellow path winds its way through the garden to the Gateway to the sky-blue mountains of spiritual attainment in the distance. Sky blue is the color of Divine Hope and Assurance.

The green of the garden represents growth, abundance, and ease. The yellow path represents the active mind, clear thinking, integrity and enlightenment. If an individual uses the gift of clear thinking with integrity, they can make tremendous strides on the material plane that benefit themselves and others at the same time. The promise of achievement symbolized by this card hinges on the actions of the individual.

MARY HANSON-ROBERTS DECK

The colors on this card are rich with symbolism. The Pentacle is golden in color representing gifts of the Spirit and advancement of the Soul. It is the color of prosperity and restoration and symbolizes the fulfillment of our hopes, desires and wishes. The Pentacle is being held aloft by white lilies which symbolize purified desires. The background is a violet pink cloud edged with golden yellow and a rose colored sky. Violet pink is the color of self-realization and creativity signifying that through our own talents and abilities we can achieve recognition, prosperity and abundance.

SUMMARY DEFINITION OF THE ACE OF PENTACLES

This card symbolizes the Creator's offers of material and Spiritual security and freedom from lack. The Ace of Pentacles also indicates the attainment of one's goals and prosperity. Honor, fame, money and contentment are keywords describing the attributes of this card. Material gain, power, wealth, the fruits of past labors are in the individual's hands. It indicates the fulfillment of hopes, wishes and desires.

What is the Spiritual Lesson or Challenge the Ace of Pentacles would teach us?

The Ace of Pentacles teaches us the true meaning of abundance and security. True security comes from establishing a sense of self-worth, of knowing who and what you are and what your goals are in life. Security comes from the knowledge that you are not alone and separate on the Earth Plane, that you are constantly surrounded by love and guidance if you will but accept it. Abundance is not only material in nature, but spiritual as well. True abundance and contentment cannot be experienced without the element of trust and faith.

TWO OF PENTACLES

RIDER-WAITE DECK

The figure depicted on this card is holding two pentacles which are entwined with the sign of Infinity. This shows our abundance has its roots in the infinite power of the Universe, it can never be depleted for its is perpetually self-renewing. The more we give, the more we receive, the supply is endless and eternal. The figure on the card is able to keep this flow balanced properly so that there is no struggle involved.

Behind him, on the rolling blue waves of the sea, are two ships which are struggling to maintain their balance within the crux of change. The Sea, being water, represents the Universal Sub-Conscious and the ebb and flow of energy within the universal structure. The ships aren't in any danger, but symbolize instead that change is what brings renewal into our lives. Ships also symbolize the thoughts or wishes we have. Remember the old adage: "When my ship comes in". Therefore, the ships represent the requests we send out into the universe.

MARY HANSON-ROBERTS DECK

Gold and golden brown are the dominant colors on this card. Gold represents enlightenment, restoration, and soul advancement. It also indicates the power of physical and material manifestation. Golden brown signifies the blending of enlightenment with practicality and strength on the Earth Plane. It indicates one who is spiritual, but with their feet firmly planted on the ground. It shows too, the importance of giving selfless service to others in need.

The two golden pentacles are rimmed with the color blue in the form of the Infinity symbol. This shows Divine Assurance, fulfillment of hopes, the preparation for new opportunities resulting in a new existence. The figure wears an outer tunic of brown which represents physical and mental satisfaction as well as receiving recognition from others for services rendered, or artistic and creative expressions completed.

SUMMARY DEFINITION OF THE TWO OF PENTACLES

This card represents the ability to handle two situations at once. Changes, harmony within change, and partnerships are also indicated as is increased business activity. This card indicates that management and executive positions may be offered to the individual. The individual working with this card in a layout spread has the ability to handle or juggle two situations at once.

The Two of Pentacles also symbolizes literary ability. There could be messages dealing with a literary career or something similar. News and messages in writing indicated.

What is the Spiritual Lesson or Challenge the Two of Pentacles would teach us?

The Two of Pentacles teaches us the importance of working in harmony with change. The thoughts we send out to universe requesting certain events to occur necessitate change in our lives, and many times we are ill prepared for the changes when they come, resulting in struggle rather than a smooth transition. Learning how to harmonize with the ebb and flow of energy is a challenge the Two of Pentacles offers.

THREE OF PENTACLES

RIDER-WAITE DECK

This picture shows an artisan or master craftsman dressed in purple hard at work creating something of lasting value. The purple clothing he wears symbolizes his openness to the influence of his Higher Consciousness on his creativity. It also represents his reliance on intuition and his connection to the forces of the universe. Because of his talents and abilities, he receives recognition and financial rewards from those who admire and enjoy his creativity. Three pentacles grace the archway of the cathedral, three is the number of completion and artistic expression.

MARY HANSON-ROBERTS DECK

The pillars and even the ceiling of this temple or cathedral is violet pink laced with gold. Violet Pink is the color of self-realization, creativity, and artistic expression. The golden pentacles represent enlightenment, gifts of the Spirit and advancement of the Soul. The color gold represents the power of physical and material manifestation. The golden browns of the arches symbolize the blending of spirituality with practicality and strength on the Earth Plane. There are touches of rose and pink showing through the lattice work of the window, signifying the expression of love in the individual's creations.

SUMMARY DEFINITION OF THE THREE OF PENTACLES

This card represents advancement in the creative arts. It is the symbol of the master craftsman. Three is the number of completion indicating promotions and contracts concerning creative potentials. This card indicates one who has learned their trade or talent well. The Three of Pentacles represents gain, material increase, fame, and recognition.

What is the Spiritual Lesson or Challenge the Three of Pentacles would teach us?

The Three of Pentacles teaches us the importance of being in tune with our creative intuitive nature under the guidance of the Higher Consciousness. Through our use of creative expression we serve as channels for Higher Forces in the Universe. Our challenge is to remove the self-imposed limitations on our creativity and allow it to flow freely.

FOUR OF PENTACLES

RIDER-WAITE DECK

The figure depicted on this card shows a preoccupation with material concerns. He is so worried that someone or something is going to take his possessions that he clutches them to himself in a protective manner. He is dressed in dark brown representing the material physical plane. He is almost obsessed in keeping what belongs to him safe, afraid to share his gifts with others. He has built a foundation of material possessions and security but has neglected his spiritual foundations. The dominance of the color gray shows a coming change in status whether the individual depicted on the card wants it or not.

MARY HANSON-ROBERTS DECK

The figure depicted on this card literally symbolizes an old miser, clutching his wealth tightly and dressed in rather poor looking clothing. There is a lot of dark gray around him, showing his difficulty in accepting change and transformation. His cloak is a reddish brown representing difficult karmic lessons due to past-life actions. However, the gold of the pentacles and the touches of violet here and there show that on a deep level, the miser is aware of the spiritual path he should walk. Eventually he will accept the changes in consciousness and free himself from the fear that limits him, the fear he has in loosing his material security and possessions.

SUMMARY DEFINITION OF THE FOUR OF PENTACLES

Four's in a suit of the Minor Arcana indicate the foundation upon which the individual builds, therefore it is very important that the individual learn to balance material concerns with spiritual concerns when establishing a proper foundation. The Four of Pentacles indicates power, increase and satisfaction, the gain of money and influence. It also represents undiscovered talents and abilities the individual has.

What is the Spiritual Lesson or Challenge the Four of Pentacles would teach us?

The Four of Pentacles teaches us the importance of sharing our abundance and gifts with others. Clutching our material security to us, afraid to let any of it go, dams up the flow of prosperity into our lives. It is just as important to learn discernment concerning charity to others too. We are not supposed to wantonly waste or scatter our resources just to impress others or to ease a guilty conscience. Finding the balance between giving too much and giving too little is, indeed, a spiritual challenge.

FIVE OF PENTACLES

RIDER-WAITE DECK

This card takes the meaning of the four of pentacles one step further, showing how poverty of the spirit leads to poverty in material concerns as well. This card serves as a warning to seek the Light within. It represents too much pride and ego interfering with the help that is available to the individuals depicted on the card. They have turned their faces away from the light in the church because they are so concentrated on their plight.

The white snow and their bare feet represent a lesson in self-mastery and purification. The figures are dressed in ragged clothing and one figure walks on crutches symbolizing the crippling effect past choices have left on him. In traditional terms, this card is often referred to as "The Dark Night of the Soul", symbolizing a difficult karmic learning experience designed to break through the ego's grip on the individual's soul.

MARY HANSON-ROBERTS DECK

The snow already on the ground and around the windows on this card is a violet pink in color representing a difficult lesson which will lead to self-realization as soon as the individual is willing to accept it. There is a lot of dark gray touched with light shades of purple showing the difficulty in the transition the individuals are going through, yet also promising enlightenment and release from limitations. The golden pentacles and the golden light emanating from the window of the church shows that God has not abandoned these individuals, but that He loves them enough to let them choose their own time to turn to Him.

SUMMARY DEFINITION OF THE FIVE OF PENTACLES

This card symbolizes both poverty of the soul and anxiety concerning material security. It represents a time of testing and trial, of feeling a great inner pain and experiencing the feeling of being burdened or abandoned. It shows a strong will and great endurance. Sometimes this card refers to a love gone astray or to a divorce. It is a difficult time, causing upheaval in the individual's life, but ultimately leading them into the Light.

What is the Spiritual Lesson or Challenge the Five of Pentacles would teach us?

The Five of Pentacles teaches us to always seek the Light within when we are faced with difficult circumstances or choices. The Five of Pentacles emphasis the need to keep attuned to the Higher Forces and to accept the guidance offered. The Spiritual Challenge is to accept that You are Spirit. You are the child of God. No physical body can contain your spirit, or impose on you a limitation God did not create.

SIX OF PENTACLES

RIDER-WAITE DECK

This picture depicts a benevolent, generous, kind and compassionate man who shares his prosperity with others in need. He epitomizes the concept of Charity. Through the wise use of material power he provides for the welfare of others not so fortunate as he. He is giving to others as he has received for himself. The scales held in one hand represents balance and the wise use of wealth and prosperity. His tunic is white and blue symbolizing spiritual blessings, gifts of the spirit and purity. It also represents his unity with the Creator. He has accepted the opportunity to become a servant of the Higher Forces.

MARY HANSON-ROBERTS DECK

The man in this card wears a robe and hat of rich purple indicating the Higher Consciousness and the intuitional mind. The gold color of the sky and the golden pentacles indicate the power of physical and material manifestation, enlightenment, and soul advancement. Orange, the color of balance between mental and physical elements, is also present in the picture. One of the beggars is dressed in muddy green rags. Muddy Green is the color of envy, jealousy, malice, and spite. Even though the individual giving out gifts to the beggars may have been the target of those negative emotions, he has forgiven them and chosen to help the beggars anyway, an example of the true meaning of Charity.

SUMMARY DEFINITION OF THE SIX OF PENTACLES

Success and gain in material things is strongly indicated. This is signified by the seizing of an opportunity, of sharing with others and by being a channel for love and healing. There will be stabilization for the individual even in the midst of uncertainty around them. This is a sign of karmic merit, the individual will receive what they deserve and finally achieve the recognition their due. This is a card of gratification and balance.

What is the Spiritual Lesson or Challenge the Six of Pentacles would teach us?

The Six of Pentacles teaches us how even the simplest things we do for others have a profound effect on them, effects we may not even be aware of. Charity is not just a matter of giving money or material things, but it means giving of yourself to others when all they may need is just for you to listen to them.

SEVEN OF PENTACLES

RIDER-WAITE DECK

The picture on this card represents the stages of growth we all go through. The young farmer has diligently plowed and planted his field, nurtured the young plants, and now is waiting patiently for them to bear fruit so he may harvest them. He is learning an important lesson involving patience, if he allows impatience to rule him, he could lose his hard earned crop. If, however, he waits just a little longer, his patience will be rewarded with a bumper crop which represents material prosperity and security.

MARY HANSON-ROBERTS DECK

The predominance of the color green shows abundant growth has taken place in this young farmer's fields, but harvest time has not yet arrived. He will reap what he has sown when the time is right, not before. The golden pentacles on the vines near the buds of the plants represent the success and attainment he will receive once the cycle of nature has completed its rotation. He needs to have trust and faith in his own skills as a creator and know the importance of believing in himself and the gifts he is entitled to. That is the purpose of his waiting period, to teach him self-confidence and faith in his own abilities to manifest on the physical and material plane.

SUMMARY DEFINITION OF THE SEVEN OF PENTACLES

This card indicates success has not yet been fully attained, but if one is patient, success will fully materialize. The Seven of Pentacles shows a natural outcome of what was sown previously. Responsibilities, patience and hard work are key qualities needed to bring progressive change and security. The presence of this card in a layout also indicates a potentially suitable mate for the individual, a partner to share the joys and challenges of life.

What is the Spiritual Lesson or Challenge the Seven of Pentacles would teach us?

Beyond the obvious lesson in patience, the Seven of Pentacles teaches us the importance of self-confidence in our talents and abilities. We all have special qualities that need nurturing and developing. Actually, there is no such thing as an ordinary person. The unique gifts we all possess in some form or another are available to us in order to discover and then complete our function on the earth plane.

EIGHT OF PENTACLES

RIDER-WAITE DECK

This card clearly shows a young apprentice learning his trade, studying to become a master craftsman. He realizes that to achieve perfection, he must be willing to dedicate himself and work hard towards that ends. This young apprentice shows honesty, attention to details, and a single-mindedness in his work. He will attain his goal of mastery because of his dedication and devotion. Allowing the higher forces to guide and direct him, he is learning something new with each pentacle he completes.

MARY HANSON-ROBERTS DECK

The face of the young apprentice in this picture shows pleasure in a job well done. It is his first commission, his first artistic creation without supervision. The gold of the pentacles and the gold color of his tools signifies he has been utilizing his gifts of the Spirit in this endeavor. This willingness to be guided by Divine Inspiration has brought enlightenment to him. The green of his tunic shows abundance and prosperity. The violet pink color of the sky outside his workplace shows that he will receive recognition and rewards for his creative and artistic endeavors. The apprentice polishes each of the pentacles with a white cloth, showing his intentions are not just for material benefits, he is using his creativity to enhance his unity with the Creator and with the Universe.

SUMMARY DEFINITION OF THE EIGHT OF PENTACLES

This card represents the beginning of a profitable undertaking. Training, development of skills and industriousness are keywords for this card. Employment or commission to come. This card also symbolizes creativity, sometimes still in the learning stages or apprenticeship stages, but unique and special enough to be developed further.

What is the Spiritual Lesson or Challenge the Eight of Pentacles would teach us?

The Eight of Pentacles teaches us the need for dedication and commitment towards our goals in life. It is necessary to undergo stages of learning or apprenticeship before we reach the pinnacle of achievement. Sometimes these stages take time and sometimes these stages are passed through very quickly. It depends on the amount of dedication and hard work one is willing to devote to their goals. The promise of attainment is there and will not be denied us, but we must make the effort required, it will not just fall into our laps.

NINE OF PENTACLES

RIDER-WAITE DECK
An elegantly dressed woman stands in her rich and fruitful garden admiring the wild falcon which has come to rest on her hand. She has the power to bring to her that which she desires. She has an attunement with and an affinity for the forces of nature which is why the falcon has come willing to her and chooses to stay with her. Her dress is decorated with the symbols of Venus, the goddess of love.

She has the ability to attract any mate she desires because of the knowledge and wisdom she possesses. The nine pentacles symbolize the wealth and prosperity she enjoys as a result of her own creativity. This card literally means success, well being and wealth. It is a card of certain success. The color yellow dominates this card representing clear thinking, the active mind, integrity, and enlightenment.

MARY HANSON-ROBERTS DECK
This woman is richly dressed in purple and peach golds with a sapphire blue scarf or shawl draped across one shoulder. The garden she stands in and even her hair is rich and abundant, showing her powers of material and physical manifestation. There are soft pink roses nestled in her hair representing the tender, nurturing nature she possesses. In the background, three arches, each with 3 pentacles, stand tall and proud in her well endowed garden. This represents the Trinity of Trinities, the triple blessings of the Creator. She, like the Queen of Pentacles, is at-one with nature. Her whole being radiates love to all life-forms which respond to her as if mesmerized. The white castle with red topped roofs in the background represent attainment and desires that have been realized.

SUMMARY DEFINITION OF THE NINE OF PENTACLES
This card symbolizes financial freedom. Good luck in material affairs is also indicated. Luxury and ease, wealth and abundance, on both the material and the spiritual level. The Nine of Pentacles indicates popularity, achievement, and good fortune. It also represents a person with a green thumb, one who is successful in their undertakings.

The Nine of Pentacles depicts a solitary enjoyment of the good things in life by choice, even though the individual has many offers of love-relationships or partnerships should they choose to accept them. This card is a sign of completion, mystic arts, and the attainment of one's goals.

What is the Spiritual Lesson or Challenge the Nine of Pentacles would teach us?

The Nine of Pentacles teaches us that our sense of completion is not found in another person, but found within ourselves and our union with the forces of the Universe. It is a wonderful experience to share one's life with another person, but relationships or partnerships with others are not a condition for happiness or contentment. We need to learn to take joy in our own solitude, to feel complete as an individual united with the Universe. Truly, there is a difference between being lonely and having solitude. One can be lonely in a crowd. Solitude is a state which allows us to find our center, our personal core of peace and balance. Without solitude we are distracted by petty details or events and find it difficult to achieve a state of peacefulness.

TEN OF PENTACLES

RIDER-WAITE DECK
This card represents material and spiritual success.

Abundance, wealth, and prosperity; satisfaction and joy, love, marriage, and family matters are all keywords depicting the symbols on this card. The old man represents the blessings of Heaven itself, the parable from the bible of the old stranger who seeks kindness from others on his travels, who is in reality an Angel of the Lord. The dogs in the corner show that the animal nature and animal passions have been transformed, (they are gray in color), to a higher level. The arch leads to a prosperous and successful future.

This card also indicates the good ripe fruits of Karma. The seeds sown in the past have been good ones. Now is the time to reap the harvest of the hard work done in the past. The figures depicted on the card have weathered the storms of life, have endured the tests and initiations required for self-mastery, and have learned to find joy and security in the bonds they have established with each other and the family unit they have established.

MARY HANSON-ROBERTS DECK
Gold and golden brown dominate this card. Gold is for the power of physical and material manifestation shown around them. It also indicates enlightenment and restoration. The golden brown represents the perfect blending of enlightenment with practicality and strength on the earth plane. It shows they have built foundations of security not only for themselves, but for others as well. This is a card which depicts contentment and happiness. Each of the faces show the love and joy they feel because of the blessings they have received. They have created a refuge from the illusions of the earth plane while still existing on the physical plane, their gateway is always open to those who seek the path and need nourishing along the way.

SUMMARY DEFINITION OF THE TEN OF PENTACLES
This card symbolizes the good ripe fruit of a happy Karma. It represents success and fulfillment in every way. For the individual, it may mean that a soulmate has been found and a family unit begun. There is an aura of material prosperity and riches around the individual. This card signifies the completion of material fortune and happy family. Balance has been won. There is advantage

for the individual in material affairs dealing with art, music, poetry, or other creative endeavors.

What is the Spiritual Lesson or Challenge the Ten of Pentacles would teach us?

The Ten of Pentacles teaches us lessons of joy and happiness. It shows us how contentment and security is found through love and sharing. The Ten of Pentacles is a card of attainment, a card which demonstrates the reality of miracles in our lives and love which inspires them. The Challenge is to remember that you are entitled to miracles and to the blessings of The Creator.

APPENDIX
EXAMPLE OF A
NUMEROLOGY WORKSHEET

I have included blank worksheets with this book for you to use as a guide in creating your own Numerology Profile. To assist you in filling out the worksheet, I am including an example of a worksheet already filled out with the numerology data of an individual. Using the directions in Chapter One and the example given here, there should be no problem in creating your own Numerology Profile.

WORKSHEET FOR NUMEROLOGY PROFILE

DATE OF BIRTH: 3/9/1950
   3+9+1+9+5+0=27/9   (1+9+5+0=15/6)

KARMIC CHALLENGE AND SUB-CHALLENGE:

```
            3  9  6
             6  3
               3
               3
```

```
                    91  1  1   9 1  6      5  =33
FULL GIVEN NAME AT BIRTH: DIANA NASHIRA ROTHWELL
                     4   5   5  18 9  9  2 8 5  33=62/8
```

       33+8=41/5

MARRIED NAME CHANGES OR LEGAL NAME CHANGES:

```
  91  1  1  9 1 9    1  =32/5
DIANA NASHIRA KINNAN
4    5  5  18 9  2  5 5  5=49/13/4
```

       5+4=9

NICKNAMES:
```
        9  9=18/9
        DIDI
        4  4 =8        8+9=17/8
```

COMPLETED NUMEROLOGY DATA

LIFELESSON NUMBER IS:	27/9	
PATH OF DESTINY NUMBER 41/5	(for birth name)	
PATH OF DESTINY NUMBER 9	(for name changes)	
PATH OF DESTINY NUMBER 17/8	(for nicknames)	

THE SOUL NUMBER: 33   (for birth name)
THE SOUL NUMRER: 32/5   (for name changes)
THE SOUL NUMBER: 18/9   (for nicknames)

THE OUTER PERSONALITY NUMBER 62/8   (for birth name)
THE OUTER PERSONALITY NUMBER:13/4   (for name changes)
THE OUTER PERSONALITY NUMBER 8   (for nicknames)

FIRST VOWEL INDICATOR: I   (for birth name)
FIRST VOWEL INDICATOR: same   (for nickname; if needed)

MISSING LINK: 7   (from birth name)
MISSING LINK 3   (from name changes)

KARMIC CHALLENGE 3
KARMIC SUB-CHALLENGE: 3

9-YEAR CYCLES OF PROGRESSION   (your personal year number)

1988=11	3+9+1+9+8+8=38	3+8+11
1989= 3	3+9+1+9+8+9=39	3+9=12 1+2=3
1990= 4	3+9+1+9+9+0=31	3+1= 4
1991= 5	3+9+1+9+9+1=32	3+2= 5
1992=33	3+9+1+9+9+2=33	
1993= 7	3+9+1+9+9+3=34	3+4= 7
1994= 8	3+9+1+9+9+4=35	3+5= 8
1995= 9	3+9+1+9+9+5=36	3+6= 9
1996= 1	3+9+1+9+9+6=37	3+7=10 1+0=1

WORKSHEET FOR NUMEROLOGY PROFILE

THE ALPHABET AND THE NUMBERS

```
1 2 3 4 5 6  7 8 9
A B C D E F G H I
J K L M N O P Q R
S T U V W X Y Z -
```

DATE OF BIRTH:

KARMIC CHALLENGE AND SUB-CHALLENGE:

FULL GIVEN NAME AT BIRTH:

MARRIED NAME CHANGES OR LEGAL NAME CHANGES:

NICKNAMES:

COMPLETED NUMEROLOGY DATA

LIFELESSON NUMBER IS:
PATH OF DESTINY NUMBER (for birth name)
PATH OF DESTINY NUMRER:(for name changes)
PATH OF DESTINY NUMBER (for nicknames)

THE SOUL NUMBER:(for birth name)
THE SOUL NUMBER:(for name changes)
THE SOUL NUMBER:(for nicknames)

THE OUTER PERSONALITY NUMBER: (for birth name)
THE OUTER PERSONALITY NUMBER: (for name changes)
THE OUTER PERSONALITY NUMBER: (for nicknames)

FIRST VOWEL INDICATOR: (for birth name)
FIRST VOWEL INDICATOR: (for nickname; if needed)

MISSING LINK: (from birth name)
MISSING LINK: (from name changes)

KARMIC CHALLENGE:
KARMIC SUB-CHALLENGE:

9-YEAR CYCLES OF PROGRESSION   (your personal year number)

GLOSSARY OF TERMS

AGAPE: This is a term used to describe Pure Love. A love without sexual connotation. Passion has been raised to its highest level: Compassion, the giving of oneself unselfishly to help others, and Forgiveness, this is the true meaning of Agape. Agape is the form of Love Jesus gave to his disciples and to all men and women whom he acknowledged were actually his brothers and sisters, children, like himself, of the Creator. All of the great Spiritual Masters through the centuries have given "Agape" to their followers and the world in general.

ARCHETYPES: This is a term used by the psychologist Carl Jung to categorize the themes or images which are found in all religions, myths and fairy tales through out the world. The Archetypes are "molds", or the master patterns from which humankind creates its visions. These master patterns have their roots in the "collective unconscious" or "Universal Mind". In other words, "Archetypes" are unconscious patterns we use in manifesting our potentials on a creative and spiritual level.

ASCENDANT: Also known as the "Rising Sign", the Ascendant is determined by the exact time of birth and the latitude and longitude of the birth place. The Ascendant sets the Astrological Houses on a Natal Chart and represents the outer personality of an individual. It is the "mask" we wear, how other people perceive us. The Ascendant or Rising Sign is an important element in understanding one's complete personality and behavior patterns.

ASTRAL PLANE: This actually refers to the 4th dimension which exists outside of the 3rd dimension. The 3rd dimension is referred to by Physicists as the Time and Space continuum. The 3rd dimension also referred to as the Earth Plane. Mathematics has proven that the 4th dimension exists, but that it cannot be experienced in the same way as the 3rd dimension where our "physical" bodies reside. The laws of Time and Space have no substance in the 4th dimension or Astral plane. The 3rd dimension is linear, the 4th dimension is not.

The Astral Plane has many levels to it. The Lower Astral Plane is where the newly dead and earth bound spirits reside. This astral level is also the repository of the negative energy humankind gives off, both in action and thought. Energy cannot be destroyed, it can be changed and transformed, but it cannot be destroyed. Judeo-Christian Theologians refer to this plane as Purgatory. It is merely one step or level beyond the physical. This is the astral plane many people see in dreams when they are having nightmares.

ASTRAL PROJECTION: This is a term used to describe the technique of separating the "astral" body from the "physical" body. These two "bodies" are attached to one another with a silver cord. Yogi's and other spiritual Masters have mastered the technique of leaving their physical body at will, projecting their astral body wherever they choose. Most humans astral project during their sleep-state which accounts for most of the flying experiences found in dreams.

ATONEMENT: The concept of "atonement" is the acceptance of responsibility for one's errors or mistakes made in the past and the decision to expend energy toward correcting those errors. Once that decision is made to "correct" mistakes, the energy we put into the process of atonement is augmented tenfold by the Divine Mind or Christ Consciousness. To accept "atonement" is to forgive yourself for your errors and to forgive others for their mistakes. This is the first step in the process of atonement, and once it is undertaken, the gift of "grace" is activated.

ATTUNEMENT: The idea of "attunement" represents an "awakening" to True Reality, the acknowledgement of one's inner-connectedness with all living things on this planet and in the Universe. Attunement means to become one with the Forces of Creation, the Universe, with one's perception of God the Father and God the Mother. We are and always have been and always will be in "attunement" with the Creator, however, we do not always acknowledge this on a conscious level nor do we act like the creatures of Light that we are.

CHAKRA CENTERS: These are energy centers within the body which affect us physically, health-wise, emotionally, mentally, and spiritually. The centers "vibrate" or have an affinity for certain colors.

FIRST CHAKRA: Base of Spine. Red in color. Referred to as the "Root Chakra". This center is the seat of the kundalini force. It governs physical strength, sexual energy, reproductive organs, warmth, and the "here and now". Its symbol is the Square.

SECOND CHAKRA: Located in the area of the Spleen. Orange in color. It governs the emotions, appetite, energy and openness to new ideas. Its symbol is the triangle.

THIRD CHAKRA: Located in the Solar Plexus area. Yellow in color. It governs clear thinking, all learning and studying, decisions, and personal power. Its symbol is the circle.

FOURTH CHAKRA: Called the Heart Chakra. Located between the breasts. Its color is Green. It governs growth, love, and the balance between Mind, Body, and Spirit. Its symbol is the cross.

FIFTH CHAKRA: Called the Throat Chakra. Sky blue in color. It governs communication, self-expression, creativity, and healing. Its symbol is the crescent moon.

SIXTH CHAKRA: Located on the brow of the forehead. Indigo in color. It governs intuition, ESP, higher comprehension, and releasing. Its symbol is the 6-pointed star.

SEVENTH CHAKRA: The Crown Chakra. Violet in color. It governs spiritual growth and self-realization, as well as artistic expression. Its symbol is the lotus flower.

CHRIST CONSCIOUSNESS: When we use this term, it refers to that part of each of us which is in complete and absolute perfect union with the Creator. Through purification and surrender of the Ego, we achieve a "Christ" Consciousness or "Super-Consciousness". To manifest this "consciousness", one must offer forgiveness and perfect love to everyone; be totally non-judgmental and have an unconditional acceptance of all creatures. All humankind will eventually achieve this perfected state, that is why we are here on the Earth Plane; to learn how to return to that perfected state of being and to correct the errors we have made in the past which has prevented us from recognizing our True Nature. It is our destiny, as Children of Light, to become purified and one with the Universal Life Force or Creator.

CONSCIOUS MIND: This state is the analytical aspect of our minds. It concerns our thinking process, our mental state of being, the Here and Now. It means awareness, the totality of one's thoughts. Feelings and impressions, knowing and ideas; these are a few words which also describe the meaning of this word.

DESCENDANT: 7TH HOUSE: This house of the Natal Horoscope Chart reveals both positive and negative behavior patterns established in previous lifetimes. However, these patterns affect your interaction with other people in partnership situations. Whether that partnership involves business, romance or marriage. This house shows what type of people you attract into your life as a result of your own subconscious energy patterns and the messages you send out into the universe. More emphasis is placed on this house in a Karmic Evaluation than in a regular Natal Chart.

EARTH PLANE: This is a term which refers to the physical manifestation of this planet. It deals with the presence of the physical body on a seemingly solid planet. The Earth Plane is also our "School". It is where we learn the lessons we need in order to return home to our Father/Mother. We, as living beings, are not truly "at home" on the Earth Plane. The physical body is not our natural state. We are creatures of Light and lightness. Unfortunately, since we trapped ourselves into our heavy physical bodies, we have forgotten our true state of being.

EGO: The Ego is that part of ourselves which imposes limitations on us. It is a part of us that weaves Illusions to trap us in darkness and despair. The ego seeks to imprison us in a physical body, trying to instill in us Fear which attempts to block out Perfect Love. Ego seeks to keep us separated from our Creator and from other people. The Ego doesn't want us to realize we are immortal or that we are more than a physical body that ages, decays and eventually dies. The Ego seeks to block Truth from us, Truth which can cut through the veils of Illusion the Ego creates which prevents from knowing what we really are.

EROS: This is a term used to describe physical and sexual love. It also refers to sexual intercourse and passion between two people in love .

GRACE: This means the unmerited love and favor of God toward men and women. It is mercy and forgiveness from God to us for our past mistakes, not because we have suffered for it or made restitution, but because He/She loves us totally and unconditionally.

KARMA: This is merely the law of action and reaction. It is a Universal Law which literally means "like attracts like". The workings of karma in one's life can be summed up this way: "As you sow, so shall you reap". What you give you get back tenfold, be it positive or negative.

KUNDALINI FORCE: This force lies coiled three and a half times at the base of the spine. This is the energy which fuels our physical, mental, emotional, and spiritual body. If one merely activates it, but does not raise the energy force up through the higher Chakra Centers, this energy often results in lusty activities, a need for more sexual intercourse, the passions of the physical body begin to rule us, rather than us ruling our passions. It is a potent force that is not to be taken lightly or toyed with. It has great potential for destruction, and equal potential for great strength.

LETTING GO AND LETTING GOD: This particular phrase needs a special definition since it is used quite frequently throughout this book, especially in regards to the symbolism of color and the Tarot. To let go and let God means to release our mental and emotional hold on worries, anxieties and fears and let the Spirit of the Creator work through us and for us. Letting go releases us from the burdens we have assumed under the direction of the Ego. In letting go of problems, we demonstrate our willingness to trust in the Love which surrounds us, fills us with tranquility, and allows us to meet the challenges of life confident in the power which works to our greater good.

LIGHT WANDS: Usually made of copper, Light Wands were used as Collectors or Generators of Energy in Atlantis. Light Wands were used by healers to channel energy into a person who was suffering "dis-ease". They were also used by some Atlanteans to gain and enhance their own psychical powers. Light Wands were used to control "lesser" beings on Atlantis. The energy collected and generated by the Light Wands could be used for good or evil, since the energy channeled was neutral in nature until transmutated by the Channeler of the Wand.

LOGOS: This is a term which refers to unalterable Universal Truth. It is similar in meaning to the laws in physics, however, its meaning is much deeper and far more spiritual than the simple physical laws of the Universe. The Logos is very real, but its not tangible, its not something you can actually touch physically. It can only be experienced on an emotional, mental, and spiritual level.

MANTRA: This is an "eastern" term referring to certain sounds chanted during meditation or prayers. The mantric chants are special vibrations or "sounds" which possess the power of manifestation on the earth plane. A mantra is the "bridge" or "channel" of sound between what can be and what is. By using a mantra, one can call "reality" forth from the 4th dimension into manifestation on the physical earth plane. A mantra enhances and augments the forces of light within an individual and opens the Gateway to the Higher Consciousness or Intuitional Centers of the mind. The most famous or well-known mantra is the "OM", used in TM or Transcendental Meditation.

NADIR 4TH HOUSE: This astrological term refers to the "Roots of the Soul", that part of you which is not always revealed to others. It is your foundation in the Universe, the "Real" you without masks or veils. The 4th house describes abilities or strengths which have been developed by you over many lifetimes. These traits represent tools you have brought with you into your present incarnation to assist you in achieving your goals.

NATAL: This is an Astrological term for a chart constructed with your birth data. It comprises the month, day, year, time, and place of birth in order to "freeze" the heavens to capture the formation of the planets in the heavens when you were born.

NON-JUDGEMENT: This is a concept whereby you choose not to pass judgement on the actions, activities, expressions, or ideas of another person. Choosing to be non-judgmental means you realize that you do not know everything and therefore could not possibly be a fair "judge" of another person. You realize that you do not know all the circumstances behind an individual's actions, why they act the way they do, what motivates them, what fears may be guiding them. When you accept the right to think freely for yourself, you automatically grant others the same privilege, no matter how ridiculous their attitudes may appear to be to you.

PERFECT LOVE: There are only two real emotions: Love and Fear. Fear encompasses all of the negative emotions we are prey to when our lives are directed by the Ego. Anger, hatred, jealousy, anxiety, worry, all of these emotions are but different shades of one emotion Fear. Perfect Love casts out fear. Perfect Love is forgiveness, it is the recognition that your brother--your sister is the same as yourself, that you are your brother/sister. Perfect love is the awareness that you are one with God, and with all Life-forms.

SALVATION: This is the saving of the soul from the mistaken idea of the reality of Sin and Death. This is done through the acceptance of Atonement.

SIN: This is merely a lack of love. Sins are merely mistakes that need to be corrected rather than an evil to be punished. Sins occur when we attempt to use ourselves or others in a loveless manner.

SUB-CONSCIOUS MIND: This term refers to the deeply buried part of our consciousness which contains memories and knowledge gained from previous lifetimes. The Sub-Conscious Mind is also where our hidden fears reside, where our instinctual nature is found. The sub-conscious is the seat of many hidden desires, desires we may not even realize motivates us or cause us to react to situations the way we do.

SUPER-CONSCIOUS MIND: Simply, this means the awareness of one's union with God. The awareness that we are one with all creation. The Super-Conscious Mind is just another term for the Christ Consciousness.

12TH HOUSE: This is an astrological term for one of the houses created by the Rising Sign or Ascendant in a Natal Chart. The 12th house is the house of Karma, it refers to soul growth through suffering, forgiveness, and faith in the unknown. This house also reveals the need for atonement because of choices made in previous lifetimes which are blocking the formation of new and better behavior patterns. The 12th house shows the inner emotional levels which pertain to the subconscious and to karmic relationships which must be faced in this lifetime.

Portions of our previous lifetimes show up in the 12th house for atonement or for reward. All of our misdeeds and good deeds are revealed in some form or another in this house. This is why the 12th house is called the house of self-undoing, frustrations, confinement, secret enemies, Karma, and ultimate understanding. The 12th house forces us to face the law of cause and effect, both on a personal level and on a racial and/or national level.

UNIVERSAL SUB-CONSCIOUS MIND: This represents the collective minds of all people who have ever lived and who will ever live on the Earth Plane. It is a source of inspiration, of guidance, and Knowledge. It is under the direction of the Creator for it serves to link all sentient creatures together on a fundamental level. Pure Knowledge is found in the Universal Sub-Conscious, knowledge which is available to all who seek it.

UNCONDITIONAL ACCEPTANCE: To accept someone unconditionally, is to accept them as they are without demanding they change or alter themselves in anyway. Unconditional Acceptance means you do not impose your expectations of behavior on someone else. If you cannot accept someone totally as they present themselves to you without judgment or expectations, your acceptance of them is not real.

BIBLIOGRAPHY

Listed below are just some of the books which have inspired me on the path for enlightenment and self-realization. I share these titles with you in the hopes this book has fueled the hunger within you for more knowledge. I wish you joy and happiness as you travel your path in life. Keep on striving toward your goals filled with hope and remember you do not walk your path alone.

AS ABOVE, SO BELOW: By Alan Oken

ASTROLOGY: EVOLUTION AND REVOLUTION: By Alan Oken

CRYSTAL CLEAR: By Connie Church

NOSTRADAMUS AND THE MILLENIUM: By John Hogue

ASTROLOGY: By Marcia Moore and Mark Douglas

MOTHERPEACE: A WAY TO THE GODDESS THROUGH
     MYTH, ART, AND THE   TAROT: By Vicki Noble

DICTIONARY OF THE TAROT: By Bill Butler

NUMEROLOGY AND THE DIVINE TRIANGLE: By Faith Javane and Dusty Bunker

THE TAROT REVEALED: By Eden Gray

THE ASTROLOGICAL PRAYERBOOK: By Alda Marian Jangl

WATCH YOUR DREAMS: By Ann Ree Colton

A COURSE IN MIRACLES: By The Foundation For Inner Peace

LOVE IS LETTING GO OF FEAR: By Dr. Gerald Jampolsky

LOVE, MEDICINE AND MIRACLES: By Dr. Bernie Siegel

ILLUSIONS: By Richard Bach

AGARTHA: By Meredith Lady Young

THE EDGAR CAYCE PRIMER: By Herbert B. Puryear

THE HEALING POWER OF COLOR: By Betty Wood

AURAS: By Edgar Cayce

REINCARNATION THROUGH THE ZODIAC: By Joan Hodgson

COSMIC CRYSTALS: By Ra Bonewitz

A SPIRITUAL APPROACH TO ASTROLOGY: By Myrna Lofthus

AMULETS & BIRTHSTONES: THEIR
     ASTROLOGICAL SIGNIFICANCE: By E.Ivy A. Bannerman-Phillips

10,000 DREAMS INTERPRETED: By Gustavus Hindman Miller

HELPING YOURSELF WITH NUMEROLOGY: By Helyn Hitchcock

NUMEROLOGY AND YOUR FUTURE: By Dusty Bunker

MEDITATIONS ON THE SIGNS OF THE ZODIAC: By John Jocelyn

BOOK OF THE HOPI: By Frank Waters

REINCARNATION: THE PHOENIX
     FIRE MYSTERY: By Joseph Head and S.L. Cranston

THE SECRET POWERS OF NUMEROLOGY: By Gerie Tully

THE COMPLETE DREAM BOOK: By Edward Frank Allen

ZOLAR'S ENCYCLOPEDIA & DICTIONARY OF DREAMS: By Zolar

SUN SIGNS: By Linda Goodman

CRYSTAL LOVE: By Connie Church

MESSAGES FROM MICHAEL: By Chelsea Quinn Yarbro

SPIRIT SONG: By Mary Summer Rain

PHOENIX RISING: By Mary Summer Rain

DREAMWALKER: By Mary Summer Rain